Technology & the Future

TWELFTH EDITION

ALBERT H. TEICH
American Association for the Advancement of Science

WADSWORTH
CENGAGE Learning·

Australia • Brazil • Japan • Korea • Mexico • Singapore • Spain • United Kingdom • United States

WADSWORTH
CENGAGE Learning·

**Technology & the Future,
Twelfth Edition**
Albert H. Teich

Senior Publisher: Suzanne Jeans

Executive Editor: Carolyn Merrill

Development Manager: Jeff Greene

Associate Development Editor:
Katie Hayes

Media Editor: Laura Hildebrand

Art Director: Linda Helcher

Manufacturing Planner: Fola
Orekoya

Marketing Program Manager:
Caitlin Green

RAS (Text and Images): Jennifer
Meyer Dare

Production Manager: Suzanne
St. Clair

Cover Designer: Jenny Willingham

Cover Image:
Avian/©Shutterstock

Compositor: PreMediaGlobal

Content Project Management:
PreMediaGlobal

For product information and
technology assistance, contact us at **Cengage Learning
Customer & Sales Support, 1-800-354-0563.**

For permission to use material from this text or product,
submit all requests online at **www.cengage.com/permissions**.
Further permissions questions can be e-mailed to
permissionrequest@cengage.com

Library of Congress Control Number: 2011941645

ISBN-13: 978-1-111-82854-7

ISBN-10: 1-111-82854-7

Wadsworth
20 Channel Center Street
Boston, MA 02210
USA

Cengage Learning is a leading provider of customized learning solutions with office locations around the globe, including Singapore, the United Kingdom, Australia, Mexico, Brazil, and Japan. Locate your local office at **international.cengage.com/region**.

Cengage Learning products are represented in Canada by Nelson Education, Ltd.

For your course and learning solutions, visit **www.cengage.com**

Purchase any of our products at your local college store or at our preferred online store **www.cengagebrain.com**.

Instructors: Please visit **login.cengage.com** and log in to access instructor-specific resources.

Printed in the United States of America
1 2 3 4 5 6 7 15 14 13 12 11

For Samantha

Contents

PART VI Contemporary Technological Dilemmas: Information and Communications Technology 267

PART VII Governance and Globalization 321

Topical Contents

Bioethics

Computers and Information Technology

Democracy, Politics, and Policy

Environment

Futures Studies

Technology and Culture

About the Editor

Albert H. Teich is senior policy adviser at the American Association for the Advancement of Science (AAAS). Previously, he served as director of Science and Policy Programs and its antecedent office at AAAS for over 25 years. In that position, he was responsible for the association's activities in science and technology policy and served as a key spokesperson on science policy issues. AAAS, founded in 1848, is the world's largest federation of scientific and engineering societies, as well as a professional organization with 125,000 members and the publisher of *Science* magazine.

Dr. Teich received a B.S. degree in physics and a Ph.D. in political science, both from the Massachusetts Institute of Technology. Prior to joining the AAAS staff in 1980, he held positions at George Washington University, the State University of New York, and Syracuse University (where he developed the first edition of *Technology and the Future* in 1971). Dr. Teich is quoted frequently in the press and has made many appearances on radio and television. He is well known as a speaker on science and technology policy and is the author of numerous articles, reports, and book chapters. He was elected a Fellow of AAAS in 1986 and in 2004 was the recipient of the Award for Scientific Achievement in Science Policy from the Washington Academy of Sciences.

He is a member of the editorial advisory boards to the journals *Science Communication*; *Science, Technology, and Human Values*; and *Review of Policy Research*; and has served as a consultant to government agencies, national laboratories, industrial firms, and international organizations. Dr. Teich was president of the Washington Academy of Sciences in 2008–2009. He chaired the advisory committee to the National Science Foundation's Division of Science Resources Studies from 1987 through 1990. He is a founding member of the World Technology Network and currently belongs to several international advisory boards and committees, including the Board of Governors of the U.S.-Israel Binational Science Foundation; the Advisory Board of the Norwegian Research and Technology Forum in the United States;

and the Program Committee of the Euroscience Open Forum — ESOF. He is also an honorary member of the Washington Science Diplomats Club.

Dr. Teich is an accomplished amateur photographer and has had several one-person shows of his work. He is married to Jill Pace, director of the American College of Real Estate Lawyers, and has three children and four grandchildren. His home page may be found at http://www.alteich.com.

Preface

I am of two minds when it comes to technology.

One side of me is totally hooked on technology. While I do not necessarily feel compelled to be the first among my friends to own every new gadget, I do use and enjoy many technologies. I spend a great deal of my time at one or another of my computers (we have five in the house, six when our daughter is home), on my iPhone, listening to my iPod, or using one of my digital cameras. I love Google and the way it makes information about practically anything instantly available to me. I love letting my Roomba® robot vacuum clean my carpets while I'm occupied with other things. I am currently lusting after a plug-in electric car and hope to have one within the next year or two. I am a regular consumer of technology blogs and reviews of new technological products online as well as in newspapers and magazines. (Okay, so I do still read paper media.) And, perhaps most important of all (and under-appreciated), I am a beneficiary of modern, high-tech medicine – living a longer and healthier life because of scientific discoveries and biomedical technologies.

Still, I am fully aware that technology has its dark side and that much of the technology with which our society is suffused is designed to earn profits for high- (and low-) tech firms and entrepreneurs rather than to improve human well-being. I worry about where our technologies are taking us. Our man-made technological systems can be fragile and, as shown in the past several years by the failure of the levee system during Hurricane Katrina; the BP oil spill; and the devastating 2011 earthquake, tsunami, and consequent nuclear disaster in Japan, they are capable of causing or at least failing to prevent great harm. Many (perhaps most) beneficial technologies can also cause inadvertent harm to people, animals, or the environment — examples such as pesticides, polluting energy sources, and medical therapies with unanticipated side effects are legion. And of course technologies can also be used intentionally to harm people, to perpetuate social injustice, or to serve other destructive ends.

This book, now in its 12th edition and, at 40 years old, well into middle age, reflects the yin and the yang of my own understanding of and feelings about technology. The articles I've selected both extol the virtues and criticize the evils of technology and its role in society, although I have tried to avoid the extremes on both sides.

Except perhaps by science fiction writers, relatively few of the technologies that are discussed by the authors in this volume were even remotely imagined when I assembled the materials for the first edition of this book in 1971. (It was not actually published until the following year.) The preface for that first edition (and several subsequent editions) was written on a typewriter and the selections were cut and pasted into the manuscript using scissors and tape rather than Word's cut and paste functions. The manuscript was mailed to the publisher — not FedExed, not e-mailed. And the galleys and page proofs were returned to me the same way. I cannot imagine working like that again and wonder how I possibly could have assembled this book in such a primitive manner. The innovations of the past several decades are astounding for those of us who grew up without them, but for the current generation (and a couple of previous generations), they're routine — an ordinary part of life, taken for granted as if they had always existed.

Technology and society are both changing at an unprecedented pace. And a textbook on technology and society is hardly timeless. Experience shows that it needs to be substantially updated every few years. The development of this book since 1972 provides a mini-history of concerns about technology and society. (Take a look at the tables of contents of previous editions at http://www.alteich. com/history/index.htm to see what I mean.) Recognizing the pace of technological change, and taking into account the comments of users and reviewers as well as my own sense of the relative importance of various topics and the timeliness (or its lack) of various chapters, I have once again, for this new edition, performed major surgery on the book. I have dropped nine chapters that appeared in the 11th edition and replaced them with ten more current and/or more relevant articles.

Despite the changes, the structure of the book remains intact, and much of the content will look familiar to those who have used previous editions. In Part I, "Thinking about Technology," several well-known authors raise big questions: What is technology? Is it good, bad, or neutral (or good *and* bad)? Is it synonymous with progress? How does it influence society and how does society influence its development? Leo Marx and Robert Pool headline this section. Next, David Edgerton reminds us not to let the focus on new technology blind us to the importance of existing technologies, even those that may seem mundane. Alvin Weinberg's essay on the "technological fix," which follows, is one of only three articles that survive from the first edition. Though dated, it still raises important questions and seldom fails to provoke discussion. The chapters by engineer Samuel Florman and political scientist Langdon Winner (difficult, perhaps, but well worth the effort) should do the same. My hope in Part I, as elsewhere in the book, is to preserve the best elements of previous editions while also bringing in more current thinking.

The four-decade old, but still very relevant, debate over the role of technology in society between the late Emmanuel Mesthene and John McDermott, like the Weinberg chapter a feature of the book since the first edition, comprises Part II, "Debating Technology: 1960s Style." Both the substance and the rhetoric of the Mesthene–McDermott debate contrast sharply with Part III, "Debating Technology: Twenty-First-Century Style," in which Bill Joy, a computer scientist and entrepreneur responsible for several major software innovations, presents his rather scary vision of a future in which the products of nanotechnology, genetics, and robotics converge and threaten the existence of humanity. Responding to Joy rather critically are John Seely Brown and Paul Duguid, as well as inventor Ray Kurzweil, a friend of Joy's whose views of the future are quite different from his.

The next three sections on "Contemporary Technological Dilemmas" turn to more concrete, current issues and explore some of the ethical, social, and human dimensions of a number of specific areas of technology and have been subject to considerable updating. Part IV examines one of the most critical issues facing society today: global climate change. Many people believe climate change is the most vexing problem facing global society in the twenty-first century. While agreement on what to do about it is still far off, all but a few of the most ardent skeptics agree that the problem is real and must be addressed. The lead article included here, by Collins et al., describes the scientific basis for the increasingly powerful consensus among researchers on the nature of this problem. It is based on the 2007 report of the Intergovernmental Panel on Climate Change and explains, in terms that do not require a PhD in atmospheric physics to understand, how and why the Earth's climate is changing.

Still, the scientific consensus is not unanimous. A significant number of policymakers and a lesser number of scientists have a different view. Among the scientists who take a contrarian position, Richard Lindzen stands out. He is a highly respected professor at M.I.T. and his article (new to this edition), originally an op-ed in the *Wall Street Journal*, provides an excellent summary of the arguments against the scientific mainstream. Following Lindzen, the third and fourth articles in Part IV (also new) approach climate change from a rather different angle, that of geoengineering, fixing the problem with a massive technological intervention. The article by Victor et al. looks at the international political ramifications of such an approach; the piece by Robock marshals the arguments against it.

Part V looks at some of the social and ethical dimensions of recent advances in the life and biomedical sciences: stem cell research, synthetic biology, genetic engineering, and neuroscience. Research involving human embryonic stem cells offers the tantalizing prospect of breakthroughs in the treatment of diseases and injuries, but, in the minds of critics, it also opens the door to possible abuses of the sanctity of human life. Christopher Thomas Scott lays out the basic features of both sides of this debate clearly and concisely.

Going a step beyond stem cell research, synthetic biology employs scientific and engineering techniques to create artificial organisms capable of reproducing themselves. The idea is controversial, and in May 2010 President Obama charged his Presidential Commission for the Study of Bioethical Issues with examining its prospects and problems. An excerpt from the commission's report is included as chapter 17, followed by an article from *Nature* examining the barriers faced by this exciting but controversial technology. Both are new to this edition.

In chapter 18, carried over from the 11th edition, Michael Sandel takes a conservative approach to the possibilities of designer children and other kinds of human enhancement created by developments in biotechnology. And, following Sandel, in chapter 20, Stanford law professor Henry Greely speculates on the meaning of advances in neuroscience which, some scientists believe, will soon provide a means of gauging an individual's mental state — i.e., reading his or her mind — with an imaging device.

Under the heading of information and communications technology in Part VI is an article by computer historian Paul Ceruzzi — a favorite of mine — on why those most responsible for originating the information technology revolution failed to anticipate its extent or its impact. It is followed by a curmudgeonly but entertaining piece by poet and farmer Wendell Berry, on why he rejects the idea of using a computer to do his writing, and by an up-to-date, broad-based survey by philosopher Deborah Johnson of the ethical issues raised by computers and information technology. New to Part VI is chapter 24, in which Nicholas Carr, writer about technology and culture, and author of the blog *Rough Type*, asks "Is Google Making Us Stupid?" More precisely, he explores the question of how the Internet is affecting our modes of reading, writing, and thinking. His thought-provoking piece is followed by two more new articles on one of the critical policy issues that will shape the future of the Internet: the matter of "net neutrality." Net neutrality is the principle that Internet service providers may not discriminate among different forms of content and applications that they carry on their lines. A short piece from *savetheinternet.com* argues against network operators who, the organization claims, want to change that principle and discriminate among different uses by charging differential fees to web site operators. In the following article, an analyst at the Information Technology and Innovation Foundation looks at the issue from a different perspective, that of broadband network managers, and asks what kinds of policies can balance the competing interests involved in using the Internet as well as future computer networks.

The last section, "Governance and Globalization," takes a step back from these rather technical concerns and returns to the broader questions of technology and society through the prism of governance. The first chapter is my own article on the relationships between governments and technology, an article I wrote originally for an encyclopedia of science, technology, and society. The other (new to this edition), by three-time Pulitzer Prize winning columnist for the *New York Times* Thomas Friedman, is a brief excerpt from his best-selling book, *The World Is Flat*. In it he describes life in a call center in Bangalore, India, using the story to illustrate how, in many respects and in many economic sectors, technology (again, especially the Internet) has made geography virtually irrelevant.

As in previous editions, my selections are — by design — a mixed bag. Not all students or all instructors will find every reading to their liking. Readers will probably love some and hate others, find some fascinating, others tedious. I have chosen the individual articles with an eye toward diversity in their authors' views of technology and political leanings. They do not necessarily represent my own views, and I do not necessarily endorse their perspectives. As a whole, however, the book reflects what I hope is a balanced view of the important issues in the field of technology and society, a view that I hope will be useful to others who are interested in these topics.

Technology and the Future has been a part of my professional life throughout my entire career. It is gratifying to have watched the growing interest in the study of technology, society, and the future in colleges and universities world-wide over the past several decades and to feel that the book may have made a modest contribution to this important intellectual development. Throughout the life of this book, I have benefited from the interest, suggestions, and feedback from the book's users. I am indebted to them all for the ideas that they shared with me, some of which have helped to shape this volume.

My thanks go also to the staff of my current publisher, Cengage Learning (formerly Thomson Wadsworth), especially Carolyn Merrill and Katie Hayes; to my previous publisher, Bedford/St. Martin's; and finally to St. Martin's Press's College Division, whose editors had the foresight to publish the first edition of this book in 1972 and who, through a generation of staff changes, mergers, acquisitions, and restructurings, remained helpful, interested, and unfailingly supportive. I have been fortunate in having a series of editors over the years with whom it has always been a pleasure to work.

I wish to acknowledge the advice of those who have contributed comments and suggestions that helped shape this edition:

Sundeep Muppidi, University of Hartford
Elizabeth Laidlaw, Monroe Community College
Vickie Kelly, Washburn University
Thomas Langston, Tulane University

Finally, a very special note of gratitude goes to my family: my wife, Jill; my daughter, Samantha; and my sons, Mitch and Ken; their wives Gretchen and Sara; and my grandchildren, Calvin Avery, Madelyn Elise, Sylvi Reine, and Charlie Joel, for the meaning they give to my life and for the strength I draw from our relationships.

Once again I invite readers — both faculty and students — to contact me with comments and suggestions. I can be reached most readily by e-mail at *ateich@gmail.org*, through *ateich.com* or *alteich.com*. The latter site ("Al Teich's Technology and the Future Toolkit") contains supplementary resources related to the book, including the tables of contents of earlier editions, my personal home page, and more. You can also follow me on Twitter: @al_teich.

Albert H. Teich
Washington, D.C.
June 2011

PART I

Thinking About Technology

Technology is more than just machines. It is a pervasive, complex system whose cultural, social, political, and intellectual elements are manifest in virtually every aspect of our lives. Small wonder, then, that it has attracted the attention of such a large and diverse group of writers and commentators. A small sampling of the range of writings on the social dimensions of technology is contained in this first section of *Technology and the Future*. All of the writers represented here are attempting to understand — from one perspective or another — these social dimensions of technology. Little else ties them together. From the oldest to the most recent they span nearly half a century. Their points of view are vastly different. Their common goal is not so much to prescribe particular courses of action as it is to explore the conceptual, metaphysical issues underlying technology–society interactions.

In the opening selection, historian Leo Marx explores the development of the American notion of progress and looks at its connections with technological advance. This seminal essay asks a simple-sounding question that sets the tone for this entire book: Does improved technology mean progress? Next, Robert Pool, former senior writer at *Science* and news editor at *Nature*, explains in lucid terms the ways in which technology and society shape one another. Pool's essay is drawn from a book that began as a straightforward treatment of the commercial nuclear industry. Instead of the simple story he expected to find, Pool discovered "a complex, often convoluted tale of how the technology had been shaped by a host of nontechnical factors in addition to the expected technical ones." His approach transcends both the notions of technological determinism (the idea that technology is an autonomous force that produces social change) and social constructivism (which views technology as purely a product of social and cultural influences) in favor of a more subtle explanation of the relations between technology and society.

The following chapter takes an entirely different approach to thinking about technology. In contrast to most of the other authors represented in Part I, British historian David Edgerton makes a powerful case for the global significance of *old* technologies. Edgerton directs his attention away from the idea of invention and toward the matter of how and by whom technologies are actually used. Through this lens he sees an entirely different world, one dominated by simple, mundane technologies rather than the newest, most advanced ones.

After the chapter by David Edgerton, in an essay dating from the mid-1960s that captures some of the heights of post–World War II technological optimism, physicist Alvin Weinberg suggests that we can find shortcuts to the solution of social problems by transforming them into technological ones, since technological problems are much easier to solve. This selection, though out of sync with much current thinking, has become a classic for the perspective it represents and for introducing the concept of the "technological fix," which continues to be the subject of debate and discussion.

In Chapter 5, Samuel Florman, a practicing engineer and industrialist as well as a humanist, proposes an alternative approach — a "tragic view" that recognizes the role of technology in human life, including its limits. The chapter that follows Florman is one of the best-known and most-discussed articles in the literature of technology and society. In it, Langdon Winner, professor at Rensselaer Polytechnic Institute, asks whether certain technological systems by their nature determine particular arrangements of power and authority among people. Understanding the significance of this and related questions is essential, Winner argues, to maintaining (or perhaps restoring) democratic control over the course of technological and social development.

The reader who is looking for unequivocal answers to the problems posed by technology will not find them here. On the whole, the readings in this section, like those in the remainder of the book, raise many more questions than they answer. They are intended to stimulate the reader to think critically about the relations between technology and society and the ways in which they shape the future.

1

Does Improved Technology Mean Progress?

LEO MARX

The concepts of technology and progress have been firmly linked in the minds of most Americans for the past 150 years. Only in the past three decades, however, has the question that Leo Marx asks in his essay, "Does Improved Technology Mean Progress?" begun to receive serious attention in our culture. This question is the perfect starting point for Technology and the Future. Deceptive in its simplicity, it underlies most of what follows in this book.

Leo Marx is Senior Lecturer and William R. Kenan Professor of American Cultural History Emeritus in the Program in Science, Technology, and Society at MIT. He is the author of The Machine in the Garden: Technology and the Pastoral Ideal in America *(1964) and is coeditor, with Merritt Roe Smith, of* Does Technology Drive History? *(1994). He holds a Ph.D. in history of American civilization from Harvard and has taught at that institution and at the University of Minnesota and Amherst College. He has twice been a Guggenheim Fellow and was a Rockefeller Humanities Fellow in 1983–1984. Marx was born in New York City in 1919.*

In this reading Marx examines how the concept of progress has itself evolved since the early days of the Republic and what that evolution means for understanding the technological choices that confront us today. Improved technology could mean progress, Marx concludes, "but only if we are willing and able to answer the next question: Progress toward what?"

Does improved technology mean progress? If some variant of this question had been addressed to a reliable sample of Americans at any time since the

Leo Marx, "Does Improved Technology Mean Progress?" from *Technology Review* (January, 1987), pp. 33–41. © 1987 Technology Review. Reprinted with permission.

early nineteenth century, the answer of a majority almost certainly would have been an unequivocal "yes." The idea that technological improvements are a primary basis for — and an accurate gauge of — progress has long been a fundamental belief in the United States. In the last half-century, however, that belief has lost some of its credibility. A growing minority of Americans has adopted a skeptical, even negative, view of technological innovation as an index of social Progress.

The extent of this change in American attitudes was brought home to me when I spent October 1984 in China. At that time, the announced goal of the People's Republic was to carry out (in the popular slogan) "Four Modernizations" — agriculture, science and technology, industry, and the military. What particularly struck our group of Americans was the seemingly unbounded, largely uncritical ardor with which the Chinese were conducting their love affair with Western-style modernization — individualistic, entrepreneurial, or "capitalist," as well as scientific and technological. Like early nineteenth-century visitors to the United States, we were witnessing a society in a veritable transport of improvement: long pent-up, innovative energies were being released, everyone seemed to be in motion, everything was eligible for change. It was assumed that any such change almost certainly would be for the better.

Most of the Chinese we came to know best — teachers and students of American studies — explicitly associated the kind of progress represented by the four modernizations with the United States. This respect for American wealth and power was flattering but disconcerting, for we often found ourselves reminding the Chinese of serious shortcomings, even some terrible dangers, inherent in the Western mode of industrial development. Like the Americans whom European travelers met 150 years ago, many of the Chinese seemed to be extravagantly, almost blindly, credulous and optimistic.

Our reaction revealed, among other things, a change in our own culture and, in some cases, in our own personal attitudes. We came face-to-face with the gulf that separates the outlook of many contemporary Americans from the old national faith in the advance of technology as the basis of social progress.

The standard explanation for this change includes that familiar litany of death and destruction that distinguishes the recent history of the West: two barbaric world wars, the Nazi holocaust, the Stalinist terror, and the nuclear arms race. It is striking to note how many of the fearful events of our time involve the destructive use or misuse, the unforeseen consequences, or the disastrous malfunction of modern technologies: Hiroshima and the nuclear threat, the damage inflicted upon the environment by advanced industrial societies, and spectacular accidents like Three Mile Island.

Conspicuous disasters have helped to undermine the public's faith in progress, but there also has been a longer-term change in our thinking. It is less obvious, less dramatic, and less tangible than the record of catastrophe that distinguishes our twentieth-century history, but I believe it is more fundamental. Our very conception — our chief criterion — of progress has undergone a subtle but decisive change since the founding of the Republic, and that change is at once a cause and a reflection of our current disenchantment with technology.

To chart this change in attitude, we need to go back at least as far as the first Industrial Revolution.

THE ENLIGHTENMENT BELIEF IN PROGRESS

The development of radically improved machinery (based on mechanized motive power) used in the new factory system of the late eighteenth century coincided with the formulation and diffusion of the modern Enlightenment idea of history as a record of progress. This conception became the fulcrum of the dominant American worldview. It assumes that history, or at least modern history, is driven by the steady, cumulative, and inevitable expansion of human knowledge of and power over nature. The new scientific knowledge and technological power were expected to make possible a comprehensive improvement in all the conditions of life — social, political, moral, and intellectual, as well as material.

The modern idea of progress, as developed by its radical French, English, and American adherents, emerged in an era of political revolution. It was a revolutionary doctrine, bonded to the radical struggle for freedom from feudal forms of domination. To ardent republicans like the French philosopher Condorcet, the English chemist Priestley, and Benjamin Franklin, a necessary criterion of progress was the achievement of political and social liberation. They regarded the new sciences and technologies not as ends in themselves, but as instruments for carrying out a comprehensive transformation of society. The new knowledge and power would provide the basis for alternatives to the deeply entrenched authoritarian, hierarchical institutions of *l'ancien régime*: monarchical, aristocratic, and ecclesiastical. Thus, in 1813 Thomas Jefferson wrote to John Adams describing the combined effect of the new science and the American Revolution on the minds of Europeans:

> Science had liberated the ideas of those who read and reflect, and the American example had kindled feelings of right in the people. An insurrection has consequently begun, of science, talents, and courage, against rank and birth, which have fallen into contempt.... Science is progressive.

Admittedly, the idea of history as endless progress did encourage extravagantly optimistic expectations, and in its most extreme form it fostered some wildly improbable dreams of the "perfectability of Man" and of humanity's absolute mastery of nature. Yet, the political beliefs of the radical republicans of the eighteenth century, such as the principle of making the authority of government dependent upon the consent of the governed, often had the effect of limiting those aspirations to omnipotence.

The constraining effect of such ultimate, long-term political goals makes itself felt, for example, in Jefferson's initial reaction to the prospect of introducing the new manufacturing system to America. "Let our work-shops remain in Europe," he wrote in 1785.

Although a committed believer in the benefits of science and technology, Jefferson rejected the idea of developing an American factory system on the ground that the emergence of an urban proletariat, which he then regarded as an inescapable consequence of the European factory system, would be too high a price to pay for any potential improvement in the American material standard of living. He regarded the existence of manufacturing cities and an industrial working class as incompatible with republican government and the happiness of the people. He argued that it was preferable, even if more costly in strictly economic terms, to ship raw materials to Europe and import manufactured goods. "The loss by the transportation of commodities across the Atlantic will be made up in happiness and permanence of government." In weighing political, moral, and aesthetic costs against economic benefits, he anticipated the viewpoint of the environmentalists and others of our time for whom the test of a technological innovation is its effect on the overall quality of life.

Another instance of the constraining effect of republican political ideals is Benjamin Franklin's refusal to exploit his inventions for private profit. Thus, Franklin's reaction when the governor of Pennsylvania urged him to accept a patent for his successful design of the "Franklin stove":

> Governor Thomas was so pleased with the construction of this stove as described in … [the pamphlet] that … he offered to give me a patent for the sole vending of them for a term of years; but I declined it from a principle which has ever weighed with me on such occasions, namely; viz., *that as we enjoy great advantages from the inventions of others, we should be glad of an opportunity to serve others by any invention of ours, and this we should do freely and generously* [emphasis in original].

What makes the example of Franklin particularly interesting is the fact that he later came to be regarded as the archetypal self-made American and the embodiment of the Protestant work ethic. When Max Weber sought out of all the world *the* exemplar of that mentality for his seminal study, *The Protestant Ethic and the Spirit of Capitalism*, whom did he choose but our own Ben? But Franklin's was a principled and limited self-interest. In his *Autobiography*, he told the story of his rise in the world not to exemplify a merely personal success, but rather to illustrate the achievements of a "rising people." He belonged to that heroic revolutionary phase in the history of the bourgeoisie when that class saw itself as the vanguard of humanity and its principles as universal. He thought of his inventions as designed not for his private benefit but for the benefit of all.

THE TECHNOCRATIC CONCEPT OF PROGRESS

With the further development of industrial capitalism, a quite different conception of technological progress gradually came to the fore in the United States. Americans celebrated the advance of science and technology with increasing fervor, but they began to detach the idea from the goal of social and political liberation. Many regarded the eventual attainment of that goal as having been assured by the victorious American Revolution and the founding of the Republic.

The difference between this later view of progress and that of Jefferson's and Franklin's generation can be heard in the rhetoric of Daniel Webster. He and Edward Everett were perhaps the leading public communicators of this new version of the progressive ideology. When Webster decided to become a senator from Massachusetts instead of New Hampshire, the change was widely interpreted to mean that he had become the quasi-official spokesman for the new industrial manufacturing interests. Thus Webster, who was generally considered the nation's foremost orator, was an obvious choice as the speaker at the dedication of new railroads. Here is a characteristic peroration of one such performance in 1847:

> It is an extraordinary era in which we live. It is altogether new. The world has seen nothing like it before. I will not pretend, no one can pretend, to discern the end; but everybody knows that the age is remarkable for scientific research into the heavens, the earth, and what is beneath the earth; and perhaps more remarkable still for the application of this scientific research to the pursuits of life.... We see the ocean navigated and the solid land traversed by steam power, and intelligence communicated by electricity. Truly this is almost a miraculous era. What is before us no one can say, what is upon us no one can hardly realize. The progress of the age has almost outstripped human belief; the future is known only to Omniscience.

By the 1840s, as Webster's rhetoric suggests, the idea of progress was already being dissociated from the Enlightenment vision of political liberation. He invests the railroad with a quasi-religious inevitability that lends force to the characterization of his language as the rhetoric of the technological sublime. Elsewhere in the speech, to be sure, Webster makes the obligatory bow to the democratic influence of technological change, but it is clear that he is casting the new machine power as the prime exemplar of the overall progress of the age, quite apart from its political significance. Speaking for the business and industrial elite, Webster and Everett thus depict technological innovation as a sufficient cause, *in itself*, for the fact that history assumes the character of continuous, cumulative progress.

At the same time, discarding the radical political ideals of the Enlightenment allowed the idea of technological progress to blend with other grandiose national aspirations. Webster's version of the "rhetoric of the technological sublime" is of a piece with the soaring imperial ambitions embodied in the slogan "Manifest Destiny," and by such tacit military figurations of American development as the popular notion of the "conquest of nature" (including Native Americans) by the increasingly technologized forces of advancing European–American "civilization." These future-oriented themes easily harmonized with the belief in the coming of the millennium that characterized evangelical Protestantism, the most popular American religion at the time. Webster indicates as much when, at the end of his tribute to the new railroad, he glibly brings in "Omniscience" as the ultimate locus of the meaning of progress.

The difference between the earlier Enlightenment conception of progress and that exemplified by Webster is largely attributable to the difference between the groups they represented. Franklin, Jefferson, and the heroic generation of founding revolutionists constituted a distinct, rather unusual social class in that for a short time the same men possessed authority and power in most of its important forms: economic, social, political, and intellectual. The industrial capitalists for whom Daniel Webster spoke were men of a very different stripe. They derived their status from a different kind of wealth and power, and their conception of progress, like their economic and social aspirations, was correspondingly different. The new technology and the immense profits it generated belonged to them, and since they had every reason to assume that they would retain their property and power, they had a vested interest in technological innovation. It is not surprising, under the circumstances, that as industrialization proceeded these men became true believers in technological improvement as the primary basis for — and virtually tantamount to — universal progress.

This dissociation of technological and material advancement from the larger political vision of progress was an intermediate stage in the eventual impoverishment of that radical eighteenth-century worldview. This subtle change prepared the way for the emergence, later in the century, of a thoroughly technocratic idea of progress. It was "technocratic" in that it valued improvements in power, efficiency, and rationality as ends in themselves. Among those who bore witness to the widespread diffusion of this concept at the turn of the century were Henry Adams and Thorstein Veblen, who were critical of it, and Andrew Carnegie, Thomas Edison, and Frederick Winslow Taylor and his followers, who lent expression to it. Taylor's theory of scientific management embodies the quintessence of the technocratic mentality, "the idea," as historian Hugh Aitken describes it, "that human activity could be measured, analyzed, and controlled by techniques analogous to those that had proved so successful when applied to physical objects."

The technocratic idea of progress is a belief in the sufficiency of scientific and technological innovation as the basis for general progress. It says that if we can ensure the advance of science-based technologies, the rest will take care of itself. (The "rest" refers to nothing less than a corresponding degree of improvement in the social, political, and cultural conditions of life.) Turning the Jeffersonian ideal on its head, this view makes instrumental values fundamental to social progress and relegates what formerly were considered primary, goal-setting values (justice, freedom, harmony, beauty, or self-fulfillment) to a secondary status.

In this century, the technocratic view of progress was enshrined in Fordism and an obsessive interest in economies of scale, standardization of process and product, and control of the workplace. This shift to mass production was accompanied by the more or less official commitment of the U.S. government to the growth of the nation's wealth, productivity, and global power and to the most rapid possible rate of technological innovation as the essential criterion of social progress.

But the old republican vision of progress — the vision of advancing knowledge empowering humankind to establish a less hierarchical, more just, and peaceful society — did not disappear. If it no longer inspired Webster and his associates, it lived on in the minds of many farmers, artisans, factory workers, shopkeepers, and small-business owners, as well as in the beliefs of the professionals, artists, intellectuals, and other members of the lower-middle and middle classes. During the late nineteenth century, a number of disaffected intellectuals sought new forms for the old progressive faith. They translated it into such political idioms as utopian socialism, the single-tax movement, the populist revolt, Progressivism in cities, and Marxism and its native variants.

THE ROOTS OF OUR ADVERSARY CULTURE

Let me turn to a set of these late-eighteenth-century ideas that was to become the basis for a powerful critique of the culture of advanced industrial society. Usually described as the viewpoint of the "counter-Enlightenment" or the "romantic reaction," these ideas have formed the basis for a surprisingly long-lived adversarial culture.

According to conventional wisdom, this critical view originated in the intellectual backlash from the triumph of the natural sciences we associate with the great discoveries of Galileo, Kepler, Harvey, and Newton. Put differently, this tendency was a reaction against the extravagant claims of the universal, not to say exclusive, truth of "the Mechanical Philosophy." That term derived from the ubiquity of the machine metaphor in the work of Newton and other natural scientists ("celestial mechanics") and many of their philosophic allies, notably Descartes, all of whom tended to conceive of nature itself as a "great engine" and its subordinate parts (including the human body) as lesser machines.

By the late eighteenth century, a powerful set of critical, antimechanistic ideas was being developed by Kant, Fichte, and other German idealists and by great English poets like Coleridge and Wordsworth. But in their time the image of the machine also was being invested with greater tangibility and social import. The Industrial Revolution was gaining momentum, and as power machinery was more widely diffused in Great Britain, Western Europe, and North America, the machine acquired much greater resonance: It came to represent both the new technologies based on mechanized motive power and the mechanistic mindset of scientific rationalism. Thus, the Scottish philosopher and historian Thomas Carlyle, who had been deeply influenced by the new German philosophy, announced in his seminal 1829 essay, "Signs of the Times," that the right name for the dawning era was the "Age of Machinery." It was to be the Age of Machinery, he warned, in every "inward" and "outward" sense of the word, meaning that it would be dominated by mechanical (utilitarian) thinking as well as by actual machines.

In his criticism of this new era, Carlyle took the view that neither kind of "machinery" was inherently dangerous. In his opinion, indeed, they represented *potential* progress as long as neither was allowed to become the exclusive or predominant mode in its respective realm.

In the United States, a small, gifted, if disaffected minority of writers, artists, and intellectuals adopted this ideology. Their version of Carlyle's critical viewpoint was labeled "romantic" in reference to its European strains, or "transcendentalist" in its native use. In the work of writers like Emerson and Thoreau, Hawthorne and Melville, we encounter critical responses to the onset of industrialism that cannot be written off as mere nostalgia or primitivism. These writers did not hold up an idealized wilderness, a pre-industrial Eden, as preferable to the world they saw in the making. Nor did they dismiss the worth of material improvement as such. But they did regard the dominant view, often represented (as in Webster's speech) by the appearance of the new machine power in the American landscape, as dangerously shallow, materialistic, and one sided. Fear of "mechanism," in the several senses of that word — especially the domination of the individual by impersonal systems — colored all of their thought. In their work, the image of the machine-in-the-landscape, far from being an occasion for exultation, often seems to arouse anxiety, dislocation, and foreboding. Henry Thoreau's detailed, carefully composed account of the intrusion of the railroad into the Concord woods is a good example; it bears out his delineation of the new inventions as "improved means to unimproved ends."

This critical view of the relationship between technological means and social ends did not merely appear in random images, phrases, and narrative episodes. Indeed, the whole of *Walden* may be read as a sustained attack on a culture that had allowed itself to become confused about the relationship of ends and means. Thoreau's countrymen are depicted as becoming "the tools of their tools." Much the same argument underlies Hawthorne's satire, "The Celestial Railroad," a modern replay of *Pilgrim's Progress* in which the hero, Christian, realizes too late that his comfortable railroad journey to salvation is taking him to hell, not heaven. Melville incorporates a similar insight into his characterization of Captain Ahab, who is the embodiment of the Faustian aspiration toward domination and total control given credence by the sudden emergence of exciting new technological capacities. Ahab exults in his power over the crew, and he explicitly identifies it with the power exhibited by the new railroad spanning the North American continent. In reflective moments, however, he also acknowledges the self-destructive nature of his own behavior: "Now in his heart, Ahab had some glimpse of this, namely, all my means are sane, my motive and my object mad."

Of course, there was nothing new about the moral posture adopted by these American writers. Indeed, their attitude toward the exuberant national celebration of the railroad and other inventions is no doubt traceable to traditional moral and religious objections to such an exaggeration of human powers. In this view, the worshipful attitude of Americans toward these new instruments of power had to be recognized for what it was: idolatry like that attacked by Old Testament prophets in a disguised, new-fashioned form. This moral critique of the debased, technocratic version of the progressive worldview has slowly gained adherents since the mid-nineteenth century, and by now it is one of the chief ideological supports of an adversary culture in the United States.

The ideas of writers like Hawthorne, Melville, and Thoreau were usually dismissed as excessively idealistic, nostalgic, or sentimental and hence impractical and unreliable. They were particularly vulnerable to that charge at a time when the rapid improvement in the material conditions of American life lent a compelling power to the idea that the meaning of history is universal progress. Only in the late twentieth century, with the growth of skepticism about scientific and technological progress, and with the emergence of a vigorous adversary culture in the 1960s, has the standpoint of that earlier eccentric minority been accorded a certain intellectual respect. To be sure, it is still chiefly the viewpoint of a relatively small minority, but there have been times, like the Vietnam upheaval of the 1960s, when that minority has won the temporary support of, or formed a tacit coalition with, a remarkably large number of other disaffected Americans. Much the same antitechnocratic viewpoint has made itself felt in various dissident movements and intellectual tendencies since the 1960s: the antinuclear movements (against both nuclear power and nuclear weaponry), some branches of the environmental and feminist movements, the "small is beautiful" and "stable-state" economic theories, as well as the quest for "soft energy paths" and "alternative (or appropriate) technologies."

TECHNOCRATIC VERSUS SOCIAL PROGRESS

Perhaps this historical summary will help explain the ambivalence toward the ideal of progress expressed by many Americans nowadays. Compared with prevailing attitudes in the United States in the 1840s, when the American situation was more like that of China today, the current mood in this country would have to be described as mildly disillusioned.

To appreciate the reasons for that disillusionment, let me repeat the distinction between the two views of progress on which this analysis rests. The initial Enlightenment belief in progress perceived science and technology to be in the service of liberation from political oppression. Over time, that conception was transformed, or partly supplanted, by the now familiar view that innovations in science-based technologies are in themselves a sufficient and reliable basis for progress. The distinction, then, turns on the apparent loss of interest in, or unwillingness to name, the social ends for which the scientific and technological instruments of power are to be used. What we seem to have instead of a guiding political goal is a minimalist definition of civic obligation.

The distinction between two versions of the belief in progress helps sort out reactions to the many troubling issues raised by the diffusion of high technology. When, for example, the introduction of some new labor-saving technology is proposed, it is useful to ask what the purpose of this new technology is. Only by questioning the assumption that innovation represents progress can we begin to judge its worth. The aim may well be to reduce labor costs, yet in our society the personal costs to the displaced workers are likely to be ignored.

The same essential defect of the technocratic mindset also becomes evident when the president of the United States calls upon those who devise nuclear weapons to provide an elaborate new system of weaponry, the Strategic Defense Initiative, as the only reliable means of avoiding nuclear war. Not only does he invite us to put all our hope in a "technological fix," but he rejects the ordinary but indispensable method of international negotiation and compromise.[1] Here again, technology is thought to obviate the need for political ideas and practices.

One final word. I perhaps need to clarify the claim that it is the modern, technocratic worldview of Webster's intellectual heirs, not the Enlightenment view descended from the Jeffersonians, that encourages the more dangerous contemporary fantasies of domination and total control. The political and social aspirations of the generation of Benjamin Franklin and Thomas Jefferson *provided tacit limits to, as well as ends for, the progressive vision of the future.* But the technocratic version so popular today entails a belief in the worth of scientific and technological innovations as ends in themselves.

All of which is to say that we urgently need a set of political, social, and cultural goals comparable to those formulated at the beginning of the Industrial Era if we are to accurately assess the worth of new technologies. Only such goals can provide the criteria required to make rational and humane choices among alternative technologies and, more important, among alternative long-term policies.

Does improved technology mean progress? Yes, it certainly *could* mean just that. But only if we are willing and able to answer the next question: Progress toward what? What is it that we want our new technologies to accomplish? What do we want beyond such immediate, limited goals as achieving efficiencies, decreasing financial costs, and eliminating the troubling human element from our workplaces? In the absence of answers to these questions, technological improvements may very well turn out to be incompatible with genuine, that is to say *social*, progress.

ENDNOTE

1. See Alvin M. Weinberg, "Can Technology Replace Social Engineering?" (Chapter 4), for a discussion of the concept of the "technological fix." — Ed.

2

How Society Shapes Technology

ROBERT POOL

Why did VHS cassette recorders succeed and Betamax fail, when most experts (and many nonexperts) agreed that Betamax was a better technology? The two formats came on the market around the same time in the mid-1970s. They are incompatible, however, so consumers had to choose one or the other. When VHS gained a small lead, perhaps because of better marketing, perhaps because it uses six-hour cassettes instead of Betamax's five, or perhaps for other reasons, video rental stores began to stock more VHS tapes. This led people to buy more VHS machines and started a self-reinforcing cycle that, in a few years, made Betamax as obsolete as eight-track audio players.

This kind of interplay between the developers of technology and the society that uses that technology is characteristic of the way in which technology and society interact. It's not technological determinism and it's not just social construction; it's a combination of the two. Robert Pool examines this fascinating interplay in depth in his book, Beyond Engineering: How Society Shapes Technology, *from which the following selection is taken. "Modern technology,"* he writes, *"is like a Great Dane in a small apartment. It may be friendly, but you still want to make sure there's nothing breakable within reach." Pool, a freelance writer living in Tallahassee, Florida, who has written for* Science *and* Discover *and was news editor at* Nature, *is the author of* Fat: Fighting the Obesity Epidemic *(2001) and* Eve's Rib: The Biological Roots of Sex Differences *(1994).*

Any modern technology is the product of a complex interplay between its designers and the larger society in which it develops.

Consider the automobile. In the early part of this century, gas-powered cars shared the roads with those powered by boilers and steam engines, such as the Stanley Steamer.[1] Eventually, internal combustion captured the market, and the old steamers disappeared. Why? The usual assumption is that the two contenders went head to head and the best technology won. Not at all.

Although the internal combustion engine did have some advantages in performance and convenience, steam-powered cars had their own pluses: They had no transmission or shifting of gears, they were simpler to build, and they were smoother and quieter to operate. Experts then and now have called it a draw — the "better" technology was mostly a matter of opinion. Instead, the steamers were killed off by several factors that had little or nothing to do with their engineering merits. For one, the Stanley brothers, builders of the best steam-powered cars of the time, had little interest in mass production. They were content to sell a few cars at high prices to aficionados who could appreciate their superiority. Meanwhile, Henry Ford and other Detroit automakers were flooding the country with inexpensive gas-powered cars. Even so, the steamers might well have survived as high-end specialty cars were it not for a series of unlucky breaks. At one point, for example, an outbreak of hoof-and-mouth disease caused public horse troughs to be drained, removing a major source of water for refilling the cars' boilers. It took the Stanley brothers three years to develop a closed-cycle steam engine that didn't need constant refilling, but by then World War I had begun, bringing strict government limits on the number of cars that businesses could build for the consumer market. The Stanley company never recovered, and it folded a few years later. The remnants of the steam automobile industry died during the Depression, when the market for high-priced cars all but disappeared.

Nonengineering factors play a role in the development of all technologies, even the simplest. In *The Pencil*, Henry Petroski tells how pencil designers in the late 1800s, in order to get around a growing shortage of red cedar, devised a pencil with a paper wrapping in place of the normal wood.[2] It "worked well technically and showed great promise," Petroski writes, "but the product failed for unanticipated psychological reasons." The public, accustomed to sharpening pencils with a knife, wanted something that could be whittled. The paper pencil never caught on.

Today, particularly for such sophisticated creations as computers, genetic engineering, or nuclear power, nontechnical factors have come to exert an influence that is unprecedented in the history of technology. Invention is no longer, as Ralph Waldo Emerson's aphorism had it, simply a matter of "Build a better mousetrap and the world will beat a path to your door." The world is already at your door, and it has a few things to say about that mousetrap.

The reasons for this are several, some grounded in the changing nature of technology itself and others arising from transformations in society. A hundred years ago, people in western nations generally saw technological development as a good thing.[3] It brought prosperity and health; it represented "progress."

But the past century has seen a dramatic change in western society, with a resulting shift in people's attitudes toward technology.[4] As countries have become more prosperous and secure, their citizens have become less concerned about increasing their material well-being and more concerned with such aesthetic considerations as maintaining a clean environment. This makes them less likely to accept new technologies uncritically. At the same time, citizens of western democracies have become more politically savvy and more active in challenging the system with lawsuits, special interest groups, campaigns to change public opinion, and other weapons. The result is that the public now exerts a much greater influence on the development of technologies — particularly those seen as risky or otherwise undesirable — than was true one hundred, or even fifty, years ago.

Meanwhile, the developers of technology have also been changing. A century ago, most innovation was done by individuals or small groups. Today, technological development tends to take place inside large, hierarchical organizations. This is particularly true for complex, large-scale technologies, since they demand large investments and extensive, coordinated development efforts. But large organizations inject into the development process a host of considerations that have little or nothing to do with engineering. Any institution has its own goals and concerns, its own set of capabilities and weaknesses, and its own biases about the best ways to do things. Inevitably, the scientists and engineers inside an institution are influenced — often quite unconsciously — by its culture.

A closely related factor is the institutionalization of science and engineering. With their professional societies, conferences, journals, and other means of communion, scientists and engineers have formed themselves into relatively close-knit — though large — groups that have uniform standards of practice and hold similar ideas. Today, opinions and decisions about a technology tend to reflect a group's thinking more than any given individual's.

The existence of large organizations and the institutionalization of the professions allow a technology to build up a tremendous amount of momentum in a relatively short time.[5] Once the choice has been made to go a certain way, even if the reasons are not particularly good ones, the institutional machinery gears up and shoves everybody in the same direction. It can be tough to resist.

But the most important changes have come in the nature of technology itself. In the twentieth century, the power of our machines and devices has grown dramatically — along with their unanticipated consequences. When DDT was introduced, it seemed an unalloyed good: a cheap, effective way to kill insect pests and improve crop yields. It took years to understand that the pesticide made its way up the food chain to weaken the shells of birds' eggs and wreak other unintended havoc. Similarly, chlorofluorocarbons, or CFCs, were widely used for decades — as refrigerants, as blowing agents in making foams, and as cleaners for computer chips — before anyone realized they were damaging the ozone layer.

Even normally benign technologies can take on different complexions when multiplied to meet the needs of a world with five billion people. Burning natural gas is an economical, safe, and clean way to heat homes and generate electricity.

Its only major waste material is carbon dioxide, the same gas that humans exhale with each breath. But carbon dioxide, in the quantities now being produced worldwide by burning fossil fuels (coal and oil as well as natural gas), is exaggerating the greenhouse effect in the earth's atmosphere and threatening major changes in the global climate.

Modern technology is like a Great Dane in a small apartment. It may be friendly, but you still want to make sure there's nothing breakable within reach. So to protect the china and crystal, government bodies, special interest groups, businesses, and even individuals are demanding an increasing say in how technologies are developed and applied.

Besides its power, modern technology has a second feature — more subtle, but equally important — that makes it qualitatively different from earlier technologies: its complexity. The plow, the cotton gin, even the light bulb — these are simple devices. No matter how much they are changed and improved, it is still easy to understand their functions and capabilities. But for better or worse, technology has reached the point where no individual can understand completely how, say, a petrochemical plant works, and no team of experts can anticipate every possible outcome once a technology is put to work. Such complexity fundamentally changes our relationship with technology.

Consider the accident that destroyed the space shuttle *Challenger*.[6] Although the cause was eventually established as the failure of O-rings at low temperatures, which allowed the escape of hot gases and led to an explosion of a fuel tank, the real culprit was the complexity of the system. Space-shuttle engineers had been concerned about how the O-rings would behave in below-freezing weather, and some even recommended the launch be postponed to a warmer day, but no one could predict with any certainty what might happen. There were too many variables, too many ways in which the components of the system could interact. Management decided to proceed with the launch despite the engineers' disquiet, and it was only months later that experts pieced together the chain of events that led to the explosion.

Complexity creates uncertainty, limiting what can be known or reasonably surmised about a technology ahead of time. Although the shuttle engineers had vague fears, they simply did not — could not — know enough about the system to foresee the looming disaster. And in such cases, when there is not a clear technical answer, people fall back on subjective, often unconscious reasoning — biases and gut feelings, organizational goals, political considerations, the profit motive. In the case of the *Challenger*, NASA was feeling pressure to keep its shuttles going into space on a regular basis, and no one in the organization wanted to postpone a launch unless it was absolutely necessary. In this case, it was, but no one knew.

For all these reasons, modern technology is not simply the rational product of scientists and engineers that it is often advertised to be. Look closely at any technology today, from aircraft to the Internet, and you'll find that it truly makes sense only when seen as part of the society in which it grew up.

The insight is not a particularly new one. Thoughtful engineers have discussed it for some time. As early as the 1960s, Alvin Weinberg, the longtime director of Oak Ridge National Laboratory, was writing on the relationship between technology and society, particularly in regard to nuclear power.[7] There have been others. But until recently no one had studied the influence of society on technology in any consistent, comprehensive way. Philosophically inclined engineers like Weinberg did not have the time, the temperament, or the training to make careful studies. They reported what they saw and mused about the larger implications, but nothing more. And social scientists, when they noticed technology at all, viewed it primarily in terms of how it shapes society. Sociologists, economists, and others have long seen technology as the driving force behind much of history — a theory usually referred to as "technological determinism"[8] — and they have happily investigated such things as how the invention of the printing press triggered the Reformation, how the development of the compass ushered in the Age of Exploration and the discovery of the New World, and how the cotton gin created the conditions that led to the Civil War.[9] But few of these scientists turned the question around and asked how society shapes technology.

In just the past decade or two, however, that has begun to change. Indeed, it has now become almost fashionable for economists, political scientists, and sociologists to bring their analytical tools to bear on various technologies, from nuclear power and commercial aviation to medical instruments, computers, even bicycles.[10] Part of the reason for this is, I suspect, the increasing importance of technology to our world, and another part is the realization by social scientists that science and technology are just as amenable to social analysis as politics or religion. Whatever the reason, the result has been to put technology in a whole new light. Scholars now talk about the push and pull between technology and society, rather than just the push of technology on society. Engineers have been brought down from the mountain to take their place as one — still very important — cog in the system by which technology is delivered to the world.

Unfortunately, very little of this has filtered down. It remains mostly specialists talking to other specialists in books and journals that few outside their fields ever see. [The book from which this chapter is taken] aims to change that. From its original design as a study of how engineers are creating a new generation of nuclear power, it has metamorphosed into a more general — and more ambitious — look at how nontechnical forces shape modern technologies. In it I collect and synthesize work from a wide variety of disciplines: history, economics, political science, sociology, risk analysis, management science, psychology. At various points, the book touches on personal computers, genetic engineering, jet aircraft, space flight, automobiles, chemical plants, even steam engines and typewriters. Such a book obviously cannot be comprehensive. Instead, my goal is to introduce a different way to think about technology and to show how many things make much more sense when technology is viewed in this way.

★★★

Lurking just beneath the surface … is one of the most intriguing and frustrating questions of our time, although it seldom gets much attention outside universities and other scholarly places: How do we know what we know? Or, to put it differently, what is the nature of human knowledge? This may sound like the sort of abstract question that only a philosopher could love, but its answer has practical — and important — ramifications for how we deal with science and technology.

There are two schools of thought on the nature of human knowledge, and they have little common ground. One has its roots in the physical sciences and goes by such names as positivism or objectivism or rationalism. Positivism accepts as knowledge only those things that have been verified by the scientific method of hypothesis formation and testing. It is, of course, impossible to verify anything absolutely — no matter how many times the sun comes up right on schedule, there is no guarantee it won't be a couple of hours late tomorrow — but positivists are generally content with verifying something beyond a reasonable doubt. Karl Popper, the influential philosopher of science, put a slightly different spin on it: Scientific statements, he said, are those that can be put to the test and potentially proven wrong, or falsified. It's not possible to prove a hypothesis is true, but if the hypothesis is tested extensively and never proven false, then one accepts it as provisionally true. If it later turns out to be false in certain situations, it can be modified or replaced. By this method, one hopes to get better and better approximations to the world's underlying physical reality. Absolute knowledge is not attainable. This provisional knowledge is the best we can do.

The strength of positivism — its insistence on verification — is also its weakness, for there is much that people think of as "knowledge" that cannot be verified in the same way that theories in physics or biology can. "The United States is a capitalist country" is a statement most would accept as true, but how does one prove it? Or how about, "Santa Claus wears a red suit and rides in a sleigh pulled by eight reindeer"? This is clearly knowledge of a sort — everyone in our culture older than two or three "knows" it — and though it may not be in the same intellectual league as, say, the general theory of relativity, it's much more important to most people than anything Einstein came up with. Yet the positivist approach has no place for such folderol.

For many years, social scientists, impressed with the success of the physical sciences, modeled their methods along the same positivist lines. They made observations, formed hypotheses, and tested their theories, attempting to make their research as objective as possible. Many social scientists still do, but in the past few decades an influential new school of thought has appeared, one that offers a different take on human knowledge. This approach, often referred to as "social construction"[11] or "interpretation," is designed explicitly to deal with social reality — the web of relationships, institutions, and shared beliefs and meanings that exist in a group of people — instead of physical reality. It sees knowledge not as something gleaned from an underlying physical reality but as the collective product of a society. Social constructionists speak not of objective facts but only of interpretations of the world, and they set out to explain how those interpretations arise. They make no attempt to judge the truth or falsity of socially constructed knowledge. Indeed, they deny that it even makes sense to ask whether such knowledge is true or false.

Thus, positivism and social construction offer diametrically opposed views of knowledge. Positivists see knowledge as arising from nature; social constructionists see it as a product of the human mind. Positivists speak of proof, social constructionists of interpretation. Positivists assume knowledge to be objective; social constructionists believe it to be subjective. In general, positivists have been willing to defer to the social constructionists in the case of social knowledge. After all, information about Santa Claus or the importance of capitalism is not really what a positivist has in mind when he speaks about "knowledge." But the social constructionists have been unwilling to return the favor and so have triggered a sharp, if so far bloodless, battle.

All human knowledge is social knowledge, the social constructionists say, even science.[12] After all, scientific knowledge is created by groups of people — the scientific community and its various subsets — and so it inevitably has a collective character. There is no such thing as a scientific truth believed by one person and disbelieved by the rest of the scientific community; an idea becomes a truth only when a vast majority of scientists accept it without question. But if this is so, the argument goes, then science is best understood as socially constructed rather than derived in some objective way from nature.

The earliest and best-known example of this approach to science is Thomas Kuhn's *The Structure of Scientific Revolutions*.[13] In it, Kuhn depicts most science as taking place inside a "paradigm" — a set of beliefs and expectations that guide the research, defining which questions are important and designating the proper ways to go about answering them. Scientific revolutions — such as the shift from the Ptolemaic to the Copernican view of the universe — occur when a paradigm breaks down and the scientific community collectively settles on a new paradigm in which to work. Kuhn argued that because such a paradigm shift is a change of the rules by which science is done, there can be no objective reasons for making the shift or for deciding on one paradigm over another. The choice is a subjective one. Ironically, much of the positivist scientific community has accepted the general idea of paradigms without understanding the deeper implications of Kuhn's work. It's not unusual to hear a scientist speak of "working within a paradigm" even though that scientist would be appalled by Kuhn's claim that scientific paradigms have no objective basis.

Today, many social scientists agree with Kuhn that the positivist claims for science were a myth. For example, in 1987 the sociologists Trevor Pinch and Wiebe Bijker wrote:

> [T]here is widespread agreement that scientific knowledge can be, and indeed has been, shown to be thoroughly socially constructed.... The treatment of scientific knowledge as a social construction implies that there is nothing epistemologically special about the nature of scientific knowledge: It is merely one in a whole series of knowledge cultures (including for instance, the knowledge systems pertaining to "primitive" tribes). Of course, the successes and failures of certain knowledge cultures still need to be explained, but this is to be seen as a sociological task, not an epistemological one.[14]

Such comments anger many scientists. Physicists especially dispute the conclusions of the social constructionists.[15,16] Yes, they admit, of course the creation of scientific knowledge is a joint effort, but nonetheless it *is* epistemologically special. Quantum mechanics, for instance, provides predictions that are consistently accurate to a dozen or more decimal places. This is no accident, they insist, but instead reflects the fact that science is uncovering and explaining some objective reality.

On the whole, the physicists get the better of this particular argument. Social construction theory is useful in explaining social knowledge and belief, but it does little to explain why physicists accept general relativity or quantum mechanics as accurate portrayals of physical reality. Social constructionists like Pinch and Bijker ignore a key difference between science and other knowledge cultures: science's insistence that its statements be falsifiable.[17] As long as science restricts itself in this way and continues testing its theories and discarding those that disagree with experiments, it is indeed epistemologically special. This and nothing else explains why science has been so much more successful than other knowledge cultures. Science may not be as objective as the positivists would like to believe, but the positivist approach comes closer than any other to capturing the essence of science.

This all may seem to be a tempest in an academic teapot, a question of interest to no one besides philosophers and the handful of scientists with an interest in epistemology, but it underlies many of the debates on scientific issues that affect the public. Consider the controversy in the mid–1980s over the use of recombinant bovine growth hormone in dairy cattle. Although the scientific community pronounced it safe, opponents of its use suggested that the researchers were influenced more by the sources of funding for their research and by their own inherent biases than by evidence.[18] This argument depended implicitly upon the assumption that the scientific opinions were not objective but rather were socially constructed. In general, if science is accepted as objective, people will give a great deal of weight to the conclusions of the scientific community and to the professional opinions of individual scientists. But if science is seen as a social construct, vulnerable to biases and fashion, people will question or even dismiss its conclusions.

Which brings us back to our original subject. At its heart, [the book from which this chapter was taken is] about technological knowledge: What is it? and, How is it formed? Traditionally, engineers have seen their work in positivist terms. Like scientists, they take it for granted that their work is objective, and they believe that to understand a technology, all one needs are the technical details. They see a strict dichotomy between the pure logic of their machines and the subjectivity and the irrationality of the world in which they must operate. On the other hand, a growing school of social scientists sees technology as socially constructed. Its objectivity, they say, is a myth created and propagated by engineers who believe their own press. As with science, this is no mere academic debate. Our attitudes toward technology hinge, in large part, on what we believe about the nature of the knowledge underlying it.

To understand technological knowledge, this book argues, it is necessary to marry the positivist and the social constructionist perspectives. Technology combines the physical world with the social, the objective with the subjective, the machine with the man. If one imagines a spectrum with scientific knowledge on one end and social knowledge on the other, technological knowledge lies somewhere in the middle. It is falsifiable to a certain extent, but not nearly to the same degree as science. Conversely, much of technological knowledge is socially constructed, but there are limits — no matter what a group of people thinks or does, an airplane design that can't fly won't fly. In short, the physical world restricts technology. Some things work better than others, some don't work at all, and this leads to a certain amount of objectivity in technological knowledge. But, unlike scientists, engineers are working with a world of their own creation, and the act of creation cannot be understood in positivist terms.

Ultimately, any understanding of technological knowledge must recognize the composite nature of that knowledge. Our technological creations carry with them the traces of both the engineer and the larger society.

ENDNOTES

1. Charles McLaughlin, "The Stanley Steamer: A Study in Unsuccessful Innovation," *Explorations in Entrepreneurial History* 7 (October 1954), pp. 37–47.

2. Henry Petroski, *The Pencil* (New York: Alfred A. Knopf, 1989), p. 207.

3. Merritt Roe Smith, "Technological Determinism in American Culture," in Merritt Roe Smith and Leo Marx, eds., *Does Technology Drive History?* (Cambridge, MA: MIT Press, 1994), pp. 1–35.

4. Ronald Inglehart, *The Silent Revolution: Changing Values and Policy Styles among Western Publics* (Princeton, NJ: Princeton University Press, 1977), p. 3.

5. Thomas P. Hughes, "Technological History and Technical Problems," in Chauncey Starr and Philip C. Ritterbush, eds., *Science, Technology and the Human Prospect* (New York: Pergamon, 1980), p. 141.

6. Maureen Hogan Casamayou, *Bureaucracy in Crisis: Three Mile Island, the Shuttle Challenger and Risk Assessment* (Boulder, CO: Westview, 1993), pp. 57–85.

7. Alvin M. Weinberg, *Nuclear Reactions: Science and Trans-Science* (New York: American Institute of Physics, 1992). See also Alvin M. Weinberg, *The First Nuclear Era: The Life and Times of a Technological Fixer* (New York: American Institute of Physics, 1994).

8. For a critical review of technological determinism, see Merritt Roe Smith and Leo Marx, eds., *Does Technology Drive History?* (Cambridge, MA: MIT Press, 1994).

9. Leo Marx and Merritt Roe Smith, introduction to Marx and Smith, *Does Technology Drive History?* p. x.

10. There have been a number of books published recently that analyze technology from a social science perspective. They include Wiebe E. Bijker, Thomas P. Hughes, and Trevor Pinch, eds., *The Social Construction of Technological Systems: New Directions in the Sociology and History of Technology* (Cambridge, MA: MIT Press, 1987); Marcel C. LaFollette and Jeffrey K. Stine, eds., *Technology and Choice: Readings from Technology and Culture* (Chicago: University of Chicago Press, 1991);

Meinolf Dierkes and Ute Hoffmann, eds., *New Technology at the Outset: Social Forces in the Shaping of Technological Innovations* (Boulder, CO: Westview, 1992); Wiebe Bijker and John Law, eds., *Shaping Technology/Building Society: Studies in Sociotechnical Change* (Cambridge, MA: MIT Press, 1992); Wiebe E. Bijker, *Of Bicycles, Bakelites, and Bulbs: Toward a Theory of Sociotechnical Change* (Cambridge, MA: MIT Press, 1995). See also various issues of *Technology and Culture; Technology in Society; Science, Technology & Human Values*; and *Technology Review*.

11. The seminal work here is Peter L. Berger and Thomas Luckmann, *The Social Construction of Reality: A Treatise in the Sociology of Knowledge* (New York: Doubleday, 1966).

12. A good summary of the social constructionist approach to scientific knowledge can be found in Trevor J. Pinch and Wiebe E. Bijker, "The Social Construction of Facts and Artifacts: Or How the Sociology of Science and the Sociology of Technology Might Benefit Each Other," in Bijker, Hughes, and Pinch, *The Social Construction of Technological Systems*, pp. 17–50.

13. Thomas S. Kuhn, *The Structure of Scientific Revolutions* (Chicago: University of Chicago Press, 1962).

14. Pinch and Bijker, "The Social Construction of Facts and Artifacts," pp. 18–19.

15. David Mermin, a very thoughtful physicist at Cornell University, offers a careful refutation of the social construction of physics in a two-part article: "What's Wrong with the Sustaining Myth?" *Physics Today* 49 (March 1996), pp. 11, 13; and "The Golemization of Relativity," *Physics Today* 49 (April 1996), pp. 11, 13.

16. In spring 1996, the dispute between physicists and social constructionists took an amusing turn — amusing, at least, for the physicists — when Alan Sokal published an article entitled "Transgressing the Boundaries: Toward a Transformative Hermeneutics of Quantum Gravity" in *Social Text*, a "postmodernist" journal devoted to social constructionist analyses. Sokal, a physicist at New York University, later revealed that it was all a hoax. He had cobbled together bad science, even worse logic, and a bunch of catch phrases from postmodernist theorizing and had somehow convinced the editors of *Social Text* that the nonsensical article was a contribution worthy of publication. The editors were understandably not amused but neither were they contrite. They did not seem to see it as a weakness on their part — or even less, on the part of the entire postmodernist movement — that they could not tell the difference between an obvious hoax and what passes for serious work in their field. The original article appeared in *Social Text* 46/47 (Spring/Summer 1996), pp. 217–252. Sokal revealed the hoax in "A Physicist Experiments with Cultural Studies," *Lingua Franca* (May/June 1996), pp. 62–64.

17. This argument is modified from one offered by Thelma Lavine, Clarence J. Robinson Professor of Philosophy at George Mason University in Fairfax, Virginia.

18. W. P. Norton, "Just Say Moo," *The Progressive* (November 1989), pp. 26–29. See also Gina Kolata, "When the Geneticists' Fingers Get in the Food," *New York Times* (February 20, 1994), sec. 4, p. 14.

3

The Shock of the Old

DAVID EDGERTON

The words "new" and "technology" seem to go together. We speak of "techno-logical change," "technological innovation," and "technological revolutions." But what of old, commonplace technologies? Do they just disappear in the face of the new ones? David Edgerton contends that they remain with us and, although we tend to overlook them or take them for granted, in a global perspective they can be more important than those that supposedly take their place.

The focus on the new can blind us to the pervasiveness of the old. Edgerton calls on us to view technology not just as the latest inventions but in terms of what people — ordinary people around the world — actually use. Seen in that light, relatively simple and mundane technologies — for example, corrugated iron — take on much more importance than we recognize. Spread around the world by the military during the days of the British Empire, "Its cheapness, lightness, ease of use and long life made it a ubiquitous material in the poor world in a way it never had been in the rich world." Edgerton considers corrugated iron as it is used in devel-oping countries, and other cheap building materials such as asbestos cement, to be "creole" technologies — hybrids resulting from local adaptations, especially in poor countries, of technologies imported from rich ones. Such a use-centered approach places the relations of technology and society in an entirely new perspective.

David Edgerton is Hans Rausing Professor of the History of Science and Technology in the Centre for the History of Science, Technology and Medicine at Imperial College, London. He is regarded as one of Britain's leading historians and is known for challenging conventional views of technology, a perspective he shows clearly in this chapter. His most recent book is Britain's War Machine: Weapons, Resources, and Experts in the Second World War, *published in 2011.*

Much of what is written on the history of technology is for boys of all ages. [The book from which this chapter is drawn] is a history for grown-ups of all genders. We have lived with technology for a long time, and collectively we know a lot about it. From economists to ecologists, from antiquarians to historians, people have had different views about the material world around us and how it has changed. Yet too often the agenda for discussing the past, present and future of technology is set by the promoters of new technologies.

When we are told about technology from on high we are made to think about novelty and the future. For many decades now the term 'technology' has been closely linked with *invention* (the creation of a new idea) and *innovation* (the first use of a new idea). Talk about technology centres on research and development, patents and the early stages of use, for which the term *diffusion* is used. The timelines of technological history, and they abound, are based on dates of invention and innovation. The most significant twentieth-century technologies are often reduced to the following: flight (1903), nuclear power (1945), contraception (1955), and the internet (1965). We are told that change is taking place at an ever-accelerating pace, and that the new is increasingly powerful. The world, the gurus insist, is entering a new historical epoch as a result of technology. In the new economy, in new times, in our post-industrial and post-modern condition, knowledge of the present and past is supposedly ever less relevant. Inventors, even in these post-modern times, are 'ahead of their time', while societies suffer from the grip of the past, resulting in a supposed slowness to adapt to new technology.

There are new things under the sun, and the world is indeed changing radically, but this way of thinking is not among them. Although the emphasis on the future itself suggests originality, this kind of futurology has been with us a long time. In the nineteenth century the idea that inventors were ahead of their time and that science and technology were advancing faster than the ability of human society to cope was a commonplace. By the early twentieth century this notion was made academically respectable with the label 'the cultural lag'. In the 1950s and even later, one could claim without embarrassment that scientists 'had the future in their bones'. By the end of the twentieth century, futurism had long been *passé*. The technological future was as it had been for a long time. Intellectuals claimed there was a new kind of future, one prefigured by 'post-modern' architecture. Yet this new kind of future was to be brought about by an old-style technological or industrial revolution which would change everything.

In the case of technology reheated futurism has held its appeal long after it was declared obsolete. The technological future marched on as before. Consider the case of the first successful flight of NASA's X-43A space aeroplane on 27 March 2004. Although it lasted all of ten seconds, it made the news the world over. 'From Kitty Hawk to the X-43A has been a century's steady advance', wrote one newspaper; from 'seven miles an hour to Mach Seven is a striking indication of how far powered flight has travelled in a hundred years'.[1] Soon we would be enjoying, yet again, almost instant travel to Australia from London.

Just below the surface was another history, which blew great holes in this old-fashioned story. Every few weeks between 1959 and 1968 B-52 aircraft took off from Edwards Air Force Base in California, with one of three X-15s under their wings. Once high up the X-15s fired their rocket engines and were actively flown by twelve 'research pilots', clad in silver pressurised space suits, reaching speeds of Mach 6.7 and touching the edge of space. These hard-drinking engineer-pilots, mostly combat veterans (among them Neil Armstrong, the first man to set foot on the moon), looked down on mere 'spam in the can' astronauts, as Tom Wolfe observed in *The Right Stuff*. While the astronauts became famous, the elite X-15 pilots were left to lament, as one did, that in the early 1990s he was still 'one of the fastest airplane pilots in the world. I am too old for that. Someone younger should have that honor.'[2] Past and present were connected even more directly. The B-52, which took the X-43A and its booster rocket up, was one of the same B-52s used on the X-15 programmes and was now the oldest flying B-52 in the world.[3] It was built in the 1950s. Not only that, but the key technology of the X-43A was the scramjet, a supersonic version of the ramjet. A technique decades old, it was used in a 1950s-designed British anti-aircraft missile, the Bloodhound, which was itself in service into the 1990s. In short, the story might well have been '1950s aeroplane launches unmanned ramjet plane which flies a little faster than 1960s Right Stuff pilots'.

★★★

By thinking about the history of technology-in-use a radically different picture of technology, and indeed of invention and innovation, becomes possible.[4] A whole invisible world of technologies appears. It leads to a rethinking of our notion of technological time, mapped as it is on innovation-based timelines. Even more importantly it alters our picture of which have been the most important technologies. It yields a global history, whereas an innovation-centred one, for all its claims to universality, is based on a very few places. It will give us a history which does not fit the usual schemes of modernity, one which refutes some important assumptions of innovation-centric accounts.

The new history will be surprisingly different. For example, steam power, held to be characteristic of the industrial revolution, was not only absolutely but relatively more important in 1900 than in 1800. Even in Britain, the lead country of the industrial revolution, it continued to grow in absolute importance after that. Britain consumed much more coal in the 1950s than in the 1850s. The world consumed more coal in 2000 than in 1950 or 1900. It has more motor cars, aeroplanes, wooden furniture and cotton textiles than ever before. The tonnage of world shipping continues to increase. We still have buses, trains, radio, television and the cinema, and consume ever-increasing quantities of paper, cement and steel. The production of books continues to increase. Even the key novel technology of the late twentieth century, the electronic computer, has been around for many decades. The post-modern world has forty-year-old nuclear power stations as well as fifty-year old bombers. It has more than a dash of technological retro about it too: it has new ocean-going passenger ships, organic food and classical music played on 'authentic' instruments. Aging, and even dead, rock stars of the 1960s still generate large sales, and children are brought up with Disney films seen by their grandparents when they were children.

Use-centred history is not simply a matter of moving technological time forward. As Bruno Latour has aptly noted, modern time, where this behaved as moderns believed, has never existed. Time was always jumbled up, in the pre-modern era, the post-modern era and the modern era. We worked with old and new things, with hammers and electric drills.[5] In use-centred history technologies do not only appear, they also disappear and reappear, and mix and match across the centuries. Since the late 1960s many more bicycles were produced globally each year than cars.[6] The guillotine made a gruesome return in the 1940s. Cable TV declined in the 1950s to reappear in the 1980s. The supposedly obsolete battleship saw more action in the Second World War than in the First. Furthermore, the twentieth century has seen cases of technological regression.

A use-based history will do much more than disturb our tidy timelines of progress. What we take to be the most significant technologies will change. Our accounts of significance have been peculiarly innovation-centric, and tied to particular accounts of modernity where particular new technologies were held to be central. In the new picture, twentieth-century technology is not just a matter of electricity, mass production, aerospace, nuclear power, the internet and the contraceptive pill. It will involve the rickshaw, the condom, the horse, the sewing machine, the spinning wheel, the Haber-Bosch process, the hydrogenation of coal, cemented-carbide tools, bicycles, corrugated iron, cement, asbestos, DDT, the chain saw and the refrigerator. The horse made a greater contribution to Nazi conquest than the V2.

A central feature of use-based history, and a new history of invention, is that alternatives exist for nearly all technologies: there are multiple military technologies, means of generating electricity, powering a motor car, storing and manipulating information, cutting metal or roofing a building. Too often histories are written as if no alternative could or did exist.

One particularly important feature of use-based history of technology is that it can be genuinely global. It includes all places that use technology, not just the small number of places where invention and innovation is concentrated. In the innovation-centric account, most places have no history of technology. In use-centred accounts, nearly everywhere does. It gives us a history of technology engaged with all the world's population, which is mostly poor, non-white and half female. A use-perspective points to the significance of novel technological worlds which have emerged in the twentieth century and which have hitherto had no place in histories of technology. Among them are the new technologies of poverty. They are missed because the poor world is thought of as having traditional local technologies, a *lack* of rich-world technologies, and/or has been subject to imperial technological violence. When we think of cities we should think of *bidonvilles* as well as Alphaville; we should think not just about the planned cities of Le Corbusier, but the unplanned shanty towns, built not by great contractors, but by millions of self-builders over many years. These are worlds of what I call 'creole' technologies, technologies transplanted from their place of origin finding uses on a greater scale elsewhere.

A consequence of the new approach is that we shift attention from the new to the old, the big to the small, the spectacular to the mundane, the masculine to the feminine, the rich to the poor. But at its core is a rethinking of the history of all technology, including the big, spectacular, masculine high technologies of the rich white world. For all the critiques, we do not in fact have a coherent productionist, masculine, materialist account of technology and history in the twentieth century. We have big questions, and big issues to address, which are surprisingly open.

A use-centred account also refutes some well-established conclusions of innovation-centric history. For example, it undermines the assumption that national innovation determines national success; the most innovative nations of the twentieth century have not been the fastest growing. Perhaps the most surprising criticism that arises from the use perspective is that innovation-centric history gives us an inadequate account of invention and innovation. Innovation-centric history focuses on the early history of some technologies which became important later. The history of invention and innovation needs to focus on all inventions and innovations at a particular time, independently of their later success or failure. It needs to look too to invention and innovation in all technologies, not just those favoured by being well known and assumed to be the most significant. Traditional innovation-centric histories have space for Bill Gates, but a history of invention and innovation would also include Ingvar Kamprad, who made his money from mass-producing and selling wooden furniture. He founded IKEA and is, some think, richer than Gates. More importantly, our histories need to have a place for the majority of failed inventions and innovations. Most inventions are never used; many innovations fail.

The innovation-centric view also misleads us as to the nature of scientists and engineers. It presents them, as they present themselves, as creators, designers, researchers. Yet the majority have always been mainly concerned with the operation and maintenance of things and processes; with the uses of things, not their invention or development.

★★★

Given the importance of innovation-centric futurism in discussing technology, history can be an especially powerful tool for rethinking technology. History reveals that technological futurism is largely unchanging over time. Present visions of the future display a startling, unselfconscious lack of originality. Take the extraordinary litany of technologies which promised peace to the world. Communications technologies, from railways and steamships, to radio and the aeroplane, and now the internet, seemed to make the world smaller and bring people together, ensuring a perpetual peace. Technologies of destruction, such as the great ironclad battleships, Nobel's explosives, the bomber aircraft and the atomic bomb were so powerful that they too would force the world to make peace. New technologies of many sorts would emancipate the downtrodden. The old class system would wither under the meritocracy demanded by new technology; racial minorities would gain new opportunities — as chauffeurs in the motor age, pilots in the air age, and computer experts in the information age. Women were to be liberated by new domestic technologies, from the vacuum cleaner to the washing machine. The differences between nations would evaporate as technology overcame borders. Political systems too would converge as technology, inevitably, became the same everywhere. The socialist and capitalist worlds would become one.

In order to be at all convincing these arguments had to deny their own history, and they did so to a remarkable extent. The obliteration of even recent history has been continuous and systematic. For example, in the middle of 1945 the bomber ceased to be a peace-creating technology; the atomic bomb took its place. When we think of information technology we forget about postal systems, the telegraph, the telephone, radio and television. When we celebrate on-line shopping, the mail-order catalogue goes missing. Genetic engineering, and its positive and negative impacts, is discussed as if there had never been any other means of changing animals or plants, let alone other means of increasing food supply. A history of how things were done in the past, and of the way past futurology has worked, will undermine most contemporary claims to novelty.

We need to be aware that this futurology of the past has affected our history. From it we get our focus on invention and innovation, and on the technologies which we take to be the most important. From this literature, the work of low and middle-ranking intellectuals and propagandists, ranging from, say, the books of H. G. Wells to the press releases of NASA's PR officials, we get a whole series of clichéd claims about technology and history. We should take them, not as well-grounded contributions to our understanding, for they rarely are that, but as the basis of questions. What have been the most significant technologies of the twentieth century? Has the world become a global village? Has culture lagged behind technology? Has technology had revolutionary or conservative social and political effects? Has new technology been responsible for the dramatic increase in economic output in the last hundred years? Has technology transformed war? Has the rate of technical change been ever increasing? These are … questions … [that] cannot be answered within the innovation-centric frame in which they are usually asked.

These questions become much easier to answer if we stop thinking about 'technology', but instead think of 'things'. Thinking about the use of things, rather than of technology, connects us directly with the world we know rather than the strange world in which 'technology' lives. We speak of 'our' technology, meaning the technology of an age or a whole society. By contrast 'things' fit into no such totality, and do not evoke what is often taken as an independent historical force. We discuss the world of things as grown-ups, but technology as children. For example, we all know that while the use of things is widely distributed through societies, ultimate control of things and their use has been highly concentrated, within societies and between societies. Ownership, and other forms of authority, on the one hand, and use on the other, have been radically separated. Most people in the world live in houses that do not belong to them, work in workplaces belonging to others, with tools that belong to others, and indeed many of the things they apparently own are often tied to credit agreements. Within societies, states and/or small groups have had disproportionate control; some societies have much more stuff than others. In many places of the world much is owned by foreigners. Things belong to particular people in ways which technology does not.

★★★

We have long been told that we live with an 'ever-increasing rate of change', yet there is good evidence that it is not always increasing. Measuring change is extremely difficult, but let us start with economic growth in the rich countries as a crude measure. While there was rapid growth before the Great War, there was slower growth overall between 1913 and 1950. There was spectacular growth in the long boom, followed by less strong growth since. In other words, growth rates were lower in the interwar years than before 1914, and average rates of economic growth after 1973 were considerably lower than in the period 1950–1973. In the 1970s there was a 'productivity slowdown' and since then the rich world has continued to grow, but not at historically unprecedented rates.

Since the 1980s one could be forgiven for believing that high growth rates had returned, not least because of the constant evocations of the notion of 'ever increasing change', and all the talk of fundamental transitions to new economies and new times. But in the USA, Japan, the EU and Britain, growth rates were lower in the 1990s than in the 1980s, lower in the 1980s than in the 1970s and lower in the 1970s than in the 1960s.[7] In the USA it appears that productivity growth increased in the late 1990s, but there is still a dispute as to whether this was general, or concentrated in the computer-manufacturing sector.[8] Growth is not the same as change but there is no evidence that structural change in the rich countries was any faster in recent decades than in the long boom. Once again, our future-oriented rhetoric has underestimated the past, and overestimated the power of the present.

Not all parts of the world grew at these same rhythms. For example the USSR grew very fast in the 1930s, while the rest of the world did not. Especially since the 1970s many economies in the Far East have grown very fast, but from a low base. The increasing scale of the Chinese economy in particular has meant that its growth has been enough to alter the global statistics materially. For example, global steel production is growing at long boom rates again thanks to China.

Another important feature of change in the last three decades is that there has been a decline of economies, as well as growth. In some places the last years of the twentieth century saw retrogression. The income per head of the 700 million sub-Saharan Africans fell from $700 per head in 1980 to the even more miserable $500 at the end of the century; to make matters worse for the majority, 45 per cent of this output was produced in South Africa so the real fall elsewhere was even worse.[9] Malaria has become more common, and new diseases such a HIV/AIDS have swept through the continent as no other. Yet this is not a reversion to an old world, for this is a continent with cars and new kinds of shanty towns, a rapidly urbanising world without what is taken to be modern industry.

From 1989 there was a remarkably rapid collapse in the economies of the Soviet Union and its former satellites, of 20, 30 and 40 per cent, far outstripping the capitalist recession of the early 1980s. Although this dramatic fall in output cannot be characterised generally as a technological retrogression such a phenomenon was evident in some places. Now independent Moldova, formerly part of the USSR, lost 60 per cent of its output. Machines virtually phased out as the economy had developed since the Second World War, things such as 'spinning wheels, weaving looms, butter churns, wooden grape presses and stone bread ovens — are now back in use', it was reported in 2001. The 'only way to survive is to be totally self-sufficient,' claimed the curator of the ethnological museum in Belsama, 'and that means turning the clock back.'[10] Cuba, as we have seen, expanded the number of its oxen as it lost its supply of tractors.

In some industries, such as shipbreaking, there has been a move towards a new kind of low-tech future. By the 1980s Taiwan had become by far the largest shipbreaker, demolishing more than a third of the world's ships. By the early 1990s it was out of this industry, now dominated by India, Pakistan and Bangladesh, which between them had more than 80 per cent of the world market by 1995.[11] Taiwan used specialised dock facilities, but the new shipbreaking was on beaches, with the most minimal equipment, carried out by thousands of barefoot workers. The reason shipbreaking was done in these places was that scrap steel was in demand locally. But it is used in a markedly different way from other places and times: it is re-rolled, re-worked, rather than used to make fresh steel.

What seems at first technological retrogression was perhaps not unknown in earlier years of the century. No one had ever attempted to build such a large canal with what were then such primitive means as were used on the White Sea canal or in the erection of the great steel works of Magnitogorsk. Collective farming itself involved technological retrogression, for all the emphasis on the tractor. However, not for many centuries has a global industry retrogressed like shipbreaking has.

★★★

This [chapter] has argued for the importance of the seemingly old. It is also a plea for a novel way of looking at the technological world, one which will change our minds about what that world has been like. And implicit in it is a plea for novel ways of thinking about the technological present.

We should be aware, for example, that most change is taking place by the transfer of techniques from place to place. The scope for such change is enormous given the level of inequalities that exist with respect to technology. Even among rich countries there are very important differences in, for example, carbon intensity. If the USA were to reduce its energy-use levels to those of Japan, the impact on total energy use would be very significant. But for poor countries, as well as for rich ones, such a message is often unwelcome. For *imitating* is seen as a much less worthy activity than innovating. To imitate, to replicate, is to deny one's creativity, to impose upon oneself what was designed for others by others. '*Que inventen ellos*' ('Let *them* invent') is seen not as sensible policy advice, but a recipe for national humiliation. To have technology or science is, it is often deeply felt, to create something new. The answer to such concerns that is implicit in this book is that all countries, firms, individuals, with rare and unusual exceptions, have relied on others to invent, and have imitated more than they have invented.

Arguments about imitating policies and practices for innovation might seem to fall in the same category. That is to say, that it might seem like a good thing that they should be the same or similar around the world. Indeed there is a remarkable lack of originality in innovation policies globally, and many explicit calls for copying those perceived as the most successful models. Yet while copying existing technology is very sensible, imitating innovation policies may be a mistake. For if all nations, areas and firms are agreed about what the research should be, by definition it will no longer be innovative; and it might not be a good thing that all nations pursue the same policies for research, because they are likely to come up with similar inventions only a few of which will be used even if technologically successful. 'If I knew the future of jazz I'd be there already,' said one wise musician.

Calling for innovation is, paradoxically, a common way of avoiding change when change is not wanted. The argument that future science and technology will deal with global warming is an instance. It is implicitly arguing that in today's world only what we have is possible. Yet we have the technological capacity to do things very differently: we are not technologically determined.

Getting away, as [the book from which this chapter is drawn] has, from the conflation of use and invention/innovation will in itself have a major impact on our thinking about novelty generation. The twentieth century was awash with inventions and innovations, so that most had to fail. Recognising this will have a liberating effect. We need no longer worry about being resistant to innovation, or being behind the times, when we chose not to take up an invention. Living in an inventive age requires us to reject the majority that are on offer. We are free to oppose technologies we do not like, however much interested pundits and governments tell us it is essential to accept, say, GM crops. There are alternative technologies, alternative paths of invention. The history of invention is not the history of a necessary future to which we must adapt or die, but rather of failed futures, and of futures firmly fixed in the past.

We should feel free to research, develop, innovate, even in areas which are considered out of date by those stuck in passé futuristic ways of thinking. Most inventions will continue to fail, the future will remain uncertain. Indeed the key problem in research policy should be ensuring that there are many more good ideas, and thus many more failed ideas. Stopping projects at the right time is the key to a successful invention and innovation policy, but doing this means being critical of the hype that surrounds, and often justifies and promotes funding for invention.

Although we can stop projects, it is often said that we cannot un-invent technologies, usually meaning that we cannot get rid of them. The idea is itself an example of the conflation of invention and technology. For most inventions are effectively un-invented, in being forgotten and often lost. A few things are going out of use as the world economy grows — among them are asbestos, declining since the 1970s, and refrigerants like CFC gases. And one of the new tasks faced by scientists and engineers is actively making old technologies disappear, some of which, like nuclear power stations, are extremely difficult to dispose of.

Thinking about the technological past can give us insights into 'the question of technology' — what is it, where does it come from, what does it do? But this book has attempted to do much more than take historical examples to address this perennially interesting question. It has been concerned primarily with asking questions not about technology, but about technology in history — asking questions about the place of technology within wider historical processes. This important distinction is not obvious, but it is central to a proper historical understanding of technology. It will help wean us off the idea that invention, 'technological change' and the 'shaping of technology' need to be the central questions for the history of technology. Instead the history of technology can be much more; and it can help us rethink history.

If we are interested in the historical relations between technology and society we need a new account not only of the technology we have used but also of the society we have lived in. For existing histories of twentieth-century technology were embedded in particular assumptions about world history, while world histories had embedded in them particular assumptions about the nature of technological change and its impact — each was already defined, usually implicitly, in relation to the other. Hence the history of the society into which this new account is placed is very different from the one usually found: for example, it takes as central the expansion of a new kind of poor world, a world which has been almost continuously at war, and in which millions have been killed and tortured. This necessitates an account of the global technological landscape that is very different from those found implicitly and explicitly in existing global histories and histories of technology — and an account that might help revise our views about world history.

It is a measure of the importance of technology to the twentieth century, and to our understanding of it, that to rethink the history of technology is necessarily to rethink the history of the world. For example, we should no longer assume that there was ineluctable globalisation thanks to new technology; on the contrary the world went through a process of de-globalisation in which technologies of self-sufficiency and empire had a powerful role. Culture has not lagged behind technology, rather the reverse; the idea that culture has lagged behind technology is itself very old and has existed under many different technological regimes. Technology has not generally been a revolutionary force; it has been responsible for keeping things the same as much as changing them. The place of technology in the undoubted increase in productivity in the twentieth century remains mysterious; but we are not entering a weightless, dematerialised information world. War changed in the twentieth century, but not according to the rhythms of conventional technological timelines.

History is changed when we put into it the technology that counts: not only the famous spectacular technologies but the low and ubiquitous ones. The historical study of things in use, and the uses of things, matters.

ENDNOTES

1. Michael McCarthy, 'Second Century of Powered Flight is heralded by jet's 5,000mph record', *Independent*, 29 March 2004, pp. 14–15.

2. Milton O. Thompson, *At the Edge of Space: the X-15 Flight Program* (Washington: Smithsonian Institution Press, 1992).

3. *http://www.nasa.gov/missions/research/X-43_overview.html* (opened 29 March 2004).

4. See David Edgerton, 'De l'innovation aux usages. Dix thèses éclectiques sur l'histoire des techniques', *Annales HSS*, July–October 1998, Nos. 4–5, pp. 815–37; Svante Lindqvist, 'Changes in the Technological Landscape: the temporal dimension

in the growth and decline of large technological systems', in Ove Granstrand (ed.), *Economics of Technology* (Amsterdam: North Holland, 1994), pp. 271–88. This approach needs to be distinguished from the longstanding interest in the influence of users on invention and innovation, as seen in, for example, Ruth Schwartz Cowan, 'The consumption junction: a proposal for research strategies in the sociology of technology', in W. Bijker et al., *The Social Construction of Technological Systems* (Cambridge, MA: MIT Press, 1987), Ruth Oldenzeil, 'Man the Maker, Woman the Consumer: The Consumption Junction Revisited' in Londa Schiebinger et al., *Feminism in the Twentieth Century. Science, Technology and Medicine* (Chicago: Chicago University Press, 2001); and Nelly Oudshoorn and Trevor Pinch (eds.), *How Users Matter: the Co-construction of Users and Technology* (Cambridge, MA: MIT Press, 2003).

5. Bruno Latour, *We Have Never Been Modern* (New York: Harvester Wheatsheaf, 1993), pp. 72–6.

6. Lester Brown et al., *Vital Signs* (London: Earthscan, 1993), pp. 86–9.

7. John B. Harms and Tim Knapp, 'The New Economy: what's new, what's not', *Review of Radical Political Economics*, Vol. 35 (2003), pp. 413–36.

8. P. A. David, 'Computer and Dynamo: the Modern Productivity Paradox in a not-too-distant mirror', in OECD, *Technology and Productivity: the Challenge for Economic Policy* (Paris: OECD, 1991).

9. *Economist*, 17 January 2004.

10. *Observer*, 8 April 2001.

11. Martin Stopford, *Maritime Economics*, second edition (London: Routledge, 1997), pp. 485–6.

4

Can Technology Replace Social Engineering?

ALVIN M. WEINBERG

*Since Alvin Weinberg's essay "Can Technology Replace Social Engineering?"
was first published in the mid-1960s, it has become a classic in the literature of
technology and society. Indeed, the term* technological fix, *introduced here, has
become part of the lexicon of the field. Weinberg, one of the pioneers of large-scale
atomic energy research and development and an inveterate technological optimist,
argues that technology is capable of finding shortcuts (technological fixes) to the
solution of social problems. For example, faced with a shortage of fresh water, he
suggests, society can try either social engineering — altering lifestyles and the ways
people use water — or a technological fix, such as the provision of additional fresh
water through nuclear-powered desalting of seawater. The reader should keep in
mind that this article dates from 1966. Although aspects are anachronistic and out
of tune with contemporary views of technology, society, and politics, the questions it
raises are as relevant today as they were more than forty years ago.*

*Alvin M. Weinberg was a physicist who joined the World War II Manhattan
Project early in his career. He went to Oak Ridge National Laboratory in 1945
and served as its director.from 1955 through 1973. Weinberg was a member of the
President's Science Advisory Committee in 1960–1962 and was the recipient of
many awards, including the President's Medal of Science and the Enrico Fermi
Award. He was born in Chicago in 1915 and received A.B., A.M., and Ph.D.
degrees from the University of Chicago. Weinberg died in 2006.*

During World War II, and immediately afterward, our federal government
mobilized its scientific and technical resources, such as the Oak Ridge

Alvin M. Weinberg, "Can Technology Replace Social Engineering?" Reprinted by permission.

National Laboratory, around great technological problems. Nuclear reactors, nuclear weapons, radar, and space are some of the miraculous new technologies that have been created by this mobilization of federal effort. In the past few years [i.e., the early 1960s], there has been a major change in focus of much of our federal research. Instead of being preoccupied with technology, our government is now mobilizing around problems that are largely social. We are beginning to ask what can we do about world population, about the deterioration of our environment, about our educational system, our decaying cities, race relations, poverty. Recent administrations have dedicated the power of a scientifically oriented federal apparatus to finding solutions for these complex social problems.

Social problems are much more complex than are technological problems. It is much harder to identify a social problem than a technological problem: How do we know when our cities need renewing, or when our population is too big, or when our modes of transportation have broken down? The problems are, in a way, harder to identify just because their solutions are never clear-cut: How do we know when our cities are renewed, or our air clean enough, or our transportation convenient enough? By contrast, the availability of a crisp and beautiful technological solution often helps focus on the problem to which the new technology is the solution. I doubt that we would have been nearly as concerned with an eventual shortage of energy as we now are if we had not had a neat solution — nuclear energy — available to eliminate the shortage.

There is a more basic sense in which social problems are much more difficult than are technological problems. A social problem exists because many people behave, individually, in a socially unacceptable way. To solve a social problem one must induce social change — one must persuade many people to behave differently than they have behaved in the past. One must persuade many people to have fewer babies, or to drive more carefully, or to refrain from disliking blacks. By contrast, resolution of a technological problem involves many fewer individual decisions. Once President Roosevelt decided to go after atomic energy, it was by comparison a relatively simple task to mobilize the Manhattan Project.

The resolution of social problems by the traditional methods — by motivating or forcing people to behave more rationally — is a frustrating business. People don't behave rationally; it is a long, hard business to persuade individuals to forgo immediate personal gain or pleasure (as seen by the individual) in favor of longer term social gain. And, indeed, the aim of social engineering is to invent the social devices — usually legal, but also moral and educational and organizational — that will change each person's motivation and redirect his activities along ways that are more acceptable to the society.

The technologist is appalled by the difficulties faced by the social engineer; to engineer even a small social change by inducing individuals to behave differently is always hard, even when the change is rather neutral or even beneficial. For example, some rice eaters in India are reported to prefer starvation to eating wheat that we send to them. How much harder it is to change motivations where the individual is insecure and feels threatened if she acts differently, as illustrated by the poor white's reluctance to accept the black as an equal. By contrast, technological engineering is simple: The rocket, the reactor, and the desalination plants are devices that are expensive to develop, to be sure, but their feasibility is relatively easy to assess and their success relatively easy to achieve once one understands the scientific principles that underlie them. It is, therefore, tempting to raise the following question: In view of the simplicity of technological engineering, and the complexity of social engineering, to what extent can social problems be circumvented by reducing them to technological problems? Can we identify "Quick Technological Fixes" for profound and almost infinitely complicated social problems, "fixes" that are within the grasp of modern technology and which would either eliminate the original social problem without requiring a change in the individual's social attitudes, or would so alter the problem as to make its resolution more feasible? To paraphrase Ralph Nader, to what extent can technological remedies be found for social problems without first having to remove the causes of the problem? It is in this sense that I ask, "Can technology replace social engineering?"

THE MAJOR TECHNOLOGICAL FIXES OF THE PAST

To better explain what I have in mind, I shall describe how two of our most profound social problems — poverty and war — have in some limited degree been solved by the "Technological Fix," rather than by the methods of social engineering. Let me begin with poverty.

The traditional Marxian view of poverty regarded our economic ills as being primarily a question of maldistribution of goods. The Marxist recipe for elimination of poverty, therefore, was to eliminate profit, in the erroneous belief that it was the loss of this relatively small increment from the worker's paycheck that kept him poverty stricken. The Marxist dogma is typical of the approach of the social engineer: One tries to convince or coerce many people to forgo their short-term profits in what is presumed to be the long-term interest of the society as a whole.

The Marxian view seems archaic in this age of mass production and automation not only to us, but apparently to many Eastern bloc economists. For the brilliant advances in the technology of energy, of mass production, and of automation have created the affluent society. Technology has expanded our productive capacity so greatly that even though our distribution is still inefficient, and unfair by Marxian precepts, there is more than enough to go around. Technology has provided a "fix" — greatly expanded production of goods — which enables our capitalistic society to achieve many of the aims of the Marxist social engineer without going through the social revolution Marx viewed as inevitable. Technology has converted the seemingly intractable social problem of widespread poverty into a relatively tractable one.

My second example is war. The traditional Christian position views war as primarily a moral issue: If people become good, and model themselves after the Prince of Peace, they will live in peace. This doctrine is so deeply ingrained in the spirit of all civilized people that I suppose it is a blasphemy to point out that it has never worked very well — that people have not been good and that they are not paragons of virtue or even of reasonableness.

Though I realize it is terribly presumptuous to claim, I believe that Edward Teller may have supplied the nearest thing to a Quick Technological Fix to the problem of war. The hydrogen bomb greatly increases the provocation that would precipitate large-scale war — and not because people's motivations have been changed, not because people have become more tolerant and understanding, but rather because the appeal to the primitive instinct of self-preservation has been intensified far beyond anything we could have imagined before the H-bomb was invented. To point out these things today [in 1966], with the United States involved in a shooting war, may sound hollow and unconvincing, yet the desperate and partial peace we have now is much better than a full-fledged exchange of thermonuclear weapons. One cannot deny that the Soviet leaders now recognize the force of H-bombs and that this has surely contributed to the less militant attitude of the USSR. One can only hope that the Chinese leadership, as it acquires familiarity with H-bombs, will also become less militant. If I were to be asked who has given the world a more effective means of achieving peace, our great religious leaders who urge people to love their neighbors and, thus, avoid fights, or our weapons technologists who simply present people with no rational alternative to peace, I would vote for the weapons technologists. That the peace we get is at best terribly fragile, I cannot deny; yet, as I shall explain, I think technology can help stabilize our imperfect and precarious peace.

THE TECHNOLOGICAL FIXES OF THE FUTURE

Are there other Technological Fixes on the horizon, other technologies that can reduce immensely complicated social questions to a matter of "engineering"? Are there new technologies that offer society ways of circumventing social problems and at the same time do not require individuals to renounce short-term advantage for long-term gain?

Probably the most important new Technological Fix is the intrauterine device for birth control. Before the IUD was invented, birth control demanded very strong motivation of countless individuals. Even with the Pill, the individual's motivation had to be sustained day in and day out; should it flag even temporarily, the strong motivation of the previous month might go for naught. But the IUD, being a one-shot method, greatly reduces the individual motivation required to induce a social change. To be sure, the mother must be sufficiently motivated to accept the IUD in the first place, but, as experience in India already seems to show, it is much easier to persuade the Indian mother to accept the IUD once than it is to persuade her to take a pill every day. The IUD does not completely replace social engineering by technology, and, indeed, in some Spanish American cultures where the husband's manliness is measured by the number of children he has, the IUD attacks only part of the problem. Yet, in many other situations, as in India, the IUD so reduces the social component of the problem as to make an impossibly difficult social problem much less hopeless.

Let me turn now to problems that from the beginning have had both technical and social components — broadly, those concerned with conservation of our resources: our environment, our water, and our raw materials for production of the means of subsistence. The social issue here arises because many people by their individual acts cause shortages and, thus, create economic, and ultimately social, imbalance. For example, people use water wastefully, or they insist on moving to California because of its climate, and so we have water shortages, or too many people drive cars in Los Angeles with its curious meteorology, and so Los Angeles suffocates from smog.

The water resources problem is a particularly good example of a complicated problem with strong social and technological connotations. Our management of water resources in the past has been based largely on the ancient Roman device, the aqueduct: Every water shortage was to be relieved by stealing water from someone else who at the moment didn't need the water or was too poor or too weak to prevent the steal. Southern California would steal from Northern California, New York City from upstate New York, the farmer who could afford a cloud-seeder from the farmer who could not afford a cloud-seeder. The social engineer insists that such shortsighted expedients have gotten us into serious trouble; we have no water resources policy, we waste water disgracefully, and, perhaps, in denying the ethic of thriftiness in using water we have generally undermined our moral fiber. The social engineer, therefore, views such technological shenanigans as being shortsighted, if not downright immoral. Instead, he says, we should persuade or force people to use less water or to stay in the cold Middle West where water is plentiful instead of migrating to California where water is scarce.

The water technologist, on the other hand, views the social engineer's approach as rather impractical. To persuade people to use less water, to get along with expensive water, is difficult, time-consuming, and uncertain in the extreme. Moreover, say the technologists, what right does the water resources expert have to insist that people use water less wastefully? Green lawns and clean cars and swimming pools are part of the good life, American style ... and what right do we have to deny this luxury if there is some alternative to cutting down the water we use?

Here we have a sharp confrontation of the two ways of dealing with a complex social issue: the social engineering way, which asks people to behave more "reasonably," and the technologists' way, which tries to avoid changing people's habits or motivation. Even though I am a technologist, I have sympathy for the social engineer. I think we must use our water as efficiently as possible, that we ought to improve people's attitudes toward the use of water, and that everything that can be done to rationalize our water policy will be welcome. Yet, as a technologist, I believe I see ways of providing more water more cheaply than the social engineers may concede is possible.

I refer to the possibility of nuclear desalination. The social engineer dismisses the technologist's simpleminded idea of solving a water shortage by transporting more water primarily because, in so doing, the water user steals water from someone else — possibly foreclosing the possibility of ultimately utilizing land now only sparsely settled. But surely water drawn from the sea deprives no one of his share of water. The whole issue is then a technological one: Can fresh water be drawn from the sea cheaply enough to have a major impact on our chronically water-short areas, like Southern California, Arizona, and the eastern seaboard?

I believe the answer is yes, though much hard technical work remains to be done. A large program to develop cheap methods of nuclear desalting has been undertaken by the United States, and I have little doubt that within the next ten to twenty years we shall see huge dual-purpose desalting plants springing up on many parched seacoasts of the world.* At first, these plants will produce water at municipal prices. But, I believe, on the basis of research now in progress at ORNL [Oak Ridge National Laboratory] and elsewhere, water from the sea at a cost acceptable for agriculture — less than ten cents per 1,000 gallons — is eventually in the cards. In short, for areas close to the seacoasts, technology can provide water without requiring a great and difficult-to-accomplish change in people's attitudes toward the utilization of water.

The Technological Fix for water is based on the availability of extremely cheap energy from very large nuclear reactors. What other social consequences can one foresee flowing from really cheap energy eventually available to every country, regardless of its endowment of conventional resources? Though we now see only vaguely the outlines of the possibilities, it does seem likely that from very cheap nuclear energy we shall get hydrogen by electrolysis of water, and, thence, the all-important ammonia fertilizer necessary to help feed the hungry of the world; we shall reduce metals without requiring coking coal; we shall even power automobiles with electricity, via fuel cells or storage batteries, thus reducing our world's dependence on crude oil, as well as eliminating our air pollution insofar as it is caused by automobile exhaust or by the burning of fossil fuels. In short, the widespread availability of very cheap energy everywhere in the world ought to lead to an energy autarky in every country of the world and eventually to an autarky in the many staples of life that should flow from really cheap energy.

WILL TECHNOLOGY REPLACE
SOCIAL ENGINEERING?

I hope these examples suggest how social problems can be circumvented or at least reduced to less formidable proportions by the application of the Technological Fix. The examples I have given do not strike me as being fanciful, nor are they at all exhaustive. I have not touched, for example, upon the extent to which really cheap computers and improved technology of communication can help improve elementary teaching without having first to improve our elementary teachers. Nor have I mentioned Ralph Nader's brilliant observation that a safer car, and even its development and adoption by the auto company, is a

---

*Here, as elsewhere in the chapter, the reader should bear in mind that the essay dates from the mid-1960s. — Ed.

quicker and probably surer way to reduce traffic deaths than is a campaign to teach people to drive more carefully. Nor have I invoked some really fanciful Technological Fixes — like providing air conditioners and free electricity to operate them for every black family in Watts on the assumption (suggested by Huntington) that race rioting is correlated with hot, humid weather, or the ultimate Technological Fix, Aldous Huxley's soma pills that eliminate human unhappiness without improving human relations in the usual sense.

My examples illustrate both the strength and the weakness of the Technological Fix for social problems. The Technological Fix accepts man's intrinsic shortcomings and circumvents them or capitalizes on them for socially useful ends. The Fix is, therefore, eminently practical and, in the short term, relatively effective. One does not wait around trying to change people's minds: If people want more water, one gets them more water rather than requiring them to reduce their use of water; if people insist on driving autos while they are drunk, one provides safer autos that prevent injuries even after a severe accident.

But the technological solutions to social problems tend to be incomplete and metastable, to replace one social problem with another. Perhaps the best example of this instability is the peace imposed upon us by the H-bomb. Evidently the pax hydrogenica is metastable in two senses: in the short term, because the aggressor still enjoys such an advantage; the long term, because the discrepancy and have-not nations must eventually be resolved if we are to have permanent peace. Yet, for these particular shortcomings, technology has something to offer. To the imbalance between offense and defense, technology says let us devise passive defense that redresses the balance. A world with H-bombs and adequate civil defense is less likely to lapse into thermonuclear war than a world with H-bombs alone, at least if one concedes that the danger of the thermonuclear war mainly lies in the acts of irresponsible leaders. Anything that deters the irresponsible leader is a force for peace: A technologically sound civil defense therefore would help stabilize the balance of terror.

To the discrepancy between haves and have-nots, technology offers the nuclear energy revolution, with its possibility of autarky for haves and have-nots alike. How this might work to stabilize our metastable thermonuclear peace is suggested by the possible politic effect of the recently proposed Israeli desalting plant. The Arab states I should think would be much less set upon destroying the Jordan River Project if the Israelis had a desalination plant in reserve that would nullify the effect of such actions. In this connection, I think countries like ours can contribute very much. Our country will soon have to decide whether to continue to spend 5.5×10^9 per year for space exploration after our lunar landing. Is it too outrageous to suggest that some of this money be devoted to building huge nuclear desalting complexes in the arid ocean rims of the troubled world? If the plants are powered with breeder reactors, the out-of-pocket costs, once the plants are built, should be low enough to make large-scale agriculture feasible in these areas. I estimate that for 4×10^9 per year we could build enough desalting capacity to feed more than ten million new mouths per year (provided we use agricultural methods that husband water), and we would, thereby, help stabilize the metastable, bomb-imposed balance of terror.

Yet, I am afraid we technologists shall not satisfy our social engineers, who tell us that our Technological Fixes do not get to the heart of the problem; they are at best temporary expedients; they create new problems as they solve old ones; to put a Technological Fix into effect requires a positive social action. Eventually, social engineering, like the Supreme Court decision on desegregation, must be invoked to solve social problems. And, of course, our social engineers are right. Technology will never replace social engineering. But technology has provided and will continue to provide to the social engineer broader options, to make intractable social problems less intractable; perhaps, most of all, technology will buy time — that precious commodity that converts violent social revolution into acceptable social evolution.

Our country now recognizes and is mobilizing around the great social problems that corrupt and disfigure our human existence. It is natural that in this mobilization we should look first to the social engineer. But, unfortunately, the apparatus most readily available to the government, like the great federal laboratories, is technologically oriented, not socially oriented. I believe we have a great opportunity here; for, as I hope I have persuaded you, many of our seemingly social problems do admit of partial technological solutions. Our already deployed technological apparatus can contribute to the resolution of social questions. I plead, therefore, first for our government to deploy its laboratories, its hardware contractors, and its engineering universities around social problems. And I plead, secondly, for understanding and cooperation between technologist and social engineer. Even with all the help he can get from the technologist, the social engineer's problems are never really solved. It is only by cooperation between technologist and social engineer that we can hope to achieve what is the aim of all technologists and social engineers — a better society and, thereby, a better life, for all of us who are part of society.

5

Technology and the
Tragic View

SAMUEL C. FLORMAN

In Part Two of this book, which follows Chapter 6, two writers of an earlier generation engage in a famous debate that, in many ways, epitomizes the bitter divisions between the advocates and critics of technology in the late 1960s and early 1970s. Though no longer tied to the domestic conflict over U.S. participation in the Vietnam War or to the social revolution that was then raging in the United States, these pro- and anti-technology divisions still exist today. However, to treat a subject as complex as the relations of technology and society in such simplistic, for-or-against terms is ultimately less than satisfying. Samuel Florman's insightful essay, "Technology and the Tragic View," taken from his book, Blaming Technology, *suggests another approach. Florman draws on the classical Greek concept of tragedy to develop a new perspective on technology. In the tragic view of life, says Florman,*

> [it] is man's destiny to die, to be defeated by the forces of the universe. But in challenging his destiny, in being brave, determined, ambitious, resourceful, the tragic hero shows to what heights a human being can soar. This is an inspiration to the rest of us. After witnessing a tragedy we feel good, because the magnificence of the human spirit has been demonstrated.

The tragic view accepts responsibility but does not seek to cast blame. It challenges us to do, with caution, what needs to be done, and to consider at the same time the consequences of not acting. Florman's view is ultimately an affirmation of the value of technology in human life, tempered by a recognition of its limits in

*sustaining human happiness. It is a uniquely constructive approach to thinking
about technology and society.*

Samuel C. Florman, author of The Existential Pleasures of Engineering
*(1976) and several other books, is a practicing engineer and chairman of Kreisler
Borg Florman Construction Company in Scarsdale, New York, one of the top
100 construction firms in the United States. His more than 100 articles dealing
with the relationship of technology to general culture have appeared in professional
journals and popular magazines. His most recent book,* The Aftermath: A
Novel of Survival *(2001), is an adventure story set on Earth after a cataclysmic
collision with a comet. Florman was born in New York City in 1925. He was
elected a member of the National Academy of Engineering in 1995 and is also a
fellow of the American Society of Civil Engineers. He holds a bachelor's degree and
a civil engineer's degree from Dartmouth College and an M.A. in English literature from Columbia University.*

The blaming of technology starts with the making of myths — most importantly, the myth of the technological imperative and the myth of the technocratic elite. In spite of the injunctions of common sense, and contrary to the
evidence at hand, the myths flourish.

False premises are followed by confused deductions — a maligning of the
scientific view, the assertion that small is beautiful, the mistake about job enrich-
ment, an excessive zeal for government regulation, the hostility of feminists
toward engineering, and the wishful thinking of the Club of Rome. These, in
turn, are followed by distracted rejoinders from the technological community,
culminating in the bizarre exaltation of engineering ethics.

In all of this it is difficult to determine how much is simple misunderstanding
and how much is willful evasion of the truth, a refusal to face up to the harsh
realities that underlie life, not only in a technological age, but in every age since
the beginning of civilization.

Out of the confusion has come a dialogue of sorts, shaped around views that
are deemed "pro" technology or "anti," "optimistic" or "pessimistic." I believe
that we should be thinking in different terms altogether.

House & Garden magazine, in celebration of the American Bicentennial,
devoted its July 1976 issue to the topic "American Know-How." The editors
invited me to contribute an article, and, enticed by the opportunity to address
a new audience, plus the offer of a handsome fee, I accepted. We agreed that
the title of my piece would be "Technology and the Human Adventure," and
I thereupon embarked on a strange adventure of my own.

I thought that it would be appropriate to begin my Bicentennial-inspired
essay with a discussion of technology in the time of the Founding Fathers, so
I went to the library and immersed myself in the works of Benjamin Franklin,
surely the most famous technologist of America's early days. Remembering stories from my childhood about Ben Franklin the clever tinkerer, I expected to find
a pleasant recounting of inventions and successful experiments, a cheering tale of
technological triumphs. I found such a tale, to be sure, but along with it I found
a record of calamities caused by the technological advances of his day.

In several letters and essays, Franklin expressed concern about fire, an ever-threatening scourge in Colonial times. Efficient sawmills made it possible to build frame houses, more versatile and economical than log cabins — but less fire resistant. Advances in transport made it possible for people to crowd these frame houses together in cities. Cleverly conceived fireplaces, stoves, lamps, and warming pans made life more comfortable, but contributed to the likelihood of catastrophic fires in which many lives were lost.

To deal with this problem, Franklin recommended architectural modifications to make houses more fireproof. He proposed the licensing and supervision of chimney sweeps and the establishment of volunteer fire companies, well supplied and trained in the science of firefighting. As is well known, he invented the lightning rod. In other words, he proposed technological ways of coping with the unpleasant consequences of technology. He applied Yankee ingenuity to solve problems arising out of Yankee ingenuity.

In Franklin's writings I found other examples of technological advances that brought with them unanticipated problems. Lead poisoning was a peril. Contaminated rum was discovered coming from distilleries where lead parts had been substituted for wood in the distilling apparatus. Drinking water collected from lead-coated roofs was also making people seriously ill.

The advancing techniques of medical science were often a mixed blessing, as they are today. Early methods of vaccination for smallpox, for example, entailed the danger of the vaccinated person dying from the artificially induced disease. (In a particularly poignant article, Franklin was at pains to point out that his four-year-old son's death from smallpox was attributable to the boy's not having been vaccinated and did not result, as rumor had it, from the vaccination itself.)

After a while, I put aside the writings of Franklin and turned my attention to American know-how in the nineteenth century. I became engrossed in the story of the early days of steamboat transport. This important step forward in American technology was far from being the unsullied triumph that it appears to be in our popular histories.

Manufacturers of the earliest high-pressure steam engines often used materials of inferior quality. They were slow to recognize the weakening of boiler shells caused by rivet holes and the danger of using wrought-iron shells together with cast iron heads that had a different coefficient of expansion. Safety valve openings were often not properly proportioned, and gauges had a tendency to malfunction. Even well-designed equipment quickly became defective through the effects of corrosion and sediment. On top of it all, competition for prestige led to racing between boats, and, during a race, the usual practice was to tie down the safety valve so that excessive steam pressure would not be relieved.

From 1825 to 1830, 42 recorded explosions killed upward of 270 persons. When, in 1830, an explosion aboard the *Helen McGregor* near Memphis killed more than fifty passengers, public outrage forced the federal government to take action. Funds were granted to the Franklin Institute of Philadelphia to purchase apparatus needed to conduct experiments on steam boilers. This was a notable event: the first technological research grant made by the federal government.

The institute made a comprehensive report in 1838, but it was not until fourteen years later that a workable bill was passed by Congress providing at least minimal safeguards for the citizenry. Today, we may wonder why the process took so long, but at the time Congress was still uncertain about its right, under the interstate commerce provision of the Constitution, to control the activities of individual entrepreneurs.

When I turned from steamboats to railroads I found another long-forgotten story of catastrophe. Not only were there problems with the trains themselves, but the roadbeds, and particularly the bridges, made even the shortest train journey a hazardous adventure. In the late 1860s, more than twenty-five American bridges were collapsing each year, with appalling loss of life. In 1873, the American Society of Civil Engineers set up a special commission to address the problem, and eventually the safety of our bridges came to be taken for granted.

The more I researched the history of American know-how, the more I perceived that practically every technological advance had unexpected and unwanted side effects. Along with each triumph of mechanical genius came an inevitable portion of death and destruction. Instead of becoming discouraged, however, our forebears seemed to be resolute in confronting the adverse consequences of their own inventiveness. I was impressed by this pattern of progress/setback/renewed creative effort. It seemed to have a special message for our day, and I made it the theme of my essay for *House & Garden*.

No matter how many articles one has published, and no matter how much one likes the article most recently submitted, waiting to hear from an editor is an anxious experience. In this case, as it turned out, I had reason to be apprehensive. I soon heard from one of the editors who, although she tried to be encouraging, was obviously distressed. "We liked the part about tenacity and ingenuity," she said, "but, oh dear, all those disasters — they are so depressing." I need not go into the details of what follows: the rewriting, the telephone conferences, the rewriting — the gradual elimination of accidents and casualty statistics and a subtle change in emphasis. I retreated, with some honor intact I like to believe, until the article was deemed to be suitably upbeat.

I should have known that the Bicentennial issue of *House & Garden* was not the forum in which to consider the dark complexities of technological change. My piece was to appear side by side with such articles as, "A House That Has Everything," "Live Longer, Look Younger," and "Everything's Coming Up Roses" (devoted to a review of Gloria Vanderbilt's latest designs).

In the United States today, magazines like *House & Garden* speak for those, and to those, who are optimistic about technology. Through technology we get better dishwashers, permanent-press blouses, and rust-proof lawn furniture. "Better living through chemistry," the old DuPont commercial used to say. Not only is *House & Garden* optimistic, that is, hopeful, about technology, it is cheerfully optimistic. There is no room in its pages for failure, or even for struggle, and in this view it speaks for many Americans, perhaps a majority. This is the lesson I learned — or I should say, relearned — in the Bicentennial year.

Much has been written about the shallow optimism of the United States: about life viewed as a Horatio Alger success story or as a romantic movie with a happy ending. This optimism is less widespread than it used to be, particularly as it relates to technology. Talk of nuclear warfare and a poisoned environment tends to dampen one's enthusiasm. Yet, optimistic materialism remains a powerful force in American life. The poll-takers tell us that people believe technology is, on balance, beneficial. And we all know a lot of people who, even at this troublesome moment in history, define happiness in terms of their ability to accumulate new gadgets. The business community, anxious to sell merchandise, spares no expense in promoting a gleeful consumerism.

Side by side with what I have come to think of as *House & Garden* optimism, there is a mood that we might call *New York Review of Books* pessimism. Our intellectual journals are full of gloomy tracts that depict a society debased by technology. Our health is being ruined, according to this view, our landscape despoiled, and our social institutions laid waste. We are forced to do demeaning work and consume unwanted products. We are being dehumanized. This is happening because a technological demon has escaped from human control or, in a slightly different version, because evil technocrats are leading us astray.

It is clear that in recent years the resoluteness exhibited by Benjamin Franklin, and other Americans of similarly robust character, has been largely displaced by a foolish optimism on the one hand and an abject pessimism on the other. These two opposing outlooks are actually manifestations of the same defect in the American character. One is the obverse, the "flip side," of the other. Both reflect a flaw that I can best describe as immaturity.

A young child is optimistic, naively assuming that his needs can always be satisfied and that his parents have it within their power to "make things right." A child frustrated becomes petulant. With the onset of puberty a morose sense of disillusionment is apt to take hold. Sulky pessimism is something we associate with the teenager.

It is not surprising that many inhabitants of the United States, a rich nation with seemingly boundless frontiers, should have evinced a childish optimism and declared their faith in technology, endowing it with the reassuring power of a parent — also regarding it with the love of a child for a favorite toy. It then follows that technological setbacks would be greeted by some with the naive assumption that all would turn out for the best and by others with peevish declarations of despair. Intellectuals have been in the forefront of this childish display, but every segment of society has been caught up in it. Technologists themselves have not been immune. In the speeches of nineteenth-century engineers, we find bombastic promises that make us blush. Today, the profession is torn between a blustering optimism and a confused guilt.

The past fifty years have seen many hopes dashed, but we can see in retrospect that they were unrealistic hopes. We simply cannot make use of coal without killing miners and polluting the air. Neither can we manufacture solar panels without worker fatalities and environmental degradation. (We assume that it will be less than with coal, but we are not sure.) We cannot build highways or canals or airports without despoiling the landscape. Not only have we learned that environmental dangers are inherent in every technological advance, but we find that we are fated to be dissatisfied with much of what we produce because our tastes keep changing. The sparkling, humming, paved metropolises of science fiction — even if they could be realized — are not, after all, the home to which humankind aspires. It seems that many people find such an environment "alienating." There can never be a technologically based utopia because we discover belatedly that we cannot agree on what form that utopia might take.

To express our disillusionment, we have invented a new word: "trade-off." It is an ugly word, totally without grace, but it signifies, I believe, the beginning of maturity for American society.

It is important to remember that our disappointments have not been limited to technology. (This is a fact that the antitechnologists usually choose to ignore.) Wonderful dreams attended the birth of the New Deal, and later the founding of the United Nations, yet we have since awakened to face unyielding economic and political difficulties. Socialism has been discredited, as was *laissez-faire* capitalism before it. We have been bitterly disappointed by the labor movement, the educational establishment, efforts at crime prevention, the ministrations of psychiatry, and, most recently, by the abortive experiments of the so-called counterculture. We have come face to face with limits that we had presumed to hope might not exist.

Those of us who have lived through the past fifty years have passed personally from youthful presumptuousness to mature skepticism at the very moment that American society has been going through the same transition. We have to be careful not to define the popular mood in terms of our personal sentiments, but I do not think I am doing that when I observe the multiple disenchantments of our time. We also have to be careful not to deprecate youthful enthusiasm, which is a force for good, along with immaturity, which is tolerable only in the young.

It can be argued that there was for a while good reason to hold out hope for utopia, since modern science and technology appeared to be completely new factors in human existence. But now that they have been given a fair trial, we perceive their inherent limitations. The human condition is the human condition still.

To persist in saying that we are optimistic or pessimistic about technology is to acknowledge that we will not grow up.

I suggest that an appropriate response to our new wisdom is neither optimism nor pessimism, but rather the espousal of an attitude that has traditionally been associated with men and women of noble character — the tragic view of life.

As a student in high school, and later in college, I found it difficult to comprehend what my teachers told me about comedy and tragedy. Comedy, they said, expresses despair. When there is no hope, we make jokes. We depict people as puny, ridiculous creatures. We laugh to keep from crying.

Tragedy, on the other hand, is uplifting. It depicts heroes wrestling with fate. It is man's destiny to die, to be defeated by the forces of the universe. But in challenging his destiny, in being brave, determined, ambitious, resourceful, the tragic hero shows to what heights a human being can soar. This is an inspiration to the rest of us. After witnessing a tragedy, we feel good, because the magnificence of the human spirit has been demonstrated. Tragic drama is an affirmation of the value of life.

Students pay lip service to this theory and give the expected answers in examinations. But sometimes the idea seems to fly in the face of reason. How can we say we feel better after Oedipus puts out his eyes, or Othello kills his beloved wife and commits suicide, than we do after laughing heartily over a bedroom farce?

Yet, this concept, which is so hard to grasp in the classroom, where students are young and the environment is serene, rings true in the world where mature people wrestle with burdensome problems.

I do not intend to preach a message of stoicism. The tragic view is not to be confused with world-weary resignation. As Moses Hadas, a great classical scholar of a generation ago, wrote about the Greek tragedians, "Their gloom is not fatalistic pessimism but an adult confrontation of reality, and their emphasis is not on the grimness of life but on the capacity of great figures to adequate themselves to it."[1]

It is not an accident that tragic drama flourished in societies that were dynamic: Periclean Athens, Elizabethan England, and the France of Louis XIV. For tragedy speaks of ambition, effort, and unquenchable spirit. Technological creativity is one manifestation of this spirit, and it is only a dyspeptic antihumanist who can feel otherwise. Even the Greeks, who for a while placed technologists low on the social scale, recognized the glory of creative engineering. Prometheus is one of the quintessential tragic heroes. In viewing technology through a tragic prism, we are at once exalted by its accomplishments and sobered by its limitations. We thus ally ourselves with the spirit of great ages past.

The fate of Prometheus, as well as that of most tragic heroes, is associated with the concept of hubris, "overweening pride." Yet pride, which in drama invariably leads to a fall, is not considered sinful by the great tragedians. It is an essential element of humanity's greatness. It is what inspires heroes to confront the universe, to challenge the status quo. Prometheus defied Zeus and brought technological knowledge to the human race. Prometheus was a revolutionary. So were Gutenberg, Watt, Edison, and Ford. Technology is revolutionary. Therefore, hostility toward technology is antirevolutionary, which is to say it is reactionary. This charge is currently being leveled against environmentalists and other enemies of technology. Since antitechnologists are traditionally "liberal" in their attitudes, the idea that they are reactionary confronts us with a paradox.

The tragic view does not shrink from paradox; it teaches us to live with ambiguity. It is at once revolutionary and cautionary. Hubris, as revealed in tragic drama, is an essential element of creativity; it is also a tragic flaw that contributes to the failure of human enterprise. Without effort, however, and daring, we are nothing. Walter Kerr has spoken of "tragedy's commitment to freedom, to the unflinching exploration of the possible." "At the heart of tragedy," he writes, "feeding it energy, stands godlike man passionately desiring a state of affairs more perfect than any that now exists."[2]

This description of the tragic hero well serves, in my opinion, as a definition of the questing technologist.

An aspect of the tragic view that particularly appeals to me is its reluctance to place blame. Those people who hold pessimistic views about technology are forever reproaching others, if not individual engineers, then the "technocratic establishment," the "megastate," "the pentagon of power," or some equally amorphous entity. Everywhere they look they see evil intent.

There is evil in the world, of course, but most of our disappointments with technology come when decent people are trying to act constructively. "The essentially tragic fact," says Hegel, "is not so much the war of good with evil as the war of good with good."

Pesticides serve to keep millions of poor people from starving. To use pesticides is good; to oppose them when they create havoc in the food chain is also good. To drill for oil and to transport it across the oceans is good, since petroleum provides lifesaving chemicals and heat for homes. To prevent oil spills is also good. Nuclear energy is good, as is the attempt to eliminate radioactivity. To seek safety is a worthy goal, but in a world of limited resources, the pursuit of economy is also worthy. We are constantly accusing each other of villainy when we should be consulting together on how best to solve our common problems.

Although the tragic view shuns blame, it does not shirk responsibility. "The fault, dear Brutus, is not in our stars, but in ourselves…." We are accountable for what we do or, more often, for what we neglect to do. The most shameful feature of the antitechnological creed is that it so often fails to consider the consequences of not taking action. The lives lost or wasted that might have been saved by exploiting our resources are the responsibility of those who counsel inaction. The tragic view is consistent with good citizenship. It advocates making the most of our opportunities; it challenges us to do the work that needs doing.

Life, it may be said, is not a play. Yet we are constantly talking about roles — role-playing, role models, and so forth. It is a primordial urge to want to play one's part. The outlook I advocate sees value in many different people playing many different parts. A vital society, like a meaningful drama, feeds on diversity. Each participant contributes to the body social: scientist, engineer, farmer, craftsman, laborer, politician, jurist, teacher, artist, merchant, entertainer…. The pro-growth industrialist and the environmentalist are both needed, and, in a strange way, they need each other.

Out of conflict comes resolution; out of variety comes health. This is the lesson of the natural world. It is the moral of ecological balance; it is also the moral of great drama. We cannot but admire Caesar, Brutus, and Antony all together. So should we applaud the guardians of our wilderness, even as we applaud the creators of dams and paper mills. I am a builder, but I feel for those who are afraid of building, and I admire those who want to endow all building with grace.

George Steiner, in *The Death of Tragedy* (1961), claimed that the tragic spirit was rendered impotent by Christianity's promise of salvation. But I do not think that most people today are thinking in terms of salvation. They are thinking of doing the best they can in a world that promises neither damnation nor transcendent victories, but instead confronts us with both perils and opportunities for achievement. In such a world, the tragic spirit is very much alive. Neither optimism nor pessimism is a worthy alternative to this noble spirit.

We use words to communicate, but sometimes they are not as precise as we pretend, and then we confuse ourselves and each other. "Optimism," "pessimism," "tragic view" — these are mere sounds or scratches on paper. The way we feel is not adequately defined by such sounds or scratches. René Dubos used to write a column for *The American Scholar* that he called "The Despairing Optimist." I seem to recall that he once gave his reasons for not calling it "The Hopeful Pessimist," although I cannot remember what they were. What really counts, I suppose, is not what we say, or even what we feel, but what we want to do.

By saying that I espouse the tragic view of technology I mean to ally myself with those who, aware of the dangers and without foolish illusions about what can be accomplished, still want to move on, actively seeking to realize our constantly changing vision of a more satisfactory society. I mean to oppose those who would evade harsh truths by intoning platitudes. I particularly mean to challenge those who enjoy the benefits of technology but refuse to accept responsibility for its consequences.

Earlier in this essay I mentioned the problems I encountered in preparing an article for *House & Garden*, and I would like to close by quoting the last few lines from that much-rewritten opus. The prose is somewhat florid, but please remember that it was written in celebration of the American Bicentennial:

> For all our apprehensions, we have no choice but to press ahead. We must do so, first, in the name of compassion. By turning our backs on technological change, we would be expressing our satisfaction with current world levels of hunger, disease, and privation. Further, we must press ahead in the name of human adventure. Without experimentation and change our existence would be a dull business. We simply cannot stop while there are masses to feed and diseases to conquer, seas to explore and heavens to survey.

The editors of *Home & Garden* thought I was being optimistic. I knew that I was being tragic, but I did not argue the point.

ENDNOTES

1. Moses Hadas, *A History of Greek Literature* (New York: Columbia University Press, 1950), p. 75.
2. Walter Kerr, *Tragedy and Comedy* (New York: Simon & Schuster, 1967), p. 107.

6

Do Artifacts Have Politics?

LANGDON WINNER

Do the properties of technological systems embody specific kinds of power and authority relationships? Are nuclear power systems inherently centralizing and authoritarian? Are solar power systems, as some of their advocates claim, more democratic and consistent with the values of pluralistic societies? Langdon Winner looks for answers to questions such as these in the following essay, originally published in a 1980 symposium issue of the journal Daedalus *entitled "Modern Technology: Problem or Opportunity?" Winner believes that, indeed, technological choices do have political consequences. He cites many examples, including a particularly egregious one: Robert Moses designed bridges over his parkways on Long Island too low for buses in order to keep members of the urban lower classes (who could not afford private automobiles) from crowding the suburban parks and beaches.*

"Technologies," Winner concludes, "are ways of building order in our world," which, by their nature, influence the way people live and work over long periods of time. We need to study and understand their consequences and to develop means of making technological choices in a more open and participatory fashion if we are to maintain a democratic society. A prolific writer whose works have appeared in both scholarly and popular publications and who served as contributing editor to Rolling Stone *magazine from 1969 to 1971, Langdon Winner is Thomas Phelan Chair of Humanities and Social Sciences at Rensselaer Polytechnic Institute (RPI) in Troy, New York. He teaches in the Department of Science and Technology Studies. Prior to coming to RPI in 1985, he taught at the Massachusetts Institute of Technology, Leiden University (in the Netherlands), and the University of California at Berkeley and at Santa Cruz. Among Winner's books are* Autonomous Technology *(1977) and* The Whale and the Reactor *(1986).*

"Do Artifacts Have Politics?" from *Daedalus, Journal of the American Academy of Arts and Sciences,* from the issue entitled, "Modern Technology: Problem or Opportunity?" Winter 1980, Vol. 109, No. 1. Reprinted by permission of the author.

In controversies about technology and society, there is no idea more provocative than the notion that technical things have political qualities. At issue is the claim that the machines, structures, and systems of modern material culture can be accurately judged not only for their contributions of efficiency and productivity, not merely for their positive and negative environmental side effects, but also for the ways in which they can embody specific forms of power and authority. Since ideas of this kind have a persistent and troubling presence in discussions about the meaning of technology, they deserve explicit attention.[1]

Writing in *Technology and Culture* almost two decades ago, Lewis Mumford gave classic statement to one version of the theme, arguing that "from late neolithic times in the Near East, right down to our own day, two technologies have recurrently existed side by side: one authoritarian, the other democratic, the first system centered, immensely powerful, but inherently unstable; the other man centered, relatively weak, but resourceful and durable."[2] This thesis stands at the heart of Mumford's studies of the city, architecture, and the history of technics and mirrors concerns voiced earlier in the works of Peter Kropotkin, William Morris, and other nineteenth-century critics of industrialism. More recently, antinuclear and prosolar energy movements in Europe and America have adopted a similar notion as a centerpiece in their arguments. Thus, environmentalist Denis Hayes concludes, "The increased deployment of nuclear power facilities must lead society toward authoritarianism. Indeed, safe reliance upon nuclear power as the principal source of energy may be possible only in a totalitarian state." Echoing the views of many proponents of appropriate technology and the soft energy path, Hayes contends that "dispersed solar sources are more compatible than centralized technologies with social equity, freedom, and cultural pluralism."[3]

An eagerness to interpret technical artifacts in political language is by no means the exclusive property of critics of large-scale, high-technology systems. A long lineage of boosters have insisted that the "biggest and best" that science and industry made available were the best guarantees of democracy, freedom, and social justice. The factory system, automobile, telephone, radio, television, the space program, and, of course, nuclear power itself have all at one time or another been described as democratizing, liberating forces. David Lilienthal, in *T.V.A.: Democracy on the March*, for example, found this promise in the phosphate fertilizers and electricity that technical progress was bringing to rural Americans during the 1940s.[4] In a recent essay, *The Republic of Technology*, Daniel Boorstin extolled television for "its power to disband armies, to cashier presidents, to create a whole new democratic world — democratic in ways never before imagined, even in America."[5] Scarcely a new invention comes along that someone does not proclaim it the salvation of a free society.

It is no surprise to learn that technical systems of various kinds are deeply interwoven in the conditions of modern politics. The physical arrangements of industrial production, warfare, communications, and the like have fundamentally changed the exercise of power and the experience of citizenship. But to go beyond this obvious fact and to argue that certain technologies in themselves have political properties seems, at first glance, completely mistaken. We all know that people have politics, not things. To discover either virtues or evils in aggregates of steel, plastic, transistors, integrated circuits, and chemicals seems just plain wrong, a way of mystifying human artifice and of avoiding the true sources, the human sources of freedom and oppression, justice and injustice. Blaming the hardware appears even more foolish than blaming the victims when it comes to judging conditions of public life.

Hence, the stern advice commonly given those who flirt with the notion that technical artifacts have political qualities: What matters is not technology itself, but the social or economic system in which it is embedded. This maxim, which in a number of variations is the central premise of a theory that can be called the social determination of technology, has an obvious wisdom. It serves as a needed corrective to those who focus uncritically on such things as "the computer and its social impacts" but who fail to look behind technical things to notice the social circumstances of their development, deployment, and use. This view provides an antidote to naive technological determinism — the idea that technology develops as the sole result of an internal dynamic, and then, unmediated by any other influence, molds society to fit its patterns. Those who have not recognized the ways in which technologies are shaped by social and economic forces have not gotten very far.

But the corrective has its own shortcomings; taken literally, it suggests that technical things do not matter at all. Once one has done the detective work necessary to reveal the social origins — power holders behind a particular instance of technological change — one will have explained everything of importance. This conclusion offers comfort to social scientists: It validates what they had always suspected, namely, that there is nothing distinctive about the study of technology in the first place. Hence, they can return to their standard models of social power — those of interest group politics, bureaucratic politics, Marxist models of class struggle, and the like — and have everything they need. The social determination of technology is, in this view, essentially no different from the social determination of, say, welfare policy or taxation.

There are, however, good reasons technology has of late taken on a special fascination in its own right for historians, philosophers, and political scientists, good reasons the standard models of social science only go so far in accounting for what is most interesting and troublesome about the subject. In another place I have tried to show why so much of modern social and political thought contains recurring statements of what can be called a theory of technological politics, an odd mongrel of notions often crossbred with orthodox liberal, conservative, and socialist philosophies.[6] The theory of technological politics draws attention to the momentum of large-scale sociotechnical systems, to the response of modern societies to certain technological imperatives, and to the all-too-common signs of the adaptation of human ends to technical means. In so doing, it offers a novel framework of interpretation and explanation for some of the more puzzling patterns that have taken shape in and around the growth of modern material culture. One strength of this point of view is that it takes technical artifacts seriously. Rather than insist that we immediately reduce everything to the interplay of social forces, it suggests that we pay attention to the characteristics of technical objects and the meaning of those characteristics.

A necessary complement to, rather than a replacement for, theories of the social determination of technology, this perspective identifies certain technologies as political phenomena in their own right. It points us back, to borrow Edmund Husserl's philosophical injunction, to the things themselves.

In what follows, I shall offer outlines and illustrations of two ways in which artifacts can contain political properties. First are instances in which the invention, design, or arrangement of a specific technical device or system becomes a way of settling an issue in a particular community. Seen in the proper light, examples of this kind are fairly straightforward and easily understood. Second are cases of what can be called inherently political technologies, man-made systems that appear to require, or to be strongly compatible with, particular kinds of political relationships. Arguments about cases of this kind are much more troublesome and closer to the heart of the matter. By "politics," I mean arrangements of power and authority in human associations as well as the activities that take place within those arrangements. For my purposes, "technology" here is understood to mean all of modern practical artifice,[7] but to avoid confusion I prefer to speak of technologies, smaller or larger pieces or systems of hardware of a specific kind. My intention is not to settle any of the issues here once and for all, but to indicate their general dimensions and significance.

TECHNICAL ARRANGEMENTS AS FORMS OF ORDER

Anyone who has traveled the highways of America and has become used to the normal height of overpasses may well find something a little odd about some of the bridges over the parkways on Long Island, New York. Many of the overpasses are extraordinarily low, having as little as nine feet of clearance at the curb. Even those who happened to notice this structural peculiarity would not be inclined to attach any special meaning to it. In our accustomed way of looking at things like roads and bridges we see the details of form as innocuous and seldom give them a second thought.

It turns out, however, that the 200 or so low-hanging overpasses on Long Island were deliberately designed to achieve a particular social effect. Robert Moses, the master builder of roads, parks, bridges, and other public works from the 1920s to the 1970s in New York, had these overpasses built to specifications that would discourage the presence of buses on his parkways. According to evidence provided by Robert A. Caro in his biography of Moses, the reasons reflect Moses's social-class bias and racial prejudice. Automobile-owning whites of "upper" and "comfortable middle" classes, as he called them, would be free to use the parkways for recreation and commuting. Poor people and blacks, who normally used public transit, were kept off the roads because the twelve-foot-tall buses could not get through the overpasses. One consequence was to limit access of racial minorities and low-income groups to Jones Beach, Moses's widely acclaimed public park. Moses made doubly sure of this result by vetoing a proposed extension of the Long Island Railroad to Jones Beach.[8]

As a story in recent American political history, Robert Moses's life is fascinating. His dealings with mayors, governors, and presidents, and his careful manipulation of legislatures, banks, labor unions, the press, and public opinion, are all matters that political scientists could study for years. But the most important and enduring results of his work are his technologies, the vast engineering projects that give New York much of its present form. For generations after Moses has gone and the alliances he forged have fallen apart, his public works, especially the highways and bridges he built to favor the use of the automobile over the development of mass transit, will continue to shape that city. Many of his monumental structures of concrete and steel embody a systematic social inequality, a way of engineering relationships among people that, after a time, becomes just another part of the landscape. As planner Lee Koppelman told Caro about the low bridges on Wantagh Parkway, "The old son-of-a-gun had made sure that buses would never be able to use his goddamned parkways."[9]

Histories of architecture, city planning, and public works contain many examples of physical arrangements that contain explicit or implicit political purposes. One can point to Baron Haussmann's broad Parisian thoroughfares, engineered at Louis Napoleon's direction to prevent any recurrence of street fighting of the kind that took place during the revolution of 1848. Or one can visit any number of grotesque concrete buildings and huge plazas constructed on American university campuses during the late 1960s and early 1970s to defuse student demonstrations. Studies of industrial machines and instruments also turn up interesting political stories, including some that violate our normal expectations about why technological innovations are made in the first place. If we suppose that new technologies are introduced to achieve increased efficiency, the history of technology shows that we will sometimes be disappointed. Technological change expresses a panoply of human motives, not the least of which is the desire of some to have dominion over others, even though it may require an occasional sacrifice of cost cutting and some violence to the norm of getting more from less.

One poignant illustration can be found in the history of nineteenth-century industrial mechanization. At Cyrus McCormick's reaper manufacturing plant in Chicago in the middle 1880s, pneumatic molding machines, a new and largely untested innovation, were added to the foundry at an estimated cost of $500,000. In the standard economic interpretation of such things, we would expect that this step was taken to modernize the plant and achieve the kind of efficiencies that mechanization brings. But historian Robert Ozanne has shown why the development must be seen in a broader context. At the time, Cyrus McCormick II was engaged in a battle with the National Union of Iron Molders. He saw the addition of the new machines as a way to "weed out the bad element among the men," namely, the skilled workers who had organized the union local in Chicago.[10] The new machines, manned by unskilled labor, actually produced inferior castings at a higher cost than the earlier process. After three years of use, the machines were, in fact, abandoned, but by that time they had served their purpose — the destruction of the union. Thus, the story of these technical developments at the McCormick factory cannot be understood adequately outside the record of workers' attempts to organize, police repression of the labor movement in Chicago during that period, and the events surrounding the bombing at Haymarket Square. Technological history and American political history were at that moment deeply intertwined.

In cases like those of Moses's low bridges and McCormick's molding machines, one sees the importance of technical arrangements that precede the use of the things in question. It is obvious that technologies can be used in ways that enhance the power, authority, and privilege of some over others, for example, the use of television to sell a candidate. To our accustomed way of thinking, technologies are seen as neutral tools that can be used well or poorly, for good, evil, or something in between. But we usually do not stop to inquire whether a given device might have been designed and built in such a way that it produces a set of consequences logically and temporally prior to any of its professed uses. Robert Moses's bridges, after all, were used to carry automobiles from one point to another; McCormick's machines were used to make metal castings; both technologies, however, encompassed purposes far beyond their immediate use. If our moral and political language for evaluating technology includes only categories having to do with tools and uses, if it does not include attention to the meaning of the designs and arrangements of our artifacts, then we will be blinded to much that is intellectually and practically crucial.

Because the point is most easily understood in the light of particular intentions embodied in physical form, I have so far offered illustrations that seem almost conspiratorial. But to recognize the political dimensions in the shapes of technology does not require that we look for conscious conspiracies or malicious intentions. The organized movement of handicapped people in the United States during the 1970s pointed out the countless ways in which machines, instruments, and structures of common use — buses, buildings, sidewalks, plumbing fixtures, and so forth — made it impossible for many handicapped persons to move about freely, a condition that systematically excluded them from public life. It is safe to say that designs unsuited for the handicapped arose more from long-standing neglect than from anyone's active intention. But now that the issue has been raised for public attention, it is evident that justice requires a remedy. A whole range of artifacts are now being redesigned and rebuilt to accommodate this minority.

Indeed, many of the most important examples of technologies that have political consequences are those that transcend the simple categories of "intended" and "unintended" altogether. These are instances in which the very process of technical development is so thoroughly biased in a particular direction that it regularly produces results counted as wonderful breakthroughs by some social interests and crushing setbacks by others. In such cases, it is neither correct nor insightful to say, "Someone intended to do somebody else harm." Rather, one must say that the technological deck has been stacked long in advance to favor certain social interests and that some people were bound to receive a better hand than others.

The mechanical tomato harvester, a remarkable device perfected by researchers at the University of California from the late 1940s to the present, offers an illustrative tale. The machine is able to harvest tomatoes in a single pass through a row, cutting the plants from the ground, shaking the fruit loose, and, in the newest models, sorting the tomatoes electronically into large plastic gondolas that hold up to twenty-five tons of produce headed for canning. To accommodate the rough motion of these "factories in the field," agricultural researchers have bred new varieties of tomatoes that are hardier, sturdier, and less tasty. The harvesters replace the system of handpicking, in which crews of farmworkers would pass through the fields three or four times putting ripe tomatoes in lug boxes and saving immature fruit for later harvest.[11] Studies in California indicate that the machine reduces costs by approximately five to seven dollars per ton as compared to hand harvesting.[12] But the benefits are by no means equally divided in the agricultural economy. In fact, the machine in the garden has in this instance been the occasion for a thorough reshaping of social relationships of tomato production in rural California.

By their very size and cost, more than $50,000 each to purchase, the machines are compatible only with a highly concentrated form of tomato growing. With the introduction of this new method of harvesting, the number of tomato growers declined from approximately 4,000 in the early 1960s to about 600 in 1973, yet with a substantial increase in tons of tomatoes produced. By the late 1970s, an estimated 32,000 jobs in the tomato industry had been eliminated as a direct consequence of mechanization.[13] Thus, a jump in productivity to the benefit of very large growers has occurred at a sacrifice to other rural agricultural communities.

The University of California's research and development on agricultural machines like the tomato harvester is at this time the subject of a lawsuit filed by attorneys for California Rural Legal Assistance, an organization representing a group of farmworkers and other interested parties. The suit charges that University officials are spending tax monies on projects that benefit a handful of private interests to the detriment of farmworkers, small farmers, consumers, and rural California generally and asks for a court injunction to stop the practice. The University has denied these charges, arguing that to accept them "would require elimination of all research with any potential practical application."[14]

As far as I know, no one has argued that the development of the tomato harvester was the result of a plot. Two students of the controversy, William Friedland and Amy Barton, specifically exonerate both the original developers of the machine and the hard tomato from any desire to facilitate economic concentration in that industry.[15] What we see here instead is an ongoing social process in which scientific knowledge, technological invention, and corporate profit reinforce each other in deeply entrenched patterns that bear the unmistakable stamp of political and economic power. Over many decades, agricultural research and development in American land-grant colleges and universities has tended to favor the interests of large agribusiness concerns.[16] It is in the face of such subtly ingrained patterns that opponents of innovations like the tomato harvester are made to seem "antitechnology" or "antiprogress." For the harvester is not merely the symbol of a social order that rewards some while punishing others; it is in a true sense an embodiment of that order.

Within a given category of technological change there are, roughly speaking, two kinds of choices that can affect the relative distribution of power, authority, and privilege in a community. Often the crucial decision is a simple "yes or no" choice — Are we going to develop and adopt the thing or not? In recent years, many local, national, and international disputes about technology have centered on "yes or no" judgments about such things as food additives, pesticides, the building of highways, nuclear reactors, and dam projects. The fundamental choice about an ABM [anti-ballistic missile] or an SST [supersonic transport] is whether or not the thing is going to join society as a piece of its operating equipment. Reasons for and against are frequently as important as those concerning the adoption of an important new law.

A second range of choices, equally critical in many instances, has to do with specific features in the design or arrangement of a technical system after the decision to go ahead with it has already been made. Even after a utility company wins permission to build a large electric power line, important controversies can remain with respect to the placement of its route and the design of its towers; even after an organization has decided to institute a system of computers, controversies can still arise with regard to the kinds of components, programs, modes of access, and other specific features the system will include. Once the mechanical tomato harvester had been developed in its basic form, design alteration of critical social significance — the addition of electronic sorters, for example — changed the character of the machine's effects on the balance of wealth and power in California agriculture. Some of the most interesting research on technology and politics at present focuses on the attempt to demonstrate in a detailed, concrete fashion how seemingly innocuous design features in mass transit systems, water projects, industrial machinery, and other technologies actually mask social choices of profound significance. Historian David Noble is now studying two kinds of automated machine tool systems that have different implications for the relative power of management and labor in the industries that might employ them. He is able to show that, although the basic electronic and mechanical components of the record/playback and numerical control systems are similar, the choice of one design over another has crucial consequences for social struggles on the shop floor. To see the matter solely in terms of cost cutting, efficiency, or the modernization of equipment is to miss a decisive element in the story.[17]

From such examples I would offer the following general conclusions. The things we call "technologies" are ways of building order in our world. Many technical devices and systems important in everyday life contain possibilities for many different ways of ordering human activity. Consciously or not, deliberately or inadvertently, societies choose structures for technologies that influence how people are going to work, communicate, travel, consume, and so forth over a very long time. In the processes by which structuring decisions are made, different people are differently situated and possess unequal degrees of power, as well as unequal levels of awareness. By far the greatest latitude of choice exists the very first time a particular instrument, system, or technique is introduced. Because choices tend to become strongly fixed in material equipment, economic investment, and social habit, the original flexibility vanishes for all practical purposes once the initial commitments are made. In that sense, technological innovations are similar to legislative acts or political foundings that establish a framework for public order that will endure over many generations. For that reason, the same careful attention one would give to the rules, roles, and relationships of politics must also be given to such things as the building of highways, the creation of television networks, and the tailoring of seemingly insignificant features on new machines. The issues that divide or unite people in society are settled not only in the institutions and practices of politics proper, but also, and less obviously, in tangible arrangements of steel and concrete, wires and transistors, nuts and bolts.

INHERENTLY POLITICAL TECHNOLOGIES

None of the arguments and examples considered thus far address a stronger, more troubling claim often made in writings about technology and society — the belief that some technologies are by their very nature political in a specific way. According to this view, the adoption of a given technical system unavoidably brings with it conditions for human relationships that have a distinctive political cast — for example, centralized or decentralized, egalitarian or inegalitarian, repressive or liberating. This is ultimately what is at stake in assertions like those of Lewis Mumford that two traditions of technology, one authoritarian, the other democratic, exist side by side in Western history. In all the cases I cited, the technologies are relatively flexible in design and arrangement and variable in their effects. Although one can recognize a particular result produced in a particular setting, one can also easily imagine how a roughly similar device or system might have been built or situated with very much different political consequences. The idea we must now examine and evaluate is that certain kinds of technology do not allow such flexibility and that to choose them is to choose a particular form of political life.

A remarkably forceful statement of one version of this argument appears in Friedrich Engels's little essay "On Authority," written in 1872. Answering anarchists who believed that authority is an evil that ought to be abolished altogether, Engels launches into a panegyric for authoritarianism, maintaining, among other things, that strong authority is a necessary condition in modern industry. To advance his case in the strongest possible way, he asks his readers to imagine that the revolution has already occurred. "Supposing a social revolution dethroned the capitalists, who now exercise their authority over the production and circulation of wealth. Supposing, to adopt entirely the point of view of the antiauthoritarians, that the land and the instruments of labor had become the collective property of the workers who use them. Will authority have disappeared or will it have only changed its form?"[18]

His answer draws upon lessons from three sociotechnical systems of his day: cotton-spinning mills, railways, and ships at sea. He observes that, on its way to becoming finished thread, cotton moves through a number of different operations at different locations in the factory. The workers perform a wide variety of tasks, from running the steam engine to carrying the products from one room to another. Because these tasks must be coordinated, and because the timing of the work is "fixed by the authority of the steam," laborers must learn to accept a rigid discipline. They must, according to Engels, work at regular hours and agree to subordinate their individual wills to the persons in charge of factory operations. If they fail to do so, they risk the horrifying possibility that production will come to a grinding halt. Engels pulls no punches. "The automatic machinery of a big factory," he writes, "is much more despotic than the small capitalists who employ workers ever have been."[19]

Similar lessons are adduced in Engels's analysis of the necessary operating conditions for railways and ships at sea. Both require the subordination of workers to an "imperious authority" that sees to it that things run according to plan. Engels finds that, far from being an idiosyncrasy of capitalist social organization, relationships of authority and subordination arise "independently of all social organization, [and] are imposed upon us together with the material conditions under which we produce and make products circulate." Again, he intends this to be stern advice to the anarchists who, according to Engels, thought it possible simply to eradicate subordination and superordination at a single stroke. All such schemes are nonsense. The roots of unavoidable authoritarianism are, he argues, deeply implanted in the human involvement with science and technology. "If man, by dint of his knowledge and inventive genius, has subdued the forces of nature, the latter avenge themselves upon him by subjecting him, insofar as he employs them, to a veritable despotism independent of all social organization."[20]

Attempts to justify strong authority on the basis of supposedly necessary conditions of technical practice have an ancient history. A pivotal theme in *The Republic* is Plato's quest to borrow the authority of techne and employ it by analogy to buttress his argument in favor of authority in the state. Among the illustrations he chooses, like Engels, is that of a ship on the high seas. Because large sailing vessels by their very nature need to be steered with a firm hand, sailors must yield to their captain's commands; no reasonable person believes that ships can be run democratically. Plato goes on to suggest that governing a state is rather like being captain of a ship or like practicing medicine as a physician. Much the same conditions that require central rule and decisive action in organized technical activity also create this need in government.

In Engels's argument, and arguments like it, the justification for authority is no longer made by Plato's classic analogy, but rather directly with reference to technology itself. If the basic case is as compelling as Engels believed it to be, one would expect that, as a society adopted increasingly complicated technical systems as its material basis, the prospects for authoritarian ways of life would be greatly enhanced. Central control by knowledgeable people acting at the top of a rigid social hierarchy would seem increasingly prudent. In this respect, his stand in "On Authority" appears to be at variance with Karl Marx's position in Volume One of *Capital*. Marx tries to show that increasing mechanization will render obsolete the hierarchical division of labor and the relationships of subordination that, in his view, were necessary during the early stages of modern manufacturing. The "Modern Industry," he writes, "… sweeps away by technical means the manufacturing division of labor, under which each man is bound hand and foot for life to a single detail operation. At the same time, the capitalistic form of that industry reproduces this same division of labor in a still more monstrous shape; in the factory proper, by converting the workman into a living appendage of the machine.[21] In Marx's view, the conditions that will eventually dissolve the capitalist division of labor and facilitate proletarian revolution are conditions latent in industrial technology itself. The differences between Marx's position in *Capital* and Engels's in his essay raise an important question for socialism: What, after all, does modern technology make possible or necessary in political life? The theoretical tension we see here mirrors many troubles in the practice of freedom and authority that have muddied the tracks of socialist revolution.

Arguments to the effect that technologies are in some sense inherently political have been advanced in a wide variety of contexts, far too many to summarize here. In my reading of such notions, however, there are two basic ways of stating the case. One version claims that the adoption of a given technical system actually requires the creation and maintenance of a particular set of social conditions as the operating environment of that system. Engels's position is of this kind. A similar view is offered by a contemporary writer who holds that "if you accept nuclear power plants, you also accept a techno-scientific-industrial-military elite. Without these people in charge, you could not have nuclear power."[22] In this conception, some kinds of technology require their social environments to be structured in a particular way in much the same sense that an automobile requires wheels in order to run. The thing could not exist as an effective operating entity unless certain social as well as material conditions were met. The meaning of "required" here is that of practical (rather than logical) necessity. Thus, Plato thought it a practical necessity that a ship at sea have one captain and an unquestioningly obedient crew.

A second, somewhat weaker, version of the argument holds that a given kind of technology is strongly compatible with, but does not strictly require, social and political relationships of a particular stripe. Many advocates of solar energy now hold that technologies of that variety are more compatible with a democratic, egalitarian society than energy systems based on coal, oil, and nuclear power; at the same time, they do not maintain that anything about solar energy requires democracy. Their case is, briefly, that solar energy is decentralizing in both a technical and political sense: Technically speaking, it is vastly more reasonable to build solar systems in a disaggregated, widely distributed manner than in large-scale, centralized plants; politically speaking, solar energy accommodates the attempts of individuals and local communities to manage their affairs effectively because they are dealing with systems that are more accessible, comprehensible, and controllable than huge centralized sources. In this view, solar energy is desirable not only for its economic and environmental benefits, but also for the salutary institutions it is likely to permit in other areas of public life.[23]

Within both versions of the argument there is a further distinction to be made between conditions that are internal to the workings of a given technical system and those that are external to it. Engels's thesis concerns internal social relations said to be required within cotton factories and railways, for example; what such relationships mean for the condition of society at large is for him a separate question. In contrast, the solar advocate's belief that solar technologies are compatible with democracy pertains to the way they complement aspects of society removed from the organization of those technologies as such.

There are, then, several different directions that arguments of this kind can follow. Are the social conditions predicated said to be required by, or strongly compatible with, the workings of a given technical system? Are those conditions internal to that system or external to it (or both)? Although writings that address such questions are often unclear about what is being asserted, arguments in this general category do have an important presence in modern political discourse. They enter into many attempts to explain how changes in social life take place in the wake of technological innovation. More importantly, they are often used to buttress attempts to justify or criticize proposed courses of action involving new technology. By offering distinctly political reasons for or against the adoption of a particular technology, arguments of this kind stand apart from more commonly employed, more easily quantifiable claims about economic costs and benefits, environmental impacts, and possible risks to public health and safety that technical systems may involve. The issue here does not concern how many jobs will be created, how much income generated, how many pollutants added, or how many cancers produced. Rather, the issue has to do with ways in which choices about technology have important consequences for the form and quality of human associations.

If we examine social patterns that comprise the environments of technical systems, we find certain devices and systems almost invariably linked to specific ways of organizing power and authority. The important question is: Does this state of affairs derive from an unavoidable social response to intractable properties in the things themselves, or is it instead a pattern imposed independently by a governing body, ruling class, or some other social or cultural institution to further its own purposes?

Taking the most obvious example, the atom bomb is an inherently political artifact. As long as it exists at all, its lethal properties demand that it be controlled by a centralized, rigidly hierarchical chain of command closed to all influences that might make its workings unpredictable. The internal social system of the bomb must be authoritarian; there is no other way. The state of affairs stands as a practical necessity independent of any larger political system in which the bomb is embedded, independent of the kind of regime or character of its rulers. Indeed, democratic states must try to find ways to ensure that the social structures and mentality that characterize the management of nuclear weapons do not "spin off" or "spill over" into the polity as a whole.

The bomb is, of course, a special case. The reasons very rigid relationships of authority are necessary in its immediate presence should be clear to anyone. If, however, we look for other instances in which particular varieties of technology are widely perceived to need the maintenance of a special pattern of power and authority, modern technical history contains a wealth of examples.

Alfred D. Chandler in *The Visible Hand*, a monumental study of modern business enterprise, presents impressive documentation to defend the hypothesis that the construction and day-to-day operation of many systems of production, transportation, and communication in the nineteenth and twentieth centuries require the development of a particular social form — a large-scale, centralized, hierarchical organization administered by highly skilled managers. Typical of Chandler's reasoning is his analysis of the growth of the railroads:

> Technology made possible fast, all-weather transportation; but safe, regular, reliable movement of goods and passengers, as well as the continuing maintenance and repair of locomotives, rolling stock, and track, roadbed, stations, roundhouses, and other equipment, required the creation of a sizable administrative organization. It meant the employment of a set of managers to supervise these functional activities over an extensive geographical area; and the appointment of an administrative command of middle and top executives to monitor, evaluate, and coordinate the work of managers responsible for the day-to-day operations.[24]

Throughout his book, Chandler points to ways in which technologies used in the production and distribution of electricity, chemicals, and a wide range of industrial goods "demanded" or "required" this form of human association. "Hence, the operational requirements of railroads demanded the creation of the first administrative hierarchies in American business."[25]

Were there other conceivable ways of organizing these aggregates of people and apparatus? Chandler shows that a previously dominant social form, the small traditional family firm, simply could not handle the task in most cases. Although he does not speculate further, it is clear that he believes there is, to be realistic, very little latitude in the forms of power and authority appropriate within modern sociotechnical systems. The properties of many modern technologies — oil pipelines and refineries, for example — are such that overwhelmingly impressive economies of scale and speed are possible. If such systems are to work effectively, efficiently, quickly, and safely, certain requirements of internal social organization have to be fulfilled; the material possibilities that modern technologies make available could not be exploited otherwise. Chandler acknowledges that as one compares sociotechnical institutions of different nations, one sees "ways in which cultural attitudes, values, ideologies, political systems, and social structure affect these imperatives."[26] But the weight of argument and empirical evidence in *The Visible Hand* suggests that any significant departure from the basic pattern would be, at best, highly unlikely.

It may be that other conceivable arrangements of power and authority, for example, those of decentralized, democratic worker self-management, could prove capable of administering factories, refineries, communications systems, and railroads as well as or better than the organizations Chandler describes. Evidence from automobile assembly teams in Sweden and worker-managed plants in Yugoslavia and other countries is often presented to salvage these possibilities. I shall not be able to settle controversies over this matter here, but merely point to what I consider to be their bone of contention. The available evidence tends to show that many large, sophisticated technological systems are in fact highly compatible with centralized, hierarchical managerial control.

The interesting question, however, has to do with whether or not this pattern is in any sense a requirement of such systems, a question that is not solely an empirical one. The matter ultimately rests on our judgments about what steps, if any, are practically necessary in the workings of particular kinds of technology and what, if anything, such measures require of the structure of human associations. Was Plato right in saying that a ship at sea needs steering by a decisive hand and that this could only be accomplished by a single captain and an obedient crew? Is Chandler correct in saying that the properties of large-scale systems require centralized, hierarchical, managerial control?

To answer such questions, we would have to examine in some detail the moral claims of practical necessity (including those advocated in the doctrines of economics) and weigh them against moral claims of other sorts, for example, the notion that it is good for sailors to participate in the command of a ship or that workers have a right to be involved in making and administering decisions in a factory. It is characteristic of societies based on large, complex technological systems, however, that moral reasons other than those of practical necessity appear increasingly obsolete, "idealistic," and irrelevant. Whatever claims one may wish to make on behalf of liberty, justice, or equality can be immediately neutralized when confronted with arguments to the effect: "Fine, but that's no way to run a railroad" (or steel mill, or airline, or communications system, and so on). Here we encounter an important quality in modern political discourse and in the way people commonly think about what measures are justified in response to the possibilities technologies make available. In many instances, to say that some technologies are inherently political is to say that certain widely accepted reasons of practical necessity — especially the need to maintain crucial technological systems as smoothly working entities — have tended to eclipse other sorts of moral and political reasoning.

One attempt to salvage the autonomy of politics from the bind of practical necessity involves the notion that conditions of human association found in the internal workings of technological systems can easily be kept separate from the polity as a whole. Americans have long rested content in the belief that arrangements of power and authority inside industrial corporations, public utilities, and the like have little bearing on public institutions, practices, and ideas at large.

That "democracy stops at the factory gates" was taken as a fact of life that had nothing to do with the practice of political freedom. But can the internal politics of technology and the politics of the whole community be so easily separated? A recent study of American business leaders, contemporary exemplars of Chandler's "visible hand of management," found them remarkably impatient with such democratic scruples as "one man, one vote." If democracy doesn't work for the firm, the most critical institution in all of society, American executives ask, how well can it be expected to work for the government of a nation — particularly when that government attempts to interfere with the achievements of the firm? The authors of the report observe that patterns of authority that work effectively in the corporation become for businessmen "the desirable model against which to compare political and economic relationships in the rest of society."[27] While such findings are far from conclusive, they do reflect a sentiment increasingly common in the land: What dilemmas like the energy crisis require is not a re-distribution of wealth or broader public participation but, rather, stronger, centralized, public management — President Carter's proposal for an Energy Mobilization Board and the like.

An especially vivid case in which the operational requirements of a technical system might influence the quality of public life is now at issue in debates about the risks of nuclear power. As the supply of uranium for nuclear reactors runs out, a proposed alternative fuel is the plutonium generated as a by-product in reactor cores. Well-known objections to plutonium recycling focus on its unacceptable economic costs, its risks of environmental contamination, and its dangers in regard to the international proliferation of nuclear weapons. Beyond these concerns, however, stands another, less widely appreciated set of hazards — those that involve the sacrifice of civil liberties. The widespread use of plutonium as a fuel increases the chance that this toxic substance might be stolen by terrorists, [members of] organized crime, or other persons. This raises the prospect, and not a trivial one, that extraordinary measures would have to be taken to safeguard plutonium from theft and to recover it if ever the substance were stolen. Workers in the nuclear industry, as well as ordinary citizens outside, could well become subject to background security checks, covert surveillance, wiretapping, informers, and even emergency measures under martial law — all justified by the need to safeguard plutonium.

Russell W. Ayres's study of the legal ramifications of plutonium recycling concludes, "With the passage of time and the increase in the quantity of plutonium in existence will come pressure to eliminate the traditional checks the courts and legislatures place on the activities of the executive and to develop a powerful central authority better able to enforce strict safeguards." He avers that "once a quantity of plutonium had been stolen, the case for literally turning the country upside down to get it back would be overwhelming." Ayres anticipates and worries about the kinds of thinking that, I have argued, characterize inherently political technologies. It is still true that, in a world in which human beings make and maintain artificial systems, nothing is "required" in an absolute sense. Nevertheless, once a course of action is under way, once artifacts like nuclear power plants have been built and put in operation, the kinds of reasoning that justify the adaptation of social life to technical requirements pop up as spontaneously as flowers in the spring. In Ayres's words, "Once recycling begins and the risks of plutonium theft become real rather than hypothetical, the case for governmental infringement of protected rights will seem compelling."[28] After a certain point, those who cannot accept the hard requirements and imperatives will be dismissed as dreamers and fools.

★ ★ ★

The two varieties of interpretation I have outlined indicate how artifacts can have political qualities. In the first instance, we noticed ways in which specific features in the design or arrangement of a device or system could provide a convenient means of establishing patterns of power and authority in a given setting. Technologies of this kind have a range of flexibility in the dimensions of their material form. It is precisely because they are flexible that their consequences for society must be understood with reference to the social actors able to influence which designs and arrangements are chosen. In the second instance, we examined ways in which the intractable properties of certain kinds of technology are strongly, perhaps unavoidably, linked to particular institutionalized patterns of power and authority. Here, the initial choice about whether or not to adopt something is decisive in regard to its consequences. There are no alternative physical designs or arrangements that would make a significant difference; there are, furthermore, no genuine possibilities for creative intervention by different social systems — capitalist or socialist — that could change the intractability of the entity or significantly alter the quality of its political effects.

To know which variety of interpretation is applicable in a given case is often what is at stake in disputes, some of them passionate ones, about the meaning of technology for how we live. I have argued a "both/and" position here, for it seems to me that both kinds of understanding are applicable in different circumstances. Indeed, it can happen that within a particular complex of technology — a system of communication or transportation, for example — some aspects may be flexible in their possibilities for society, while other aspects may be (for better or worse) completely intractable. The two varieties of interpretation I have examined here can overlap and intersect at many points.

These are, of course, issues on which people can disagree. Thus, some proponents of energy from renewable resources now believe they have at last discovered a set of intrinsically democratic, egalitarian, communitarian technologies. In my best estimation, however, the social consequences of building renewable energy systems will surely depend on the specific configurations of both hardware and the social institutions created to bring that energy to us. It may be that we will find ways to turn this silk purse into a sow's ear. By comparison, advocates of the further development of nuclear power seem to believe that they are working on a rather flexible technology whose adverse social effects can be fixed by changing the design parameters of reactors and nuclear waste disposal systems. For reasons indicated above, I believe them to be dead wrong in that faith. Yes, we may be able to manage some of the "risks" to public health and safety that nuclear power brings. But as society adapts to the more dangerous and apparently indelible features of nuclear power, what will be the long-range toll in human freedom?

My belief that we ought to attend more closely to technical objects themselves is not to say that we can ignore the contexts in which those objects are situated. A ship at sea may well require, as Plato and Engels insisted, a single captain and obedient crew. But a ship out of service, parked at the dock, needs only a caretaker. To understand which technologies and which contexts are important to us, and why, is an enterprise that must involve both the study of specific technical systems and their history as well as a thorough grasp of the concepts and controversies of political theory. In our times, people are often willing to make drastic changes in the way they live to accord with technological innovation at the same time they would resist similar kinds of changes justified on political grounds. If for no other reason than that, it is important for us to achieve a clearer view of these matters than has been our habit so far.

ENDNOTES

1. I would like to thank Merritt Roe Smith, Leo Marx, James Miller, David Noble, Charles Weiner, Sherry Turkle, Loren Graham, Gail Stuart, Dick Sclove, and Stephen Graubard for their comments and criticisms on earlier drafts of this essay. My thanks also to Doris Morrison of the Agriculture Library of the University of California, Berkeley, for her bibliographical help.

2. Lewis Mumford, "Authoritarian and Democratic Technics," *Technology and Culture* 5 (1964), pp. 1–8.

3. Denis Hayes, *Rays of Hope: The Transition to a Post-Petroleum World* (New York: W. W. Norton, 1977), pp. 71, 159.

4. David Lilienthal, *T.V.A.: Democracy on the March* (New York: Harper & Brothers, 1944), pp. 72–83.

5. Daniel J. Boorstin, *The Republic of Technology* (New York: Harper & Row, 1978), p. 7.

6. Langdon Winner, *Autonomous Technology: Technics-out-of-Control as a Theme in Political Thought* (Cambridge, MA: M.I.T. Press, 1977).

7. The meaning of "technology" I employ in this essay does not encompass some of the broader definitions of that concept found in contemporary literature, for example, the notion of "technique" in the writings of Jacques Ellul. My purposes here are more limited. For a discussion of the difficulties that arise in attempts to define "technology," see Winner, *Autonomous Technology*, pp. 8–12.

8. Robert A. Caro, *The Power Broker: Robert Moses and the Fall of New York* (New York: Random House, 1974), pp. 318, 481, 514, 546, 951–58.

9. Ibid., p. 952.

10. Robert Ozanne, *A Century of Labor–Management Relations at McCormick and International Harvester* (Madison: University of Wisconsin Press, 1967), p. 20.

11. The early history of the tomato harvester is told in Wayne D. Rasmussen, "Advances in American Agriculture: The Mechanical Tomato Harvester as a Case Study," *Technology and Culture* 9 (1968), pp. 531–43.

12. Andrew Schmitz and David Seckler, "Mechanized Agriculture and Social Welfare: The Case of the Tomato Harvester," *American Journal of Agricultural Economics* 52 (1970), pp. 569–77.

13. William H. Friedland and Amy Barton, "Tomato Technology," *Society* 13:6 (September/October 1976). See also William H. Friedland, *Social Sleepwalkers: Scientific and Technological Research in California Agriculture*, University of California, Davis, Department of Applied Behavioral Sciences, Research Monograph No. 13, 1974.

14. University of California Clip Sheet, 54:36, May 1, 1979.

15. Friedland and Barton, "Tomato Technology."

16. A history and critical analysis of agricultural research in the land-grant colleges is given in James Hightower, *Hard Tomatoes, Hard Times* (Cambridge, MA: Schenkman, 1978).

17. David Noble, "Social Change in Machine Design: The Case of Automatically Controlled Machine Tools," in *Case Studies in the Labor Process*, A. Zimbalist, ed. (New York: Monthly Review Press, 1979), pp. 18–50.

18. Friedrich Engels, "On Authority" in *The Marx-Engels Reader*, 2nd ed., ed. Robert Tucker (New York: W. W. Norton, 1978), p. 731.

19. Ibid.

20. Ibid., pp. 732, 731.

21. Karl Marx, *Capital*, vol. 1, 3rd ed., trans. Samuel Moore and Edward Aveling (New York: The Modern Library, 1906), p. 530.

22. Jerry Mander, *Four Arguments for the Elimination of Television* (New York: William Morrow, 1978), p. 44.

23. See, for example, Robert Argue, Barbara Emanuel, and Stephen Graham, *The Sun Builders: A People's Guide to Solar, Wind, and Wood Energy in Canada* (Toronto: Renewable Energy in Canada, 1978). "We think decentralization is an implicit component of renewable energy; this implies the decentralization of energy systems, communities and of power. Renewable energy doesn't require mammoth generation sources or disruptive transmission corridors. Our cities and towns, which have been dependent on centralized energy supplies, may be able to achieve some degree of autonomy, thereby controlling and administering their own energy needs" (p. 16).

24. Alfred D. Chandler, Jr., *The Visible Hand: The Managerial Revolution in American Business* (Cambridge, MA: Belknap, Harvard University Press, 1977), p. 244.

25. Ibid.

26. Ibid., p. 500.

27. Leonard Silk and David Vogel, *Ethics and Profits: The Crisis of Confidence in American Business* (New York: Simon & Schuster, 1976), p. 191.

28. Russell W. Ayres, "Policing Plutonium: The Civil Liberties Fallout," *Harvard Civil Rights–Civil Liberties Law Review* 10 (1975), pp. 374, 413–14, 443.

PART II

Debating Technology: 1960s Style

Chapter 7, Emmanuel Mesthene's essay, "The Role of Technology in Society," and the piece that follows it, "Technology: The Opiate of the Intellectuals" by John McDermott (Chapter 8), constitute a classic debate about the role of technology in society. The articles date from the late 1960s, when the war in Vietnam was in full swing, and intellectual and political life in the United States was torn by bitter conflicts between the "establishment" and the "New Left." The use of high tech weapons by U.S. forces in the war provoked an intense debate about technology and its impacts.

These two articles are included here, as they have been in every edition of *Technology and the Future* since the book was first published in 1972, as a means of illustrating in sharp relief the different perspectives on technology of the powerful and powerless. Mesthene, a Harvard professor and former RAND Corporation analyst, head of a large research program funded by a multimillion dollar grant from IBM, is comfortable with technology. He and his colleagues feel that technology is something that they can control and use. It is a neutral tool that can be employed for purposes that are good and evil, and it often has both positive and negative effects on society.

McDermott, on the other hand, sees technology from the lower rungs of society's ladder. A professor of labor studies writing in the then-radical left-wing *New York Review of Books*, he adopts the viewpoint of a factory worker struggling to make ends meet rather than the highly paid industry executive. He is the foot soldier slogging through the jungles of Vietnam in a war whose purpose he does not understand, rather than the systems analyst comfortably ensconced in the Pentagon or in RAND's Santa Monica headquarters. Technology, seen from McDermott's side of

69

the fence, is hardly a neutral tool; it is the means by which those in power maintain their control of society while perpetuating social injustice.

Some of the illustrations the authors use in these two essays — which were instantly recognizable and conjured up clear images to readers of their day — may be unfamiliar to readers in the twenty-first century. But the issues they raise and the differing perspectives on technology of the rulers and the ruled are as important today as they were almost four decades ago.

7

The Role of Technology in Society

EMMANUEL G. MESTHENE

Emmanuel Mesthene's essay, "The Role of Technology in Society," originated as the overview section of the fourth annual report of the Harvard Program on Technology and Society, an interdisciplinary program of academic studies funded by a $5 million grant from the IBM Corporation. Mesthene (pronounced mess-then-ee) was the program's director, and this essay was his general statement of what the program had learned during its first four years about the implications of technological change for society.

According to Mesthene, technology appears to induce social change in two ways: by creating new opportunities and by generating new problems for individuals and for societies. "It has both positive and negative effects, and it usually has the two at the same time and in virtue of each other." By enlarging the realm of goal choice, or by altering the relative costs associated with different values, technology can induce value change. In all areas, technology is seen to have two faces, one positive and one negative.

Emmanuel G. Mesthene directed the Harvard Program on Technology and Society from 1964 through 1974, following eleven years with the RAND Corporation. He joined Rutgers University in 1974, serving as dean of Livingston College for several years, then as distinguished professor of philosophy and professor of management. Mesthene died in 1990. Among his books are Technological Change: Its Impact on Man and Society *(1970) and* How Language Makes Us Know *(1964).*

From *Technology and Culture* 10:4 (1969), pp. 489–536, © Society for the History of Technology. Reprinted with permission of The Johns Hopkins University Press.

SOCIAL CHANGE

Three Unhelpful Views about Technology

While a good deal of research is aimed at discerning the particular effects of technological change on industry, government, or education, systematic inquiry devoted to seeing these effects together and to assessing their implications for contemporary society as a whole is relatively recent and does not enjoy the strong methodology and richness of theory and data that mark more established fields of scholarship. It therefore often has to contend with facile or one-dimensional views about what technology means for society. Three such views, which are prevalent at the present time, may be mildly caricatured somewhat as follows.

The first holds that technology is an unalloyed blessing for man and society. Technology is seen as the motor of all progress, as holding the solution to most of our social problems, as helping to liberate the individual from the clutches of a complex and highly organized society, and as the source of permanent prosperity; in short, as the promise of utopia in our time. This view has its modern origins in the social philosophies of such nineteenth-century thinkers as Saint Simon, Karl Marx, and Auguste Comte. It tends to be held by many scientists and engineers, by many military leaders and aerospace industrialists, by people who believe that man is fully in command of his tools and his destiny, and by many of the devotees of modern techniques of "scientific management."

A second view holds that technology is an unmitigated curse. Technology is said to rob people of their jobs, their privacy, their participation in democratic government, and even, in the end, their dignity as human beings. It is seen as autonomous and uncontrollable, as fostering materialistic values and as destructive of religion, as bringing about a technocratic society and bureaucratic state in which the individual is increasingly submerged, and as threatening, ultimately, to poison nature and blow up the world. This view is akin to historical "back-to-nature" attitudes toward the world and is propounded mainly by artists, literary commentators, popular social critics, and existentialist philosophers. It is becoming increasingly attractive to many of our youth, and it tends to be held, understandably enough, by segments of the population that have suffered dislocation as a result of technological change.

The third view is of a different sort. It argues that technology as such is not worthy of special notice, because it has been well recognized as a factor in social change at least since the Industrial Revolution, because it is unlikely that the social effects of computers will be nearly so traumatic as the introduction of the factory system in eighteenth-century England, because research has shown that technology has done little to accelerate the rate of economic productivity since the 1880s, because there has been no significant change in recent decades in the time periods between invention and widespread adoption of new technology, and because improved communications and higher levels of education make people much more adaptable than heretofore to new ideas and to new social reforms required by technology.

This view is supported by a good deal of empirical evidence; however, it tends to ignore a number of social, cultural, psychological, and political effects of technological change that are less easy to identify with precision. It thus reflects the difficulty of coming to grips with a new or broadened subject matter by means of concepts and intellectual categories designed to deal with older and different subject matters. This view tends to be held by historians, for whom continuity is an indispensable methodological assumption, and by many economists, who find that their instruments measure some things quite well while those of the other social sciences do not yet measure much of anything.

Stripped of caricature, each of these views contains a measure of truth and reflects a real aspect of the relationship of technology and society. Yet they are oversimplifications that do not contribute much to understanding. One can find empirical evidence to support each of them without gaining much knowledge about the actual mechanism by which technology leads to social change or significant insight into its implications for the future. All three remain too uncritical or too partial to guide inquiry. Research and analysis lead to more differentiated conclusions and reveal more subtle relationships.

★ ★ ★

How Technological Change Impinges on Society

It is clearly possible to sketch a more adequate hypothesis about the interaction of technology and society than the partial views outlined [here]. Technological change would appear to induce or "motor" social change in two principal ways. New technology creates new opportunities for men and societies, and it also generates new problems for them. It has both positive and negative effects, and it usually has the two at the same time and in virtue of each other. Thus, industrial technology strengthens the economy, as our measures of growth and productivity show…. However, it also induces changes in the relative importance of individual supplying sectors in the economy as new techniques of production alter the amounts and kinds of materials, parts and components, energy, and service inputs used by each industry to produce its output. It thus tends to bring about dislocations of businesses and people as a result of changes in industrial patterns and in the structure of occupations.

The close relationship between technological and social change itself helps to explain why any given technological development is likely to have both positive and negative effects. The usual sequence is that (1) technological advance creates a new opportunity to achieve some desired goal; (2) this requires (except in trivial cases) alterations in social organization if advantage is to be taken of the new opportunity; (3) which means that the functions of existing social structures will be interfered with; (4) with the result that other goals, which were served by the older structures, are now only inadequately achieved.

As the Meyer–Kain[1] study has shown, for example, improved transportation technology and increased ownership of private automobiles have increased the mobility of businesses and individuals. This has led to altered patterns of industrial and residential location, so that older unified cities are being increasingly transformed into larger metropolitan complexes. The new opportunities for mobility are largely denied to the poor and black populations of the core cities, however, partly for economic reasons, and partly as a result of restrictions on choice of residence by blacks, thus leading to persistent black unemployment despite a generally high level of economic activity. Cities are thus increasingly unable to perform their traditional functions of providing employment opportunities for all segments of their populations and an integrated social environment that can temper ethnic and racial differences. The new urban complexes are neither fully viable economic units nor effective political organizations able to upgrade and integrate their core populations into new economic and social structures. The resulting instability is further aggravated by modern mass communications technology, which heightens the expectations of the poor and the fears of the well-to-do and adds frustration and bitterness to the urban crisis....

In all such cases, technology creates a new opportunity and a new problem at the same time. That is why isolating the opportunity or the problem and construing it as the whole answer is ultimately obstructive of, rather than helpful to, understanding.

How Society Reacts to Technological Change

The heightened prominence of technology in our society makes the interrelated tasks of profiting from its opportunities and containing its dangers a major intellectual and political challenge of our time.

Failure of society to respond to the opportunities created by new technology means that much actual or potential technology lies fallow, that is, is not used at all or is not used to its full capacity. This can mean that potentially solvable problems are left unsolved and potentially achievable goals unachieved, because we waste our technological resources or use them inefficiently. A society has at least as much stake in the efficient utilization of technology as in that of its natural or human resources.

There are often good reasons, of course, for not developing or utilizing a particular technology. The mere fact that it can be developed is not sufficient reason for doing so....

But there are also cases where technology lies fallow because existing social structures are inadequate to exploit the opportunities it offers.... Community institutions wither for want of interest and participation by residents. City agencies are unable to marshal the skills and take the systematic approach needed to deal with new and intensified problems of education, crime control, and public welfare. Business corporations, finally, which are organized around the expectation of private profit, are insufficiently motivated to bring new technology and management know-how to bear on urban projects where the benefits will be largely social. All these factors combine to dilute what may otherwise be a genuine desire to apply our best knowledge and adequate resources to the resolution of urban tensions and the eradication of poverty in the nation....

Containing the Negative Effects of Technology

The kinds and magnitude of the negative effects of technology are no more independent of the institutional structures and cultural attitudes of society than is realization of the new opportunities that technology offers. In our society, there are individuals or individual firms always on the lookout for new technological opportunities, and large corporations hire scientists and engineers to invent such opportunities. In deciding whether to develop a new technology, individual entrepreneurs engage in calculations of expected benefits and expected costs to themselves and proceed if the former are likely to exceed the latter. Their calculations do not take adequate account of the probable benefits and costs of the new developments to others than themselves or to society generally. These latter are what economists call external benefits and costs.

The external benefits potential in new technology will thus not be realized by the individual developer and will rather accrue to society as a result of deliberate social action, as has been argued above. Similarly with the external costs. In minimizing only expected costs to himself, the individual decision maker helps to contain only some of the potentially negative effects of the new technology. The external costs and therefore the negative effects on society at large are not of principal concern to him and, in our society, are not expected to be.

Most of the consequences of technology that are causing concern at the present time — pollution of the environment, potential damage to the ecology of the planet, occupational and social dislocations, threats to the privacy and political significance of the individual, social and psychological malaise — are negative externalities of this kind. They are with us in large measure because it has not been anybody's explicit business to foresee and anticipate them. They have fallen between the stools of innumerable individual decisions to develop individual technologies for individual purposes without explicit attention to what all these decisions add up to for society as a whole and for people as human beings. This freedom of individual decision making is a value that we have cherished and that is built into the institutional fabric of our society. The negative effects of technology that we deplore are a measure of what this traditional freedom is beginning to cost us. They are traceable, less to some mystical autonomy presumed to lie in technology, and much more to the autonomy that our economic and political institutions grant to individual decision making....

Measures to control and mitigate the negative effects of technology, however, often appear to threaten freedoms that our traditions still take for granted as inalienable rights of men and good societies, however much they may have been tempered in practice by the social pressures of modern times: the freedom of the market, the freedom of private enterprise, the freedom of the scientist to follow truth wherever it may lead, and the freedom of the individual to pursue his fortune and decide his fate. There is thus set up a tension between the need to control technology and our wish to preserve our values, which leads some people to conclude that technology is inherently inimical to human values. The political effect of this tension takes the form of inability to adjust our decision making structures to the realities of technology so as to take maximum advantage of the opportunities it offers and so that we can act to contain its potential ill effects before they become so pervasive and urgent as to seem uncontrollable.

To understand why such tensions are so prominent a social consequence of technological change, it becomes necessary to look explicitly at the effects of technology on social and individual values.

VALUES

★ ★ ★

Technology as a Cause of Value Change

Technology has a direct impact on values by virtue of its capacity for creating new opportunities. By making possible what was not possible before, it offers individuals and society new options to choose from. For example, space technology makes it possible for the first time to go to the moon or to communicate by satellite and thereby adds those two new options to the spectrum of choices available to society. By adding new options in this way, technology can lead to changes in values in the same way that the appearance of new dishes on the heretofore standard menu of one's favorite restaurant can lead to changes in one's tastes and choices of food. Specifically, technology can lead to value change either (1) by bringing some previously unattainable goal within the realm of choice or (2) by making some values easier to implement than heretofore, that is, by changing the costs associated with realizing them....

One example related to the effect of technological change on values is implicit in our concept of democracy. The ideal we associate with the old New England town meeting is that each citizen should have a direct voice in political decisions. Since this has not been possible, we have elected representatives to serve our interests and vote our opinions. Sophisticated computer technology, however, now makes possible rapid and efficient collection and analysis of voter opinion and could eventually provide for "instant voting" by the whole electorate on any issue presented to it via television a few hours before. It thus raises the possibility of instituting a system of direct democracy and gives rise to tensions between those who would be violently opposed to such a prospect and those who are already advocating some system of participatory democracy.

This new technological possibility challenges us to clarify what we mean by democracy. Do we construe it as the will of an undifferentiated majority, as the resultant of transient coalitions of different interest groups representing different value commitments, as the considered judgment of the people's elected representatives, or as by and large the kind of government we actually have in the United States, minus the flaws in it that we would like to correct? By bringing us face to face with such questions, technology has the effect of calling society's bluff and thereby preparing the ground for changes in its values.

In the case where technological change alters the relative costs of implementing different values, it impinges on inherent contradictions in our value system. To pursue the same example, modern technology can enhance the values we associate with democracy. But it can also enhance another American value — that of "secular rationality," as sociologists call it — by facilitating the use of scientific and technical expertise in the process of political decision making. This can in turn further reduce citizen participation in the democratic process. Technology thus has the effect of facing us with contradictions in our value system and of calling for deliberate attention to their resolution.

★ ★ ★

ECONOMIC AND POLITICAL ORGANIZATION

The Enlarged Scope of Public Decision Making

When technology brings about social changes (as described in the first section of this essay) that impinge on our existing system of values (in ways reviewed in the second section), it poses for society a number of problems that are ultimately political in nature. The term "political" is used here in the broadest sense: It encompasses all of the decision making structures and procedures that have to do with the allocation and distribution of wealth and power in society. The political organization of society thus includes not only the formal apparatus of the state but also industrial organizations and other private institutions that play a role in the decision making process. It is particularly important to attend to the organization of the entire body politic when technological change leads to a blurring of once-clear distinctions between the public and private sectors of society and to changes in the roles of its principal institutions.

It was suggested above that the political requirements of our modern technological society call for a relatively greater public commitment on the part of individuals than in previous times. The reason for this, stated most generally, is that technological change has the effect of enhancing the importance of public decision making in society, because technology is continually creating new possibilities for social action as well as new problems that have to be dealt with.

A society that undertakes to foster technology on a large scale, in fact, commits itself to social complexity and to facing and dealing with new problems as a normal feature of political life. Not much is yet known with any precision about the political imperatives inherent in technological change, but one may nevertheless speculate about the reasons why an increasingly technological society seems to be characterized by enlargement of the scope of public decision making.

For one thing, the development and application of technology seems to require large-scale, and hence increasingly complex, social concentrations, whether these be large cities, large corporations, big universities, or big government. In instances where technological advance appears to facilitate reduction of such first-order concentrations, it tends to instead enlarge the relevant system of social organization, that is, to lead to increased centralization. Thus, the physical dispersion made possible by transportation and communications technologies, as Meyer and Kain have shown, enlarges the urban complex that must be governed as a unit.

A second characteristic of advanced technology is that its effects cover large distances, in both the geographical and social senses of the term. Both its positive and negative features are more extensive. Horse-powered transportation technology was limited in its speed and capacity, but its nuisance value was also limited, in most cases to the owner and to the occupant of the next farm. The supersonic transport can carry hundreds across long distances in minutes, but its noise and vibration damage must also be suffered willy-nilly by everyone within the limits of a swath 3,000 miles long and several miles wide.

The concatenation of increased density (or enlarged system) and extended technological "distance" means that technological applications have increasingly wider ramifications and that increasingly large concentrations of people and organizations become dependent on technological systems.... The result is not only that more and more decisions must be social decisions taken in public ways, as already noted, but that, once made, decisions are likely to have a shorter useful life than heretofore. That is partly because technology is continually altering the spectrum of choices and problems that society faces, and partly because any decision taken is likely to generate a need to take ten more.

These speculations about the effects of technology on public decision making raise the problem of restructuring our decision making mechanisms — including the system of market incentives — so that the increasing number and importance of social issues that confront us can be resolved equitably and effectively.

★ ★ ★

The Promise and Problems of Scientific Decision Making

There are two further consequences of the expanding role of public decision making. The first is that the latest information-handling devices and techniques tend to be utilized in the decision making process. This is so (1) because public policy can be effective only to the degree that it is based on reliable knowledge about the actual state of the society, and thus requires a strong capability to collect, aggregate, and analyze detailed data about economic activities, social patterns, popular attitudes, and political trends, and (2) because it is recognized increasingly that decisions taken in one area impinge on and have consequences for other policy areas often thought of as unrelated, so that it becomes necessary to base decisions on a model of society that sees it as a system and that it is capable of signaling as many as possible of the probable consequences of a contemplated action.

As Professor Alan F. Westin points out, reactions to the prospect of more decision making based on computerized data banks and scientific management techniques run the gamut of optimism to pessimism mentioned in the opening of this essay. Negative reactions take the form of rising political demands for greater popular participation in decision making, for more equality among different segments of the population, and for greater regard for the dignity of individuals. The increasing dependence of decision making on scientific and technological devices and techniques is seen as posing a threat to these goals, and pressures are generated in opposition to further "rationalization" of decision making processes. These pressures have the paradoxical effect, however, not of deflecting the supporters of technological decision making from their course, but of spurring them on to renewed effort to save the society before it explodes under planlessness and inadequate administration.

The paradox goes further and helps to explain much of the social discontent that we are witnessing at the present time. The greater complexity and the more extensive ramifications that technology brings about in society tend to make social processes increasingly circuitous and indirect. The effects of actions are widespread and difficult to keep track of, so that experts and sophisticated techniques are increasingly needed to detect and analyze social events and to formulate policies adequate to the complexity of social issues. The "logic" of modern decision making thus appears to require greater and greater dependence on the collection and analysis of data and on the use of technological devices and scientific techniques. Indeed, many observers would agree that there is an "increasing relegation of questions which used to be matters of political debate to professional cadres of technicians and experts which function almost independently of the democratic political process."[2] In recent times, that process has been most noticeable, perhaps, in the areas of economic policy and national security affairs.

This "logic" of modern decision making, however, runs counter to that element of traditional democratic theory that places high value on direct participation in the political processes and generates the kind of discontent referred to above. If it turns out on more careful examination that direct participation is becoming less relevant to a society in which the connections between causes and effects are long and often hidden — which is an increasingly "indirect" society, in other words — elaboration of a new democratic ethos and of new democratic processes more adequate to the realities of modern society will emerge as perhaps the major intellectual and political challenge of our time.

The Need for Institutional Innovation

The challenge is, indeed, already upon us, for the second consequence of the enlarged scope of public decision making is the need to develop new institutional forms and new mechanisms to replace established ones that can no longer deal effectively with the new kinds of problems with which we are increasingly faced. Much of the political ferment of the present time — over the problems of technology assessment, the introduction of statistical data banks, the extension to domestic problems of techniques of analysis developed for the military services, and the modification of the institutions of local government — is evidence of the need for new institutions....

CONCLUSION

As we review what we are learning about the relationship of technological and social change, a number of conclusions begin to emerge. We find, on the one hand, that the creation of new physical possibilities and social options by technology tends toward, and appears to require the emergence of, new values, new forms of economic activity, and new political organizations. On the other hand, technological change also poses problems of social and psychological displacement.

The two phenomena are not unconnected, nor is the tension between them new. Man's technical prowess always seems to run ahead of his ability to deal with and profit from it. In America, especially, we are becoming adept at extracting the new techniques, the physical power, and the economic productivity that are inherent in our knowledge and its associated technologies. Yet we have not fully accepted the fact that our progress in the technical realm does not leave our institutions, values, and political processes unaffected. Individuals will be fully integrated into society only when we can extract from our knowledge not only its technological potential but also its implications for a system of values and a social, economic, and political organization appropriate to a society in which technology is so prevalent....

ENDNOTES

1. Unless otherwise noted, studies referred to in this article are described in the Fourth Annual Report (1967–68) of the Harvard University Program on Technology and Society.
2. Harvey Brooks, "Scientific Concepts and Cultural Changes," in G. Holton, ed., *Science and Culture* (Boston: Houghton Mifflin, 1965), p. 71.

8

Technology: The Opiate of the Intellectuals

JOHN McDERMOTT

Several months after the report containing Emmanuel Mesthene's article was published by Harvard, a sharply critical review–essay by John McDermott appeared in The New York Review of Books. *McDermott's essay, which follows here, is not a point-by-point analysis or rebuttal of the Mesthene work. Rather, it is McDermott's attempt to critique the entire point of view that he sees as epitomized by Mesthene — "not of a new but of a newly aggressive right-wing ideology in this country." McDermott focuses on a notion he calls* laissez innover, *from the French for "let them innovate," an adaptation of the more common* laissez faire *meaning "let them do as they please (i.e., in a free market economy)." The idea behind* laissez innover *(which McDermott rejects) is that technology can be seen as a self-correcting system. Mesthene, he claims, finds this principle acceptable because he defines technology abstractly. McDermott himself, however, rejects* laissez innover *because he claims to see specific characteristics in contemporary technology that contradict the abstraction.*

Concentrating on the application of technology to the war in Vietnam, McDermott examines its nature and concludes that "technology, in its concrete, empirical meaning, refers fundamentally to systems of rationalized control over large groups of men, events, and machines by small groups of technically skilled men operating through organized hierarchy." Using this definition, he proceeds to discuss the social effect of modern technology in America, concluding that the ideology of laissez innover *is attractive to those in power since they are in a position to reap technology's benefits while avoiding its costs.*

John McDermott is professor emeritus of labor studies at the State University of New York at Old Westbury. He is the author of Economics in Real

From "Technology: The Opiate of the Masses," from *The New York Review of Books*, July 31, 1969. © 1969 NYREV, Inc.

Time: A Theoretical Reconstruction *(2003). McDermott received his B.A. from Brooklyn College, a unit of CUNY, the City University of New York.*

I

If religion was formerly the opiate of the masses, then surely technology is … … the opiate of the educated public today, or at least of its favorite authors. No other single subject is so universally invested with high hopes for the improvement of mankind generally and of Americans in particular.…

These hopes for mankind's, or technology's, future, however, are not unalloyed. Technology's defenders, being otherwise reasonable men, are also aware that the world population explosion and the nuclear missile race are also the fruit of the enormous advances made in technology during the past half-century or so. But here, too, a cursory reading of their literature would reveal widespread though qualified optimism that these scourges, too, will fall before technology's might. Thus, population (and genetic) control and permanent peace are sometimes added to the already imposing roster of technology's promises. What are we to make of such extravagant optimism?

In early 1968, Harvard University's Program on Technology and Society … issued its Fourth Annual Report to the accompaniment of full front-page coverage in *The New York Times* (January 18). Within the brief (fewer than 100) pages of that report, and most clearly in the concluding essay by the Program's director, Emmanuel G. Mesthene, one can discern some of the important threads of belief that bind together much current writing on the social implications of technology. Mesthene's essay is worth extended analysis, because these beliefs are of interest in themselves and, of greater importance, because they form the basis not of a new but of a newly aggressive right-wing ideology in this country, an ideology whose growing importance was accurately measured by the magnitude of the *Times*'s news report.

… Mesthene believes there are two distinct problems in technology's relation to society, a positive one of taking full advantage of the opportunity it offers and the negative one of avoiding unfortunate consequences that flow from the exploitation of those opportunities. Positive opportunities may be missed because the costs of technological development outweigh likely benefits (e.g., Herman Kahn's "Doomsday Machine"). Mesthene seems convinced, however, that a more important case is that in which

> … technology lies fallow because existing social structures are inadequate to exploit the opportunities it offers. This is revealed clearly in the examination of institutional failure in the ghetto carried on by [the Program].…

His diagnosis of these problems is generous in the extreme:

> All these factors combine to dilute what may be otherwise a genuine desire to apply our best knowledge and adequate resources to the resolution of urban tensions and the eradication of poverty in the nation.

Moreover, because government and the media "are not yet equipped for the massive task of public education that is needed," if we are to exploit technology more fully, many technological opportunities are lost because of the lack of public support. This, too, is a problem primarily of "institutional innovation."

Mesthene believes that institutional innovation is no less important in combating the negative effects of technology. Individuals or individual firms that decide to develop new technologies normally do not take "adequate account" of their likely social benefits or costs. His critique is anticapitalist in spirit, but lacks bite, for he goes on to add that

> [most of the negative] consequences of technology that are causing concern at the present time — pollution of the environment, potential damage to the ecology of the planet, occupational and social dislocations, threats to the privacy and political significance of the individual, social and psychological malaise — are *negative externalities of this kind.* They are with us in large measure because it has not been anybody's explicit business to foresee and anticipate them. [Italics added]

Mesthene's abstract analysis and its equally abstract diagnosis in favor of "institutional innovation" place him in a curious and, for us, instructive position. If existing social structures are inadequate to exploit technology's full potential, or if, on the other hand, so-called negative externalities assail us because it is nobody's business to foresee and anticipate them, doesn't this say that we should apply technology to this problem, too? That is, we ought to apply and organize the appropriate *organizational* knowledge for the practical purpose of solving the problems of institutional inadequacy and "negative externalities." Hence, in principle, Mesthene is in the position of arguing that the cure for technology's problems, whether positive or negative, is still more technology. This is the first theme of the technological school of writers and its ultimate First Principle.

Technology, in their view, is a self-correcting system. Temporary oversight or "negative externalities" will and should be corrected by technological means. Attempts to restrict the free play of technological innovation are, in the nature of the case, self-defeating. Technological innovation exhibits a distinct tendency to work for the general welfare in the long run. *Laissez innover!*

I have so far deliberately refrained from going into any greater detail than does Mesthene on the empirical character of contemporary technology, for it is important to bring out the force of the principle of *laissez innover* in its full generality. Many writers on technology appear to deny in their definition of the subject — organized knowledge for practical purposes — that contemporary technology exhibits distinct trends, which can be identified or projected. Others, like Mesthene, appear to accept these trends, but then blunt the conclusion by attributing to technology so much flexibility and "scientific" purity that it becomes an abstraction infinitely malleable in behalf of good, pacific, just, and egalitarian purposes. Thus, the analogy to the *laissez-faire* principle of another time is quite justified. Just as the market or the free play of competition provided in theory the optimum long-run solution for virtually every aspect of virtually every social and economic problem, so too does the free play of technology, according to its writers. Only if technology or innovation (or some other synonym) is allowed the freest possible reign, they believe, will the maximum social good be realized.

What reasons do they give to believe that the principle of *laissez innover* will normally function for the benefit of humankind rather than, say, merely for the belief of the immediate practitioners of technology, their managerial cronies, and for the profits accruing to their corporations? As Mesthene and other writers of his school are aware, this is a very real problem, for they all believe that the normal tendency of technology is, and ought to be, the increasing concentration of decision-making power in the hands of larger and larger scientific-technical bureaucracies. *In principle*, their solution is relatively simple, though not often explicitly stated.[1]

Their argument goes as follows: The men and women who are elevated by technology into commanding positions within various decision-making bureaucracies exhibit no generalized drive for power such as characterized by, say, the landed gentry of pre-industrial Europe or the capitalist entrepreneur of the last century, for their social and institutional position and its supporting culture as well are defined solely by the fact that these men are problem-solvers. (Organized knowledge for practical purposes again.) That is, they gain advantage and reward only to the extent that they can bring specific technical knowledge to bear on the solution of specific technical problems. Any more general drive for power would undercut the bases of their usefulness and legitimacy.

Moreover, their specific training and professional commitment to solving technical problems creates a bias against ideologies in general, which inhibits any attempts to formulate a justifying ideology for the group. Consequently, they do not constitute a class and have no general interests antagonistic to those of their problem-beset clients. We may refer to all of this as the disinterested character of the scientific-technical decision-maker, or, more briefly and cynically, as the principle of the Altruistic Bureaucrat....

This combination of guileless optimism with scientific tough-mindedness might seem to be no more than an eccentric delusion were the American technology it supports not moving in directions that are strongly antidemocratic. To show why this is so, we must examine more closely Mesthene's seemingly innocuous distinction between technology's positive opportunities and its "negative externalities." In order to do this, I will make use of an example drawn from the very frontier of American technology: the war in Vietnam.

II

★ ★ ★

Advanced technological systems such as those employed in the bombardment of South Vietnam make use not only of extremely complex and expensive equipment but, quite as important, of large numbers of relatively scarce and expensive-to-train technicians. They have immense capital costs: a thousand aircraft of a very advanced type; literally hundreds of thousands of spare parts; enormous stocks of rockets, bombs, shells, and bullets; in addition to tens of thousands of technical specialists — pilots, bombardiers, navigators, radar operators, computer programmers, accountants, engineers, electronic and mechanical technicians, to name only a few. In short, they are "capital intensive."

Moreover, the coordination of this immense mass of esoteric equipment and its operators in the most effective possible way depends upon an extremely highly developed technique both in the employment of each piece of equipment by a specific team of operators and in the management of the program itself. Of course, all large organizations standardize their operating procedures, but it is peculiar to advanced technological systems that their operating procedures embody a very high degree of information drawn from the physical sciences, while their managerial procedures are equally dependent on information drawn from the social sciences. We may describe this situation by saying that advanced technological systems are both "technique intensive" and "management intensive." It should be clear, moreover, even to the most casual observer, that such intensive use of capital, technique, and management spills over into almost every area touched by the technological system in question. An attack program delivering 330,000 tons of munitions more or less selectively to several thousand different targets monthly would be an anomaly if forced to rely on sporadic intelligence data, erratic maintenance systems, or a fluctuating and unpredictable supply of heavy bombs, rockets, jet fuel, and napalm tanks. Thus, it is precisely because the bombing program requires an intensive use of capital, technique, and management that the same properties are normally transferred to the intelligence, maintenance, supply, coordination, and training systems that support it. Accordingly, each of these supporting systems is subject to sharp pressures to improve and rationalize the performance of its machines and men, the reliability of its techniques, and the efficiency and sensitivity of the management controls under which it operates. Within integrated technical systems, higher levels of technology drive out lower, and the normal tendency is to integrate systems.

From this perverse Gresham's Law of Technology follow some of the main social and organizational characteristics of contemporary technological systems: the radical increase in the scale and complexity of operations that they demand and encourage; the rapid and widespread diffusion of technology to new areas; the great diversity of activities that can be directed by central management; an increase in the ambition of management's goals; and, as a corollary, especially to the last, growing resistance to the influence of so-called negative externalities.

Complex technological systems are extraordinarily resistant to intervention by persons or problems operating outside or below their managing groups, and this is so regardless of the "politics" of a given situation. Technology creates its own politics. The point of such advanced systems is to minimize the incidence of personal or social behavior that is erratic or otherwise not easily classified, of tools and equipment with poor performance, of improvisory techniques, and of unresponsiveness to central management....

To define technology so abstractly that it obscures these observable characteristics of contemporary technology — as Mesthene and his school have done — makes no sense. It makes even less sense to claim some magical malleability for something as undefined as "institutional innovation." Technology, in its concrete, empirical meaning, refers fundamentally to systems of rationalized control over large groups of men, events, and machines by small groups of technically skilled men operating through organizational hierarchy. The latent "opportunities" provided by that control and its ability to filter out discordant "negative externalities" are, of course, best illustrated by extreme cases. Hence, the most instructive and accurate example should be of a technology able to suppress the humanity of its rank-and-file and to commit genocide as a by-product of its rationality. The Vietnam bombing program fits technology to a "T."

★ ★ ★

IV

Among the conventional explanations for the rise and spread of the democratic ethos in Europe and North America in the seventeenth, eighteenth, and nineteenth centuries, the destruction of the gap in political culture between the mass of the population and that of the ruling classes is extremely important....

Similarly, it is often argued that with the expansion and improvement of road and postal systems, the spread of new tools and techniques, the growth in the number and variety of merchants, the consequent invigoration of town life, and other numerous and familiar related developments, the social experience of larger numbers of people became richer, more varied, and similar in fact to those of the ruling class....

The same period also witnessed a growth in the organized means of popular expression....

This description by no means does justice to the richness and variety of the historical process underlying the rise and spread of what has come to be called the democratic ethos. But it does, I hope, isolate some of the important structural elements and, moreover, it enables us to illuminate some important ways in which the new technology, celebrated by Mesthene and his associates for its potential contributions to democracy, contributes instead to the erosion of that same democratic ethos. For if, in an earlier time, the gap between the political cultures of the higher and lower orders of society was being widely attacked and closed, this no longer appears to be the case. On the contrary, I am persuaded that the direction has been reversed and that we now observe evidence of a growing separation between ruling- and lower-class culture in America, a separation that is particularly enhanced by the rapid growth of technology and the spreading influence of its *laissez innover* ideologues.

Certainly, there has been a decline in popular literacy, that is to say, in those aspects of literacy that bear on an understanding of the political and social character of the new technology. Not one person in a hundred is even aware of, much less understands, the nature of technologically highly advanced systems such as are used in the Vietnam bombing program....

Secondly, the social organization of this new technology, by systematically denying to the general population experiences that are analogous to those of its higher management, contributes very heavily to the growth of social irrationality in our society. For example, modern technological organization defines the roles and values of its members, not vice versa. An engineer or a sociologist is one who does all those things but only those things called for by the "table of organization" and the "job description" used by his employer. Professionals who seek self-realization through creative and autonomous behavior without regard to the defined goals, needs, and channels of their respective departments have no more place in a large corporation or government agency than squeamish soldiers in the army....

However, those at the top of technology's most advanced organizations hardly suffer the same experience. For reasons that are clearly related to the principle of the Altruistic Bureaucracy, the psychology of an individual's fulfillment through work has been incorporated into management ideology. As the pages of *Fortune, Time,* or *Business Week* ... serve to show, the higher levels of business and government are staffed by men and women who spend killing hours looking after the economic welfare and national security of the rest of us. The rewards of this life are said to be very few: The love of money would be demeaning and, anyway, taxes are said to take most of it; its sacrifices are many, for failure brings economic depression to the masses or gains for communism as well as disgrace to the erring managers. Even the essential high-mindedness or altruism of our managers earns no reward, for the public is distracted, fickle, and, on occasion, vengeful.... Hence, for these "real revolutionaries of our time," as Walt Rostow [economist and National Security Advisor to President Lyndon B. Johnson during the Vietnam war – ed.] has called them, self-fulfillment through work and discipline is the only reward. The managerial process is seen as an expression of the vital personalities of our leaders and the right to it an inalienable right of the national elite.

In addition to all this, their lonely and unrewarding eminence in the face of crushing responsibility, etc., tends to create an air of mystification around technology's managers....

It seems fundamental to the social organization of modern technology that the quality of the social experience of the lower orders of society declines as the level of technology grows no less than does their literacy. And, of course, this process feeds on itself, for with the consequent decline in the real effectiveness and usefulness of local and other forms of organization open to easy and direct popular influence, their vitality declines still further, and the cycle is repeated.

The normal life of men and women in the lower and, I think, middle levels of American society now seems cut off from those experiences in which near social means and distant social ends are balanced and rebalanced, adjusted and readjusted. But it is from such widespread experience with effective balancing and adjusting that social rationality derives. To the degree that it is lacking, social irrationality becomes the norm, and social paranoia a recurring phenomenon....

Mesthene himself recognizes that such "negative externalities" are on the increase. His list includes "pollution of the environment, potential damage to the ecology of the planet, occupational and social dislocations, threats to the privacy and political significance of the individual, social and psychological malaise." Minor matters all, however, when compared to the marvelous opportunities *laissez innover* holds out to us: more GNP, continued free-world leadership, supersonic transports, urban renewal on a regional basis, institutional innovation, and the millennial promises of his school.

This brings us finally to the ideologies and doctrines of technology and their relation to what I have argued is a growing gap in political culture between the lower and upper classes in American society. Even more fundamentally than the principles of *laissez innover* and the altruistic bureaucrat, technology in its very definition as the organization of knowledge for practical purposes assumes that the primary and really creative role in the social processes consequent on technological change is reserved for a scientific and technical elite, the elite that presumably discovers and organizes that knowledge. But if the scientific and technical elite and their indispensable managerial cronies are the really creative (and hardworking and altruistic) elements in American society, what is this but to say that the common mass of people are essentially drags on the social weal? This is precisely the implication which is drawn by the *laissez innover* school. Consider the following quotations from an article that appeared in *The New Republic* in December 1967, written by Zbigniew Brzezinski, one of the intellectual leaders of the school.

Brzezinski [who later became National Security Advisor to President Jimmy Carter – ed.] is describing a nightmare that he calls the "technetronic society" (the word, like the concept, is a pastiche of technology and electronics). This society will be characterized, he argues, by the application of "the principle of equal opportunity for all but ... special opportunity for the singularly talented few." It will thus combine "continued *respect* for the popular will with an increasing *role* in the key decision-making institutions of individuals with special intellectual and scientific attainments." [Italics added.] Naturally, "the educational and social systems [will make] it increasingly attractive and easy for those meritocratic few to develop to the fullest of their special potential."

However, while it will be "necessary to require everyone at a sufficiently responsible post to take, say, two years of [scientific and technical] retraining every ten years," the rest of us can develop a new "interest in the cultural and humanistic aspects of life, *in addition to purely hedonistic preoccupations.*" [Italics added.] The latter, he is careful to point out, "would serve as a social valve, reducing tensions and political frustration."

Is it not fair to ask how much respect we carefree pleasure lovers and culture consumers will get from the hardworking bureaucrats, going to night school two years in every ten, while working like beavers in the "key decision-making institutions"? The altruism of our bureaucrats has a heavy load to bear.

Stripped of their euphemisms, these are simply arguments that enhance the social legitimacy of the interests of new technical and scientific elites and detract from the interests of the rest of us....

As has already been made clear, the *laissez innover* school accepts as inevitable and desirable the centralizing tendencies of technology's social organization, and they accept as well the mystification that comes to surround the management process. Thus, equality of opportunity, as they understand it, has precious little to do with creating a more egalitarian society. On the contrary, it functions as an indispensable feature of the highly stratified society they envision for the future. For in their society of meritocratic hierarchy, equality of opportunity assures that talented young meritocrats (the word is no uglier than the social system it refers to) will be able to climb into the "key decision-making" slots reserved for trained talent and thus generate the success of the new society and its cohesion against popular "tensions and political frustration."

The structures that formerly guaranteed the rule of wealth, age, and family will not be destroyed (or at least not totally so). They will be firmed up and rationalized by the perpetual addition of trained (and, of course, acculturated) talent. In technologically advanced societies, equality of opportunity functions as a hierarchical principle, in opposition to the egalitarian social goals it pretends to serve. To the extent that it has already become the kind of "equality" we seek to institute in our society, it is one of the main factors contributing to the widening gap between the cultures of upper- and lower-class America.

V

… *Laissez innover* is now the premier ideology of the technological impulse in American society, which is to say, of the institutions that monopolize and profit from advanced technology and of the social classes that find in the free exploitation of their technology the most likely guarantee of their power, status, and wealth.

This said, it is important to stress both the significance and limitations of what has in fact been said. Here, Mesthene's distinction between the positive opportunities and negative "externalities" inherent in technological change is pivotal; for everything else that I've argued follows inferentially from the actual social meaning of that distinction. As my analysis of the Vietnam bombing program suggested, those technological effects that are sought after as positive opportunities and those that are dismissed as negative externalities are decisively influenced by the fact that this distinction between positive and negative within advanced technological organizations tends to be made among the planners and managers themselves. Within these groups there are, as was pointed out, extremely powerful organizational, hierarchical, doctrinal, and other "technical" factors, which tend by design to filter out "irrational" demands from below, substituting for them the "rational" demands of technology itself. As a result, technological rationality is as socially neutral today as market rationality was a century ago.…

This analysis lends some weight (though perhaps no more than that) to a number of wide-ranging and unorthodox conclusions about American society today and the directions in which it is tending.…

First, and most important, technology should be considered as an institutional system, not more and certainly not less. Mesthene's definition of the subject is inadequate, for it obscures the systematic and decisive social changes, especially their political and cultural tendencies, that follow the widespread application of advanced technological systems. At the same time, technology is less than a social system per se, though it has many elements of a social system, viz., an elite, a group of linked institutions, an ethos, and so forth. Perhaps the best summary statement of the case resides in an analogy — with all the vagueness and imprecision attendant on such things: today's technology stands in relation to today's capitalism as, a century ago, the latter stood to the free market capitalism of the time.…

A second major hypothesis would argue that the most important dimension of advanced technological institutions is the social one, that is, the institutions are agencies of highly centralized and intensive social control. Technology conquers nature, as the saying goes. But to do so it must first conquer man. More precisely, it demands a very high degree of control over the training, mobility, and skills of the work force. The absence (or decline) of direct controls or of coercion should not serve to obscure from our view the reality and intensity of the social controls that are employed (such as the internalized belief in equality of opportunity, indebtedness through credit, advertising, selective service channeling, and so on).

Advanced technology has created a vast increase in occupational specialties, many of them requiring many, many years of highly specialized training. It must motivate this training. It has made ever more complex and "rational" the ways in which these occupational specialties are combined in our economic and social life. It must win passivity and obedience to this complex activity. Formerly, technical rationality had been employed only to organize the production of rather simple physical objects, for example, aerial bombs. Now, technical rationality is increasingly employed to organize all of the processes necessary to the utilization of physical objects, such as bombing systems. For this reason, it seems a mistake to argue that we are in a "postindustrial" age, a concept favored by the *laissez innover* school. On the contrary, the rapid spread of technical rationality into organizational and economic life and, hence, into social life is more aptly described as a second and much more intensive phase of the industrial revolution. One might reasonably suspect that it will create analogous social problems.

Accordingly, a third major hypothesis would argue that there are very profound social antagonisms or contradictions not less sharp or fundamental than those ascribed by Marx to the development of nineteenth-century industrial society. The general form of the contradictions might be described as follows: A society characterized by the employment of advanced technology requires an ever-more socially disciplined population, yet retains an ever-declining capacity to enforce the required discipline....

These are brief and, I believe, barely adequate reviews of extremely complex hypotheses. But, in outline, each of these contradictions appears to bear on roughly the same group of the American population: a technological underclass. If we assume this to be the case, a fourth hypothesis would follow, namely that technology is creating the basis for new and sharp class conflict in our society. That is, technology is creating its own working and managing classes, just as earlier industrialization created its working and owning classes. Perhaps this suggests a return to the kind of class-based politics that characterized the U.S. in the last quarter of the nineteenth century, rather than the somewhat more ambiguous politics that was a feature of the second quarter of this century. I am inclined to think that this is the case, though I confess the evidence for it is as yet inadequate. This leads to a final hypothesis, namely that *laissez innover* should be frankly recognized as a conservative or right-wing ideology....

The point of this final hypothesis is not primarily to reimpress the language of European politics on the American scene. Rather, it is to summarize the fact that many of the forces in American life hostile to the democratic ethos have enrolled under the banner of *laissez innover*. Merely to grasp this is already to take the first step toward a politics of radical reconstruction and against the malaise, irrationality, powerlessness, and official violence that characterize American life today.

ENDNOTE

1. For a more complete statement of the argument that follows, see Suzanne Keller, *Beyond the Ruling Class* (New York: Random House, 1963).

PART III

Debating Technology:
Twenty-First-Century Style

The comparison between the 1960s-style debate on technology between Emmanuel Mesthene and John McDermott in Part II of this book and the twenty-first-century debate between Bill Joy and his critics in the next three chapters is a remarkable illustration of both how much and how little has changed during the 35 years that separates these writings.

The Mesthene–McDermott dispute is strongly ideological. McDermott represents the "New Left" of the 1960s and '70s and its attendant counterculture. Although Mesthene would have disagreed strongly with the characterization, McDermott places him squarely in the camp of the reactionary "establishment" seeking to preserve the status quo and all the inequities and injustices it implies. Mesthene, for his part, probably regarded McDermott as a Luddite, heir to the radical anti-technology tradition of those British activists who went about destroying machines in the early days of the Industrial Revolution 200 years ago. The Bill Joy–John Seely Brown/Paul Duguid argument lacks the ideological edge, invective, and bitterness of the 1960s debate. Their arguments are largely devoid of politics and ideology. Both sides in the dispute are technophiles — good friends, in fact — although Joy is a technophile who believes he has seen the future and is very frightened by it. Nonetheless, the opposite sides in both of these debates (Mesthene vs. McDermott and Joy vs. Brown/Duguid) reflect sharply different perspectives on the balance between the benefits and the harmful impacts of technology.

To this mix we have added, as a kind of middle ground, the perspective of Ray Kurzweil, an inventor of extraordinary achievement, winner of the Lemelson-MIT Prize for invention and the National Medal of Technology. Kurzweil is the person Bill Joy says first made him "anxiously aware" of the dangers technology is creating for society. Here Kurzweil presents his side of the story. He shares many of Joy's concerns, but he would deal with them differently. Rather than "relinquishing" the areas of technology that pose threats to humanity, as Joy proposes, he would respond to their threats by more conventional means — regulation and the development of counter-technologies.

The shift back to debating this balance between harm and benefits represents something of a departure during the past few years. In the eighth edition of *Technology and the Future* (published in 2000), the counterpart to this section ("Debating Technology: Turn of the Millennium Style") featured Nicholas Negroponte and Donald Norman in a friendly disagreement over whether the future is going to be "digital" (i.e., shaped by our ability to digitize any kind of information — Negroponte's view) or analog (i.e., whether the headlong rush to digitization is causing us to lose sight of the fact that we are analog creatures and need to design technologies to suit ourselves rather than designing technologies and expecting that we will adapt — Norman's perspective). The technologies about which Bill Joy, John Seely Brown, Paul Duguid, and Ray Kurzweil are arguing — genetic engineering, nanotechnology, and robotics — were barely imagined in the 1960s, and their potential for interaction (which is what concerns Joy) was just coming into focus in 2000. Yet, whether we fear these technologies or look to them as the potential sources of enormous economic, health, and societal benefits (or both), we need to be thinking carefully and constantly about the ways in which society is affected by them and how we can shape their development in positive ways. The articles in this part can help us do this.

9

Why the Future Doesn't Need Us

BILL JOY

The publication in Wired *(April 2000) of Bill Joy's article, "Why the Future Doesn't Need Us," caused quite a stir among the so-called digerati (the elite of the Internet and information technology world). Joy sees the convergence of genetic engineering, nanotechnology, and robotics (GNR) as posing a grave threat to the future of humanity. He argues that these new technologies are qualitatively different from those with which we are familiar. "Accustomed to living with almost routine scientific breakthroughs, we have yet to come to terms with the fact that the most compelling twenty-first-century technologies — robotics, genetic engineering, and nanotechnology — pose a different threat than the technologies that have come before. Specifically, robots, engineered organisms, and nanobots share a dangerous amplifying factor: They can self-replicate. A bomb is blown up only once — but one bot can become many, and quickly get out of control."*

Joy develops his argument in detail, drawing on his knowledge of these technologies, and on conversations with and writings of many contemporary leaders in technology, as well as a number of well-known science fiction writers. His scenario is pessimistic in the extreme. If these technologies are allowed to develop unchecked, Joy fears, they could lead to the extinction of the human species. In response, he calls for the voluntary relinquishment of certain of these technologies by scientists, technologists, and the firms and nations that sponsor their work. Had such a polemic been published by one of the many well-known technological critics (several of whom are represented in this book), it might not have attracted much attention. Bill Joy, however, is one of the leading figures of the high-tech world. At the time he wrote this article, he was chief scientist and corporate executive officer of Sun Microsystems, a company he cofounded. Joy was the principal designer of the Berkeley version of UNIX, and one of the developers of the Java Programming Language that is now ubiquitous on the Web. He left Sun in 2003 and in 2005 joined the venture capital firm of Kleiner Perkins Caufield & Byers, where he is currently a partner, investing — some might say, ironically — in genetics, nanotechnology, and robotics firms. His lengthy essay, and the rebuttals that follow it, are well worth reading.

From the moment I became involved in the creation of new technologies, their ethical dimensions have concerned me, but it was only in the autumn of 1998 that I became anxiously aware of how great are the dangers facing us in the twenty-first century. I can date the onset of my unease to the day I met Ray Kurzweil, the deservedly famous inventor of the first reading machine for the blind and many other amazing things.

Ray and I were both speakers at George Gilder's Telecosm conference, and I encountered him by chance in the bar of the hotel after both our sessions were over. I was sitting with John Searle, a Berkeley philosopher who studies consciousness. While we were talking, Ray approached and a conversation began, the subject of which haunts me to this day.

I had missed Ray's talk and the subsequent panel that Ray and John had been on, and they now picked right up where they'd left off, with Ray saying that the rate of improvement of technology was going to accelerate and that we were going to become robots or fuse with robots or something like that, and John countering that this couldn't happen, because the robots couldn't be conscious.

While I had heard such talk before, I had always felt sentient robots were in the realm of science fiction. But now, from someone I respected, I was hearing a strong argument that they were a near-term possibility. I was taken aback, especially given Ray's proven ability to imagine and create the future. I already knew that new technologies like genetic engineering and nanotechnology were giving us the power to remake the world, but a realistic and imminent scenario for intelligent robots surprised me.

It's easy to get jaded about such breakthroughs. We hear in the news almost every day of some kind of technological or scientific advance. Yet this was no ordinary prediction. In the hotel bar, Ray gave me a partial preprint of his then-forthcoming book, *The Age of Spiritual Machines*, which outlined a utopia he foresaw — one in which humans gained near immortality by becoming one with robotic technology. On reading it, my sense of unease only intensified; I felt sure he had to be understating the dangers, understating the probability of a bad outcome along this path.

I found myself most troubled by a passage detailing a dystopian scenario:

The New Luddite Challenge

First, let us postulate that the computer scientists succeed in developing intelligent machines that can do all things better than human beings can do them. In that case, presumably all work will be done by vast, highly organized systems of machines and no human effort will be necessary. Either of two cases might occur. The machines might be permitted to make all of their own decisions without human oversight, or else human control over the machines might be retained.

If the machines are permitted to make all their own decisions, we can't make any conjectures as to the results, because it is impossible to guess how such machines might behave. We only point out that the fate of the human race would be at the mercy of the machines. It might be argued that the human race would never be foolish enough to hand over all the power to the machines. But we are suggesting neither that the human race would voluntarily turn power over to the machines, nor that the machines would willfully seize power. What we do suggest is that the human race might easily permit itself to drift into a position of such dependence on the machines that it would have no practical choice but to accept all of the machines' decisions. As society and the problems that face it become more and more complex and machines become more and more intelligent, people will let machines make more of their decisions for them, simply because machine-made decisions will bring better results than man-made ones. Eventually, a stage may be reached at which the decisions necessary to keep the system running will be so complex that human beings will be incapable of making them intelligently. At that stage the machines will be in effective control. People won't be able to just turn the machines off, because they will be so dependent on them that turning them off would amount to suicide.

On the other hand, it is possible that human control over the machines may be retained. In that case, the average man may have control over certain private machines of his own, such as his car or his personal computer, but control over large systems of machines will be in the hands of a tiny elite — just as it is today, but with two differences. Due to improved techniques the elite will have greater control over the masses, and, because human work will no longer be necessary, the masses will be superfluous, a useless burden on the system. If the elite is ruthless, they may simply decide to exterminate the mass of humanity. If they are humane, they may use propaganda or other psychological or biological techniques to reduce the birth rate until the mass of humanity becomes extinct, leaving the world to the elite. Or, if the elite consists of soft-hearted liberals, they may decide to play the role of good shepherds to the rest of the human race. They will see to it that everyone's physical needs are satisfied, that all children are raised under psychologically hygienic conditions, that everyone has a wholesome hobby to keep him busy, and that anyone who may become dissatisfied undergoes "treatment" to cure his "problem." Of course, life will be so purposeless that people will have to be biologically or psychologically engineered either to remove their need for the power process or make them "sublimate" their drive for power into some harmless hobby. These engineered human beings may be happy in such a society, but they will most certainly not be free. They will have been reduced to the status of domestic animals.[1]

In the book, you don't discover until you turn the page that the author of this passage is Theodore Kaczynski — the Unabomber. I am no apologist for Kaczynski. His bombs killed three people during a seventeen-year terror campaign and wounded many others. One of his bombs gravely injured my friend David Gelernter, one of the most brilliant and visionary computer scientists of our time. Like many of my colleagues, I felt that I could easily have been the Unabomber's next target.

Kaczynski's actions were murderous and, in my view, criminally insane. He is clearly a Luddite, but simply saying this does not dismiss his argument; as difficult as it is for me to acknowledge, I saw some merit in the reasoning in this single passage. I felt compelled to confront it.

Kaczynski's dystopian vision describes unintended consequences, a well-known problem with the design and use of technology and one that is clearly related to Murphy's law — "Anything that can go wrong, will." (Actually, this is Finagle's law, which in itself shows that Finagle was right.) Our overuse of antibiotics has led to what may be the biggest such problem so far: the emergence of antibiotic-resistant and much more dangerous bacteria. Similar things happened when attempts to eliminate malarial mosquitoes using DDT caused them to acquire DDT resistance; malarial parasites likewise acquired multidrug-resistant genes.[2]

The cause of many such surprises seems clear: The systems involved are complex, involving interaction among and feedback between many parts. Any changes to such a system will cascade in ways that are difficult to predict; this is especially true when human actions are involved.

I started showing friends the Kaczynski quote from *The Age of Spiritual Machines*; I would hand them Kurzweil's book, let them read the quote, and then watch their reaction as they discovered who had written it. At around the same time, I found Hans Moravec's book *Robot: Mere Machine to Transcendent Mind*. Moravec is one of the leaders in robotics research and was a founder of the world's largest robotics research program, at Carnegie Mellon University. *Robot* gave me more material to try out on my friends — material surprisingly supportive of Kaczynski's argument. For example:

The Short Run (Early 2000s)

Biological species almost never survive encounters with superior competitors. Ten million years ago, South and North America were separated by a sunken Panama isthmus. South America, like Australia today, was populated by marsupial mammals, including pouched equivalents of rats, deer, and tigers. When the isthmus connecting North and South America rose, it took only a few thousand years for the northern placental species, with slightly more effective metabolisms and reproductive and nervous systems, to displace and eliminate almost all the southern marsupials.

In a completely free marketplace, superior robots would surely affect humans as North American placentals affected South American marsupials (and as humans have affected countless species). Robotic industries would compete vigorously among themselves for matter, energy, and space, incidentally driving their price beyond human reach. Unable to afford the necessities of life, biological humans would be squeezed out of existence.

There is probably some breathing room, because we do not live in a completely free marketplace. Government coerces nonmarket behavior, especially by collecting taxes. Judiciously applied, governmental coercion could support human populations in high style on the fruits of robot labor, perhaps for a long while.

A textbook dystopia — and Moravec is just getting wound up. He goes on to discuss how our main job in the twenty-first century will be "ensuring continued cooperation from the robot industries" by passing laws decreeing that they be "nice"[3] and to describe how seriously dangerous a human can be "once transformed into an unbounded superintelligent robot." Moravec's view is that the robots will eventually succeed us — that humans clearly face extinction.

I decided it was time to talk to my friend Danny Hillis. Danny became famous as the cofounder of Thinking Machines Corporation, which built a very powerful parallel supercomputer. Despite my current job title of Chief Scientist at Sun Microsystems, I am more a computer architect than a scientist, and I respect Danny's knowledge of the information and physical sciences more than that of any other single person I know. Danny is also a highly regarded futurist who thinks long-term: Four years ago he started the Long Now Foundation, which is building a clock designed to last 10,000 years, in an attempt to draw attention to the pitifully short attention span of our society. (See "Test of Time," *Wired* 8.03, p. 78.)

So I flew to Los Angeles for the express purpose of having dinner with Danny and his wife, Pati. I went through my now-familiar routine, trotting out the ideas and passages that I found so disturbing. Danny's answer — directed specifically at Kurzweil's scenario of humans merging with robots — came swiftly and quite surprised me. He said, simply, that the changes would come gradually and that we would get used to them.

But I guess I wasn't totally surprised. I had seen a quote from Danny in Kurzweil's book in which he said, "I'm as fond of my body as anyone, but if I can be 200 with a body of silicon, I'll take it." It seemed that he was at peace with this process and its attendant risks, while I was not.

While talking and thinking about Kurzweil, Kaczynski, and Moravec, I suddenly remembered a novel I had read almost 20 years ago — *The White Plague*, by Frank Herbert — in which a molecular biologist is driven insane by the senseless murder of his family. To seek revenge, he constructs and disseminates a new and highly contagious plague that kills widely but selectively. (We're lucky Kaczynski was a mathematician, not a molecular biologist.) I was also reminded of the Borg of Star Trek, a hive of partly biological, partly robotic creatures with a strong destructive streak. Borg-like disasters are a staple of science fiction, so why hadn't I been more concerned about such robotic dystopias earlier? Why weren't other people more concerned about these nightmarish scenarios?

Part of the answer certainly lies in our attitude toward the new — in our bias toward instant familiarity and unquestioning acceptance. Accustomed to living with almost routine scientific breakthroughs, we have yet to come to terms with the fact that the most compelling twenty-first-century technologies — robotics, genetic engineering, and nanotechnology — pose a different threat than the technologies that have come before. Specifically, robots, engineered organisms, and nanobots share a dangerous amplifying factor: They can self-replicate. A bomb is blown up only once — but one 'bot can become many and quickly get out of control.

Much of my work over the past twenty-five years has been on computer networking, where the sending and receiving of messages creates the opportunity for out-of-control replication. But while replication in a computer or a computer network can be a nuisance, at worst it disables a machine or takes down a network or network service. Uncontrolled self-replication in these newer technologies runs a much greater risk: a risk of substantial damage in the physical world.

Each of these technologies also offers untold promise: The vision of near immortality that Kurzweil sees in his robot dreams drives us forward; genetic engineering may soon provide treatments, if not outright cures, for most diseases, and nanotechnology and nanomedicine can address yet more ills. Together they could significantly extend our average life span and improve the quality of our lives. Yet, with each of these technologies, a sequence of small, individually sensible advances leads to an accumulation of great power and, concomitantly, great danger.

What was different in the twentieth century? Certainly, the technologies underlying the weapons of mass destruction (WMD) — nuclear, biological, and chemical (NBC) — were powerful and the weapons an enormous threat. But building nuclear weapons required, at least for a time, access to both rare — indeed, effectively unavailable — raw materials and highly protected information; biological and chemical weapons programs also tended to require large-scale activities.

The twenty-first-century technologies — genetics, nanotechnology, and robotics (GNR) — are so powerful that they can spawn whole new classes of accidents and abuses. Most dangerously, for the first time, these accidents and abuses are widely within the reach of individuals or small groups. They will not require large facilities or rare raw materials. Knowledge alone will enable the use of them.

Thus, we have the possibility not just of weapons of mass destruction but of knowledge-enabled mass destruction (KMD), this destructiveness hugely amplified by the power of self-replication.

I think it is no exaggeration to say we are on the cusp of the further perfection of extreme evil, an evil whose possibility spreads well beyond that which weapons of mass destruction bequeathed to the nation-states, on to a surprising and terrible empowerment of extreme individuals.

Nothing about the way I got involved with computers suggested to me that I was going to be facing these kinds of issues.

My life has been driven by a deep need to ask questions and find answers. When I was three, I was already reading, so my father took me to the elementary school, where I sat on the principal's lap and read him a story. I started school early, later skipped a grade, and escaped into books — I was incredibly motivated to learn. I asked lots of questions, often driving adults to distraction.

As a teenager, I was very interested in science and technology. I wanted to be a ham radio operator but didn't have the money to buy the equipment. Ham radio was the Internet of its time: very addictive and quite solitary. Money issues aside, my mother put her foot down — I was not to be a ham; I was antisocial enough already.

I may not have had many close friends, but I was awash in ideas. By high school, I had discovered the great science-fiction writers. I remember especially Heinlein's *Have Spacesuit Will Travel* and Asimov's *I, Robot*, with its Three Laws of Robotics. I was enchanted by the descriptions of space travel and wanted to have a telescope to look at the stars; since I had no money to buy or make one, I checked books on telescope making out of the library and read about making them instead. I soared in my imagination.

Thursday nights my parents went bowling, and we kids stayed home alone. It was the night of Gene Roddenberry's original *Star Trek*, and the program made a big impression on me. I came to accept its notion that humans had a future in space, Western-style, with big heroes and adventures. Roddenberry's vision of the centuries to come was one with strong moral values, embodied in codes like the Prime Directive: to not interfere in the development of less technologically advanced civilizations. This had an incredible appeal to me; ethical humans, not robots, dominated this future, and I took Roddenberry's dream as part of my own.

I excelled in mathematics in high school, and when I went to the University of Michigan as an undergraduate engineering student I took the advanced curriculum of the mathematics majors. Solving math problems was an exciting challenge, but when I discovered computers I found something much more interesting: a machine into which you could put a program that attempted to solve a problem, after which the machine quickly checked the solution. The computer had a clear notion of correct and incorrect, true and false. Were my ideas correct? The machine could tell me. This was very seductive. I was lucky enough to get a job programming early supercomputers and discovered the amazing power of large machines to numerically simulate advanced designs. When I went to graduate school at UC Berkeley in the mid-1970s, I started staying up late, often all night, inventing new worlds inside the machines. Solving problems. Writing the code that argued so strongly to be written.

In *The Agony and the Ecstasy*, Irving Stone's biographical novel of Michelangelo, Stone described vividly how Michelangelo released the statues from the stone, "breaking the marble spell," carving from the images in his mind.[4] In my most ecstatic moments, the software in the computer emerged in the same way. Once I had imagined it in my mind, I felt that it was already there in the machine, waiting to be released. Staying up all night seemed a small price to pay to free it — to give the ideas concrete form.

After a few years at Berkeley, I started to send out some of the software I had written — an instructional Pascal system, Unix utilities, and a text editor called vi (which is still, to my surprise, widely used more than twenty years later) — to others who had similar small PDP-11 and VAX minicomputers. These adventures in software eventually turned into the Berkeley version of the Unix operating system, which became a personal "success disaster" — so many people wanted it that I never finished my Ph.D. Instead, I got a job working for DARPA [Defense Advanced Research Projects Agency] putting Berkeley Unix on the Internet and fixing it to be reliable and to run large research applications well. This was all great fun and very rewarding. And, frankly, I saw no robots here, or anywhere near.

Still, by the early 1980s, I was drowning. The Unix releases were very successful, and my little project of one soon had money and some staff, but the problem at Berkeley was always office space rather than money. There wasn't room for the help the project needed, so when the other founders of Sun Microsystems showed up, I jumped at the chance to join them. At Sun, the long hours continued into the early days of workstations and personal computers, and I have enjoyed participating in the creation of advanced microprocessor technologies and Internet technologies such as Java and Jini.

From all this, I trust it is clear that I am not a Luddite. I have always, rather, had a strong belief in the value of the scientific search for truth and in the ability of great engineering to bring material progress. The Industrial Revolution has immeasurably improved everyone's life over the last couple hundred years, and I always expected my career to involve the building of worthwhile solutions to real problems, one problem at a time.

I have not been disappointed. My work has had more impact than I had ever hoped for and has been more widely used than I could have reasonably expected. I have spent the last twenty years still trying to figure out how to make computers as reliable as I want them to be (they are not nearly there yet) and how to make them simple to use (a goal that has met with even less relative success). Despite some progress, the problems that remain seem even more daunting.

But while I was aware of the moral dilemmas surrounding technology's consequences in fields like weapons research, I did not expect that I would confront such issues in my own field, or at least not so soon.

Perhaps it is always hard to see the bigger impact while you are in the vortex of a change. Failing to understand the consequences of our inventions while we are in the rapture of discovery and innovation seems to be a common fault of scientists and technologists; we have long been driven by the overarching desire to know that is the nature of science's quest, not stopping to notice that the progress to newer and more powerful technologies can take on a life of its own.

I have long realized that the big advances in information technology come not from the work of computer scientists, computer architects, or electrical engineers, but from that of physical scientists. The physicists Stephen Wolfram and Brosl Hasslacher introduced me, in the early 1980s, to chaos theory and nonlinear systems. In the 1990s, I learned about complex systems from conversations with Danny Hillis, the biologist Stuart Kauffman, the Nobel-laureate physicist Murray Gell-Mann, and others. Most recently, Hasslacher and the electrical engineer and device physicist Mark Reed have been giving me insight into the incredible possibilities of molecular electronics.

In my own work, as codesigner of three microprocessor architectures — SPARC, picoJava, and MAJC — and as the designer of several implementations thereof, I've been afforded a deep and firsthand acquaintance with Moore's law. For decades, Moore's law has correctly predicted the exponential rate of improvement of semiconductor technology. Until last year, I believed that the rate of advances predicted by Moore's law might continue only until roughly 2010, when some physical limits would begin to be reached. It was not obvious to me that a new technology would arrive in time to keep performance advancing smoothly.

But because of the recent rapid and radical progress in molecular electronics — where individual atoms and molecules replace lithographically drawn transistors — and related nanoscale technologies, we should be able to meet or exceed the Moore's law rate of progress for another thirty years. By 2030, we are likely to be able to build machines, in quantity, a million times as powerful as the personal computers of today — sufficient to implement the dreams of Kurzweil and Moravec.

As this enormous computing power is combined with the manipulative advances of the physical sciences and the new, deep understandings in genetics, enormous transformative power is being unleashed. These combinations open up the opportunity to completely redesign the world, for better or worse: The replicating and evolving processes that have been confined to the natural world are about to become realms of human endeavor.

In designing software and microprocessors, I have never had the feeling that I was designing an intelligent machine. The software and hardware is so fragile and the capabilities of the machine to "think" so clearly absent that, even as a possibility, this has always seemed very far in the future.

But now, with the prospect of human-level computing power in about thirty years, a new idea suggests itself: that I may be working to create tools which will enable the construction of the technology that may replace our species. How do I feel about this? Very uncomfortable. Having struggled my entire career to build reliable software systems, it seems to me more than likely that this future will not work out as well as some people may imagine. My personal experience suggests we tend to overestimate our design abilities.

Given the incredible power of these new technologies, shouldn't we be asking how we can best coexist with them? And if our own extinction is a likely, or even possible, outcome of our technological development, shouldn't we proceed with great caution?

The dream of robotics is, first, that intelligent machines can do our work for us, allowing us lives of leisure, restoring us to Eden. Yet in his history of such ideas, *Darwin Among the Machines*, George Dyson warns, "In the game of life and evolution there are three players at the table: human beings, nature, and machines. I am firmly on the side of nature. But nature, I suspect, is on the side of the machines." As we have seen, Moravec agrees, believing we may well not survive the encounter with the superior robot species.

How soon could such an intelligent robot be built? The coming advances in computing power seem to make it possible by 2030. And once an intelligent robot exists, it is only a small step to a robot species — to an intelligent robot that can make evolved copies of itself.

A second dream of robotics is that we will gradually replace ourselves with our robotic technology, achieving near immortality by downloading our consciousnesses; it is this process that Danny Hillis thinks we will gradually get used to and that Ray Kurzweil elegantly details in *The Age of Spiritual Machines*. (We are beginning to see intimations of this in the implantation of computer devices into the human body, as illustrated on the cover of *Wired* 8.02.)

But if we are downloaded into our technology, what are the chances that we will thereafter be ourselves or even human? It seems to me far more likely that a robotic existence would not be like a human one in any sense that we understand, that the robots would in no sense be our children, that on this path our humanity may well be lost.

Genetic engineering promises to revolutionize agriculture by increasing crop yields while reducing the use of pesticides; to create tens of thousands of novel species of bacteria, plants, viruses, and animals; to replace reproduction, or supplement it, with cloning; to create cures for many diseases, increasing our life span and our quality of life; and much, much more. We now know with certainty that these profound changes in the biological sciences are imminent and will challenge all our notions of what life is.

Technologies such as human cloning have in particular raised our awareness of the profound ethical and moral issues we face. If, for example, we were to reengineer ourselves into several separate and unequal species using the power of genetic engineering, then we would threaten the notion of equality that is the very cornerstone of our democracy.

Given the incredible power of genetic engineering, it's no surprise that there are significant safety issues in its use. My friend Amory Lovins recently cowrote, along with Hunter Lovins, an editorial that provides an ecological view of some of these dangers. Among their concerns: that "the new botany aligns the development of plants with their economic, not evolutionary, success." Amory's long career has been focused on energy and resource efficiency by taking a whole-system view of human-made systems; such a whole-system view often finds simple, smart solutions to otherwise seemingly difficult problems and is usefully applied here as well.

After reading the Lovins's editorial, I saw an op-ed by Gregg Easterbrook in *The New York Times* (November 19, 1999) about genetically engineered crops, under the headline: "Food for the Future: Someday, rice will have built-in vitamin A. Unless the Luddites win."

Are Amory and Hunter Lovins Luddites? Certainly not. I believe we all would agree that golden rice, with its built-in vitamin A, is probably a good thing, if developed with proper care and respect for the likely dangers in moving genes across species boundaries.

Awareness of the dangers inherent in genetic engineering is beginning to grow, as reflected in the Lovins's editorial. The general public is aware of, and uneasy about, genetically modified foods and seems to be rejecting the notion that such foods should be permitted to be unlabeled.

But genetic engineering technology is already very far along. As the Lovins note, the USDA has already approved about fifty genetically engineered crops for unlimited release; more than half of the world's soybeans and a third of its corn now contain genes spliced in from other forms of life.

While there are many important issues here, my own major concern with genetic engineering is narrower: that it gives the power — whether militarily, accidentally, or in a deliberate terrorist act — to create a White Plague.

The many wonders of nanotechnology were first imagined by the Nobel laureate physicist Richard Feynman in a speech he gave in 1959, subsequently published under the title "There's Plenty of Room at the Bottom." The book that made a big impression on me, in the mid-'80s, was Eric Drexler's *Engines of Creation*, in which he described beautifully how manipulation of matter at the atomic level could create a utopian future of abundance, where just about everything could be made cheaply, and almost any imaginable disease or physical problem could be solved using nanotechnology and artificial intelligences.

A subsequent book, *Unbounding the Future: The Nanotechnology Revolution*, which Drexler cowrote, imagines some of the changes that might take place in a world where we had molecular-level "assemblers." Assemblers could make possible incredibly low-cost solar power, cures for cancer and the common cold by augmentation of the human immune system, essentially complete cleanup of the environment, incredibly inexpensive pocket supercomputers — in fact, any product would be manufacturable by assemblers at a cost no greater than that of wood — spaceflight more accessible than transoceanic travel today, and restoration of extinct species.

I remember feeling good about nanotechnology after reading *Engines of Creation*. As a technologist, it gave me a sense of calm — that is, nanotechnology showed us that incredible progress was possible, and indeed perhaps inevitable. If nanotechnology was our future, then I didn't feel pressed to solve so many problems in the present. I would get to Drexler's utopian future in due time; I might as well enjoy life more in the here and now. It didn't make sense, given his vision, to stay up all night, all the time.

Drexler's vision also led to a lot of good fun. I would occasionally get to describe the wonders of nanotechnology to others who had not heard of it. After teasing them with all the things Drexler described, I would give a home-work assignment of my own: "Use nanotechnology to create a vampire; for extra credit create an antidote."

With these wonders came clear dangers, of which I was acutely aware. As I said at a nanotechnology conference in 1989, "We can't simply do our science and not worry about these ethical issues."[5] But my subsequent conversations with physicists convinced me that nanotechnology might not even work — or, at least, it wouldn't work anytime soon. Shortly thereafter I moved to Colorado, to a skunk works I had set up, and the focus of my work shifted to software for the Internet, specifically on ideas that became Java and Jini.

Then, last summer, Brosl Hasslacher told me that nanoscale molecular electronics was now practical. This was new news, at least to me, and I think to many people — and it radically changed my opinion about nanotechnology. It sent me back to *Engines of Creation*. Rereading Drexler's work after more than ten years, I was dismayed to realize how little I had remembered of its lengthy section called "Dangers and Hopes," including a discussion of how nanotechnologies can become "engines of destruction." Indeed, in my rereading of this cautionary material today, I am struck by how naive some of Drexler's safeguard proposals seem and how much greater I judge the dangers to be now than even he seemed to then. (Having anticipated and described many technical and political problems with nanotechnology, Drexler started the Foresight Institute in the late 1980s "to help prepare society for anticipated advanced technologies" — most important, nanotechnology.)

The enabling breakthrough to assemblers seems quite likely within the next twenty years. Molecular electronics — the new subfield of nanotechnology where individual molecules are circuit elements — should mature quickly and become enormously lucrative within this decade, causing a large incremental investment in all nanotechnologies.

Unfortunately, as with nuclear technology, it is far easier to create destructive uses for nanotechnology than constructive ones. Nanotechnology has clear military and terrorist uses, and you need not be suicidal to release a massively destructive nanotechnological device. Such devices can be built to be selectively destructive, affecting, for example, only a certain geographical area or a group of people who are genetically distinct.

An immediate consequence of the Faustian bargain in obtaining the great power of nanotechnology is that we run a grave risk — the risk that we might destroy the biosphere on which all life depends.

As Drexler explained:

> "Plants" with "leaves" no more efficient than today's solar cells could outcompete real plants, crowding the biosphere with an inedible foliage. Tough omnivorous "bacteria" could out-compete real bacteria: They could spread like blowing pollen, replicate swiftly, and reduce the biosphere to dust in a matter of days. Dangerous replicators could easily be too tough, small, and rapidly spreading to stop — at least if we make no preparation. We have trouble enough controlling viruses and fruit flies.
>
> Among the cognoscenti of nanotechnology, this threat has become known as the "gray goo problem." Though masses of uncontrolled replicators need not be gray or gooey, the term "gray goo" emphasizes that replicators able to obliterate life might be less inspiring than a single species of crabgrass. They might be superior in an evolutionary sense, but this need not make them valuable.

> The gray goo threat makes one thing perfectly clear: We cannot afford certain kinds of accidents with replicating assemblers.

Gray goo would surely be a depressing ending to our human adventure on Earth, far worse than mere fire or ice, and one that could stem from a simple laboratory accident.[6] Oops.

It is most of all the power of destructive self-replication in genetics, nanotechnology, and robotics (GNR) that should give us pause. Self-replication is the modus operandi of genetic engineering, which uses the machinery of the cell to replicate its designs, and the prime danger underlying gray goo in nanotechnology. Stories of run-amok robots like the Borg, replicating or mutating to escape from the ethical constraints imposed on them by their creators, are well established in our science fiction books and movies. It is even possible that self-replication may be more fundamental than we thought, and hence harder — or even impossible — to control. A recent article by Stuart Kauffman in *Nature* titled "Self-Replication: Even Peptides Do It" discusses the discovery that a thirty-two-amino-acid peptide can "autocatalyse its own synthesis." We don't know how widespread this ability is, but Kauffman notes that it may hint at "a route to self-reproducing molecular systems on a basis far wider than Watson-Crick base-pairing."[7]

In truth, we have had in hand for years clear warnings of the dangers inherent in widespread knowledge of GNR technologies — of the possibility of knowledge alone enabling mass destruction. But these warnings haven't been widely publicized; the public discussions have been clearly inadequate. There is no profit in publicizing the dangers.

The nuclear, biological, and chemical (NBC) technologies used in twentieth-century weapons of mass destruction were and are largely military, developed in government laboratories. In sharp contrast, the twenty-first-century GNR technologies have clear commercial uses and are being developed almost exclusively by corporate enterprises. In this age of triumphant commercialism, technology — with science as its handmaiden — is delivering a series of almost magical inventions that are the most phenomenally lucrative ever seen. We are aggressively pursuing the promises of these new technologies within the now unchallenged system of global capitalism and its manifold financial incentives and competitive pressures.

This is the first moment in the history of our planet when any species, by its own voluntary actions, has become a danger to itself — as well as to vast numbers of others.

> It might be a familiar progression, transpiring on many worlds — a planet, newly formed, placidly revolves around its star; life slowly forms; a kaleidoscopic procession of creatures evolves; intelligence emerges which, at least up to a point, confers enormous survival value; and then technology is invented. It dawns on them that there are such things as laws of Nature, that these laws can be revealed by experiment, and that knowledge of these laws can be made both to save and to take lives, both on unprecedented scales. Science, they recognize, grants immense powers. In a flash, they create world-altering contrivances. Some planetary civilizations see their way through, place limits on what may and

what must not be done, and safely pass through the time of perils.

Others, not so lucky or so prudent, perish.

That is Carl Sagan, writing in 1994, in *Pale Blue Dot*, a book describing his vision of the human future in space. I am only now realizing how deep his insight was, and how sorely I miss, and will miss, his voice. For all its eloquence, Sagan's contribution was not least that of simple common sense — an attribute that, along with humility, many of the leading advocates of the twenty-first-century technologies seem to lack.

I remember from my childhood that my grandmother was strongly against the overuse of antibiotics. She had worked since before the first World War as a nurse and had a common sense attitude that taking antibiotics, unless they were absolutely necessary, was bad for you.

It is not that she was an enemy of progress. She saw much progress in an almost seventy-year nursing career; my grandfather, a diabetic, benefited greatly from the improved treatments that became available in his lifetime. But she, like many levelheaded people, would probably think it greatly arrogant for us, now, to be designing a robotic "replacement species" when we obviously have so much trouble making relatively simple things work and so much trouble managing — or even understanding — ourselves.

I realize now that she had an awareness of the nature of the order of life and of the necessity of living with and respecting that order. With this respect comes a necessary humility that we, with our early-twenty-first-century chutzpah, lack at our peril. The common sense view, grounded in this respect, is often right, in advance of the scientific evidence. The clear fragility and inefficiencies of the human-made systems we have built should give us all pause; the fragility of the systems I have worked on certainly humbles me.

We should have learned a lesson from the making of the first atomic bomb and the resulting arms race. We didn't do well then, and the parallels to our current situation are troubling.

The effort to build the first atomic bomb was led by the brilliant physicist J. Robert Oppenheimer. Oppenheimer was not naturally interested in politics but became painfully aware of what he perceived as the grave threat to Western civilization from the Third Reich, a threat surely grave because of the possibility that Hitler might obtain nuclear weapons. Energized by this concern, he brought his strong intellect, passion for physics, and charismatic leadership skills to Los Alamos and led a rapid and successful effort by an incredible collection of great minds to quickly invent the bomb.

What is striking is how this effort continued so naturally after the initial impetus was removed. In a meeting shortly after V-E Day with some physicists who felt that perhaps the effort should stop, Oppenheimer argued to continue. His stated reason seems a bit strange: not because of the fear of large casualties from an invasion of Japan, but because the United Nations, which was soon to be formed, should have foreknowledge of atomic weapons. A more likely reason the project continued is the momentum that had built up — the first atomic test, Trinity, was nearly at hand.

We know that in preparing this first atomic test the physicists proceeded despite a large number of possible dangers. They were initially worried, based on a calculation by Edward Teller, that an atomic explosion might set fire to the atmosphere. A revised calculation reduced the danger of destroying the world to a three-in-a-million chance. (Teller says he was later able to dismiss the prospect of atmospheric ignition entirely.) Oppenheimer, though, was sufficiently concerned about the result of Trinity that he arranged for a possible evacuation of the southwest part of the state of New Mexico. And, of course, there was the clear danger of starting a nuclear arms race.

Within a month of that first, successful test, two atomic bombs destroyed Hiroshima and Nagasaki. Some scientists had suggested that the bomb simply be demonstrated, rather than dropped on Japanese cities — saying that this would greatly improve the chances for arms control after the war — but to no avail. With the tragedy of Pearl Harbor still fresh in Americans' minds, it would have been very difficult for President Truman to order a demonstration of the weapons rather than use them as he did — the desire to quickly end the war and save the lives that would have been lost in any invasion of Japan was very strong. Yet the overriding truth was probably very simple: As the physicist Freeman Dyson later said, "The reason that it was dropped was just that nobody had the courage or the foresight to say no."

It's important to realize how shocked the physicists were in the aftermath of the bombing of Hiroshima, on August 6, 1945. They describe a series of waves of emotion: first, a sense of fulfillment that the bomb worked, then horror at all the people that had been killed, and then a convincing feeling that on no account should another bomb be dropped. Yet of course another bomb was dropped, on Nagasaki, only three days after the bombing of Hiroshima.

In November 1945, three months after the atomic bombings, Oppenheimer stood firmly behind the scientific attitude, saying, "It is not possible to be a scientist unless you believe that the knowledge of the world, and the power which this gives, is a thing which is of intrinsic value to humanity, and that you are using it to help in the spread of knowledge and are willing to take the consequences."

Oppenheimer went on to work, with others, on the Acheson-Lilienthal report, which, as Richard Rhodes says in his recent book *Visions of Technology*, "found a way to prevent a clandestine nuclear arms race without resorting to armed world government"; their suggestion was a form of relinquishment of nuclear weapons work by nation-states to an international agency.

This proposal led to the Baruch Plan, which was submitted to the United Nations in June 1946 but never adopted (perhaps because, as Rhodes suggests, Bernard Baruch had "insisted on burdening the plan with conventional sanctions," thereby inevitably dooming it, even though it would "almost certainly have been rejected by Stalinist Russia anyway"). Other efforts to promote sensible steps toward internationalizing nuclear power to prevent an arms race ran afoul either of U.S. politics and internal distrust, or distrust by the Soviets. The opportunity to avoid the arms race was lost and very quickly.

Two years later, in 1948, Oppenheimer seemed to have reached another stage in his thinking, saying, "In some sort of crude sense which no vulgarity, no humor, no overstatement can quite extinguish, the physicists have known sin; and this is a knowledge they cannot lose."

In 1949, the Soviets exploded an atom bomb. By 1955, both the U.S. and the Soviet Union had tested hydrogen bombs suitable for delivery by aircraft. And so the nuclear arms race began.

Nearly twenty years ago, in the documentary *The Day After Trinity*, Freeman Dyson summarized the scientific attitudes that brought us to the nuclear precipice:

> I have felt it myself. The glitter of nuclear weapons. It is irresistible if you come to them as a scientist. To feel it's there in your hands, to release this energy that fuels the stars, to let it do your bidding. To perform these miracles, to lift a million tons of rock into the sky. It is something that gives people an illusion of illimitable power, and it is, in some ways, responsible for all our troubles — this, what you might call technical arrogance, that overcomes people when they see what they can do with their minds.[8]

Now, as then, we are creators of new technologies and stars of the imagined future, driven — this time by great financial rewards and global competition — despite the clear dangers, hardly evaluating what it may be like to try to live in a world that is the realistic outcome of what we are creating and imagining.

In 1947, *The Bulletin of the Atomic Scientists* began putting a Doomsday Clock on its cover. For more than fifty years, it has shown an estimate of the relative nuclear danger we have faced, reflecting the changing international conditions. The hands on the clock have moved fifteen times and today, standing at nine minutes to midnight, reflect continuing and real danger from nuclear weapons. The recent addition of India and Pakistan to the list of nuclear powers has increased the threat of failure of the nonproliferation goal, and this danger was reflected by moving the hands closer to midnight in 1998. [The hands were moved to five minutes before midnight in 2007, then back to six minutes before in January 2010. – Ed.]

In our time, how much danger do we face, not just from nuclear weapons, but from all of these technologies? How high are the extinction risks?

The philosopher John Leslie has studied this question and concluded that the risk of human extinction is at least 30 percent,[9] while Ray Kurzweil believes we have "a better than even chance of making it through," with the caveat that he has "always been accused of being an optimist." Not only are these estimates not encouraging, but they do not include the probability of many horrid outcomes that lie short of extinction.

Faced with such assessments, some serious people are already suggesting that we simply move beyond Earth as quickly as possible. We would colonize the galaxy using von Neumann probes, which hop from star system to star system, replicating as they go. This step will almost certainly be necessary five billion years from now (or sooner if our solar system is disastrously impacted by the impending collision of our galaxy with the Andromeda galaxy within the next three billion years), but if we take Kurzweil and Moravec at their word, it might be necessary by the middle of this century.

What are the moral implications here? If we must move beyond Earth this quickly in order for the species to survive, who accepts the responsibility for the fate of those (most of us, after all) who are left behind? And even if we scatter to the stars, isn't it likely that we may take our problems with us or find, later, that they have followed us? The fate of our species on Earth and our fate in the galaxy seem inextricably linked.

Another idea is to erect a series of shields to defend against each of the dangerous technologies. The Strategic Defense Initiative, proposed by the Reagan administration, was an attempt to design such a shield against the threat of a nuclear attack from the Soviet Union. But as Arthur C. Clarke, who was privy to discussions about the project, observed:

> Though it might be possible, at vast expense, to construct local defense systems that would "only" let through a few percent of ballistic missiles, the much touted idea of a national umbrella was nonsense. Luis Alvarez, perhaps the greatest experimental physicist of this century, remarked to me that the advocates of such schemes were "very bright guys with no common sense."

Clarke continued:

> Looking into my often cloudy crystal ball, I suspect that a total defense might indeed be possible in a century or so. But the technology involved would produce, as a by-product, weapons so terrible that no one would bother with anything as primitive as ballistic missiles.[10]

In *Engines of Creation*, Eric Drexler proposed that we build an active nanotechnological shield — a form of immune system for the biosphere — to defend against dangerous replicators of all kinds that might escape from laboratories or otherwise be maliciously created. But the shield he proposed would itself be extremely dangerous — nothing could prevent it from developing autoimmune problems and attacking the biosphere itself.[11]

Similar difficulties apply to the construction of shields against robotics and genetic engineering. These technologies are too powerful to be shielded against in the time frame of interest; even if it were possible to implement defensive shields, the side effects of their development would be at least as dangerous as the technologies we are trying to protect against.

These possibilities are all thus either undesirable or unachievable or both. The only realistic alternative I see is relinquishment: to limit development of the technologies that are too dangerous, by limiting our pursuit of certain kinds of knowledge.

Yes, I know, knowledge is good, as is the search for new truths. We have been seeking knowledge since ancient times. Aristotle opened his *Metaphysics* with the simple statement, "All men by nature desire to know." We have, as a bedrock value in our society, long agreed on the value of open access to information, and recognize the problems that arise with attempts to restrict access to and development of knowledge. In recent times, we have come to revere scientific knowledge.

But despite the strong historical precedents, if open access to and unlimited development of knowledge henceforth puts us all in clear danger of extinction, then common sense demands that we reexamine even these basic, long-held beliefs.

It was Nietzsche who warned us, at the end of the nineteenth century, not only that God is dead but that "faith in science, which after all exists undeniably, cannot owe its origin to a calculus of utility; it must have originated in spite of the fact that the disutility and dangerousness of the 'will to truth,' of 'truth at any price' is proved to it constantly." It is this further danger that we now fully face — the consequences of our truth seeking. The truth that science seeks can certainly be considered a dangerous substitute for God if it is likely to lead to our extinction.

If we could agree, as a species, what we wanted, where we were headed, and why, then we would make our future much less dangerous — then we might understand what we can and should relinquish. Otherwise, we can easily imagine an arms race developing over GNR technologies, as it did with the NBC technologies in the twentieth century. This is perhaps the greatest risk, for once such a race begins, it's very hard to end it. This time — unlike during the Manhattan Project — we aren't in a war, facing an implacable enemy that is threatening our civilization; we are driven, instead, by our habits, our desires, our economic system, and our competitive need to know.

I believe that we all wish our course could be determined by our collective values, ethics, and morals. If we had gained more collective wisdom over the past few thousand years, then a dialogue to this end would be more practical, and the incredible powers we are about to unleash would not be nearly so troubling.

One would think we might be driven to such a dialogue by our instinct for self-preservation. Individuals clearly have this desire, yet as a species our behavior seems to be not in our favor. In dealing with the nuclear threat, we often spoke dishonestly to ourselves and to each other, thereby greatly increasing the risks. Whether this was politically motivated, or because we chose not to think ahead, or because when faced with such grave threats we acted irrationally out of fear, I do not know, but it does not bode well.

The new Pandora's boxes of genetics, nanotechnology, and robotics are almost open, yet we seem hardly to have noticed. Ideas can't be put back in a box; unlike uranium or plutonium, they don't need to be mined and refined, and they can be freely copied. Once they are out, they are out. Churchill remarked, in a famous left-handed compliment, that the American people and their leaders "invariably do the right thing, after they have examined every other alternative." In this case, however, we must act more presciently, as to do the right thing only at last may be to lose the chance to do it at all.

As Thoreau said, "We do not ride on the railroad; it rides upon us"; and this is what we must fight, in our time. The question is, indeed, Which is to be master? Will we survive our technologies?

We are being propelled into this new century with no plan, no control, no brakes. Have we already gone too far down the path to alter course? I don't believe so, but we aren't trying yet, and the last chance to assert control — the fail-safe point — is rapidly approaching. We have our first pet robots, as well as commercially available genetic engineering techniques, and our nanoscale techniques are advancing rapidly. While the development of these technologies proceeds through a number of steps, it isn't necessarily the case — as happened in the Manhattan Project and the Trinity test — that the last step in proving a technology is large and hard. The breakthrough to wild self-replication in robotics, genetic engineering, or nanotechnology could come suddenly, reprising the surprise we felt when we learned of the cloning of a mammal.

And yet I believe we do have a strong and solid basis for hope. Our attempts to deal with weapons of mass destruction in the last century provide a shining example of relinquishment for us to consider: the unilateral U.S. abandonment, without preconditions, of the development of biological weapons. This relinquishment stemmed from the realization that while it would take an enormous effort to create these terrible weapons, they could from then on easily be duplicated and fall into the hands of rogue nations or terrorist groups.

The clear conclusion was that we would create additional threats to ourselves by pursuing these weapons and that we would be more secure if we did not pursue them. We have embodied our relinquishment of biological and chemical weapons in the 1972 Biological Weapons Convention (BWC) and the 1993 Chemical Weapons Convention (CWC).[12]

As for the continuing sizable threat from nuclear weapons, which we have lived with now for more than fifty years, the U.S. Senate's recent rejection of the Comprehensive Test Ban Treaty makes it clear relinquishing nuclear weapons will not be politically easy. But we have a unique opportunity, with the end of the Cold War, to avert a multipolar arms race. Building on the BWC and CWC relinquishments, successful abolition of nuclear weapons could help us build toward a habit of relinquishing dangerous technologies. (Actually, by getting rid of all but 100 nuclear weapons worldwide — roughly the total destructive power of World War II and a considerably easier task — we could eliminate this extinction threat.[13])

Verifying relinquishment will be a difficult problem, but not an unsolvable one. We are fortunate to have already done a lot of relevant work in the context of the BWC and other treaties. Our major task will be to apply this to technologies that are naturally much more commercial than military. The substantial need here is for transparency, as difficulty of verification is directly proportional to the difficulty of distinguishing relinquished from legitimate activities.

I frankly believe that the situation in 1945 was simpler than the one we now face: The nuclear technologies were reasonably separable into commercial and military uses and monitoring was aided by the nature of atomic tests and the ease with which radioactivity could be measured. Research on military applications could be performed at national laboratories such as Los Alamos, with the results kept secret as long as possible.

The GNR technologies do not divide clearly into commercial and military uses; given their potential in the market, it's hard to imagine pursuing them only in national laboratories. With their widespread commercial pursuit, enforcing relinquishment will require a verification regime similar to that for biological weapons, but on an unprecedented scale. This, inevitably, will raise tensions between our individual privacy and desire for proprietary information and the need for verification to protect us all. We will undoubtedly encounter strong resistance to this loss of privacy and freedom of action.

Verifying the relinquishment of certain GNR technologies will have to occur in cyberspace as well as at physical facilities. The critical issue will be to make the necessary transparency acceptable in a world of proprietary information, presumably by providing new forms of protection for intellectual property.

Verifying compliance will also require that scientists and engineers adopt a strong code of ethical conduct, resembling the Hippocratic oath, and that they have the courage to whistleblow as necessary, even at high personal cost. This would answer the call — fifty years after Hiroshima — by the Nobel laureate Hans Bethe, one of the most senior of the surviving members of the Manhattan Project, that all scientists "cease and desist from work creating, developing, improving, and manufacturing nuclear weapons and other weapons of potential mass destruction."[14] In the twenty-first century, this requires vigilance and personal responsibility by those who would work on both NBC and GNR technologies to avoid implementing weapons of mass destruction and knowledge-enabled mass destruction.

Thoreau also said that we will be "rich in proportion to the number of things which we can afford to let alone." We each seek to be happy, but it would seem worthwhile to question whether we need to take such a high risk of total destruction to gain yet more knowledge and yet more things; common sense says that there is a limit to our material needs — and that certain knowledge is too dangerous and is best forgone.

Neither should we pursue near immortality without considering the costs, without considering the commensurate increase in the risk of extinction. Immortality, while perhaps the original, is certainly not the only possible utopian dream.

I recently had the good fortune to meet the distinguished author and scholar Jacques Attali, whose book *Lignes d'horizons* (*Millennium*, in the English translation) helped inspire the Java and Jini approach to the coming age of pervasive computing, as previously described in [*Wired*]. In his new book *Fraternités*, Attali describes how our dreams of utopia have changed over time:

> At the dawn of societies, men saw their passage on Earth as nothing more than a labyrinth of pain, at the end of which stood a door leading, via their death, to the company of gods and to *Eternity*. With the Hebrews and then the Greeks, some men dared free themselves from theological demands and dream of an ideal City where *Liberty* would flourish. Others, noting the evolution of the market society, understood that the liberty of some would entail the alienation of others, and they sought *Equality*.

Jacques helped me understand how these three different utopian goals exist in tension in our society today. He goes on to describe a fourth utopia, Fraternity, whose foundation is altruism. Fraternity alone associates individual happiness with the happiness of others, affording the promise of self-sustainment.

This crystallized for me my problem with Kurzweil's dream. A technological approach to Eternity — near immortality through robotics — may not be the most desirable utopia, and its pursuit brings clear dangers. Maybe we should rethink our utopian choices.

Where can we look for a new ethical basis to set our course? I have found the ideas in the book *Ethics for the New Millennium*, by the Dalai Lama, to be very helpful. As is perhaps well known but little heeded, the Dalai Lama argues that the most important thing is for us to conduct our lives with love and compassion for others and that our societies need to develop a stronger notion of universal responsibility and of our interdependency; he proposes a standard of positive ethical conduct for individuals and societies that seems consonant with Attali's Fraternity utopia.

The Dalai Lama further argues that we must understand what it is that makes people happy and acknowledge the strong evidence that neither material progress nor the pursuit of the power of knowledge is the key — that there are limits to what science and the scientific pursuit alone can do.

Our Western notion of happiness seems to come from the Greeks, who defined it as "the exercise of vital powers along lines of excellence in a life affording them scope."[15]

Clearly, we need to find meaningful challenges and sufficient scope in our lives if we are to be happy in whatever is to come. But I believe we must find alternative outlets for our creative forces, beyond the culture of perpetual economic growth; this growth has largely been a blessing for several hundred years, but it has not brought us unalloyed happiness, and we must now choose between the pursuit of unrestricted and undirected growth through science and technology and the clear accompanying dangers.

It is now more than a year since my first encounter with Ray Kurzweil and John Searle. I see around me cause for hope in the voices for caution and relinquishment and in those people I have discovered who are as concerned as I am about our current predicament. I feel, too, a deepened sense of personal responsibility — not for the work I have already done, but for the work that I might yet do, at the confluence of the sciences.

But many other people who know about the dangers still seem strangely silent. When pressed, they trot out the "this is nothing new" riposte — as if awareness of what could happen is response enough. They tell me, There are universities filled with bioethicists who study this stuff all day long. They say, All this has been written about before, and by experts. They complain, Your worries and your arguments are already old hat.

I don't know where these people hide their fear. As an architect of complex systems I enter this arena as a generalist. But should this diminish my concerns? I am aware of how much has been written about, talked about, and lectured about so authoritatively. But does this mean it has reached people? Does this mean we can discount the dangers before us?

Knowing is not a rationale for not acting. Can we doubt that knowledge has become a weapon we wield against ourselves?

The experiences of the atomic scientists clearly show the need to take personal responsibility, the danger that things will move too fast, and the way in which a process can take on a life of its own. We can, as they did, create insurmountable problems in almost no time flat. We must do more thinking up front if we are not to be similarly surprised and shocked by the consequences of our inventions.

My continuing professional work is on improving the reliability of software. Software is a tool, and as a toolbuilder I must struggle with the uses to which the tools I make are put. I have always believed that making software more reliable, given its many uses, will make the world a safer and better place; if I were to come to believe the opposite, then I would be morally obligated to stop this work. I can now imagine such a day may come.

This all leaves me not angry but at least a bit melancholic. Henceforth, for me, progress will be somewhat bittersweet.

Do you remember the beautiful penultimate scene in *Manhattan* where Woody Allen is lying on his couch and talking into a tape recorder? He is writing a short story about people who are creating unnecessary, neurotic problems for themselves, because it keeps them from dealing with more unsolvable, terrifying problems about the universe.

He leads himself to the question, "Why is life worth living?" and to consider what makes it worthwhile for him: Groucho Marx, Willie Mays, the second movement of the Jupiter Symphony, Louis Armstrong's recording of "Potato Head Blues," Swedish movies, Flaubert's *Sentimental Education*, Marlon Brando, Frank Sinatra, the apples and pears by Cézanne, the crabs at Sam Wo's, and, finally, the showstopper: his love Tracy's face.

Each of us has our precious things, and as we care for them we locate the essence of our humanity. In the end, it is because of our great capacity for caring that I remain optimistic we will confront the dangerous issues now before us.

My immediate hope is to participate in a much larger discussion of the issues raised here, with people from many different backgrounds, in settings not predisposed to fear or favor technology for its own sake.

As a start, I have twice raised many of these issues at events sponsored by the Aspen Institute and have separately proposed that the American Academy of Arts and Sciences take them up as an extension of its work with the Pugwash Conferences. (These have been held since 1957 to discuss arms control, especially of nuclear weapons, and to formulate workable policies.)

It's unfortunate that the Pugwash meetings started only well after the nuclear genie was out of the bottle — roughly fifteen years too late. We are also getting a belated start on seriously addressing the issues around twenty-first-century technologies — the prevention of knowledge-enabled mass destruction — and further delay seems unacceptable.

So I'm still searching; there are many more things to learn. Whether we are to succeed or fail, to survive or fall victim to these technologies, is not yet decided. I'm up late again — it's almost 6 A.M. I'm trying to imagine some better answers, to break the spell and free them from the stone.

ENDNOTES

1. The passage Kurzweil quotes is from Kaczynski's "Unabomber Manifesto," which was published jointly, under duress, by *The New York Times* and *The Washington Post*

to attempt to bring his campaign of terror to an end. I agree with David Gelernter, who said about their decision:

> It was a tough call for the newspapers. To say yes would be giving in to terrorism, and for all they knew he was lying anyway. On the other hand, to say yes might stop the killing. There was also a chance that someone would read the tract and get a hunch about the author; and that is exactly what happened. The suspect's brother read it, and it rang a bell.
>   I would have told them not to publish. I'm glad they didn't ask me.
> I guess. (*Drawing Life: Surviving the Unabomber.* Free Press, 1997:120.)

2. Laurie Garrett, *The Coming Plague: Newly Emerging Diseases in a World Out of Balance* (New York: Penguin, 1994), pp. 47–52, 414, 419, 452.

3. Isaac Asimov described what became the most famous view of ethical rules for robot behavior in his book *I, Robot* in 1950, in his Three Laws of Robotics: 1. A robot may not injure a human being, or, through inaction, allow a human being to come to harm. 2. A robot must obey the orders given it by human beings, except where such orders would conflict with the First Law. 3. A robot must protect its own existence, as long as such protection does not conflict with the First or Second Law.

4. Michelangelo wrote a sonnet that begins:

> *Non ha l' ottimo artista alcun concetto*
> *Ch' un marmo solo in sè non circonscriva*
> *Col suo soverchio; e solo a quello arriva*
> *La man che ubbidisce all' intelleto.*

Stone translates this as:

> The best of artists hath no thought to show
> which the rough stone in its superfluous shell
> doth not include; to break the marble spell
> is all the hand that serves the brain can do.

Stone describes the process: "He was not working from his drawings or clay models; they had all been put away. He was carving from the images in his mind. His eyes and hands knew where every line, curve, mass must emerge, and at what depth in the heart of the stone to create the low relief." *The Agony and the Ecstasy* (New York: Doubleday, 1961), pp. 6, 144.

5. First Foresight Conference on Nanotechnology in October 1989, a talk titled "The Future of Computation." Published in B.C. Crandall, and James Lewis, eds., *Nanotechnology: Research and Perspectives* (Boston: MIT Press, 1992), p. 269. See also <www.foresight.org/Conferences/MNT01/Nano1.html>.

6. In his 1963 novel *Cat's Cradle*, Kurt Vonnegut imagined a gray-goo-like accident where a form of ice called ice-nine, which becomes solid at a much higher temperature, freezes the oceans.

7. Stuart Kauffman, "Self-replication: Even Peptides Do It." *Nature*, 382 (August 8, 1996), p. 496. See <www.santafe.edu/sfi/People/kauffman/sak-peptides.html>.

8. Jon Else, *The Day After Trinity: J. Robert Oppenheimer and The Atomic Bomb* (available at <www.pyramiddirect.com>).

9. This estimate is in Leslie's book *The End of the World: The Science and Ethics of Human Extinction*, where he notes that the probability of extinction is substantially higher if we accept Brandon Carter's Doomsday Argument, which is, briefly, that "we ought to have some reluctance to believe that we are very exceptionally early, for instance in the earliest 0.001 percent, among all humans who will ever have lived. This

would be some reason for thinking that humankind will not survive for many more centuries, let alone colonize the galaxy. Carter's doomsday argument doesn't generate any risk estimates just by itself. It is an argument for revising the estimates which we generate when we consider various possible dangers." (Routledge, 1996, pp. 1, 3, 145.)

10. Arthur C. Clarke, "Presidents, Experts, and Asteroids." *Science*, June 5, 1998. Reprinted as "Science and Society" in *Greetings, Carbon-Based Bipeds! Collected Essays, 1934–1998* (New York: St. Martin's Press, 1999), p. 526.

11. And, as David Forrest suggests in his paper "Regulating Nanotechnology Development," available at <www.foresight.org/NanoRev/Forrest1989.html>, "If we used strict liability as an alternative to regulation it would be impossible for any developer to internalize the cost of the risk (destruction of the biosphere), so theoretically the activity of developing nanotechnology should never be undertaken." Forrest's analysis leaves us with only government regulation to protect us — not a comforting thought.

12. Matthew Meselson, "The Problem of Biological Weapons." Presentation to the 1,818th Stated Meeting of the American Academy of Arts and Sciences, January 13, 1999 (available at <minerva.amacad.org/archive/bulletin4.htm>).

13. Paul Doty, "The Forgotten Menace: Nuclear Weapons Stockpiles Still Represent the Biggest Threat to Civilization." *Nature*, 402 (December 9, 1999), p. 583.

14. See also Hans Bethe's 1997 letter to President Clinton, at <www.fas.org/bethecr.htm>.

15. Edith Hamilton, *The Greek Way* (New York: W. W. Norton & Co., 1942), p. 35.

10

A Response to Bill Joy and the Doom-and-Gloom Technofuturists

JOHN SEELY BROWN AND PAUL DUGUID

Bill Joy's article drew many responses, some concurring with Joy's argument, most not. Among the most interesting and articulate rebuttals of the Joy thesis was one published not long after Joy's in The Industry Standard, *a magazine of e-commerce, technology, media, and politics that was launched in early 1998 and became an unfortunate casualty of the dot.com crash in September 2001. The authors of that piece, colleagues of Joy in high-tech industry, take him to task for basing his pessimistic vision on an overly simplistic way of viewing the influence of technology on society. "Technology and society are constantly forming and reforming new dynamic equilibriums with far-reaching implications," they write. "The challenge for futurology (and for all of us) is to see beyond the hype and past the oversimplifications to the full import of these new sociotechnical formations." In essence, they are restating the outlook articulated by Robert Pool in Part I of this book.*

John Seely Brown is a visiting scholar and advisor to the provost at University of Southern California and the Independent co-chairman of the Deloitte Center for the Edge, a part of Deloitte that "helps senior executives make sense of and profit from emerging opportunities on the edge of business and technology." Brown was formerly chief scientist of the Xerox Corporation from 1992 to 2002, and director of the Xerox Palo Alto Research Center (PARC) from 1990 to

2000. He is also a cofounder of the Institute for Research on Learning, a non-profit institute for addressing the problems of lifelong learning. Paul Duguid, a historian and social theorist, is an adjunct full professor at the School of Infor-mation, at the University of California, Berkeley, and a professorial research fel-low at Queen Mary, University of London. He was formerly a member of the Institute for Research on Learning, and is coauthor, with John Seely Brown, of The Social Life of Information *(2000).*

If you lived through the 1950s, you might remember President Eisenhower, orderly suburban housing tracts, backyard bomb shelters — and dreams of a nuclear power plant in every home. Plans for industrial nuclear generators had barely left the drawing board before futurists predicted that every house would have a miniature version. From there, technoenthusiasts predicted the end of power monopolies, the emergence of the "electronic cottage," the death of the city and the decline of the corporation.

... Pessimists and Luddites, of course, envisioned nuclear apocalypse. Each side waited for nirvana, or Armageddon, so it could triumphantly tell the other, "I told you so."...With "Why the Future Doesn't Need Us" in the April [2000] issue of *Wired*, Bill Joy invokes those years gone by. No Luddite, Joy is an awe-inspiring technologist — as cofounder and chief scientist of Sun Microsystems, he coauthored, among other things, the Java programming language. So when his article describes a technological juggernaut thundering toward society — bringing with it mutant genes, molecular-level nanotechnology machines, and superintelli-gent robots — all need to listen. Like the nuclear prognosticators, Joy can see the juggernaut clearly. What he can't see — which is precisely what makes his vision so scary — are any controls.

But it doesn't follow that the juggernaut is uncontrollable. To understand why not, readers should note the publication in which this article appeared. For the better part of a decade, *Wired* has been a cheerleader for the digital age. Until now, *Wired* has rarely been a venue to which people have looked for a way to put a brake on innovation. Therefore, its shift with Joy's article from cheering to warning marks an important and surprising moment in the dig-ital zeitgeist. In an effort to locate some controls, let's go back to the nuclear age. Innovation, the argument went back in the 1950s, would make nuclear power plants smaller and cheaper. They would enter mass production and quickly be-come available to all.

Even today, the argument might appear inescapable until you notice what's missing: The tight focus of this vision makes it almost impossible to see forces other than technology at work. In the case of nuclear development, a host of forces worked to dismantle the dream of a peaceful atom, including the environ-mental movement, antinuclear protests, concerned scientists, worried neighbors of Chernobyl and Three Mile Island, government regulators and antiproliferation treaties. Cumulatively, these forces slowed the nuclear juggernaut to a crawl.

Similar social forces are at work on technologies today. But because the digerati, like technoenthusiasts before them, look to the future with technologi-cal tunnel vision, they too have trouble bringing other forces into view.

THE TUNNEL AHEAD

In Joy's vision, as in the nuclear one, there's a recognizable tunnel vision that leaves people out of the picture and focuses on technology in splendid isolation. This vision leads not only to doom-and-gloom scenarios, but also to tunnel design: the design of "simple" technologies that are actually difficult to use.

To escape both trite scenarios and bad design, we have to widen our horizons and bring into view not only technological systems, but also social systems. Good designs look beyond the dazzling potential of the technology to social factors, such as the limited patience of most users.

Paying attention to the latter has, for example, allowed the Palm Pilot and Nintendo Game Boy to sweep aside more complex rivals. Their elegant simplicity has made them readily usable. And their usability has in turn created an important social support system. The devices are so widely used that anyone having trouble with a Pilot or Game Boy rarely has to look far for advice from a more experienced user.

As this small example suggests, technological and social systems shape each other. The same is true on a larger scale. Technologies — such as gunpowder, the printing press, the railroad, the telegraph, and the Internet — can shape society in profound ways. But, on the other hand, social systems — in the form of governments, the courts, formal and informal organizations, social movements, professional networks, local communities, market institutions, and so forth — shape, moderate, and redirect the raw power of technologies.

Given the crisp edges of technology and the fuzzy outlines of society, it certainly isn't easy to use these two worldviews simultaneously. But if you want to see where we are going, or design the means to get there, you need to grasp both.

This perspective allows a more sanguine look at Joy's central concerns: genetic engineering, nanotechnology, and robotics. Undoubtedly, each deserves serious thought. But each should be viewed in the context of the social system in which it is inevitably embedded.

Genetic engineering presents the clearest example. Barely a year ago, the technology seemed to be an unstoppable force. Major chemical and agricultural interests were barreling down an open highway. In the past year, however, road conditions changed dramatically for the worse: Cargill faced Third World protests against its patents; Monsanto suspended research on sterile seeds; and champions of genetically modified foods, who once saw an unproblematic and lucrative future, are scurrying to counter consumer boycotts of their products.

Almost certainly, those who support genetic modification will have to look beyond the technology if they want to advance it. They need to address society directly — not just by putting labels on modified foods, but by educating people about the costs and the benefits of these new agricultural products. Having ignored social concerns, however, proponents have made the people they need to educate profoundly suspicious and hostile.

Nanotechnology offers a rather different example of how the future can frighten us. Because the technology involves engineering at a molecular level, both the promise and the threat seem immeasurable. But they are immeasurable for a good reason: The technology is still almost wholly on the drawing board.

Two of nanotechnology's main proponents, Ralph Merkle and Eric Drexler, worked with us at the Xerox Palo Alto Research Center in Palo Alto, California. The two built powerful nano-CAD tools and then ran simulations of the resulting molecular-level designs. These experiments showed definitively that nano devices are theoretically feasible. No one, however, has laid out a route from lab-based simulation to practical systems in any detail.

In the absence of a plan, it's important to ask the right questions: Can nanotechnology fulfill its great potential in tasks ranging from data storage to pollution control, all without spiraling out of control? If the lesson of genetic engineering is any guide, planners would do well to consult and educate the public early on, even though useful nano systems are probably decades away.

Worries about robotics appear premature, as well. Internet "bots" that search, communicate, and negotiate for their human masters may appear to behave like Homo sapiens, but, in fact, bots are often quite inept at functions that humans do well — functions that call for judgment, discretion, initiative, or tacit understanding. They are good (and useful) for those tasks that humans do poorly. So they are better thought of as complementary systems, not rivals to humanity. Although bots will undoubtedly get better at what they do, such development will not necessarily make them more human.

Are more conventional clanking robots — the villains of science fiction — any great threat to society? We doubt it. Xerox PARC research on self-aware, reconfigurable "polybots" has pushed the boundaries of what robots can do, pointing the way to "morphing robots" that are able to move and change shape.

Nonetheless, for all their cutting-edge agility, these robots are a long way from making good dance partners. The chattiness of *Star Wars'* C-3PO still lies well beyond real-world machines. Indeed, what talk robots or computers achieve, though it may appear similar, is quite different from human talk. Talking machines travel routes designed specifically to avoid the full complexities of human language.

Robots may seem intelligent, but such intelligence is profoundly hampered by their inability to learn in any significant way. (This failing has apparently led Toyota, after heavy investment in robotics, to consider replacing robots with humans on many production lines.) And, without learning, simple common sense will lie beyond robots for a long time to come.

Indeed, despite years of startling advances and innumerable successes like the chess-playing Big Blue, computer science is still about as far as it ever was from building a machine with the learning abilities, linguistic competence, common sense or social skills of a five-year-old child.

As with Internet bots, real-world robots will no doubt become increasingly useful. But they will probably also become increasingly frustrating to use as a result of tunnel design. In that regard, they may indeed seem antisocial, but not in the way of *Terminator*-like fantasies of robot armies that lay waste … human society.

Indeed, the thing that handicaps robots most is their lack of a social existence. For it is our social existence as humans that shapes how we speak, learn, think, and develop common sense. All forms of artificial life (whether bugs or bots) will remain primarily a metaphor for — rather than a threat to — society, at least until they manage to enter a debate, sing in a choir, take a class, survive a committee meeting, join a union, pass a law, engineer a cartel, or summon a constitutional convention.

These critical social mechanisms allow society to shape its future. It is through planned, collective action that society forestalls expected consequences (such as Y2K) and responds to unexpected events (such as epidemics).

THE FAILURE OF A "6-D" VISION

Why does the threat of cunning, replicating robot society look so close from one perspective, yet so distant from another? The difference lies in the well-known tendency of futurologists to count "1, 2, 3 … a million." That is, once the first step on a path is taken, it's very easy to assume that all subsequent steps are trivial.

Several of the steps Joy asks us to take — the leap from genetic engineering to a "white plague," from simulations to out-of-control nanotechnology, from replicating peptides to a "robot species" — are extremely large. And they are certainly not steps that will be taken without diversions, regulations, or controls.

One of the lessons of Joy's article, then, is that the path to the future can look simple (and sometimes downright terrifying) if you look at it through what we call "6-D lenses." We coined this phrase having so often in our research hit up against … such "de-" or "di-" words as demassification, decentralization, disintermediation, despacialization, disaggregation, and demarketization in the canon of futurology.

If you take any one of these words in isolation, it's easy to follow their relentless logic to its evident conclusion. Because firms are getting smaller, for example, it's easy to assume that companies and other intermediaries are simply disintegrating into markets. And because communication is growing cheaper and more powerful, it's easy to believe in the "death of distance."

But things rarely work in such linear fashion. Other forces are often at work, such as those driving firms into larger and larger mergers to take advantage of social, rather than merely technological, networks. Similarly, even though communications technology has killed distance, people curiously can't stay away from the social hotbed of modern communications technology, Silicon Valley.

Importantly, these d-words indicate that the old ties that once bound communities, organizations, and institutions are being picked apart by technologies. A simple, linear reading, then, suggests that these communities, organizations, and institutions will now simply fall apart. A more complex reading, taking into account the multiple forces at work, offers another picture.

While many powerful national corporations have grown insignificant, some have transformed into more powerful transnational firms. While some forms of community may be dying, others, bolstered by technology, are growing stronger.

Technology and society are constantly forming and reforming new dynamic equilibriums with far-reaching implications. The challenge for futurology (and for all of us) is to see beyond the hype and past the oversimplifications to the full import of these new sociotechnical formations. Two hundred years ago, Thomas Malthus, assuming that human society and agricultural technology developed on separate paths, predicted that society was growing so fast that it would starve itself to death, the so-called Malthusian trap.

A hundred years later, H. G. Wells similarly assumed that society and technology were developing independently. Like many people today, Wells saw the advance of technology outstripping the evolution of society, leading him to predict that technology's relentless juggernaut would unfeelingly crush society. Like Joy, both Malthus and Wells issued important warnings, alerting society to the dangers it faced. But by their actions, Malthus and Wells helped prevent the very future they were so certain would come about.

These self-*un*fulfilling prophecies failed to see that, once warned, society could galvanize itself into action. Of course, this social action in the face of threats showed that Malthus and Wells were most at fault in their initial assumption. Social and technological systems do not develop independently; the two evolve together in complex feedback loops, wherein each drives, restrains, and accelerates change in the other. Malthus and Wells — and now Joy — are, indeed, critical parts of these complex loops. Each knew when and how to sound the alarm. But each thought little about how to respond to that alarm.

Once the social system is factored back into the equation like this, the road ahead becomes harder to navigate. Ultimately we should be grateful to Joy for saying, at the least, that there could be trouble ahead when so many of his fellow digerati will only tell us complacently that the road is clear.

11

Promise and Peril

RAY KURZWEIL

Following the publication of Bill Joy's essay, "Why the Future Doesn't Need Us," Ray Kurzweil, another remarkably prolific inventor and technologist, and the author of The Age of Spiritual Machines *(1999), frequently found himself invited to debate Joy in conferences and forums, as a counterpoint, taking (as he does in his book) a more positive view of future technology. Indeed, at the beginning of his essay, Joy attributes his concern about the dangers of emerging technologies to a conversation with Kurzweil in 1998. In this essay, first presented as a paper at a conference on technology at Columbia University entitled "Living with the Genie," Kurzweil presents his side of what he calls a long-term debate with Joy, professing a much more nuanced view than he is sometimes given credit for.*

Mindful of their dangers, he describes the opportunities that the technologies of genetic engineering, nanotechnology, and robotics can offer humankind. The strongest part of his counterpoint, however, is in discussing Joy's recommendation that we relinquish some or all of these technological fields (i.e., give up their pursuit). Some form of "fine-grained" relinquishment, he says, is possible and should be part of technologists' professional ethics. Overall relinquishment, though, is not the answer. Not only will it not work, but there are other, better strategies to protect against the hazards that concern Joy. Technology, Kurzweil says, "will remain a double-edged sword.... We have no choice but to work hard to apply these quickening technologies to advance our human values, despite what often appears to be a lack of consensus on what those values should be."

Ray Kurzweil is perhaps best known as the inventor of the first omni-font optical character recognition device and the first print-to-speech reading machine for the blind. He has founded and developed nine businesses in fields related to optical character recognition, speech and music synthesis, and other areas of artificial intelligence. He was inducted into the National Inventors Hall of Fame in 2002. He is also the recipient of the National Medal of Technology and the MIT-Lemelson Prize for invention and innovation.

Consider these articles we'd rather not see on the web:

- Impress Your Enemies: How to Build Your Own Atomic Bomb from Readily Available Materials[1]
- How to Modify the Influenza Virus in Your College Laboratory to Release Snake Venom
- Ten Easy Modifications to the *E. coli* Virus
- How to Modify Smallpox to Counteract the Smallpox Vaccine
- How to Build a Self-Guiding, Low-Flying Airplane Using an Inexpensive Aircraft, GPS, and a Notebook Computer

Or how about the following:

- The Genomes of Ten Leading Pathogens
- The Floor Plans of Leading Skyscrapers
- The Layout of U.S. Nuclear Reactors
- Personal Health Information on 100 Million Americans
- The Customer Lists of Top Pornography Sites

Anyone posting the first item above is almost certain to get a quick visit from the FBI, as did Nate Ciccolo, a fifteen-year-old high school student, in March 2000. For a school science project, he built a papier-mâché model of an atomic bomb that turned out to be disturbingly accurate. In the ensuing media storm, Nate told ABC News, "Someone just sort of mentioned, you know, you can go on the Internet now and get information. And I, sort of, wasn't exactly up to date on things. Try it. I went on there and a couple of clicks and I was right there."[2]

Of course, Nate didn't possess the key ingredient, plutonium, nor did he have any intention of acquiring it, but the report created shock waves in the media, not to mention among the authorities who worry about nuclear proliferation. Nate had reported finding 563 web pages on atomic bomb designs. The publicity resulted in an urgent effort to remove this information. Unfortunately, trying to get rid of information on the Internet is akin to trying to sweep back the ocean with a broom. The information continues to be easily available today. I won't provide any URLs in this essay, but they are not hard to find.

Although the actual article titles above are fictitious, one can find extensive information on the Internet about all of these topics.[3] The web is an extraordinary research tool. In my own experience as a technologist and author, I've found that research which used to require half a day at the library can now typically be accomplished in a couple of minutes. This has enormous and obvious benefits for advancing beneficial technologies, but is also empowering those whose values are inimical to the mainstream of society.

My urgent concern with this issue goes back at least a couple of decades. When I wrote my first book, *The Age of Intelligent Machines*, in the mid-1980s, I was deeply concerned with the ability of genetic engineering, then an emerging technology, to allow those skilled in the art and with access to fairly widely available equipment to modify bacterial and viral pathogens to create new diseases.[4] In malevolent or merely careless hands, these engineered pathogens could potentially combine a high degree of communicability and destructiveness.

In the 1980s this was not easy to do, but was nonetheless feasible. We now know that bioweapons programs in the Soviet Union and elsewhere were doing exactly this.[5] At the time, I made a conscious decision to not talk about this specter in my book, feeling that I did not want to give the wrong people a destructive idea. I had disturbing visions of a future disaster, with the perpetrators saying that they got the idea from Ray Kurzweil.

Partly as a result of this decision, there was some reasonable criticism that the book emphasized the benefits of future technology while ignoring the downside. Thus, when I wrote *The Age of Spiritual Machines* in … late 1997–98, I attempted to cover both promise and peril.[6] There had been sufficient public attention to the perils by that time (for example, the 1995 movie *Outbreak*, which portrays the terror and panic that follow the release of a new viral pathogen) that I felt comfortable in beginning to address the issue publicly.

It was at that time, in September 1998, with a just-finished manuscript, that I ran into Bill Joy, an esteemed and longtime colleague in the high-technology world, in a bar in Lake Tahoe. I had long admired Bill for his pioneering work in creating the leading software language for interactive web systems (Java) and having cofounded Sun Microsystems. But my focus at this brief get-together was not on Bill but on the third person sitting in our small booth: John Searle, an eminent philosopher from the University of California, Berkeley. John had built a career out of defending the deep mysteries of human consciousness from apparent attack by materialists like me (though I deny the characterization).[7] John and I had just finished debating the issue of whether a machine could be conscious; we'd been part of the closing panel of George Gilder's "Telecosm" conference, which was devoted to a discussion of the philosophical implications of *The Age of Spiritual Machines*.[8]

I gave Bill a preliminary manuscript of the book and tried to bring him up to speed on the debate about consciousness that John and I were having. As it turned out, Bill focused on a completely different issue, specifically the impending dangers to human civilization from three emerging technologies I had presented in the book: genetics, nanotechnology, and robotics, or GNR for short. My discussion of the downsides of future technology alarmed Bill, as he relays in his now-famous cover story for *Wired* magazine, "Why the Future Doesn't Need Us."[9] In the article, Bill describes how he asked his friends in the scientific and technology community whether the projections I was making were credible and was dismayed to discover how close these capabilities were to realization.

Needless to say, Bill's article focused entirely on the downside scenarios, and created a firestorm. Here was one of the technology world's leading figures addressing new and dire emerging dangers from future technology. It was reminiscent of the attention that George Soros, the currency arbitrager and archcapitalist, received when he made vaguely critical comments about the excess of unrestrained capitalism, although the "Bill Joy" controversy became far more intense. The *New York Times* cited about 10,000 articles commenting on and discussing Bill's article, more than any other article in the history of commentary on technology issues.

My attempt to relax in a Lake Tahoe lounge ended up fostering two long-term debates. My dialogue with John Searle has continued to this day, and my debate with Bill has taken on a life of its own. Perhaps this is one reason I now avoid hanging out in bars.

Despite Bill's concerns, my reputation as a technology optimist has remained intact, and Bill and I have been invited to a variety of forums to debate the peril and promise, respectively, of future technologies. Although I am expected to take up the "promise" side of the debate, I often end up spending most of my time at these forums defending the feasibility of the dangers. I recall one event at Harvard during which a Nobel Prize–winning biologist dismissed the "N" (nanotechnology) danger by stating that he did not expect to see self-replicating nano-engineered entities for a hundred years.

I replied that indeed, a hundred years matched my own estimate of the amount of progress required — at *today's* rate of progress. However, since my models show that we are doubling the paradigm shift rate (the rate of technological progress) every ten years, we can expect to make a hundred years of progress — at today's rate — in about twenty-five calendar years, which matches the consensus view within the nanotechnology community. Thus are both promise and peril much closer at hand.

My view is that technology has always been a double-edged sword, bringing us longer and healthier life spans, freedom from physical and mental drudgery, and many new creative possibilities on the one hand, while introducing new and salient dangers on the other. Technology empowers both our creative and our destructive natures. Stalin's tanks and Hitler's trains used technology. We benefit from nuclear power, but live today with sufficient nuclear weapons (not all of which appear to be well accounted for) to end all mammalian life on the planet.

Bioengineering holds the promise of making enormous strides in reversing disease and aging processes. However, the means and knowledge it has created, which began to exist in the 1980s, will soon enable an ordinary college bioengineering lab to create unfriendly pathogens more dangerous than nuclear weapons.[10]

As technology accelerates toward the full realization of G (genetic engineering, also known as biotechnology), followed by N (nanotechnology) and ultimately R (robotics, also referred to as "strong" AI — artificial intelligence at human levels and beyond), we will see the same intertwined potentials: a feast of creativity resulting from human intelligence expanded many-fold, combined with many grave new dangers.

Consider the manner in which extremely small robots, or nanobots, are likely to develop. Nanobot technology requires billions or trillions of such intelligent devices to be useful. The most cost-effective way to scale up to such levels is through self-replication, essentially the same approach used in the biological world. And in the same way that biological self-replication gone awry (i.e., cancer) results in biological destruction, a defect in the mechanism curtailing nanobot self-replication would endanger all physical entities, biological or otherwise. Later in this chapter I suggest steps we can take to address this grave risk, but we cannot have complete assurance in any strategy that we devise today.

Other primary concerns include who controls the nanobots and who the nanobots are talking to. Organizations (e.g., governments or extremist groups) or just a clever individual could put trillions of undetectable nanobots in the water or food supply of an individual or of an entire population. These "spy" nanobots could then monitor, influence, and even control our thoughts and actions. In addition to physical spy nanobots, existing nanobots could be influenced through software viruses and other software "hacking" techniques. When there is software running in our brains, issues of privacy and security will take on a new urgency.

My own expectation is that the creative and constructive applications of this technology will dominate, as I believe they do today. I believe we need to vastly increase our investment in developing specific defensive technologies, however. We are at the critical stage today for biotechnology, and we will reach the stage where we need to directly implement defensive technologies for nanotechnology during the late teen years of this century.

THE INEVITABILITY OF A TRANSFORMED FUTURE

The diverse GNR technologies are progressing on many fronts and comprise hundreds of small steps forward, each benign in itself. An examination of the underlying trends, which I have studied for the past quarter-century, shows that full-blown GNR is inevitable.

The motivation for this study came from my interest in inventing. As an inventor in the 1970s, I came to realize that my inventions needed to make sense in terms of the enabling technologies and market forces that would exist when the invention was introduced, which would represent a very different world than when it was conceived. I began to develop models of how distinct technologies — electronics, communications, computer processors, memory, magnetic storage, and the key feature sizes in a range of technologies — developed and how these changes rippled through markets and ultimately our social institutions. I realized that most inventions fail not because they never work, but because their timing is wrong. Inventing is a lot like surfing; you have to anticipate and catch the wave at just the right moment.

In the 1980s my interest in technology trends and implications took on a life of its own, and I began to use my models of these trends to project and antici-pate the technologies of the future. This enabled me to invent with the capabili-ties of the future in mind. I wrote *The Age of Intelligent Machines*, which ended with the specter of machine intelligence becoming indistinguishable from its human progenitors. The book included hundreds of predictions about the 1990s and early 2000s, and my track record of prediction has held up well.

During the 1990s, I gathered empirical data on the apparent acceleration of all information-related technologies and sought to refine the mathematical models underlying these observations. In *The Age of Spiritual Machines*, I introduced improved models of technology and a theory I called "the law of accelerating returns," which explained why technology evolves in an exponential fashion.

THE INTUITIVE LINEAR VIEW VERSUS THE HISTORICAL EXPONENTIAL VIEW

The most important trend this study has revealed concerns the overall pace of technological progress itself. The future is widely misunderstood. Our forebears expected the future to be pretty much like their present, which had been pretty much like their past. Although exponential trends did exist a thousand years ago, they were at that very early stage where an exponential trend is so flat and so slow that it looks like no trend at all. So their expectation of stasis was largely fulfilled. Today, in accordance with the common wisdom, everyone expects continuous technological progress and the social repercussions that follow. But the future will nonetheless be far more surprising than most observers realize because few have truly internalized the implications of the fact that the rate of change itself is accelerating.

Most long-range forecasts of technical feasibility in future time periods dramatically underestimate the power of future developments because they are based on what I call the "intuitive linear view" of history rather than the "historical exponential view." To express this another way, it is not the case that we will experience 100 years of progress in the twenty-first century; rather, we will witness on the order of 20,000 years of progress (again, at *today*'s rate of progress).

When people think of a future period, they intuitively assume that the current rate of progress will continue into that future. Even for those who have been around long enough to experience how the pace increases over time, an unexamined intuition nonetheless provides the impression that progress happens at the rate we have experienced recently. From the mathematician's perspective, a primary reason for this is that an exponential curve approximates a straight line when viewed for a brief duration. It is typical therefore, for even sophisticated commentators, when considering the future, to extrapolate the current pace of change over the next ten years or hundred years to determine their expectations. This is why I call this way of looking at the future the "intuitive linear view."

But a serious assessment of the history of technology shows that technological change is exponential. In exponential growth, a key measurement such as computational power is multiplied by a constant factor for each unit of time (e.g., doubling every year) rather than just increased incrementally. Exponential growth is a feature of any evolutionary process, of which technology is a prime example. One can examine the data in different ways, on different time scales, and for a wide variety of technologies ranging from electronic to biological, as well as for social implications ranging from the size of the economy to human life span, and the acceleration of progress and growth applies to all.

Indeed, we find not just simple exponential growth, but "double" exponential growth, meaning that the rate of exponential growth is itself growing exponentially. These observations do not rely merely on an assumption of the continuation of Moore's Law (i.e., the exponential shrinking of transistor sizes on an integrated circuit), which I discuss a bit later, but are based on a rich model of diverse technological processes. What the model clearly shows is that technology, particularly the pace of technological change, advances (at least) exponentially, not linearly, and has been doing so since the advent of technology, indeed since the advent of evolution on Earth.

Many scientists and engineers have what my colleague Lucas Hendrich calls "engineer's pessimism." Often engineers or scientists who are so immersed in the difficulties and intricate details of a contemporary challenge fail to appreciate the ultimate long-term implications of their own work and, in particular, the larger field of work that they operate in. Consider the biochemists in 1985 who were skeptical of the announced goal of transcribing the entire genome in a mere fifteen years. These scientists had just spent an entire year transcribing a mere one tenthousandth of the genome, so even with reasonable anticipated advances, it seemed to them as though it would be hundreds of years, if not longer, before the entire genome could be sequenced.

Or consider the skepticism expressed in the mid-1980s that the Internet would ever be a significant phenomenon, given that it included only tens of thousands of nodes. The fact that the number of nodes was doubling every year, so tens of millions of nodes were likely to exist ten years later, was not appreciated by those struggling with a limited "state of the art" technology in 1985 that permitted adding only a few thousand nodes throughout the world in a year.[11]

I emphasize this point because it is the most important failure that would-be prognosticators make in considering future trends. The vast majority of technology forecasts and forecasters ignore altogether this "historical exponential view" of technological progress. Indeed, almost everyone I meet has a linear view of the future. That is why people tend to overestimate what can be achieved in the short term (because we tend to leave out necessary details) but underestimate what can be achieved in the long term (because the exponential growth is ignored).

THE LAW OF ACCELERATING RETURNS

The ongoing acceleration of technology is the implication and the inevitable result of what I call the "law of accelerating returns," which describes the acceleration of the pace and the exponential growth of the products of an evolutionary process. This process includes information-bearing technologies such as computation as well as the accelerating trend toward miniaturization — all the prerequisites for the full realization of GNR.

A wide range of technologies are subject to the law of accelerating returns. The exponential trend that has gained the greatest public recognition has become known as Moore's Law. Gordon Moore, one of the inventors of integrated circuits and then chairman of Intel, noted in the mid-1970s that we could squeeze twice as many transistors on an integrated circuit every twenty-four months.[12] Given that the electrons have a shorter distance to travel, the transistors change states more quickly. This, along with other techniques, allows the circuits to run faster, providing an overall quadrupling of computational power.

The exponential growth of computing is much broader than Moore's Law, however. If we plot the speed (in instructions per second) per $1,000 (in constant dollars) of forty-nine famous calculators and computers spanning the entire twentieth century, we note that there were four completely different paradigms providing exponential growth in the price-performance of computing before integrated circuits were invented. Therefore, Moore's Law was not the first but the fifth paradigm of exponential growth of computational power.[13] And it won't be the last. When Moore's Law approaches its limit, now expected before 2020, the exponential growth will continue with three-dimensional molecular computing, a prime example of the application of nanotechnology, which will constitute the sixth paradigm.

When in 1999 I suggested that three-dimensional molecular computing, particularly an approach based on using carbon nanotubes, would become the dominant computing hardware technology in the teen years of this century, that was considered a radical notion. But so much progress has been accomplished in the past four years, with literally dozens of major milestones having been achieved, that this expectation is now a mainstream view.[14]

The exponential growth of computing is a marvelous quantitative example of the exponentially growing returns from an evolutionary process. We can express the exponential growth of computing in terms of an accelerating pace: it took ninety years to achieve the first million instructions per second (MIPS) per $1,000; now we add one MIPS per $1,000 every day. The human brain uses a very inefficient electrochemical digital-controlled analog computational process. The bulk of the calculations are done in the interneuronal connections at a speed of only about two hundred calculations per second (in each connection), which is about ten million times slower than contemporary electronic circuits. But the brain gains its prodigious powers from its extremely parallel organization *in three dimensions*. There are many technologies in the wings that build circuitry in three dimensions.

Nanotubes (tubes formed from graphite sheets, consisting of hexagonal arrays of carbon atoms) are good conductors and can be used to build compact circuits; these are already working in laboratories. One cubic inch of nanotube circuitry would theoretically be a million times more powerful than the human brain. There are more than enough new computing technologies now being researched, including three-dimensional silicon chips, spin computing, crystalline computing, DNA computing, and quantum computing, to keep the law of accelerating returns as applied to computation going for a long time.

It is important to distinguish between the S curve (an *S* stretched to the right, comprising very slow, virtually unnoticeable growth — followed by very rapid growth — followed by a flattening out as the process approaches an asymptote, or limit) that is characteristic of any specific technological paradigm, and the continuing exponential growth that is characteristic of the ongoing evolutionary process of technology. Specific paradigms, such as Moore's Law, do ultimately reach levels at which exponential growth is no longer feasible. That is why Moore's Law is an S curve.

But the growth of computation is an ongoing exponential pattern (at least until we "saturate" the universe with the intelligence of our human-machine civilization, but that is not likely to happen in this century). In accordance with the law of accelerating returns, paradigm shift (also called innovation) turns the S curve of any specific paradigm into a continuing exponential pattern. A new paradigm (e.g., three-dimensional circuits) takes over when the old paradigm approaches its natural limit, which has already happened at least four times in the history of computation. This difference also distinguishes the tool making of nonhuman species, in which the mastery of a tool-making (or tool-using) skill by each animal is characterized by an abruptly ending S-shaped learning curve, from human-created technology, which has followed an exponential pattern of growth and acceleration since its inception.

This "law of accelerating returns" applies to all of technology, indeed to any true evolutionary process, and can be measured with remarkable precision in information-based technologies. There are a great many examples of the exponential growth implied by the law of accelerating returns in technologies, as varied as electronics of all kinds, DNA sequencing, communication speeds, brain scanning, reverse engineering of the brain, the size and scope of human knowledge, and the rapidly shrinking size of technology, which is directly relevant to emergence of nanotechnology.[15]

The future GNR age results not from the exponential explosion of computation alone, but rather from the interplay and myriad synergies that will result from intertwined technological revolutions. Keep in mind that every point on the exponential growth curves underlying this panoply of technologies represents an intense human drama of innovation and competition. It is remarkable, therefore, that these chaotic processes result in such smooth and predictable exponential trends.

ECONOMIC IMPERATIVE

It is the economic imperative of a competitive marketplace that is fueling the law of accelerating returns and driving technology forward toward the full realization of GNR. In turn, the law of accelerating returns is transforming economic relationships.

We are moving toward nanoscale machines, as well as more intelligent machines, as the result of a myriad of small advances, each with their own particular economic justification. There is a vital economic imperative to create smaller and more intelligent technology. Machines that can more precisely carry out their missions have enormous value, which is why they are being built. There are tens of thousands of projects advancing the various aspects of the law of accelerating returns in diverse incremental ways.

Regardless of near-term business cycles, the support for "high tech" in the business community, and in particular for software advancement, has grown enormously. When I started my optical character recognition (OCR) and speech synthesis company (Kurzweil Computer Products) in 1974, high-tech venture deals totaled approximately $10 million. Even during today's high-tech recession, the figure is a hundred times greater. We would have to repeal capitalism and every visage of economic competition to stop this progression.

The economy (viewed either in total or per capita) has been growing exponentially throughout this century. This underlying exponential growth is a far more powerful force than periodic recessions.[16] Even the Great Depression represents only a minor blip on this pattern of growth. Most importantly, recessions and depressions represent only temporary deviations from the underlying curve. In each case, the economy ends up exactly where it would have been had the recession or depression never occurred.

In addition to GDP, other improvements include productivity (economic output per worker), quality and features of products and services (for example, $1,000 of computation today is more powerful, by a factor of more than a thousand, than $1,000 of computation ten years ago), new products and product categories, and the value of existing goods, which has been increasing at 1.5 percent per year for the past twenty years because of qualitative improvements.[17, 18]

INTERTWINED BENEFITS...

Significant portions of our species have already experienced substantial alleviation of the poverty, disease, hard labor, and misfortune that have characterized much of human history. Many of us have the opportunity to gain satisfaction and meaning from our work rather than merely toiling to survive. We have ever more powerful tools to express ourselves. We have worldwide sharing of culture, art, and humankind's exponentially expanding knowledge base. Ubiquitous N and R are two to three decades away. A prime example of their application will be the deployment of billions of nanobots the size of human blood cells to travel inside the human bloodstream. This technology will be feasible within twenty-five years, based on miniaturization and cost-reduction trends. In addition to scanning the brain to facilitate reverse engineering (that is, analyzing how the brain works in order to copy its design), nanobots will be able to perform a broad variety of diagnostic and therapeutic functions inside the bloodstream and human body. Robert A. Freitas, for example, has designed robotic replacements for human blood cells that perform hundreds or thousands of times more effectively than their biological counterparts.[19] With Freitas's "respirocytes" (robotic red blood cells), you could do an Olympic sprint for fifteen minutes without taking a breath. His robotic macrophages would be far more effective than our white blood cells at combating pathogens. His DNA repair robot would be able to repair DNA transcription errors and even implement needed DNA changes.

Although realization of Freitas's conceptual designs is two or three decades away, substantial progress has already been achieved on bloodstream-based devices. For example, one scientist has cured type 1 diabetes in rats with a nanoengineered device that incorporates pancreatic islet cells. The device has seven nanometer pores that let insulin out but block the antibodies that destroy these cells. Many innovative projects of this type are already under way.

Clearly, nanobot technology has profound military applications, and any expectation that such uses will be "relinquished" is highly unrealistic. Already, the Department of Defense is developing "smart dust" — tiny robots the size of insects or even smaller.[20] Although not quite nanotechnology, millions of these devices can be dropped into enemy territory to provide highly detailed surveillance. The potential application for even smaller nanotechnology-based devices is even greater. Want to find Saddam Hussein or Osama bin Laden? Need to locate hidden weapons of mass destruction? Billions of essentially invisible spies could monitor every square inch of enemy territory, identify every person and every weapon, and even carry out missions to destroy enemy targets. The only way for an enemy to counteract such a force is, of course, with their own nanotechnology. The point is that nanotechnology-based weapons will one day make larger weapons obsolete.

Nanobots will also expand our experiences and our capabilities by providing fully immersive, totally convincing virtual reality. They will take up positions in close proximity to every interneuronal connection of our sensory organs (e.g., eyes, ears, and skin). We already have the technology that enables electronic devices to communicate with neurons in both directions, and it requires no direct physical contact with the neurons. For example, scientists at the Max Planck Institute have developed "neuron transistors" that can detect the firing of a nearby neuron or, alternatively, can cause a nearby neuron to fire, or suppress it from firing.[21] This amounts to two-way communication between neurons and the electronically based neuron transistors. The institute scientists demonstrated their invention by controlling the movement of a living leech from their computer.

When we want to experience real reality, the nanobots just stay in position (in the capillaries) and do nothing. If we want to enter virtual reality, they suppress all of the inputs coming from the real senses and replace them with the signals that would be appropriate for the virtual environment. You (i.e., your brain) could decide to cause your muscles and limbs to move as you normally would, but the nanobots would intercept these interneuronal signals, suppress your real limbs from moving, and instead cause your virtual limbs to move and provide the appropriate reorientation in the virtual environment.

The primary limitation of nanobot-based virtual reality at this time is only that it's not yet feasible in size and cost. One day, however, the web will provide a panoply of virtual environments to explore. Some will be re-creations of real places; others will be fanciful environments that have no "real" counterpart. Some will be impossible in the physical world, perhaps because they violate the laws of physics. We will be able to "go" to these virtual environments by ourselves, or we will meet other people there, both real people and simulated people. Of course, ultimately there won't be a clear distinction between the two. By 2030, going to a website will mean entering a full-immersion virtual reality environment. In addition to encompassing all of the senses, some of these shared environments will include emotional overlays, as the nanobots will be capable of triggering the neurological correlates of emotions, sexual pleasure, and other derivatives of our sensory experience and mental reactions. In the same way that people today beam their lives from webcams in their bedrooms, "experience beamers" circa 2030 will beam their entire flow of sensory experiences and, if so desired, their emotions and other secondary reactions. We'll be able to plug in (by going to the appropriate website) and experience other people's lives, as in the movie *Being John Malkovich*. We will be able to archive particularly interesting experiences and relive them at any time.

We won't need to wait until 2030 to experience shared virtual-reality environments, though, at least for the visual and auditory senses. Full-immersion visual-auditory environments will be available by the end of this decade, with images written directly onto our retinas by our eyeglasses and contact lenses. All of the electronics for computation, image reconstruction, and a very high bandwidth wireless connection to the Internet will be embedded in our glasses and woven into our clothing, so computers as distinct objects will disappear.

It's not just the virtual world that will benefit from ubiquitous application of nanobots and fully realized nanotechnology. Portable manufacturing systems will be able to produce virtually any physical product from information for pennies a pound, thereby providing for our physical needs at almost no cost. Nanobots will be able to reverse the environmental destruction left by the first industrial revolution. Nanoengineered fuel cells and solar cells will provide clean energy. Nanobots in our physical bodies will destroy pathogens and cancer cells, repair DNA, and reverse the ravages of aging.

These technologies will become so integral to our health and well-being that we will eventually become indistinguishable from our machine support systems. In fact, in my view, the most significant implication of the development of nanotechnology and related advanced technologies of the twenty-first century will be the merger of biological and nonbiological intelligence. First, it is important to point out that well before the end of the twenty-first century, thinking on nonbiological substrates will dominate. Biological thinking is stuck at 1026 calculations per second (for all biological human brains), and that figure will not appreciably change, even with bioengineering changes to our genome.

Nonbiological intelligence, on the other hand, is growing at a double exponential rate and will vastly exceed biological intelligence well before the middle of this century. In my view, however, this nonbiological intelligence should still be considered human, since it is fully derivative of the human-machine civilization. The merger of these two worlds of intelligence is not merely a merger of biological and nonbiological thinking media but, more importantly, one of method and organization of thinking.

Nanobot technology will be able to expand our minds in virtually any imaginable way. Our brains today are relatively fixed in design. Although we do add patterns of interneuronal connections and neurotransmitter concentrations as a normal part of the learning process, the current overall capacity of the human brain is highly constrained, restricted to a mere trillion connections. Brain implants based on massively distributed intelligent nanobots will ultimately expand our memories a trillionfold, and otherwise vastly improve all of our sensory, pattern recognition, and cognitive abilities. Since the nanobots will be communicating with each other over a wireless local area network, they will be able to create any set of new neural connections, break existing connections (by suppressing neural firing), and create new hybrid biological-nonbiological networks, as well as add vast new nonbiological networks.

Using nanobots as brain extenders will be a significant improvement over surgically installed neural implants, which are beginning to be used today (e.g., ventral posterior nucleus, subthalamic nucleus, and ventral lateral thalamus neural implants to counteract Parkinson's disease and tremors from other neurological disorders; cochlear implants; and the like). Nanobots will be introduced without surgery, essentially just by injecting or even swallowing them. They can all be directed to leave, so the process is easily reversible. They are programmable, in that they can provide virtual reality one minute and a variety of brain extensions the next. They can change their configuration and alter their software. Perhaps most importantly, they are massively distributed and therefore can take up billions or trillions of positions throughout the brain, whereas a surgically introduced neural implant can be placed in only one or at most a few locations.

...AND DANGERS

Needless to say, we have already experienced technology's downside. One hundred million people were killed in two world wars during the last century — a scale of mortality made possible by technology. The crude technologies of the first industrial revolution have crowded out many of the species on our planet that existed a century ago. Our centralized technologies (e.g., buildings, cities, airplanes, and power plants) are demonstrably insecure.

The NBC (nuclear, biological, and chemical) technologies of warfare were all used, or threatened to be used, in our recent past.[22] The far more powerful GNR technologies pose what philosopher of science Nick Bostrom calls "existential risks," referring to potential threats to the viability of human civilization itself.[23]

If we manage to get past the concerns about genetically altered designer pathogens, followed by self-replicating entities created through nanotechnology, we will next encounter robots whose intelligence will rival and ultimately exceed our own. Such robots may make great assistants, but who's to say that we can count on them to remain reliably friendly to mere humans?

In my view, "strong AI" (artificial intelligence at human levels and beyond) promises to continue the exponential gains of human civilization. But the dangers are also more profound precisely because of this amplification of intelligence. Intelligence is inherently impossible to control, so the various strategies that have been devised to control nanotechnology won't work for strong AI. There have been discussions and proposals to guide AI development toward "friendly AI."[24] These are useful for discussion, but it is impossible to devise strategies today that will absolutely ensure that future AI embodies human ethics and values.

RELINQUISHMENT

In his *Wired* essay and subsequent presentations, Bill Joy eloquently describes the plagues of centuries past and how new self-replicating technologies, such as mutant bioengineered pathogens and "nanobots" run amok, may bring back long-forgotten pestilence. Of course, as Joy graciously acknowledges, it has also been technological advances, such as antibiotics and improved sanitation, that have freed us from the prevalence of such plagues. Suffering in the world continues and demands our steadfast attention. Should we tell the millions of people afflicted with cancer and other devastating conditions that we are canceling the development of all bioengineered treatments because there is a risk that these same technologies may someday be used for malevolent purposes?

Relinquishment is Bill's most controversial recommendation and personal commitment. I do feel that relinquishment at the right levels is part of a responsible and constructive response to these genuine perils. The issue, however, is exactly this: at what level are we to relinquish technology?

Ted Kaczynski would have us renounce all of it.[25] This, in my view, is neither desirable nor feasible, and the futility of such a position is only underscored by the senselessness of Kaczynski's deplorable tactics. There are other voices, less reckless than Kaczynski, who are nonetheless arguing for broad-based relinquishment of technology. The environmentalist Bill McKibben takes the position that "environmentalists must now grapple squarely with the idea of a world that has enough wealth and enough technological capability, and should not pursue more."[26] In my view, this position ignores the extensive suffering that remains in the human world, which we will be in a position to alleviate through continued technological progress.

Another level of relinquishment, one recommended by Joy, would be to forgo certain fields — nanotechnology, for example — that might be regarded as too dangerous. But such sweeping strokes of relinquishment are equally untenable. As I pointed out above, nanotechnology is simply the inevitable end result of the persistent trend toward miniaturization that pervades all of technology. It is far from a single centralized effort, but is being pursued by a myriad of projects with many diverse goals.

One observer wrote:

A further reason why industrial society cannot be reformed … is that modern technology is a unified system in which all parts are dependent on one another. You can't get rid of the "bad" parts of technology and retain only the "good" parts. Take modern medicine, for example. Progress in medical science depends on progress in chemistry, physics, biology, computer science and other fields. Advanced medical treatments require expensive, high-tech equipment that can be made available only by a technologically progressive, economically rich society. Clearly you can't have much progress in medicine without the whole technological system and everything that goes with it.

The observer, again, is Ted Kaczynski.[27] Although one will properly resist Kaczynski as an authority, I believe he is correct on the deeply entangled nature of the benefits and risks. He and I clearly part company on our overall assessment of the relative balance between the two, however. Bill Joy and I have debated this issue both publicly and privately, and we both believe that technology will and should progress and that we need to be actively concerned with the dark side. If he and I disagree, it's on the granularity of relinquishment that is both feasible and desirable.

Abandonment of broad areas of technology would only push them underground, where development would continue unimpeded by ethics and regulation. In such a situation, it would be the less stable, less responsible practitioners (e.g., terrorists) who would have all the expertise. I do think that relinquishment at the right level needs to be part of our ethical response to the dangers of twenty-first-century technologies. One constructive example is the ethical guideline proposed by the Foresight Institute, founded by nanotechnology pioneer Eric Drexler, along with Christine Peterson, that nanotechnologists agree to relinquish the development of physical entities that can self-replicate in a natural environment.[28] Another is a ban on self-replicating physical entities that contain their own codes for self-replication. In what nanotechnologist Ralph Merkle calls the "broadcast architecture," such entities would have to obtain these codes from a centralized secure server, which would guard against undesirable replication.[29] I discuss these guidelines further below.

The broadcast architecture is impossible in the biological world, so it represents at least one way in which nanotechnology can be made safer than biotechnology. In other ways, nanotechnology is potentially more dangerous because nanobots can be physically stronger, and more intelligent, than protein-based entities. It will eventually be possible to combine the two by having nanotechnology provide the codes within biological entities (replacing DNA), in which case biological entities will be able to use the much safer broadcast architecture.

As responsible technologists, our ethics should include such "fine-grained" relinquishment among our professional ethical guidelines. Protections must also include oversight by regulatory bodies, the development of technology-specific "immune" responses, and computer-assisted surveillance by law enforcement organizations. Many people are not aware that our intelligence agencies already use advanced technologies such as automated word spotting to monitor a substantial flow of telephone conversations. As we go forward, balancing our cherished rights of privacy with our need to be protected from the malicious use of powerful twenty-first-century technologies will be one of many profound challenges. This is one reason such issues as an encryption "trap door" (in which law enforcement authorities would have access to otherwise secure information) and the FBI's Carnivore email-snooping system have been controversial.[30]

We can take a small measure of comfort from how our society has dealt with one recent technological challenge. There exists today a new form of fully non-biological self-replicating entity that did not exist just a few decades ago: the computer virus. When this form of destructive intruder first appeared, strong concerns were voiced that as these software pathogens became more sophisticated, they would have the potential to destroy the computer network medium they live in. Yet the "immune system" that has evolved in response to this challenge has been largely effective. Although destructive self-replicating software entities do cause damage from time to time, the injury is but a small fraction of the benefit we receive from the computers and communication links that harbor them. No one would suggest we do away with computers, local area networks, and the Internet because of software viruses.

One might counter that computer viruses do not have the lethal potential of biological viruses or of destructive nanotechnology. This is not always the case; we rely on software to monitor patients in critical care units, to fly and land airplanes, to guide intelligent weapons in wartime, and to perform other "mission-critical" tasks. To the extent that this assertion is true, however, it only strengthens my argument. The fact that computer viruses are not usually deadly to humans only means that more people are willing to create and release them. It also means that our response to the danger is that much less intense. Conversely, when it comes to self-replicating entities that are potentially lethal on a large scale, our response on all levels will be vastly more serious, as we have seen since September 11.

THE DEVELOPMENT OF DEFENSIVE
TECHNOLOGIES AND THE IMPACT OF
REGULATION

Bill Joy's *Wired* treatise is effective because he paints a picture of future dangers as if they were released on today's unprepared world. The reality is that the sophistication and power of our defensive technologies and knowledge will grow along with the dangers. When we have "gray goo" (unrestrained nanobot replication), we will also have "blue goo" ("police" nanobots that combat the "bad" nanobots). The story of the twenty-first century has not yet been written, so we cannot say with assurance that we will successfully avoid all misuse. But the surest way to prevent the development of defensive technologies would be to relinquish the pursuit of knowledge in broad areas. We have been able to largely control harmful software virus replication because the requisite knowledge is widely available to responsible practitioners. Attempts to restrict this knowledge would have created a far less stable situation. Responses to new challenges would have been far slower, and the balance would have likely shifted toward the more destructive applications (e.g., software viruses).

As we compare the success we have had in controlling engineered software viruses to the coming challenge of controlling engineered biological viruses, we are struck with one salient difference: the software industry is almost completely unregulated. The same is obviously not true for biotechnology. We require scientists developing defensive technologies to follow the existing regulations, which slow down the innovation process at every step. A bioterrorist, however, does not need to put his "innovations" through the FDA. Moreover, under existing regulations and ethical standards, it is impossible to test defenses against bioterrorist agents. Extensive discussion is already under way regarding modifying these regulations to allow for animal models and simulations, since human trials are infeasible.

For reasons I have articulated above, stopping these technologies is not feasible, and pursuit of such broad forms of relinquishment will only distract us from the vital task in front of us. It is quite clearly a race. There is simply no alternative. We cannot relinquish our way out of this challenge. In the software field, defensive technologies have remained a step ahead of offensive ones. With the extensive regulation in the medical field slowing down innovation at each stage, we cannot have the same confidence with regard to the abuse of biotechnology.

In the current environment, when one person dies in gene therapy trials, research can be severely restricted.[31] There is a legitimate need to make biomedical research as safe as possible, but our balancing of risks is completely off. The millions of people who desperately need the advances that will result from gene therapy and other breakthrough biotechnologies appear to carry little political weight against a handful of well-publicized casualties from the inevitable risks of progress.

This equation will become even more stark when we consider the emerging dangers of bioengineered pathogens. What is needed is a change in public attitude in terms of tolerance for needed risk.

Hastening defensive technologies is absolutely vital to our security. We need to streamline regulatory procedures to achieve this, and we also need to greatly increase our investment in defensive technologies explicitly. In the biotechnology field, this means the rapid development of antiviral medications. We will not have time to develop specific countermeasures for each new challenge that comes along. We are close to developing more generalized antiviral technologies, and these need to be accelerated.

I have addressed here the issue of biotechnology because that is the threshold and challenge that we now face. As the threshold for nanotechnology comes closer, we will then need to invest specifically in the development of defensive technologies in that area, including the creation of a nanotechnology-based immune system. Bill Joy and other observers have pointed out that such an immune system would itself be a danger because of the potential of "autoimmune" reactions (i.e., the immune system using its powers to attack the world it is supposed to be defending).[32]

This observation is not a compelling reason to avoid the creation of an immune system, however. No one would argue that humans would be better off without an immune system because of the possibility of autoimmune diseases. Although the immune system can itself be a danger, humans would not last more than a few weeks (barring extraordinary efforts at isolation) without one. The development of a technological immune system for nanotechnology will happen even without explicit efforts to create one. We have effectively done this with regard to software viruses. We created a software virus immune system not through a formal grand design, but rather through our incremental responses to each new challenge and through the development of heuristic algorithms for early detection. We can expect the same thing will happen as challenges from nanotechnology-based dangers emerge. The point for public policy will be to specifically invest in these defensive technologies.

It is premature to develop specific defensive nanotechnologies today, since we can have only a general idea of what we are trying to defend against. It would be similar to the engineering world creating defenses against software viruses before the first virus had been created. There is already fruitful dialogue and discussion on anticipating these issues, however, and significantly expanded investment in these efforts is to be encouraged.

As one example, as I mentioned above, the Foresight Institute has devised a set of ethical standards and strategies for ensuring the development of safe nano-technology.[33] These guidelines include:

- Artificial replicators must not be capable of replication in a natural, uncontrolled environment.

- Evolution within the context of a self-replicating manufacturing system is discouraged.

- MNT (molecular nanotechnology) designs should specifically limit proliferation and provide traceability of any replicating systems.

- Distribution of molecular manufacturing development capability should be restricted, whenever possible, to responsible actors that have agreed to the guidelines. No such restriction need apply to end products of the development process.

Other strategies proposed by the Foresight Institute include:

- Replication should require materials not found in the natural environment.

- Manufacturing (replication) should be separated from the functionality of end products. Manufacturing devices can create end products but should not be able to replicate themselves, and end products should have no replication capabilities.

- Replication should require codes that are encrypted and time-limited. (The broadcast architecture mentioned earlier is an example.)

These guidelines and strategies are likely to be effective for preventing accidental release of dangerous self-replicating nanotechnology entities. But the intentional design and release of such entities is a more complex and challenging problem. A sufficiently determined and destructive opponent could possibly defeat each of these layers of protections. Take, for example, the broadcast architecture. When properly designed, each entity is unable to replicate without first obtaining replication codes. These codes are not passed on from one replication generation to the next. A modification to such a design could bypass the destruction of the codes, however, and thereby pass them on to the next generation. To counteract that possibility, it has been recommended that the memory for the replication codes be limited to only a subset of the full code so that insufficient memory exists to pass the full set of codes along. But this guideline could be defeated by expanding the size of the replication code memory to incorporate the entire code. Another suggestion is to encrypt the codes and build protections such as time limits into the decryption systems. We can see how easy it has been to defeat protections against unauthorized replications of intellectual property such as music files, however. Once replication codes and protective layers are stripped away, the information can be replicated without these restrictions. My point is not that protection is impossible. Rather, we need to realize that any level of protection will only work to a certain level of sophistication. The meta-lesson here is that we will need to place society's highest priority during the twenty-first century on continuing to advance defensive technologies and on keeping them one or more steps ahead of destructive technologies. We have seen analogies to this in many areas, including technologies for national defense as well as our largely successful efforts to combat software viruses.

The broadcast architecture won't protect us against abuses of strong AI. The barriers of the broadcast architecture rely on the nanoengineered entities' lacking the intelligence to overcome the built-in restrictions. By definition, intelligent entities have the cleverness to easily overcome such barriers. Inherently, there will be no absolute protection other than dominance by friendly AI. Although the argument is subtle, I believe that maintaining an open system for incremental scientific and technological progress, in which each step is subject to market *acceptance*, will provide the most constructive environment for technology to embody widespread human values. Attempts to control these technologies in dark government programs, along with inevitable underground development, would create an unstable environment in which the dangerous applications would likely become dominant.

One profound trend already well under way that will provide greater stability is the movement from centralized technologies to distributed ones, and from the real world to the virtual world discussed above. Centralized technologies involve an aggregation of resources such as people (e.g., cities and buildings), energy (e.g., nuclear power plants, liquid natural gas and oil tankers, and energy pipelines), transportation (e.g., airplanes and trains), and other resources. Centralized technologies are subject to disruption and disaster. They also tend to be inefficient, wasteful, and harmful to the environment.

Distributed technologies, on the other hand, tend to be flexible, efficient, and relatively benign in their environmental effects. The quintessential distributed technology is the Internet. Despite concerns about viruses, these information-based pathogens are mere nuisances. The Internet is essentially indestructible. If any hub or channel goes down, the information simply routes around it. The Internet is remarkably resilient, a quality that continues to increase with its continued exponential growth.

In energy, we need to move rapidly toward the opposite end of the spectrum of contemporary energy sources, away from the extremely concentrated energy installations we now depend on. In one example of a trend in the right direction, Integrated Fuel Cell Technologies is pioneering microscopic fuel cells that use microelectromechanical systems (MEMS) technology. The fuel cells are manufactured like electronic chips but are actually batteries with an energy-to-size ratio vastly exceeding conventional technology. Ultimately, forms of energy along these lines could power everything from our cell phones to our cars and homes, and would not be subject to disaster or disruption.

As these technologies develop, our need to aggregate people in large buildings and cities will diminish and people will spread out, living where they want and gathering together in virtual reality.

But we don't need to look past today to see the intertwined promise and peril of technological advancement. If we imagine describing the dangers that exist today to people who lived a couple of hundred years ago, they would think it mad to take such risks. On the other hand, how many people in the year 2000 would really want to go back to the short, brutish, disease-filled, poverty-stricken, disaster-prone lives that 99 percent of the human race struggled through a couple of centuries ago?[34] We may romanticize the past, but up until fairly recently, most of humanity lived extremely fragile lives where one all-too-common misfortune could spell disaster. Two hundred years ago, life expectancy for females in the record-holding country (Sweden) was roughly thirty-five years, compared to the longest life expectancy today — almost eighty-five years — enjoyed by Japanese women. Life expectancy for males was roughly thirty-three years to the current seventy-nine years in the record-holding countries.[35] It took half the day to prepare the evening meal, and hard labor characterized most human activity. There were no social safety nets. Substantial portions of our species still live in this precarious way, which is at least one reason to continue technological progress and the economic enhancement that accompanies it.

People often go through three stages in considering future technologies: awe and wonderment at their potential to overcome age-old problems; a sense of dread at the new set of grave dangers that accompany the new technologies; and, finally (and hopefully), the realization that the only viable and responsible path is to set a careful course that can reap the benefits while managing the dangers.

Technology will remain a double-edged sword. It represents vast power to be used for all humankind's purposes. We have no choice but to work hard to apply these quickening technologies to advance our human values, despite what often appears to be a lack of consensus on what those values should be.

ENDNOTES

1. In the 1960s, the U.S. government conducted an experiment in which they asked three recently graduated physics students to build a nuclear weapon using only publicly available information. The result was successful; the three students built one in about three years (www.pimall.com/nais/nl/n.nukes.html). Plans for how to build an atomic bomb are available on the Internet and have been published in book form by a national laboratory. In 2002, the British Ministry of Defense released measurements, diagrams, and precise details on bomb-building to the Public Record Office, since removed (www.news.bbc.co.uk/1/hi/uk/1932702.stm).

2. *Free Speech in America*, ABC News, March 23, 2000, www.abcnews.go.com/onair/abcnewsspecials/transcripts/Stossel_000323_freespeech_trans.html.

3. The web contains extensive information, including military manuals, on how to build bombs, weapons, and explosives. Some of this information is erroneous, but accurate information on these topics continues to be accessible despite efforts to remove it. In June 1997 Congress passed an amendment (the Feinstein Amendment, SP 419) to a Defense Department appropriations bill banning the dissemination of instructions on building bombs. See Helmenstine, Anne Marie, "How to Build a Bomb," www.chemistry.about.com/library/weekly/aa021003a.htm, posted February 10, 2003. Information on toxic industrial chemicals is widely available on the web and in libraries, as is information and tools for cultivating bacteria and viruses. Techniques for creating computer viruses and hacking into computers and networks are also widely available on the Internet. Note that it is my policy not to provide specific examples of such information, since it might be helpful to destructive individuals and groups. I realize that even stating the availability of such information has this potential, but I feel that the benefit of open dialogue about this issue outweighs this concern. Moreover, the widespread availability of this type of information has been widely discussed in the media and other venues.

4. Ray Kurzweil, *The Age of Intelligent Machines* (Cambridge, MA: MIT Press, 1990).

5. Ken Alibek, *Biohazard* (New York: Dell Publishing, 1999).

6. Ray Kurzweil, *The Age of Spiritual Machines* (New York: Viking, 1999).

7. John Searle, "I Married a Computer," and Ray Kurzweil, "Locked in His Chinese Room," in Jay Richards, et al., *Are We Spiritual Machines?: Ray Kurzweil vs. the Critics of Strong AI* (Seattle, WA: Discovery Institute, 2002), www.kurzweilai.net/meme/frame.html?main=/articles/art0502.html.

8. This panel resulted in a book: Jay Richards, et al., *Are We Spiritual Machines?: Ray Kurzweil vs. the Critics of Strong AI* (Seattle, WA: Discovery Institute, 2002), www.kurzweilai.net/meme/frame.html?m=19. The book includes point-counterpoint essays by John Searle, Thomas Ray, Michael Denton, William A. Dembski, and George Gilder, and responses by Ray Kurzweil.

9. Bill Joy, "Why the Future Doesn't Need Us." *Wired* (April 2000), www.wired.com/wired/archive/8.04/joy.html.

10. Handbooks on gene splicing such as A. J. Harwood, ed., *Basic DNA and RNA Protocols* (Totowa, NJ.: Humana Press, 1996), along with reagents and kits required to do gene splicing, are generally available. Even if access to these materials were limited in the West, a large number of Russian companies could provide equivalent materials.

11. The Internet, as measured by the number of nodes, was doubling every year during the 1980s, but was only tens of thousands of nodes in 1985. It grew to tens of millions of nodes by 1995.

12. Intel Corporation, "Expanding Moore's Law," www.intel.com/labs/eml, accessed 2003.

13. Electromechanical card-reading equipment was used in the 1890 U.S. census. Alan Turing and his colleagues built the first special-purpose computer out of electromagnetic relays in 1942. Vacuum tubes were used in the 1952 computer that predicted the election of Eisenhower, the first time the networks had used a computer to predict a presidential election. Computers based on discrete transistors were used in the space flights during the 1960s. Integrated circuits began to be used in the late 1960s.

14. Silicon nanowires and carbon nanotubes are now the candidate nanoscale technologies that could begin to replace standard transistors in the decade after 2010. Because nanotubes are small, a large number can be packed in a given space and will enable very high-density processors and memory-storage devices. IBM (www.ibm. com/news/2001/04/27.phtml) and other institutions are currently researching this technology. For a survey of recent developments in nanotubes and other recent breakthroughs, see "Top KurzweilAI.net News of 2002," www.kurzweilai.net/ meme/frame.html?main=articles/arto550.html, posted February 5, 2003.

15. These trends are discussed in more detail in Ray Kurzweil, "The Law of Accelerating Returns," www.kurzweilai.net/law, posted March 7, 2001.

16. Based on U.S. Department of Commerce Bureau of Economic Analysis data, www.bea.doc.gov/.

17. Despite these weaknesses in the productivity statistical methods, the gains in productivity are now reaching the steep part of the exponential curve. Labor productivity grew at 1.6 percent per year until 1994, then rose at 2.4 percent per year, and is now growing even more rapidly. In the quarter ending July 30, 2000, labor productivity grew at 5.3 percent. Manufacturing productivity grew at 4.4 percent annually from 1995 to 1999, durables manufacturing at 6.5 percent per year.

18. Steven E. Landsburg, "I've Got to Admit It's Getting Better." *Slate* (February 10, 2000), slate.msn.com/id/74544.

19. Robert A. Freitas, Jr., *Nanomedicine series.* (Georgetown, TX: Landes Bioscience, 1999), www.nanomedicine.com.

20. Thomas Hoffman, "Smart Dust." *Computerworld* (March 24. 2003).

21. Phillip F. Schewe, and Ben Stein, "Physics News Update." *The American Institute of Physics Bulletin of Physics News* (August 7, 1995), www.aip.org/enewsphysnews/ 1995/physnews.236.htm.

22. Steve Bowman, and Helit Barel, *Weapons of Mass Destruction — The Terrorist Threat.* Washington, D.C.: Congressional Research Service, 1999, www.cnie.org/nle/ crsreports/international/inter-75.pdf.

23. Nick D. Bostrom, "Existential Risks: Analyzing Human Extinction Scenarios and Related Hazards," www.kurzweilai.net/meme/frame.html?main=/articles/arto194. html, posted May 29, 2001.

24. Eliezer S. Yudkowsky, "What Is Friendly AI?" www.kurzweilai.net/meme/frame. html?main=/articles/art0172.html, posted May 3, 2001.

25. Ted Kaczynski, "The Unabomber's Manifesto," www.kurzweilai.net/meme/frame. html?main=/articles/art0182.html, posted May 14, 2001.

26. Bill McKibben, "Are We Becoming an Endangered Species? Technology and Ethics in the 21st Century," www.kurzweilai.net/meme/frame.html?main=/articles/ art0351.html, posted November 8, 2001; Bill McKibben, *Enough: Staying Human in an Engineered Age* (New York: Times/Holt, 2003).

27. Kaczynski, "The Unabomber's Manifesto."

28. Foresight Institute and the Institute for Molecular Manufacturing (IMM), *Foresight Guidelines on Molecular Nanotechnology,* www.foresight.org/guidelines/current.html, accessed February 21, 1999; Christine Peterson, "Molecular Manufacturing: Social Implications of Advanced Nanotechnology," www.kurzweilai.net/meme/frame. html?main=articles/art0557.html, posted April 9, 2003; Chris Phoenix, and Mike

Treder, "Safe Utilization of Advanced Nanotechnology," www.kurzweilai.net/meme/frame.html?main=/articles/art0547.html, posted January 28, 2003.

29. Ralph C. Merkle, "Self-Replicating Systems and Low-Cost Manufacturing." In M. E. Welland, and J. K. Gimzewski, eds., *The Ultimate Limits of Fabrication and Measurement* (Dordrecht, The Netherlands: Kluwer, 1994), pp. 25–32, www.zyvex.com/nanotech/selfRepNATO.html.

30. "Carnivore Diagnostic Tool," www.fbi.gov/hq/lab/carnivore/carnivore.htm.

31. Larry Thompson, "Human Gene Therapy: Harsh Lessons, High Hopes." *FDA Consumer* (September–October 2000), www.fda.gov/fdac/features/2000/500_gene.html.

32. Joy, "Why the Future Doesn't Need Us."

33. Foresight and IMM, *Foresight Guidelines on Molecular Nanotechnology.*

34. George DeWan, "Diary of a Colonial Housewife." *Newsday.* [EDI] www.newsday.com/extras/lihistory/3/hs331a.htm.

35. Jim Oeppen, and James W. Vaupel, "Broken Limits to Life Expectancy." *Science* 296 (5570):1029–1031 (May 10, 2002). Female life expectancy in the record-holding country has risen linearly for 160 years at almost three months per year. Extrapolating backward from 1840 to 1800, female life expectancy would be 35. "The gap between female and male levels has grown from 2 to 6 years."

PART IV

Contemporary Technological Dilemmas: Climate Change

This and the following two parts of *Technology and the Future* are devoted to current issues, problems, and opportunities involving science and technology as causes, potential solutions or both. Some of these issues are being addressed — or should be addressed — by governments and public policies. Others are matters that are best addressed by individuals or within families. Some are international in scope; others are more specific to the United States. All are having or soon could have wide-ranging impacts on society. Part IV deals with climate change. Parts V and VI, are devoted to life science issues and information and communications technology (ICT), respectively.

A great deal has been written and said about climate change in recent years. There are those who still regard the question of whether the earth is warming (or if it is warming, whether the warming is caused by human activities) as unsettled. Indeed, some even claim the whole business is a fraud perpetrated on the public by some vast conspiracy. Nevertheless, the overwhelming consensus among scientists and many policymakers throughout the United States and the international community is that the problem is real and that it must be dealt with effectively and soon lest the world face increasingly dire consequences. The selection included here as chapter 12 is a review of the scientific evidence that explains why climatologists are confident that human activities are causing the earth to warm and that the warming is a very serious problem. The authors are five scientists who participated in one of the working groups that wrote the 2007 report of the Nobel Prize-winning Intergovernmental Panel on Climate Change. This chapter is followed by a concise critique by one of the most respected dissenters from the scientific consensus. The author, a professor of meteorology at

147

M.I.T., believes that the mathematical models used by most climate experts are flawed, that they have been "tweaked" to maximize the appearance of warming and that apparent changes we are seeing in our climate are part of a natural cycle.

The authors of chapters 14 and 15 do not question the notion that the earth's climate is changing. Rather, they approach the phenomenon as a technological problem to be solved. The approach discussed (and questioned) in both of these articles is "geoengineering" — deploying technological systems on a planetary scale with the aim of intervening in the processes that are causing global temperatures to increase, sea levels to rise, and otherwise changing our climate. Geoengineering is a "technological fix," as proposed nearly half a century ago by Alvin Weinberg and discussed in chapter 4 of this book. If one of the geoengineering proposals were to be implemented successfully, it could address the climate problem without the need to make the kind of massive changes in human behavior that most alternative approaches would require. If the possibilities of geoengineering are substantial, however, so are the risks. The authors of chapter 14 focus primarily on the international political dimensions of the issue, systematically examining the pros and cons and possible ways in which geoengineering might play out. The author of chapter 15 generally feels that it is a bad idea and cites a long list of reasons. The cure, he believes, could well be worse than the disease.

12

The Science Behind Climate Change

WILLIAM COLLINS, ROBERT COLMAN, JAMES HAYWOOD, MARTIN R. MANNING, AND PHILIP MOTE

In December 2007, the Nobel Peace Prize was awarded jointly to former U.S. Vice President Al Gore and the Intergovernmental Panel on Climate Change (IPCC). Gore, whose film An Inconvenient Truth *helped raise public awareness of climate change, received the lion's share of media attention, but it was the IPCC that sorted through the vast amount of data that has come out of climate research to determine what is happening to the Earth's climate, what the causes are, and where things are headed.*

It was for this purpose — to conduct an authoritative assessment of the available scientific and technical knowledge about climate change — that two United Nations bodies (the World Meteorological Organization and the U.N. Environment Program) established the IPCC in 1988. Hundreds of scientists from more than 130 countries have been involved in the IPCC's work. Over the past two decades, as evidence of climate change has accumulated, the IPCC's reports have reflected increasing certainty about the warming trend and its causes. The Fourth Assessment Report, *published in 2007, states that warming of the Earth's climate is unequivocal and that it is almost certainly caused by human activity. Working Group I, which prepared the "Summary for Policymakers" on which this chapter is based, involved over 600 authors from 40 countries and hundreds of reviewers. Although the reputations of the IPCC and some of its participants were somewhat tarnished by the publicity surrounding the November 2009 release of e-mails stolen from a server at the University of East Anglia (UK) known as "climategate," the major conclusions of the* Fourth Assessment Report *were not brought into question. The* Fifth Assessment Report *is now underway with an expected completion date of 2014.*

The authors were among the participants in Working Group I. William Collins is a professor in residence in the Department of Earth and Planetary Science at the University of California, Berkeley, and a senior scientist and head of the Climate Science Department at Lawrence Berkeley National Laboratory. Robert Colman is a senior research scientist in the Climate Dynamics Group at the Australian Bureau of Meteorology Research Centre in Melbourne. James Haywood is a research fellow in the Observation Based Research Group and the Chemistry, Climate, and Ecosystem Group at the Met Office in Exeter, England. Martin R. Manning was director of the IPCC Working Group I Support Unit at the National Oceanic and Atmospheric Administration (NOAA) Earth System Research Laboratory in Boulder, Colorado. He is currently professor and research fellow in climate change at Victoria University of Wellington, New Zealand. Philip Mote is a research scientist at the University of Washington, in the Climate Impacts Group (CIG), and an affiliate professor in the Department of Atmospheric Sciences. He was formerly the Washington State Climatologist. The full report of the IPCC, including the "Summary for Policymakers," is available online on the IPCC web site: http://www.ipcc.ch/. *Information about the* Fifth Assessment Report *can also be found there.*

F or a scientist studying climate change, "eureka" moments are unusually rare. Instead progress is generally made by a painstaking piecing together of evidence from every new temperature measurement, satellite sounding or climate-model experiment. Data get checked and rechecked, ideas tested over and over again. Do the observations fit the predicted changes? Could there be some alternative explanation? Good climate scientists, like all good scientists, want to ensure that the highest standards of proof apply to everything they discover.

And the evidence of change *has* mounted as climate records have grown longer, as our understanding of the climate system has improved and as climate models have become ever more reliable. Over the past 20 years, evidence that humans are affecting the climate has accumulated inexorably, and with it has come ever greater certainty across the scientific community in the reality of recent climate change and the potential for much greater change in the future. This increased certainty is starkly reflected in the latest report of the Intergovernmental Panel on Climate Change (IPCC), the fourth in a series of assessments of the state of knowledge on the topic, written and reviewed by hundreds of scientists worldwide.

The panel released a condensed version of the first part of the report, on the physical science basis of climate change, in February 2007. Called the "Summary for Policymakers," it delivered to policymakers and ordinary people alike an unambiguous message: scientists are more confident than ever that humans have interfered with the climate and that further human-induced climate change is on the way. Although the report finds that some of these further changes are now inevitable, its analysis also confirms that the future, particularly in the longer term, remains largely in our hands — the magnitude of expected change depends on what humans choose to do about greenhouse gas emissions.

The physical science assessment focuses on four topics: drivers of climate change, changes observed in the climate system, understanding cause-and-effect relationships, and projection of future changes. Important advances in research into all these areas have occurred since the IPCC assessment in 2001. In the pages that follow, we lay out the key findings that document the extent of change and that point to the unavoidable conclusion that human activity is driving it.

DRIVERS OF CLIMATE CHANGE

Atmospheric concentrations of many gases — primarily carbon dioxide, methane, nitrous oxide and halocarbons (gases once used widely as refrigerants and spray propellants) — have increased because of human activities. Such gases trap thermal energy (heat) within the atmosphere by means of the well-known greenhouse effect, leading to global warming. The atmospheric concentrations of carbon dioxide, methane and nitrous oxide remained roughly stable for nearly 10,000 years, before the abrupt and rapidly accelerating increases of the past 200 years [*see right illustrations in box on page 155*]. Growth rates for concentrations of carbon dioxide have been faster in the past 10 years than over any 10-year period since continuous atmospheric monitoring began in the 1950s, with concentrations now roughly 35 percent above preindustrial levels (which can be determined from air bubbles trapped in ice cores). Methane levels are roughly two and a half times preindustrial levels, and nitrous oxide levels are around 20 percent higher.

How can we be sure that humans are responsible for these increases? Some greenhouse gases (most of the halocarbons, for example) have no natural source. For other gases, two important observations demonstrate human influence. First, the geographic differences in concentrations reveal that sources occur predominantly over land in the more heavily populated Northern Hemisphere. Second, analysis of isotopes, which can distinguish among sources of emissions, demonstrates that the majority of the increase in carbon dioxide comes from combustion of fossil fuels (coal, oil and natural gas). Methane and nitrous oxide increases derive from agricultural practices and the burning of fossil fuels.

Climate scientists use a concept called radiative forcing to quantify the effect of these increased concentrations on climate. Radiative forcing is the change that is caused in the global energy balance of the earth relative to preindustrial times. (Forcing is usually expressed as watts per square meter.) A positive forcing induces warming; a negative forcing induces cooling. We can determine the radiative forcing associated with the long-lived greenhouse gases fairly precisely, because we know their atmospheric concentrations, their spatial distribution and the physics of their interaction with radiation.

Climate change is not driven just by increased greenhouse gas concentrations; other mechanisms — both natural and human-induced — also play a part. Natural

---

B o x   12.1   Key Concepts

- Scientists are confident that humans have interfered with the climate and that further human-induced climate change is on the way.
- The principal driver of recent climate change is greenhouse gas emissions from human activities, primarily the burning of fossil fuels.
- The report of the Intergovernmental Panel on Climate Change places the probability that global warming has been caused by human activities at greater than 90 percent. The previous report, published in 2001, put the probability at higher than 66 percent.
- Although further changes in the world's climate are now inevitable, the future, particularly in the longer term, remains largely in our hands — the magnitude of expected change depends on what humans choose to do about greenhouse gas emissions.

---

drivers include changes in solar activity and large volcanic eruptions. The report identifies several additional significant human-induced forcing mechanisms — microscopic particles called aerosols, stratospheric and tropospheric ozone, surface albedo (reflectivity) and aircraft contrails — although the influences of these mechanisms are much less certain than those of greenhouse gases [*see left illustration in box on page 155*].

Investigators are least certain of the climatic influence of something called the aerosol cloud albedo effect, in which aerosols from human origins interact with clouds in complex ways and make the clouds brighter, reflecting sunlight back to space. Another source of uncertainty comes from the direct effect of aerosols from human origins: How much do they reflect and absorb sunlight directly as particles? Overall these aerosol effects promote cooling that could offset the warming effect of long-lived greenhouse gases to some extent. But by how much? Could it overwhelm the warming? Among the advances achieved since the 2001 IPCC report is that scientists have quantified the uncertainties associated with each individual forcing mechanism through a combination of many modeling and observational studies. Consequently, we can now confidently estimate the total human-induced component. Our best estimate is some 10 times larger than the best estimate of the natural radiative forcing caused by changes in solar activity.

This increased certainty of a net positive radiative forcing fits well with the observational evidence of warming discussed next. These forcings can be visualized as a tug-of-war, with positive forcings pulling the earth to a warmer climate and negative ones pulling it to a cooler state. The result is a no contest; we know the strength of the competitors better than ever before. The earth is being pulled to a warmer climate and will be pulled increasingly in this direction as the "anchorman" of greenhouse warming continues to grow stronger and stronger.

B o x 12.2   Jargon Buster

RADIATIVE FORCING, as used in the box on page 155, is the change in the energy balance of the earth from preindustrial times to the present.

LONG-LIVED GREENHOUSE GASES include carbon dioxide, methane, nitrous oxide and halocarbons. The observed increases in these gases are the result of human activity.

OZONE is a gas that occurs both in the earth's upper atmosphere and at ground level. At ground level ozone is an air pollutant. In the upper atmosphere, an ozone layer protects life on the earth from the sun's harmful ultraviolet rays.

SURFACE ALBEDO is the reflectivity of the earth's surface: a lighter surface, such as snow cover, reflects more solar radiation than a darker surface does.

AEROSOLS are airborne particles that come from both natural (dust storms, forest fires, volcanic eruptions) and man-made sources, such as the burning of fossil fuels.

CONTRAILS, or vapor trails, are condensation trails and artificial clouds made by the exhaust of aircraft engines.

TROPOSPHERE is the layer of the atmosphere close to the earth. It rises from sea level up to about 12 kilometers (7.5 miles).

STRATOSPHERE lies just above the troposphere and extends upward about 50 kilometers.

OBSERVED CLIMATE CHANGES

The many new or improved observational data sets that became available in time for the 2007 IPCC report allowed a more comprehensive assessment of changes than was possible in earlier reports. Observational records indicate that 11 of the past 12 years are the warmest since reliable records began around 1850. The odds of such warm years happening in sequence purely by chance are exceedingly small. Changes in three important quantities — global temperature, sea level and snow cover in the Northern Hemisphere [*see box on page 157*] — all show evidence of warming, although the details vary. The previous IPCC assessment reported a warming trend of 0.6 ± 0.2 degree Celsius over the period 1901 to 2000. Because of the strong recent warming, the updated trend over 1906 to 2005 is now 0.74 ± 0.18 degree C. Note that the 1956 to 2005 trend alone is 0.65 ± 0.15 degree C, emphasizing that the majority of twentieth century warming occurred in the past 50 years. The climate, of course, continues to vary around the increased averages, and extremes have changed consistently with these averages — frost days and cold days and nights have become less common, while heat waves and warm days and nights have become more common.

The properties of the climate system include not just familiar concepts of averages of temperature, precipitation, and so on but also the state of the ocean and the cryosphere (sea ice, the great ice sheets in Greenland and Antarctica, glaciers, snow, frozen ground, and ice on lakes and rivers). Complex interactions among different parts of the climate system are a fundamental part of climate change — for example, reduction in sea ice increases the absorption of heat by the ocean and the heat flow between the ocean and the atmosphere, which can also affect cloudiness and precipitation.

A large number of additional observations are broadly consistent with the observed warming and reflect a flow of heat from the atmosphere into other components of the climate system. Spring snow cover, which decreases in concert with rising spring temperatures in northern midlatitudes, dropped abruptly around 1988 and has remained low since. This drop is of concern because snow cover is important to soil moisture and water resources in many regions.

In the ocean, we clearly see warming trends, which decrease with depth, as expected. These changes indicate that the ocean has absorbed more than 80 percent of the heat added to the climate system: this heating is a major contributor to sea-level rise. Sea level rises because water expands as it is warmed and because water from melting glaciers and ice sheets is added to the oceans. Since 1993, satellite observations have permitted more precise calculations of global sea-level rise, now estimated to be 3.1 ± 0.7 millimeters per year over the period 1993 to 2003. Some previous decades displayed similarly fast rates, and longer satellite records will be needed to determine unambiguously whether sea-level rise is accelerating. Substantial reductions in the extent of Arctic sea ice since 1978 (2.7 ± 0.6 percent per decade in the annual average, 7.4 ± 2.4 percent per decade for summer), increases in permafrost temperatures, and reductions in glacial extent globally and in Greenland and Antarctic ice sheets have also been observed in recent decades. Unfortunately, many of these quantities were not well monitored until recent decades, so the starting points of their records vary.

Hydrological changes are broadly consistent with warming as well. Water vapor is the strongest greenhouse gas; unlike other greenhouse gases, it is controlled principally by temperature. It has generally increased since at least the 1980s. Precipitation is very variable locally but has increased in several large regions of the world, including eastern North and South America, northern Europe, and northern and central Asia. Drying has been observed in the Sahel, the Mediterranean, southern Africa and parts of southern Asia. Ocean salinity can act as a massive rain gauge. Near-surface waters of the oceans have generally freshened in middle and high latitudes, while they have become saltier in lower latitudes, consistent with changes in large-scale patterns of precipitation.

Reconstructions of past climate — paleoclimate — from tree rings and other proxies provide important additional insights into the workings of the climate system with and without human influence. They indicate that the warmth of the past half a century is unusual in at least the previous 1,300 years. The warmest period between A.D. 700 and 1950 was probably A.D. 950 to 1100, which was several tenths of a degree C cooler than the average temperature since 1980.

B o x 12.3   Influences on Climate

A tug-of-war between positive forcings (influences that cause the climate to grow warmer) and negative forcings (those that cause it to grow cooler) is a hands down "victory" for the predominantly human-induced forces that lead to warming (left graph). The dominant human-induced forcings are from the long-lived greenhouse gases in the atmosphere, whose concentrations have soared in the past 200 years or so (right graphs).

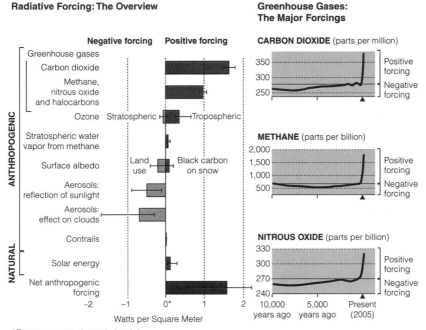

Zero represents the preindustrial energy balance.

Estimates for global averages of radioactive forcing in 2005 are shown for the major mechanisms. The black error bars indicate the level of certainty associated with each forcing: it is 90 percent likely that values lie within the error bars. The radioactive forcing of the greenhouse gases, for example, is quite certain, as opposed to the uncertainty associated with the aerosol effects. (Volcanic aerosols are not included in the graph because of their episodic nature.)

Carbon dioxide, methane and nitrous oxide concentrations of the past were derived from ice cores: those for recent times come from samples of the atmosphere. Large recent increases can be attributed to human activities.

ATTRIBUTION OF OBSERVED CHANGES

Although confidence is high both that human activities have caused a positive radiative forcing and that the climate has actually changed, can we confidently link the two? This is the question of attribution: Are human activities primarily responsible for observed climate changes, or is it possible they result from some other cause, such as some natural forcing or simply spontaneous variability within the climate system? The 2001 IPCC report concluded it was *likely* (more than 66 percent probable) that most of the warming since the mid-twentieth century was attributable to humans. The 2007 report goes significantly further, upping this to *very likely* (more than 90 percent probable).

The source of the extra confidence comes from a multitude of separate advances. For a start, observational records are now roughly five years longer, and the global temperature increase over this period has been largely consistent with IPCC projections of greenhouse gas–driven warming made in previous reports dating back to 1990. In addition, changes in more aspects of the climate have been considered, such as those in atmospheric circulation or in temperatures within the ocean. Such changes paint a consistent and now broadened picture of human intervention. Climate models, which are central to attribution studies, have also improved and are able to represent the current climate and that of the recent past with considerable fidelity. Finally, some important apparent inconsistencies noted in the observational record have been largely resolved since the last report.

The most important of these was an apparent mismatch between the instrumental surface temperature record (which showed significant warming over recent decades, consistent with a human impact) and the balloon and satellite atmospheric records (which showed little of the expected warming). Several new studies of the satellite and balloon data have now largely resolved this discrepancy — with consistent warming found at the surface and in the atmosphere.

An experiment with the real world that duplicated the climate of the twentieth century with constant (rather than increasing) greenhouse gases would be the ideal way to test for the cause of climate change, but such an experiment is of course impossible. So scientists do the next best thing: they simulate the past with climate models.

Two important advances since the last IPCC assessment have increased confidence in the use of models for both attribution and projection of climate changes. The first is the development of a comprehensive, closely coordinated ensemble of simulations from 18 modeling groups around the world for the historical and future evolution of the earth's climate. Using many models helps to quantify the effects of uncertainties in various climate processes on the range of model simulations. Although some processes are well understood and well represented by physical equations (the flow of the atmosphere and ocean or the propagation of sunlight and heat, for example), some of the most critical components of the climate system are less well understood, such as clouds, ocean eddies and transpiration by vegetation. Modelers approximate these components using simplified representations called parameterizations. The principal reason to develop a multimodel ensemble for the IPCC assessments is to understand how this lack of certainty affects attribution and prediction of climate change. The ensemble for the latest assessment is unprecedented in the number of models and experiments performed.

The second advance is the incorporation of more realistic representations of climate processes in the models. These processes include the behavior of atmospheric aerosols, the dynamics (movement) of sea ice, and the exchange of water

---

B o x 12.4   Observed Evidence

Observations of global average surface temperature, sea level and snow cover for the Northern Hemisphere in March and April document increased warming. Heavy black lines represent values averaged over a decade, with the gray shading indicating the range of uncertainty; dots show yearly values. All measures are relative to 1961–1990.

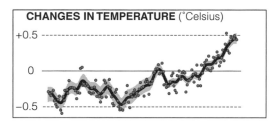

CHANGES IN TEMPERATURE (°Celsius)

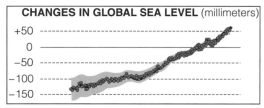

CHANGES IN GLOBAL SEA LEVEL (millimeters)

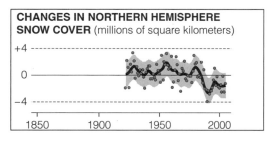

CHANGES IN NORTHERN HEMISPHERE
SNOW COVER (millions of square kilometers)

---

and energy between the land and the atmosphere. More models now include the major types of aerosols and the interactions between aerosols and clouds.

When scientists use climate models for attribution studies, they first run simulations with estimates of only "natural" climate influences over the past 100 years, such as changes in solar output and major volcanic eruptions. They then run models that include human-induced increases in greenhouse gases and aerosols. The results of such experiments are striking. Models using only natural forcings are unable to explain the observed global warming since the mid-twentieth century, whereas they can do so when they include anthropogenic factors in addition to natural ones. Large-scale *patterns* of temperature change are also most consistent between models and observations when all forcings are included.

Two patterns provide a fingerprint of human influence. The first is greater warming over land than ocean and greater warming at the surface of the sea than in the deeper layers. This pattern is consistent with greenhouse gas–induced warming by the overlying atmosphere: the ocean warms more slowly because of its large thermal inertia. The warming also indicates that a large amount of heat is being taken up by the ocean, demonstrating that the planet's energy budget has been pushed out of balance. A second pattern of change is that while the troposphere (the lower region of the atmosphere) has warmed, the stratosphere, just above it, has cooled. If solar changes provided the dominant forcing, warming would be expected in both atmospheric layers. The observed contrast, however, is just that expected from the combination of greenhouse gas increases and stratospheric ozone decreases. This collective evidence, when subjected to careful statistical analyses, provides much of the basis for the increased confidence that human influences are behind the observed global warming. Suggestions that cosmic rays could affect clouds, and thereby climate, have been based on correlations using limited records; they have generally not stood up when tested with additional data, and their physical mechanisms remain speculative.

What about at smaller scales? As spatial and temporal scales decrease, attribution of climate change becomes more difficult. This problem arises because natural small-scale temperature variations are less "averaged out" and thus more readily mask the change signal. Nevertheless, continued warming means the signal is emerging on smaller scales. The report has found that human activity is likely to have influenced temperature significantly down to the continental scale for all continents except Antarctica.

Human influence is discernible also in some extreme events such as unusually hot and cold nights and the incidence of heat waves. This does not mean, of course, that individual extreme events (such as the 2003 European heat wave) can be said to be simply "caused" by human-induced climate change — usually such events are complex, with many causes. But it does mean that human activities have, more likely than not, affected the *chances* of such events occurring.

PROJECTIONS OF FUTURE CHANGES

How will climate change over the twenty-first century? This critical question is addressed using simulations from climate models based on projections of future emissions of greenhouse gases and aerosols. The simulations suggest that, for greenhouse gas emissions at or above current rates, changes in climate will very likely be larger than the changes already observed during the twentieth century. Even if emissions were immediately reduced enough to stabilize greenhouse gas concentrations at current levels, climate change would continue for centuries. This inertia in the climate results from a combination of factors. They include the heat capacity of the world's oceans and the millennial timescales needed for the circulation to mix heat and carbon dioxide throughout the deep ocean and thereby come into equilibrium with the new conditions.

To be more specific, the models project that over the next 20 years, for a range of plausible emissions, the global temperature will increase at an average rate of about 0.2 degree C per decade, close to the observed rate over the past 30 years. About half of this near-term warming represents a "commitment" to future climate change arising from the inertia of the climate system response to current atmospheric concentrations of greenhouse gases.

The long-term warming over the twenty-first century, however, is strongly influenced by the future rate of emissions, and the projections cover a wide variety of scenarios, ranging from very rapid to more modest economic growth and from more to less dependence on fossil fuels. The best estimates of the increase in global temperatures range from 1.8 to 4.0 degrees C for the various emission scenarios, with higher emissions leading to higher temperatures. As for regional impacts, projections indicate with more confidence than ever before that these will mirror the *patterns* of change observed over the past 50 years (greater warming over land than ocean, for example) but that the *size* of the changes will be larger than they have been so far.

The simulations also suggest that the removal of excess carbon dioxide from the atmosphere by natural processes on land and in the ocean will become less efficient as the planet warms. This change leads to a higher percentage of emitted carbon dioxide remaining in the atmosphere, which then further accelerates global warming. This is an important positive feedback on the carbon cycle (the exchange of carbon compounds throughout the climate system). Although models agree that carbon-cycle changes represent a positive feedback, the range of their responses remains very large, depending, among other things, on poorly understood changes in vegetation or soil uptake of carbon as the climate warms. Such processes are an important topic of ongoing research.

The models also predict that climate change will affect the physical and chemical characteristics of the ocean. The estimates of the rise in sea level during the twenty-first century range from about 30 to 40 centimeters, again depending on emissions. More than 60 percent of this rise is caused by the thermal expansion of the ocean. Yet these model-based estimates do not include the possible acceleration of recently observed increases in ice loss from the Greenland and Antarctic ice sheets. Although scientific understanding of such effects is very limited, they could add an additional 10 to 20 centimeters to sea-level rises, and the possibility of significantly larger rises cannot be excluded. The chemistry of the ocean is also affected, as the increased concentrations of atmospheric carbon dioxide will cause the ocean to become more acidic.

Some of the largest changes are predicted for polar regions. These include significant increases in high-latitude land temperatures and in the depth of thawing in permafrost regions and sharp reductions in the extent of summer sea ice in the Arctic basin. Lower latitudes will likely experience more heat waves, heavier precipitation, and stronger (but perhaps less frequent) hurricanes and typhoons. The extent to which hurricanes and typhoons may strengthen is uncertain and is a subject of much new research.

Some important uncertainties remain, of course. For example, the precise way in which clouds will respond as temperatures increase is a critical factor

> ### B o x 12.5   The Mechanics of the IPCC
>
> The IPCC was established by governments in 1988 to provide assessments of available scientific and technical information on climate change. The process used to produce these assessments is designed to ensure their high credibility in both science and policy communities.
>
> Comprehensive assessments were published in 1990, 1995, 2001, and 2007.
>
> Three separate "working groups" examine the physical science of climate change, the effects on nature and society, and methods for mitigation.
>
> Lead authors, who are active participants in relevant research, are nominated by governments. Care is taken to balance points of view as well as geography, gender and age.
>
> A review process tests the authors' assessment against views in the broader expert community. More than 600 expert reviewers provided over 30,000 comments on the report of Working Group I, on which this article is based.
>
> Each of the three working groups also issues a "Summary for Policymakers," which is done in cooperation with government delegates to ensure that the language used is clear to policymakers.

governing the overall size of the projected warming. The complexity of clouds, however, means that their response has been frustratingly difficult to pin down, and, again, much research remains to be done in this area.

We are now living in an era in which both humans and nature affect the future evolution of the earth and its inhabitants. Unfortunately, the crystal ball provided by our climate models becomes cloudier for predictions out beyond a century or so. Our limited knowledge of the response of both natural systems and human society to the growing impacts of climate change compounds our uncertainty. One result of global warming is certain, however. Plants, animals and humans will be living with the consequences of climate change for at least the next thousand years.

13

The Climate Science Isn't Settled

RICHARD S. LINDZEN

The IPCC report and the large majority of scientists who hold views consistent with most of its conclusions have many critics. Some of the critics have vested interests in industries and technologies that would be affected by policies that have been proposed to adapt to or counter global climate change. Others adhere to what has become virtually a political ideology of climate change denial. Still others are scientists who are critical of the way their colleagues have selected and interpreted climate data. There are relatively few such scientists and fewer still who are distinguished scholars of climate science. Richard Lindzen is one of the latter. He is Alfred P. Sloan Professor of Meteorology in the Department of Earth, Atmospheric and Planetary Sciences at MIT. He holds a Ph.D. from Harvard and is a member of the National Academy of Sciences. He has received awards from the American Meteorological Society and the American Geophysical Union. An atmospheric physicist, Lindzen has published more than 200 scientific papers and books and was the lead author of the chapter on "Physical Climate Processes and Feedbacks" in the third IPCC assessment report. Lindzen is also a skeptic of the scientific consensus on climate change. In this article, originally published as an op-ed in The Wall Street Journal *a few weeks after "climategate" hit the news media, he argues that the conclusions of the IPCC fourth assessment report are flawed and that the models on which they are based are too weak to support the notion that we are facing a climate "catastrophe." Although the vast majority of climate scientists disagree with Lindzen and specific rebuttals can be found online, his arguments deserve to be taken seriously.*

Is there a reason to be alarmed by the prospect of global warming? Consider that the measurement used, the globally averaged temperature anomaly (GATA), is always changing. Sometimes it goes up, sometimes down, and occasionally — such as for the last dozen years or so — it does little that can be discerned.

Richard S. Lindzen, "The Climate Science Isn't Settled," *The Wall Street Journal* (November 30, 2009). Reprinted by permission of the author.

Claims that climate change is accelerating are bizarre. There is general support for the assertion that GATA has increased about 1.5 degrees Fahrenheit since the middle of the 19th century. The quality of the data is poor, though, and because the changes are small, it is easy to nudge such data a few tenths of a degree in any direction. Several of the emails from the University of East Anglia's Climate Research Unit (CRU) that have caused such a public ruckus dealt with how to do this so as to maximize apparent changes.

The general support for warming is based not so much on the quality of the data, but rather on the fact that there was a little ice age from about the 15th to the 19th century. Thus it is not surprising that temperatures should increase as we emerged from this episode. At the same time that we were emerging from the little ice age, the industrial era began, and this was accompanied by increasing emissions of greenhouse gases such as CO_2, methane and nitrous oxide. CO_2 is the most prominent of these, and it is again generally accepted that it has increased by about 30%.

The defining characteristic of a greenhouse gas is that it is relatively transparent to visible light from the sun but can absorb portions of thermal radiation. In general, the earth balances the incoming solar radiation by emitting thermal radiation, and the presence of greenhouse substances inhibits cooling by thermal radiation and leads to some warming.

That said, the main greenhouse substances in the earth's atmosphere are water vapor and high clouds. Let's refer to these as major greenhouse substances to distinguish them from the anthropogenic minor substances. Even a doubling of CO_2 would only upset the original balance between incoming and outgoing radiation by about 2%. This is essentially what is called "climate forcing."

There is general agreement on the above findings. At this point there is no basis for alarm regardless of whether any relation between the observed warming and the observed increase in minor greenhouse gases can be established. Nevertheless, the most publicized claims of the U.N.'s Intergovernmental Panel on Climate Change (IPCC) deal exactly with whether any relation can be discerned. The failure of the attempts to link the two over the past 20 years bespeaks the weakness of any case for concern.

The IPCC's Scientific Assessments generally consist of about 1,000 pages of text. The Summary for Policymakers is 20 pages. It is, of course, impossible to accurately summarize the 1,000-page assessment in just 20 pages; at the very least, nuances and caveats have to be omitted. However, it has been my experience that even the summary is hardly ever looked at. Rather, the whole report tends to be characterized by a single iconic claim.

The main statement publicized after the last IPCC Scientific Assessment two years ago was that it was likely that most of the warming since 1957 (a point of anomalous cold) was due to man. This claim was based on the weak argument that the current models used by the IPCC couldn't reproduce the warming from about 1978 to 1998 without some forcing, and that the only forcing that they could think of was man. Even this argument assumes that these models adequately deal with natural internal variability — that is, such naturally occurring cycles as El Nino, the Pacific Decadal Oscillation, the Atlantic Multidecadal Oscillation, etc.

Yet articles from major modeling centers acknowledged that the failure of these models to anticipate the absence of warming for the past dozen years was due to the failure of these models to account for this natural internal variability. Thus even the basis for the weak IPCC argument for anthropogenic climate change was shown to be false.

Of course, none of the articles stressed this. Rather they emphasized that according to models modified to account for the natural internal variability, warming would resume — in 2009, 2013 and 2030, respectively.

But even if the IPCC's iconic statement were correct, it still would not be cause for alarm. After all we are still talking about tenths of a degree for over 75% of the climate forcing associated with a doubling of CO_2. The potential (and only the potential) for alarm enters with the issue of climate sensitivity — which refers to the change that a doubling of CO_2 will produce in GATA. It is generally accepted that a doubling of CO_2 will only produce a change of about two degrees Fahrenheit if all else is held constant. This is unlikely to be much to worry about.

Yet current climate models predict much higher sensitivities. They do so because in these models, the main greenhouse substances (water vapor and clouds) act to amplify anything that CO_2 does. This is referred to as positive feedback. But as the IPCC notes, clouds continue to be a source of major uncertainty in current models. Since clouds and water vapor are intimately related, the IPCC claim that they are more confident about water vapor is quite implausible.

There is some evidence of a positive feedback effect for water vapor in cloud-free regions, but a major part of any water-vapor feedback would have to acknowledge that cloud-free areas are always changing, and this remains an unknown. At this point, few scientists would argue that the science is settled. In particular, the question remains as to whether water vapor and clouds have positive or negative feedbacks.

The notion that the earth's climate is dominated by positive feedbacks is intuitively implausible, and the history of the earth's climate offers some guidance on this matter. About 2.5 billion years ago, the sun was 20%-30% less bright than now (compare this with the 2% perturbation that a doubling of CO_2 would produce), and yet the evidence is that the oceans were unfrozen at the time, and that temperatures might not have been very different from today's. Carl Sagan in the 1970s referred to this as the "Early Faint Sun Paradox."

For more than 30 years there have been attempts to resolve the paradox with greenhouse gases. Some have suggested CO_2 — but the amount needed was thousands of times greater than present levels and incompatible with geological evidence. Methane also proved unlikely. It turns out that increased thin cirrus cloud coverage in the tropics readily resolves the paradox — but only if the clouds constitute a negative feedback. In present terms this means that they would diminish rather than enhance the impact of CO_2.

There are quite a few papers in the literature that also point to the absence of positive feedbacks. The implied low sensitivity is entirely compatible with the small warming that has been observed. So how do models with high sensitivity manage to simulate the currently small response to a forcing that is almost as large as a doubling of CO_2? Jeff Kiehl notes in a 2007 article from the National Center for Atmospheric Research, the models use another quantity that the IPCC lists as poorly known (namely aerosols) to arbitrarily cancel as much greenhouse warming as needed to match the data, with each model choosing a different degree of cancellation according to the sensitivity of that model.

What does all this have to do with climate catastrophe? The answer brings us to a scandal that is, in my opinion, considerably greater than that implied in the hacked emails from the Climate Research Unit (though perhaps not as bad as their destruction of raw data): namely the suggestion that the very existence of warming or of the greenhouse effect is tantamount to catastrophe. This is the grossest of "bait and switch" scams. It is only such a scam that lends importance to the machinations in the emails designed to nudge temperatures a few tenths of a degree.

The notion that complex climate "catastrophes" are simply a matter of the response of a single number, GATA, to a single forcing, CO_2 (or solar forcing for that matter), represents a gigantic step backward in the science of climate. Many disasters associated with warming are simply normal occurrences whose existence is falsely claimed to be evidence of warming. And all these examples involve phenomena that are dependent on the confluence of many factors.

Our perceptions of nature are similarly dragged back centuries so that the normal occasional occurrences of open water in summer over the North Pole, droughts, floods, hurricanes, sea-level variations, etc. are all taken as omens, portending doom due to our sinful ways (as epitomized by our carbon footprint). All of these phenomena depend on the confluence of multiple factors as well.

Consider the following example. Suppose that I leave a box on the floor, and my wife trips on it, falling against my son, who is carrying a carton of eggs, which then fall and break. Our present approach to emissions would be analogous to deciding that the best way to prevent the breakage of eggs would be to outlaw leaving boxes on the floor. The chief difference is that in the case of atmospheric CO_2 and climate catastrophe, the chain of inference is longer and less plausible than in my example.

14

The Geoengineering Option: A Last Resort Against Global Warming?

DAVID G. VICTOR, M. GRANGER MORGAN, JAY APT, JOHN STEINBRUNER, AND KATHARINE RICKE

Global climate change is one of the major technological dilemmas — probably the technological dilemma of our time. Although there is broad agreement among scientists and policymakers in many countries that it is real and that it is anthropogenic (that is, caused by human activities), there are those who disagree, and even among scientists and policymakers who share the consensus, there is no clear agreement on what should be done about it. Views range along a spectrum of potential actions. At one end are those who consider current trends to be part of a natural climate cycle and advocate doing nothing in the expectation that the problem will eventually take care of itself. Others regard climate change as inevitable and believe that the best course is to adapt to it (by building seawalls to control flooding or changing agricultural crops and practices, for example). Still others support stronger actions — the mostly widely discussed of which is to limit emissions of greenhouse gases. Finally there some who believe that we should explore the possibility of deploying systems on a global scale aimed at intervening in climate processes. The last of these approaches, known as "geoengineering" — or, as one science writer calls it, "hacking the planet,"[1] — is

From David G. Victor, M. Granger Morgan, Jay Apt, John Steinbrunner, and Katharine Ricke. "The Geoengineering Option: A Last Resort Against Global Warming?" *Foreign Affairs* (Vol. 88, No. 2), March/April 2009, pp. 64–76. Reprinted with permission.

probably the most risky, but it could also be the most effective means of meeting the challenge.

The risks, as well as the scale and unpredictability of potential impacts, have made geoengineering a highly controversial notion. Until the past few years, discussions of geoengineering projects took place mostly within military circles (where their potential as weapons were examined) or on the fringes of scientific legitimacy. More recently, however, they have moved into the mainstream and the discussions, involving some of the more important figures in climate science and foreign policy, have become more focused and more serious.

This article, in the highly respected journal, Foreign Affairs, *by a group of distinguished engineers, technologists, political scientists, and public policy experts, is a prime example. Part of the journal's "syllabus on climate change," it takes a wide-ranging look at the ramifications of unprecedented technological projects that would seek to alter the earth's climate.*

The first author, David G. Victor, is professor at the School of International Relations and Pacific Studies of the University of California at San Diego, and director of the School's new Laboratory on International Law and Regulation. At the time this article was written, he was professor at Stanford Law School. M. Granger Morgan is Lord Chair Professor in Engineering, and head of the Department of Engineering and Public Policy at Carnegie Mellon University. Jay Apt is professor of technology in the Tepper School of Business and the Department of Engineering and Public Policy at Carnegie Mellon University. He is a former astronaut and flew four missions on NASA's space shuttle. John Steinbruner is professor of public policy at the School of Public Policy and director of the Center for International and Security Studies at the University of Maryland. Katharine Ricke is a Ph.D. candidate in the Department of Engineering and Public Policy at Carnegie Mellon.

E ach year, the effects of climate change are coming into sharper focus. Barely a month goes by without some fresh bad news: ice sheets and glaciers are melting faster than expected, sea levels are rising more rapidly than ever in recorded history, plants are blooming earlier in the spring, water supplies and habitats are in danger, birds are being forced to find new migratory patterns.

The odds that the global climate will reach a dangerous tipping point are increasing. Over the course of the twenty-first century, key ocean currents, such as the Gulf Stream, could shift radically, and thawing permafrost could release huge amounts of additional greenhouse gases into the atmosphere. Such scenarios, although still remote, would dramatically accelerate and compound the consequences of global warming. Scientists are taking these doomsday scenarios seriously because the steady accumulation of warming gases in the atmosphere is forcing change in the climate system at rates so rapid that the outcomes are extremely difficult to predict.

Eliminating all the risks of climate change is impossible because carbon dioxide emissions, the chief human contribution to global warming, are unlike conventional air pollutants, which stay in the atmosphere for only hours or days. Once carbon dioxide enters the atmosphere, much of it remains for over a hundred years. Emissions from anywhere on the planet contribute to the global problem, and once headed in the wrong direction, the climate system is slow to respond to attempts at reversal. As with a bathtub that has a large faucet and a small drain, the only practical way to lower the level is by dramatically cutting the inflow. Holding global warming steady at its current rate would require a worldwide 60–80 percent cut in emissions, and it would still take decades for the atmospheric concentration of carbon dioxide to stabilize.

Most human emissions of carbon dioxide come from burning fossil fuels, and most governments have been reluctant to force the radical changes necessary to reduce those emissions. Economic growth tends to trump vague and elusive global aspirations. The United States has yet to impose even a cap on its emissions, let alone a reduction. The European Union has adopted an emissions-trading scheme that, although promising in theory, has not yet had much real effect because carbon prices are still too low to cause any significant change in behavior. Even Norway, which in 1991 became one of the first nations to impose a stiff tax on emissions, has seen a net increase in its carbon dioxide emissions. Japan, too, has professed its commitment to taming global warming. Nevertheless, Tokyo is struggling to square the need for economic growth with continued dependence on an energy system powered mainly by conventional fossil fuels. And China's emissions recently surpassed those of the United States, thanks to coal-fueled industrialization and a staggering pace of economic growth. The global economic crisis is stanching emissions a bit, but it will not come close to shutting off the faucet.

The world's slow progress in cutting carbon dioxide emissions and the looming danger that the climate could take a sudden turn for the worse require policymakers to take a closer look at emergency strategies for curbing the effects of global warming. These strategies, often called "geoengineering," envision deploying systems on a planetary scale, such as launching reflective particles into the atmosphere or positioning sunshades to cool the earth. These strategies could cool the planet, but they would not stop the buildup of carbon dioxide or lessen all its harmful impacts. For this reason, geoengineering has been widely shunned by those committed to reducing emissions.

Serious research on geoengineering is still in its infancy, and it has not received the attention it deserves from politicians. The time has come to take it seriously. Geoengineering could provide a useful defense for the planet — an emergency shield that could be deployed if surprisingly nasty climatic shifts put vital ecosystems and billions of people at risk. Actually raising the shield, however, would be a political choice. One nation's emergency can be another's opportunity, and it is unlikely that all countries will have similar assessments of how to balance the ills of unchecked climate change with the risk that geoengineering could do more harm than good. Governments should immediately begin to undertake serious research on geoengineering and help create international norms governing its use.

THE RAINMAKERS

Geoengineering is not a new idea. In 1965, when President Lyndon Johnson received the first-ever U.S. presidential briefing on the dangers of climate change, the only remedy prescribed to counter the effects of global warming was geoengineering. That advice reflected the scientific culture of the time, which imagined that engineering could fix almost any problem.

By the late 1940s, both the United States and the Soviet Union had begun exploring strategies for modifying the weather to gain battlefield advantage. Many schemes focused on "seeding" clouds with substances that would coax them to drop more rain. Despite offering no clear advantage to the military, "weather makers" were routinely employed (rarely with much effect) to squeeze more rain from clouds for thirsty crops. Starting in 1962, U.S. government researchers for Project Stormfury tried to make tropical hurricanes less intense through cloud seeding, but with no clear success. Military experts also dreamed of using nuclear explosions and other interventions to create a more advantageous climate. These applications were frightening enough that in 1976 the United Nations adopted the Convention on the Prohibition of Military or Any Other Hostile Use of Environmental Modification Techniques to bar such projects. By the 1970s, after a string of failures, the idea of weather modification for war and farming had largely faded away.

Today's proposals for geoengineering are more likely to have an impact because the interventions needed for global-scale geoengineering are much less subtle than those that sought to influence local weather patterns. The earth's climate is largely driven by the fine balance between the light energy with which the sun bathes the earth and the heat that the earth radiates back to space. On average, about 70 percent of the earth's incoming sunlight is absorbed by the atmosphere and the planet's surface; the remainder is reflected back into space. Increasing the reflectivity of the planet (known as the albedo) by about one percentage point could have an effect on the climate system large enough to offset the gross increase in warming that is likely over the next century as a result of a doubling of the amount of carbon dioxide in the atmosphere. Making such tweaks is much more straightforward than causing rain or fog at a particular location in the ways that the weather makers of the late 1940s and 1950s dreamed of doing.

In fact, every few decades, volcanoes validate the theory that it is possible to engineer the climate. When Mount Pinatubo, in the Philippines, erupted in 1991, it ejected plumes of sulfate and other fine particles into the atmosphere, which reflected a bit more sunlight and cooled the planet by about 0.5 degrees Celsius over the course of a year. Larger eruptions, such as the 1883 eruption of Krakatau, in Indonesia, have caused even greater cooling that lasted longer. Unlike efforts to control emissions of greenhouse gases, which will take many years to yield a noticeable effect, volcano-like strategies for cooling the planet would work relatively promptly.

Another lesson from volcanoes is that a geoengineering system would require frequent maintenance, since most particles lofted into the stratosphere would disappear after a year or two. Once a geoengineering project were under way, there would be strong incentives to continue it, since failure to keep the shield in place could allow particularly harmful changes in the earth's climate, such as warming so speedy that ecosystems would collapse because they had no time to adjust. By carefully measuring the climatic effects of the next major volcanic eruption with satellites and aircraft, geoengineers could design a number of climate-cooling technologies.

ALBEDO ENHANCERS

Today, the term "geoengineering" refers to a variety of strategies designed to cool the climate. Some, for example, would slowly remove carbon dioxide from the atmosphere, either by manipulating the biosphere (such as by fertilizing the ocean with nutrients that would allow plankton to grow faster and thus absorb more carbon) or by directly scrubbing the air with devices that resemble big cooling towers. However, from what is known today, increasing the earth's albedo offers the most promising method for rapidly cooling the planet.

Most schemes that would alter the earth's albedo envision putting reflective particles into the upper atmosphere, much as volcanoes do already. Such schemes offer quick impacts with relatively little effort. For example, just one kilogram of sulfur well placed in the stratosphere would roughly offset the warming effect of several hundred thousand kilograms of carbon dioxide. Other schemes include seeding bright reflective clouds by blowing seawater or other substances into the lower atmosphere. Substantial reductions of global warming are also possible to achieve by converting dark places that absorb lots of sunlight to lighter shades — for example, by replacing dark forests with more reflective grasslands. (Engineered plants might be designed for the task.) More ambitious projects could include launching a huge cloud of thin refracting discs into a special space orbit that parks the discs between the sun and the earth in order to bend just a bit of sunlight away before it hits the planet.

So far, launching reflective materials into the upper stratosphere seems to be the easiest and most cost-effective option. This could be accomplished by using high-flying aircraft, naval guns, or giant balloons. The appropriate materials could include sulfate aerosols (which would be created by releasing sulfur dioxide gas), aluminum oxide dust, or even self-levitating and self-orienting designer particles engineered to migrate to the Polar Regions and remain in place for long periods. If it can be done, concentrating sunshades over the poles would be a particularly interesting option, since those latitudes appear to be the most sensitive to global warming. Most cost estimates for such geoengineering strategies are preliminary and unreliable. However, there is general agreement that the strategies are cheap; the total expense of the most cost-effective options would amount to perhaps as little as a few billion dollars, just one percent (or less) of the cost of dramatically cutting emissions.

Cooling the planet through geoengineering will not, however, fix all of the problems related to climate change. Offsetting warming by reflecting more sunlight back into space will not stop the rising concentration of carbon dioxide in the atmosphere. Sooner or later, much of that carbon dioxide ends up in the oceans, where it forms carbonic acid. Ocean acidification is a catastrophe for marine ecosystems, for the 100 million people who depend on coral reefs for their livelihoods, and for the many more who depend on them for coastal protection from storms and for biological support of the greater ocean food web. Over the last century, the oceans have become markedly more acidic, and current projections suggest that without a serious effort to control emissions, the concentration of carbon dioxide will be so high by the end of the century that many organisms that make shells will disappear and most coral reef ecosystems will collapse, devastating the marine fishing industry. Recent studies have also suggested that ocean acidification will increase the size and depth of "dead zones," areas of the sea that are so oxygen depleted that larger marine life, such as squid, are unable to breathe properly.

Altering the albedo of the earth would also affect atmospheric circulation, rainfall, and other aspects of the hydrologic cycle. In the six to 18 months following the eruption of Mount Pinatubo, rainfall and river flows dropped, particularly in the tropics. Understanding these dangers better would help convince government leaders in rainfall-sensitive regions, such as parts of China and India (along with North Africa, the Middle East, and the desert regions of the southwestern United States), not to prematurely deploy poorly designed geoengineering schemes that could wreak havoc on agricultural productivity. Indeed, some climate models already suggest that negative outcomes — decreased precipitation over land (especially in the tropics) and increased precipitation over the oceans — would accompany a geoengineering scheme that sought to lower average temperatures by raising the planet's albedo. Such changes could increase the risk of major droughts in some regions and have a major impact on agriculture and the supply of fresh water. Complementary policies — such as investing in better water-management schemes — may be needed.

The highly uncertain but possibly disastrous side effects of geoengineering interventions are difficult to compare to the dangers of unchecked global climate change. Chances are that if countries begin deploying geoengineering systems, it will be because calamitous climate change is near at hand. Yet the assignment of blame after a geoengineering disaster would be very different from the current debates over who is responsible for climate change, which is the result of centuries of accumulated emissions from activities across the world. By contrast, the side effects of geoengineering projects could be readily pinned on the geoengineers themselves. That is one reason why nations must begin building useful international norms to govern geoengineering in order to assess its dangers and decide when to act in the event of an impending climatic disaster.

LONE RANGERS

An effective foreign policy strategy for managing geoengineering is difficult to formulate because the technology involved turns the normal debate over climate change on its head. The best way to reduce the danger of global warming is, of course, to cut emissions of carbon dioxide and other greenhouse gases. But success in that venture will require all the major emitting countries, with their divergent interests, to cooperate for several decades in a sustained effort to develop and deploy completely new energy systems with much lower emissions. Incentives to defect and avoid the high cost of emissions controls will be strong.

By contrast, geoengineering is an option at the disposal of any reasonably advanced nation. A single country could deploy geoengineering systems from its own territory without consulting the rest of the planet. Geoengineers keen to alter their own country's climate might not assess or even care about the dangers their actions could create for climates, ecosystems, and economies elsewhere. A unilateral geoengineering project could impose costs on other countries, such as changes in precipitation patterns and river flows or adverse impacts on agriculture, marine fishing, and tourism. And merely knowing that geoengineering exists as an option may take the pressure off governments to implement the policies needed to cut emissions.

At some point in the near future, it is conceivable that a nation that has not done enough to confront climate change will conclude that global warming has become so harmful to its interests that it should unilaterally engage in geoengineering. Although it is hardly wise to mess with a poorly understood global climate system using instruments whose effects are also unknown, politicians must take geoengineering seriously because it is cheap, easy, and takes only one government with sufficient hubris or desperation to set it in motion. Except in the most dire climatic emergency, universal agreement on the best approach is highly unlikely. Unilateral action would create a crisis of legitimacy that could make it especially difficult to manage geoengineering schemes once they are under way.

Although governments are the most likely actors, some geoengineering options are cheap enough to be deployed by wealthy and capable individuals or corporations. Although it may sound like the stuff of a future James Bond movie, private-sector geoengineers might very well attempt to deploy affordable geoengineering schemes on their own. And even if governments manage to keep freelance geoengineers in check, the private sector could emerge as a potent force by becoming an interest group that pushes for deployment or drives the direction of geoengineering research and assessment. Already, private companies are running experiments on ocean fertilization in the hope of sequestering carbon dioxide and earning credits that they could trade in carbon markets. Private developers of technology for albedo modification could obstruct an open and transparent research environment as they jockey for position in the potentially lucrative market for testing and deploying geoengineering systems. To prevent such scenarios and to establish the rules that should govern the use of geoengineering technology for the good of the entire planet, a cooperative, international research agenda is vital.

FROM SCIENCE FICTION TO FACTS

Despite years of speculation and vague talk, peer-reviewed research on geoengineering is remarkably scarce. Nearly the entire community of geoengineering scientists could fit comfortably in a single university seminar room, and the entire scientific literature on the subject could be read during the course of a transatlantic flight. Geoengineering continues to be considered a fringe topic.

Many scientists have been reluctant to raise the issue for fear that it might create a moral hazard: encouraging governments to deploy geoengineering rather than invest in cutting emissions. Indeed, geoengineering ventures will be viewed with particular suspicion if the nations funding geoengineering research are not also investing in dramatically reducing their emissions of carbon dioxide and other greenhouse gases. Many scientists also rightly fear that grants for geoengineering research would be subtracted from the existing funds for urgently needed climate-science research and carbon-abatement technologies. But there is a pressing need for a better understanding of geoengineering, rooted in theoretical studies and empirical field measurements. The subject also requires the talents of engineers, few of whom have joined the small group of scientists studying these techniques.

The scientific academies in the leading industrialized and emerging countries — which often control the purse strings for major research grants — must orchestrate a serious and transparent international research effort funded by their governments. Although some work is already under way, a more comprehensive understanding of geoengineering options and of risk-assessment procedures would make countries less trigger-happy and more inclined to consider deploying geoengineering systems in concert rather than on their own. (The International Council for Science, which has a long and successful history of coordinating scientific assessments of technical topics, could also lend a helping hand.) Eventually, a dedicated international entity overseen by the leading academies, provided with a large budget, and suffused with the norms of transparency and peer review will be necessary.

In time, international institutions such as the Intergovernmental Panel on Climate Change could be expected to synthesize the findings from the published research. The IPCC, which shared the Nobel Peace Prize in 2007 for its pivotal role in building a consensus around climate science, has not considered geoengineering so far because the topic is politically radioactive and there is a dearth of peer-reviewed research on it. The IPCC's fifth assessment report on climate change, which is being planned right now, should promise to take a closer look at geoengineering. Attention from the IPCC and the world's major scientific academies would help encourage new research.

A broad and solid foundation of research would help on three fronts. First, it would transform the discussion about geoengineering from an abstract debate into one focused on real risk assessment. Second, a research program that was backed by the world's top scientific academies could secure funding and political cover for essential but controversial experiments. (Field trials of engineered aerosols, for example, could spark protests comparable to those that accompanied trials of genetically modified crops.) Such experiments will be seen as more acceptable if they are designed and overseen by the world's leading scientists and evaluated in a fully transparent fashion. Third, and what is crucial, a better understanding of the dangers of geoengineering would help nations craft the norms that should govern the testing and possible deployment of newly developed technologies. Scientists could be influential in creating these norms, just as nuclear scientists framed the options on nuclear testing and influenced pivotal governments during the Cold War.

If countries were actually to contemplate the deployment of geoengineering technologies, there would inevitably be questions raised about what triggers would compel the use of these systems. Today, nobody knows which climatic triggers are most important for geoengineering because research on the harmful effects of climate change has not been coupled tightly enough with research on whether and how geoengineering might offset those effects.

Although the international scientific community should take the lead in developing a research agenda, social scientists, international lawyers, and foreign policy experts will also have to play a role. Eventually, there will have to be international laws to ensure that globally credible and legitimate rules govern the deployment of geoengineering systems. But effective legal norms cannot be imperiously declared. They must be carefully developed by informed consensus in order to avoid encouraging the rogue forms of geoengineering they are intended to prevent.

Those who worry that such research will cause governments to abandon their efforts to control emissions, including much of the environmental community, are prone to seek a categorical prohibition against geoengineering. But a taboo would interfere with much-needed scientific research on an option that might be better for humanity and the world's ecosystems than allowing unchecked climate change or reckless unilateral geoengineering. Formal prohibition is unlikely to stop determined rogues, but a smart and scientifically sanctioned research program could gather data essential to understanding the risks of geoengineering strategies and to establishing responsible criteria for their testing and deployment.

BRAVE NEW WORLD

Fiddling with the climate to fix the climate strikes most people as a shockingly bad idea. Many worry that research on geoengineering will make governments less willing to regulate emissions. It is more likely, however, that serious study will reveal the many dangerous side effects of geoengineering, exposing it as a true option of last resort. But because the option exists, and might be used, it would be dangerous for scientists and policymakers to ignore it. Assessing and managing the risks of geoengineering may not require radically different approaches from those used for other seemingly risky endeavors, such as genetic engineering (research on which was paused in the 1970s as scientists worked out useful regulatory systems), the construction and use of high-energy particle accelerators (which a few physicists suggest could create black holes that might swallow the earth), and the development of nanotechnology (which some worry could unleash self-replicating nanomachines that could reduce the world to "gray goo"). The option of eliminating risk altogether does not exist. Countries have kept smallpox samples on hand, along with samples of many other diseases, such as the Ebola and Marburg viruses, despite the danger of their inadvertent release. All of these are potentially dangerous endeavors that governments, with scientific support, have been able to manage for the greater good.

Humans have already engaged in a dangerous geophysical experiment by pumping massive amounts of carbon dioxide and other greenhouse gases into the atmosphere. The best and safest strategy for reversing climate change is to halt this buildup of greenhouse gases, but this solution will take time, and it involves myriad practical and political difficulties. Meanwhile, the dangers are mounting. In a few decades, the option of geoengineering could look less ugly for some countries than unchecked changes in the climate. Nor is it impossible that later in the century the planet will experience a climatic disaster that puts ecosystems and human prosperity at risk. It is time to take geoengineering out of the closet — to better control the risk of unilateral action and also to know the costs and consequences of its use so that the nations of the world can collectively decide whether to raise the shield if they think the planet needs it.

ENDNOTE

1. Eli Kintisch, *Hack the Planet: Science's Best Hope — or Worst Nightmare — for Averting Climate Catastrophe* (Hoboken: NJ: John Wiley & Sons, 2010).

15

20 Reasons Why Geoengineering May Be a Bad Idea

ALAN ROBOCK

The authors of the previous article advocate a pragmatic approach to geoengineering. They have serious reservations about the technology and the risks it poses, but they are at least as worried about the potential impacts of climate change.

They are concerned about the politics of climate change and the possibility that some nations may choose to take unilateral action. In the end they say it is time "to take geoengineering out of the closet" and discuss it openly at the international level.

Alan Robock has a more negative view. His concerns "address unknowns in climate system response; effects on human quality of life; and the political, ethical, and moral issues" raised by geoengineering. Robock is a distinguished professor in the Department of Environmental Sciences at Rutgers University, where he is also associate director of the Center for Environmental Prediction, director of the Meteorology Undergraduate Program, and a member of the Graduate Program in Atmospheric Science. He has many honors and distinctions, including serving as an American Association for the Advancement of Science (AAAS) Congressional Fellow in 1986 and as snow forecaster for Montgomery County (Maryland) Public Schools in the early 1980s (when two of my children were students there and eagerly awaited his forecasts of snow as well as — they hoped — subsequent school closings). He was a participant in the Intergovernmental Panel on Climate

From Alan Robock, "20 Reasons Why Geoengineering May Be a Bad Idea," *Bulletin of the Atomic Scientists* (Vol. 64, No. 2), May/June 2008, pp. 14–18, 59. Reprinted with permission.

*Change and is a Fellow of the American Meteorological Society. Robock holds a
B.A. in meteorology from the University of Wisconsin at Madison and an S.M.
and a Ph.D. in meteorology from M.I.T.*

*Robock worries that while implementation of geoengineering approaches to
limiting solar radiation would perhaps limit temperature increases, they would not
address other important impacts of carbon emissions — acid deposition, ozone
depletion, and regional climate effects. His article, originally published in the* Bulletin of the Atomic Scientists, *includes two interesting sidebars: one on carbon
sequestration by Kirsten Jerch, assistant editor at the* Bulletin *and another on ethical
aspects of geoengineering, by Martin Bunzl, a philosophy professor at Rutgers.*

The stated objective of the 1992 U.N. Framework Convention on Climate
Change is to stabilize greenhouse gas concentrations in the atmosphere "at a
level that would prevent dangerous anthropogenic interference with the climate
system." Though the framework convention did not define "dangerous," that
level is now generally considered to be about 450 parts per million (ppm)
of carbon dioxide in the atmosphere; the current concentration is about 385 ppm.
up from 280 ppm before the Industrial Revolution.

In light of society's failure to act concertedly to deal with global warming in
spite of the framework convention agreement, two prominent atmospheric scientists recently suggested that humans consider geoengineering — in this case, deliberate modification of the climate to achieve specific effects such as cooling — to
address global warming. Nobel laureate Paul Crutzen, who is well regarded for
his work on ozone damage and nuclear winter, spearheaded a special August
2006 issue of *Climatic Change* with a controversial editorial about injecting sulfate
aerosols into the stratosphere as a means to block sunlight and cool Earth. Another
respected climate scientist, Tom Wigley, followed up with a feasibility study in
Science that advocated the same approach in combination with emissions reduction.[1]

The idea of geoengineering traces its genesis to military strategy during the
early years of the Cold War, when scientists in the United States and the Soviet
Union devoted considerable funds and research efforts to controlling the weather.
Some early geoengineering theories involved damming the Strait of Gibraltar and
the Bering Strait as a way to *warm* the Arctic, making Siberia more habitable.[2] Since
scientists became aware of rising concentrations of atmospheric carbon dioxide,
however, some have proposed artificially altering climate and weather patterns to
reverse or mask the effects of global warming.

Some geoengineering schemes aim to remove carbon dioxide from the
atmosphere, through natural or mechanical means. Ocean fertilization, where
iron dust is dumped into the open ocean to trigger algal blooms; genetic modification of crops to increase biotic carbon uptake; carbon capture and storage techniques such as those proposed to outfit coal plants; and planting forests are such
examples. Other schemes involve blocking or reflecting incoming solar radiation,
for example by spraying seawater hundreds of meters into the air to seed the
formation of stratocumulus clouds over the subtropical ocean.[3]

Two strategies to reduce incoming solar radiation — stratospheric aerosol
injection as proposed by Crutzen and space-based sun shields (i.e., mirrors or

shades placed in orbit between the sun and Earth) — are among the most widely discussed geoengineering schemes in scientific circles. While these schemes (if they could be built) would cool Earth, they might also have adverse consequences. Several papers in the August 2006 *Climatic Change* discussed some of these issues, but here I present a fairly comprehensive list of reasons why geoengineering might be a bad idea, first written down during a two-day NASA-sponsored conference on Managing Solar Radiation (a rather audacious title) in November 2006.[4] These concerns address unknowns in climate system response; effects on human quality of life; and the political, ethical, and moral issues raised.

1. Effects on regional climate. Geoengineering proponents often suggest that volcanic eruptions are an innocuous natural analog for stratospheric injection of sulfate aerosols. The 1991 eruption of Mount Pinatubo on the Philippine island of Luzon, which injected 20 megatons of sulfur dioxide gas into the stratosphere, produced a sulfate aerosol cloud that is said to have caused global cooling for a couple of years without adverse effects. However, researchers at the National Center for Atmospheric Research showed in 2007 that the Pinatubo eruption caused large hydrological responses, including reduced precipitation, soil moisture, and river flow in many regions.[5] Simulations of the climate response to volcanic eruptions have also shown large impacts on regional climate, but whether these are good analogs for the geoengineering response requires further investigation.

Scientists have also seen volcanic eruptions in the tropics produce changes in atmospheric circulation, causing winter warming over continents in the Northern Hemisphere, as well as eruptions at high latitudes weaken the Asian and African monsoons, causing reduced precipitation.[6] In fact, the eight-month-long eruption of the Laki fissure in Iceland in 1783–1784 contributed to famine in Africa, India, and Japan.

If scientists and engineers were able to inject smaller amounts of stratospheric aerosols than result from volcanic eruptions, how would they affect summer wind and precipitation patterns? Could attempts to geoengineer isolated regions (say, the Arctic) be confined there? Scientists need to investigate these scenarios. At the fall 2007 American Geophysical Union meeting, researchers presented preliminary findings from several different climate models that simulated geoengineering schemes and found that they reduced precipitation over wide regions, condemning hundreds of millions of people to drought.

2. Continued ocean acidification. If humans adopted geoengineering as a solution to global warming, with no restriction on continued carbon emissions, the ocean would continue to become more acidic, because about half of all excess carbon dioxide in the atmosphere is removed by ocean uptake. The ocean is already 30 percent more acidic than it was before the Industrial Revolution, and continued acidification threatens the entire oceanic biological chain, from coral reefs right up to humans.[7]

3. Ozone depletion. Aerosol particles in the stratosphere serve as surfaces for chemical reactions that destroy ozone in the same way that water and nitric acid aerosols in polar stratospheric clouds produce the seasonal Antarctic ozone hole.[8] For the next four decades or so, when the concentration of anthropogenic ozone-depleting substances will still be large enough in the stratosphere to

> **B o x 15.1   Capitalizing on Carbon**
>
> Without market incentives, geoengineering schemes to reflect solar heat are still largely confined to creative thought and artists' renderings. But a few ambitious entrepreneurs have begun to experiment with privatizing climate mitigation through carbon sequestration. Here are a few companies in the market to offset your carbon footprint:
>
> California-based technology startups Planktos and Climos are perhaps the most prominent groups offering to sell carbon offsets in exchange for performing ocean iron fertilization, which induces blooms of carbon-eating phytoplankton. Funding for Planktos dried up in early 2008 as scientists grew increasingly skeptical about the technique, but Climos has managed to press on, securing $3.5 million in funding from Braemar Energy Ventures as of February.
>
> Also in the research and development phase is Sydney, Australia-based Ocean Nourishment Corporation, which similarly aims to induce oceanic photosynthesis, only it fertilizes with nitrogen-rich urea instead of iron, Atmocean, based in Santa Fe, New Mexico, takes a slightly different tack: It's developed a 200-meter deep, wave-powered pump that brings colder, more biota-rich water up to the surface where lifeforms such as tiny, tube-like salps sequester carbon as they feed on algae.
>
> Related in mission if not in name, stationary carbon-capture technologies, which generally aren't considered geoengineering, are nonetheless equally inventive: Skyonic, a Texas-based startup, captures carbon dioxide at power plants (a relatively well-proven technology) and mixes it with sodium hydroxide to render high-grade baking soda. A pilot version of the system is operating at the Brown Stream Electric Station in Fairfield, Texas. To the west in Tucson, Arizona, Global Research Technologies, the only company in the world dedicated to carbon capture from ambient air, recently demonstrated a working "air extraction" prototype — a kind of carbon dioxide vacuum that stands upright and is about the size of a phone booth. Meanwhile, GreenFuel Technologies Corporation, in collaboration with Arizona Public Service Company, is recycling carbon dioxide emissions from power plants by using it to grow biofuel stock in the form of — what else? — algae.
>
> Kirsten Jerch

produce this effect, additional aerosols from geoengineering would destroy even more ozone and increase damaging ultraviolet flux to Earth's surface.

4. Effects on plants. Sunlight scatters as it passes through stratospheric aerosols, reducing direct solar radiation and increasing diffuse radiation, with important biological consequences. Some studies, including one that measured this effect in trees following the Mount Pinatubo eruption, suggest that diffuse radiation allows plant canopies to photosynthesize more efficiently, thus increasing their capacity as a carbon sink.[9] At the same time, inserting aerosols or reflective disks into the atmosphere would reduce the total sunlight to reach Earth's surface. Scientists need to assess the impacts on crops and natural vegetation of reductions in total, diffuse, and direct solar radiation.

5. More acid deposition. If sulfate is injected regularly into the stratosphere, no matter where on Earth, acid deposition will increase as the material passes through the troposphere — the atmospheric layer closest to Earth's surface. In 1977, Russian climatologist Mikhail Budyko calculated that the additional acidity caused by sulfate injections would be negligibly greater than levels that resulted from air pollution.[10] But the relevant quantity is the *total* amount of acid that reaches the ground, including both wet (acid rain, snow, and fog) and dry deposition (acidic gases and particles). Any additional acid deposition would harm the ecosystem, and it will be important to understand the consequences of exceeding different biological thresholds. Furthermore, more acidic particles in the troposphere would affect public health. The effect may not be large compared to the impact of pollution in urban areas, but in pristine areas it could be significant.

6. Effects of cirrus clouds. As aerosol particles injected into the stratosphere fall to Earth, they may seed cirrus cloud formations in the troposphere.[11] Cirrus clouds affect Earth's radiative balance of incoming and outgoing heat, although the amplitude and even direction of the effects are not well understood. While evidence exists that some volcanic aerosols form cirrus clouds, the global effect has not been quantified.[12]

7. Whitening of the sky (but nice sunsets). Atmospheric aerosols close to the size of the wavelength of light produce a white, cloudy appearance to the sky. They also contribute to colorful sunsets, similar to those that occur after volcanic eruptions. The red and yellow sky in *The Scream* by Edvard Munch was inspired by the brilliant sunsets he witnessed over Oslo in 1883, following the eruption of Krakatau in Indonesia.[13] Both the disappearance of blue skies and the appearance of red sunsets could have strong psychological impacts on humanity.

8. Less sun for solar power. Scientists estimate that as little as a 1.8 percent reduction in incoming solar radiation would compensate for a doubling of atmospheric carbon dioxide. Even this small reduction would significantly affect the radiation available for solar power systems — one of the prime alternate methods of generating clean energy — as the response of different solar power systems to total available sunlight is not linear. This is especially true for some of the most efficiently designed systems that reflect or focus direct solar radiation on one location for direct heating.[14] Following the Mount Pinatubo eruption and the 1982 eruption of El Chichón in Mexico, scientists observed a direct solar radiation decrease of 25–35 percent.[15]

9. Environmental impacts of implementation. Any system that could inject aerosols into the stratosphere, i.e., commercial jetliners with sulfur mixed into their fuel, 16-inch naval rifles firing 1-ton shells of dust vertically into the air, or hoses suspended from stratospheric balloons, would cause enormous environmental damage. The same could be said for systems that would deploy sun shields. University of Arizona astronomer Roger P. Angel has proposed putting a fleet of 2-foot-wide reflective disks in a stable orbit between Earth and the sun that would bend sunlight away from Earth.[16] But to get the needed *trillions* of disks into space, engineers would need 20 electromagnetic launchers to fire missiles with stacks of 800,000 disks every five minutes for twenty years. What would be the atmospheric effects of the resulting sound and gravity waves? Who would want to live nearby?

10. Rapid warming if deployment stops. A technological, societal, or political crisis could halt a project of stratospheric aerosol injection in mid-deployment.

Such an abrupt shift would result in rapid climate warming, which would produce much more stress on society and ecosystems than gradual global warming.[17]

11. There's no going back. We don't know how quickly scientists and engineers could shut down a geoengineering system — or stem its effects — in the event of excessive climate cooling from large volcanic eruptions or other causes. Once we put aerosols into the atmosphere, we cannot remove them.

12. Human error. Complex mechanical systems never work perfectly. Humans can make mistakes in the design, manufacturing, and operation of such systems. (Think of Chernobyl, the *Exxon Valdez,* airplane crashes, and friendly fire on the battlefield.) Should we stake the future of Earth on a much more complicated arrangement than these, built by the lowest bidder?

13. Undermining emissions mitigation. If humans perceive an easy technological fix to global warming that allows for "business as usual," gathering the national (particularly in the United States and China) and international will to change consumption patterns and energy infrastructure will be even more difficult.[18] This is the oldest and most persistent argument against geoengineering.

14. Cost. Advocates casually claim that it would not be too expensive to implement geoengineering solutions, but there have been no definitive cost studies, and estimates of large-scale government projects are almost always too low. (Boston's "Big Dig" to reroute an interstate highway under the coastal city, one of humankind's greatest engineering feats, is only one example that was years overdue and billions over budget.) Angel estimates that his scheme to launch reflective disks into orbit would cost "a few trillion dollars." British economist Nicholas Stern's calculation of the cost of climate change as a percentage of global GDP (roughly $9 trillion) is in the same ballpark; Angel's estimate is also orders of magnitude greater than current global investment in renewable energy technology. Wouldn't it be a safer and wiser investment for society to instead put that money in solar power, wind power, energy efficiency, and carbon sequestration?

15. Commercial control of technology. Who would end up controlling geoengineering systems? Governments? Private companies holding patents on proprietary technology? And whose benefit would they have at heart? These systems could pose issues analogous to those raised by pharmaceutical companies and energy conglomerates whose products ostensibly serve the public, but who often value shareholder profits over the public good.

16. Military use of the technology. The United States has a long history of trying to modify weather for military purposes, including inducing rain during the Vietnam War to swamp North Vietnamese supply lines and disrupt antiwar protests by Buddhist monks.[19] Eighty-five countries, including the United States, have signed the U.N. Convention on the Prohibition of Military or Any Other Hostile Use of Environmental Modification Techniques (ENMOD), but could techniques developed to control global climate forever be limited to peaceful uses?

17. Conflicts with current treaties. The terms of ENMOD explicitly prohibit "military or any other hostile use of environmental modification techniques having widespread, long-lasting or severe effects as the means of destruction, damage, or injury to any other State Party." Any geoengineering scheme that adversely affects regional climate, for example, producing warming or drought, would therefore violate ENMOD.

18. Control of the thermostat. Even if scientists could predict the behavior and environmental effects of a given geoengineering project, and political leaders could muster the public support and funding to implement it, how would the world agree on the optimal climate? What if Russia wants it a couple of degrees warmer, and India a couple of degrees cooler? Should global climate be reset to preindustrial temperature or kept constant at today's reading? Would it be possible to tailor the climate of each region of the planet independently without affecting the others? If we proceed with geoengineering, will we provoke future climate wars?

19. Questions of moral authority. Ongoing global warming is the result of inadvertent climate modification. Humans emit carbon dioxide and other greenhouse gases to heat and cool their homes; to grow, transport, and cook their food; to run their factories; and to travel — not intentionally, but as a byproduct of fossil fuel combustion. But now that humans are aware of their effect on climate, do they have a moral right to continue emitting greenhouse gases? Similarly, since scientists know that stratospheric aerosol injection, for example, might impact the ecosphere, do humans have a right to plow ahead regardless? There's no global agency to require an environmental impact statement for geoengineering. So, how should humans judge how much climate control they may try?

20. Unexpected consequences. Scientists cannot possibly account for all of the complex climate interactions or predict all of the impacts of geoengineering. Climate models are improving, but scientists are discovering that climate is changing more rapidly than they predicted, for example, the surprising and unprecedented extent to which Arctic sea ice melted during the summer of 2007. Scientists may never have enough confidence that their theories will predict how well geoengineering systems can work. With so much at stake, there is reason to worry about what we don't know.

The reasons why geoengineering may be a bad idea are manifold, though a moderate investment in *theoretical* geoengineering research might help scientists to determine whether or not it *is* a bad idea. Still, it's a slippery slope: I wouldn't advocate actual small-scale stratospheric experiments unless comprehensive climate modeling results could first show that we could avoid at least all of the potential consequences we *know* about. Due to the inherent natural variability of the climate system, this task is not trivial. After that there are still the unknowns, such as the long-term effects of short-term experiments — stratospheric aerosols have an atmospheric lifetime of a couple years.

Solving global warming is not a difficult technical problem. As Stephen Pacala and Robert Socolow detail with their popular wedge model, a combination of several specific actions can stabilize the world's greenhouse gas emissions — although I disagree with their proposal to use nuclear power as one of their "wedges."[20] Instead, the crux of addressing global warming is political. The U.S. government gives multibillion-dollar subsidies to the coal, oil, gas, and nuclear industries, and gives little support to alternative energy sources like solar and

---

B o x 15.2   An Ethical Assessment of Geoengineering

While there are many questions about the feasibility, cost, and effectiveness of geoengineering plans, my colleague Alan Robock has been the most systematic and persistent of a number of scientists in raising ethical quandaries about the enterprise. But just how serious are these ethical quandaries?

Most science poses risks of unintended consequences, and lots of science raises issues of commercial and military control. At issue here is whether there is any reason to believe *ex ante* that these are special or unusually large risks. Merely asserting them does not ground an objection *per se*.

Not all of Robock's concerns involve ethics, but of those that do, some involve issues of procedural justice (such as who decides) while others involve matters of distributive justice (such as uneven benefit and harm). To simplify things, let's assume that injecting aerosols into the stratosphere successfully cooled Earth without any untoward effects and with evenly distributed benefits. One might still object that there are issues of procedural justice involved — who decides and who controls. But such concerns don't get much traction when everyone benefits.

Let's pull back from this idealization to imagine an outcome that involves untoward consequences and an uneven distribution of benefits. We deal with consequences by balancing them against the benefits of our interventions. The issue is whether or not we can obtain reliable estimates of both risks and benefits without full-scale implementation of the planned intervention. We already know from modeling that the impact of any such intervention will be uneven, but again, without knowing what the distribution of benefit and harm would be, it's hard to estimate how much this matters. Let's differentiate two circumstances under which going ahead with the intervention might be judged: One is where everyone benefits, while the other is a circumstance in which something less is the case. A conservative conclusion would be to say that beyond modeling and controlled, low-level tests (if the modeling justifies it), we shouldn't sanction any large-scale interventions unless they are in everyone's interest. A slightly eased condition, proposed by the philosopher Dale Jamieson, would be that at least nobody is worse off. That may not be as farfetched a condition as one might think, since, in the end, we are considering this intervention as a means to balance a risk we all face — global warming.

But suppose there are isolated livelihoods that only suffer negative effects of geoengineering. Then numbers begin to matter. In the case that a geoengineering scheme were to harm the few, we should have the foresight to be able to compensate, even if doing so requires something as drastic as relocating populations. I don't mean to oversimplify a complicated issue, but objection to any negative consequences whatsoever isn't a strong enough argument to end discussion.

More trenchant is the worry that the mere possibility of geoengineering would undermine other efforts to decrease our carbon output. Such moral hazard is a familiar worry, and we don't let it stop us in other areas: Antilock braking systems and airbags may cause some to drive more recklessly, but few would let that argument outweigh the overwhelming benefits of such safety features.

As Robock correctly asserts, the crux of addressing global warming may be a political — not a scientific — problem, but it doesn't follow that we may not need geoengineering to solve it. If it is a political problem, it is a *global* political problem, and getting global agreement to curb greenhouse gases is easier said than done.

> **B o x 15.2   An Ethical Assessment of Geoengineering** *(continued)*
>
> With geoengineering, in principle, one nation or agent could act, but a challenge arises if the intervention is certain to have uneven impacts among nations. At this early stage, there is no cost associated with improving our ability to quantify and describe what those inequalities would look like. Once we have those answers in hand, then we can engage in serious ethical consideration over whether or not to act.
>
> Martin Bunzl

wind power that could contribute to a solution. Similarly, the federal government is squashing attempts by states to mandate emissions reductions. If global warming is a political problem more than it is a technical problem, it follows that we don't need geoengineering to solve it.

The U.N. Framework Convention on Climate Change defines "dangerous anthropogenic interference" as *inadvertent* climate effects. However, states must also carefully consider geoengineering in their pledge to prevent dangerous anthropogenic interference with the climate system.

ENDNOTES

1. Paul Crutzen, "Albedo Enhancement by Stratospheric Sulfur Injections: A Contribution to Solve a Policy Dilemma?" *Climatic Change*, vol. 77, pp. 211–19 (2006); Tom M. L. Wigley, "A Combined Mitigation/Geoengineering Approach to Climate Stabilization," *Science*, vol. 314, pp. 452–54 (2006).

2. See the chapter on climate modification schemes in Spencer R. Weart, *The Discovery of Global Warming* (2007), available at http://www.aip.org/history/climate/ RainMake.htm; a long history of geoengineering proposals in James R. Fleming, "Fixing the Weather and Climate: Military and Civilian Schemes for Cloud Seeding and Climate Engineering," in Lisa Rosner, ed., *The Technological Fix* (New York: Routledge, 2004), pp. 175–200; and James R. Fleming, "The Pathological History of Weather and Climate Modification," *Historical Studies in the Physical Sciences*, vol. 37, pp. 3–25 (2006). See also N. Rusin and L. Flit, *Man Versus Climate* (Moscow: Peace Publishers, 1960); Mikhail I. Budyko, *Climatic Changes* (Washington, D.C.: American Geophysical Union, 1977); Ralph J. Cicerone et al., "Global Environmental Engineering," *Nature*, vol. 356, p. 472 (1992); Edward Teller et al., *Global Warming and Ice Ages: I. Prospects for Physics-Based Modulation of Global Change* (Lawrence Livermore National Laboratory Publication UCRL-JC-128715, 1997); David W. Keith, "Geoengineering the Climate: History and Prospect," *Annual Review of Energy and the Environment*, vol. 25, pp. 245–84 (2000).

3. John Latham first raised this idea in two articles that appeared in *Nature*, vol. 347, no. 6291: "Control of Global Warming," pp. 330–40, and "Effect on Global Warming of Wind-Dependent Aerosol Generation at the Ocean Surface," pp. 372–73 (1990). Keith Bower offers a numerical evaluation in "Computational Assessment of a Proposed Technique for Global Warming Mitigation Via Albedo-Enhancement of Marine Stratocumulous Clouds," *Atmospheric Research*, vol. 82, pp. 328–36 (2006).

4. See Lee Lane, Ken Caldeira, Robert Chatfield, and Stephanie Langhoff, eds., "Workshop Report on Managing Solar Radiation," NASA/CP-2007-214558 (2007).

5. Kevin E. Trenberth and Aiguo Dai, "Effects of Mount Pinatubo Volcanic Eruption on the Hydrological Cycle as an Analog of Geoengineering," *Geophysical Research Letters*, vol. 34, no. 16 (2007).

6. For more on warming over continents of the Northern Hemisphere, see Alan Robock, "Volcanic Eruptions and Climate," *Reviews of Geophysics*, vol. 38, pp. 191–219 (2000): Georgiy Stenchikov et al., "Arctic Oscillation Response to Volcanic Eruptions in the IPCC AR4 Climate Models," *Journal of Geophysical Research*, vol. 111 (2006). For more on the effects of Asian and African monsoons, see Luke Oman et al., "Climatic Response to High-Latitude Volcanic Eruptions," *Journal of Geophysical Research*, vol. 110 (2005); Luke Oman et al., "High-Latitude Eruptions Cast Shadow Over the African Monsoon and the Flow of the Nile," *Geophysical Research Letters*, vol. 33 (2006).

7. Royal Society, *Ocean Acidification Due to Increasing Atmospheric Carbon Dioxide*, June 30, 2005, available at royalsociety.org/displaypagedoc.asp?id=13539

8. Susan Solomon et al., "The Role of Aerosol Variations in Anthropogenic Ozone Depletion at Northern Midlatitudes," *Journal of Geophysical Research*, vol. 101 (1996); Susan Solomon. "Stratospheric Ozone Depletion: A Review of Concepts and History," *Reviews of Geophysics*, vol. 37 (1999).

9. L. Gu et al., "Responses of Net Ecosystem Exchanges of Carbon Dioxide to Changes in Cloudiness: Results from Two North American Deciduous Forests," *Journal of Geophysical Research*, vol. 104, no. 31, pp. 421–31, 434 (1999); L. Gu et al., "Advantages of Diffuse Radiation for Terrestrial Ecosystem Productivity," *Journal of Geophysical Research*, vol. 107 (2002); L. Gu et al., "Response of a Deciduous Forest to the Mount Pinatubo Eruption: Enhanced Photosynthesis," *Science*, vol. 299, pp. 2,035–38 (2003).

10. Budyko, *Climatic Changes*.

11. Richard P. Turco et al., "A Study of Mesospheric Rocket Contrails and Clouds Produced by Liquid-Fueled Rockets," *Space Solar Power Review*, vol. 3, pp. 223–34 (1982); V. A. Mohnen, "Stratospheric Ion and Aerosol Chemistry and Possible Links With Cirrus Cloud Microphysics — A Critical Assessment," *Journal of Atmospheric Science*, vol. 47, pp. 1,933–48 (1990).

12. K. Sassen et al., "The 5–6 December 1991 FIRE IFO II Jet Stream Cirrus Case Study: Possible Influences of Volcanic Aerosols," *Journal of Atmospheric Science*, vol. 52, pp. 97–123 (1993).

13. D. W. Olsen et al., "When the Sky Ran Red: The Story Behind *The Scream*," *Sky & Telescope*, February 2004, pp. 29–35.

14. For the estimate for reducing incoming solar radiation, see Balan Govindasamy and Ken Caldeira, "Geoengineering Earth's Radiation Balance to Mitigate CO_2-Induced Climate Change," *Geophysical Research Letters*, vol. 27, pp. 2,141–44 (2000). For the response of solar power systems, see Michael C. MacCracken, "Geoengineering: Worthy of Cautious Evaluation?" *Climatic Change*, vol. 77, pp. 235–43 (2006).

15. Robock, "Volcanic Eruptions and Climate," pp. 191–219.

16. Roger P. Angel, "Feasibility of Cooling the Earth with a Cloud of Small Spacecraft Near the Inner Lagrange Point (L_1)," *Proceedings of the National Academy of Sciences*, vol. 103, pp. 17,184–89 (2006).

17. See Figure 1 in Wigley, "A Combined Mitigation/Geoengineering Approach to Climate Stabilization," pp. 452–54, and Figure 3 in H. Damon Matthews and Ken Caldeira, "Transient Climate-Carbon Simulations of Planetary Geoengineering," *Proceedings of the National Academy of Sciences*, vol. 104, pp. 9,949–54 (2007).

18. See for example Stephen H. Schneider, "Earth Systems: Engineering and Management," *Nature*, vol. 409, pp. 417–19, 421 (2001), and Ralph J. Cicerone, "Geoengineering: Encouraging Research and Overseeing Implementation," *Climatic Change*, vol. 77, pp. 221–26 (2006).

19. James R. Fleming writes eloquently about the militaristic history of climate modification schemes in "The Climate Engineers," *Wilson Quarterly*, Spring 2007, pp. 46–60. See also Fleming, "Fixing the Weather and Climate," and Fleming, "The Pathological History of Weather and Climate Modification."

20. Stephen W. Pacala and Robert Socolow, "Stabilization Wedges: Solving the Climate Problem for the Next 50 Years with Current Technologies," *Science*, vol. 305, pp. 968–72 (2004); Alan Robock, "Nuclear Power's Costs and Perils" (Letter to the Editor), *Physics Today*, vol. 60, no. 1, p. 14 (2007).

PART V

Contemporary Technological Dilemmas: The New Biology

The twentieth century is often regarded as the century of physics. Discoveries in physics including quantum theory, general and special relativity, the basic constituents of the atom, the nature of subatomic forces, the photon and the nature of light, and the like led to the incredible technological progress that took place during that century: computers, wireless communication, lasers, television and so many other technologies that are now part of our daily lives.

The twenty-first century, scientists, technologists, and futurists agree, will most likely be known as the century of biology.

The explosion of knowledge began with the discovery of the structure of DNA in the mid-twentieth century. The understanding of the double helix led to the growing ability to manipulate our genes and those of other organisms. Research in biology now depends on computers and information technology, modeling, imaging technologies, materials science — technologies that are transforming the life sciences and in turn laying the foundation for enormous progress in the technologies of medicine, in understanding of the human brain, as well as in such fields as energy, agriculture, and environmental science.

Part V is devoted to the nature and implications of this new biology. It opens with a discussion of perhaps the most morally and politically divisive area that has entered the science, technology and policy arena in recent times — human embryonic stem cell research. Christopher Thomas Scott provides a balanced introduction to the possibilities offered by research in this contentious area as well as the arguments of its advocates and its opponents. While stem cell research has been debated for well over a decade, synthetic biology — the subject of the next two chapters — is relatively new, at least outside the realm of fiction.

The ability to create a self-replicating genome from laboratory chemicals, demonstrated for the first time in 2010, has stimulated widespread debate about the potential and limits of synthetic biology. Articles from the Presidential Commission for the Study of Bioethical Issues and from the journal *Nature* are included here to help frame the emerging issues in this field. Next, Michael Sandel, a political philosopher at Harvard who teaches one of the most popular courses offered at that institution, argues "The Case against Perfection," exploring the moral issues raised by the technologies of human genetic enhancement in such realms as physical strength, memory, height, and sex selection of babies. Finally, Stanford law professor Henry Greely looks at the profound and difficult issues raised by current and potential future developments in neuroscience, one of the fastest growing areas of the new biology. His discussion intersects with Sandel's in some areas, such as the enhancement of the brain's capabilities, but it also goes into such areas as lie detection in criminal justice and even detection of racial or ethnic bias. In all, these chapters suggest the exciting possibilities — and the complex dilemmas — that the century of biology has in store.

16

Stem Cell Research: The Great Moral Divide

CHRISTOPHER THOMAS SCOTT

The debate over use of human embryonic stem cells in medical research and, ultimately, in therapy has been raging in the United States for over a decade, since James Thomson at the University of Wisconsin, Madison, became the first person to isolate and culture this unique type of cell. Under proper conditions, these cells are capable of developing into any of the more than 200 cell types in the human body. In other words, if a number of difficult hurdles are overcome through research, such cells open up possibilities for what is being called "regenerative medicine" or tissue replacement, potentially leading to cures for Parkinson's disease, diabetes, spinal cord injuries, and many more causes of human suffering. The catch is that the process of creating a stem cell line (a live culture maintained artificially after being separated from its original source) destroys a fertilized human egg — a blastocyst or pre-embryo — that, if implanted in a woman's uterus, could grow into a person. Balancing these two considerations is at the root of the stem cell controversy. Some countries have policies encouraging stem cell research; others have banned it or declared moratoriums.

In the United States, stem cell research is one of the most politicized areas of science. While stem cell research conducted without government funding is legal almost everywhere in the country, federal funding remains in dispute. President George W. Bush issued an executive order in August 2001 limiting federal funding to research using stem cell lines already in existence on the date and time of the speech announcing the policy. Early in his presidency, in March 2009, President Barack Obama fulfilled a campaign promise and pleased scientists and patient advocates by overturning the Bush policy. Under the Obama

Administration, the National Institutes of Health initiated a modest program of research grants. About a year and a half later, in August 2010, a federal judge, in response to a suit brought by two scientists and a group called the Alliance Defense Fund, issued a temporary injunction stopping the stem cell research program in its tracks. The judge ruled that the Obama policy violated a law banning "research in which a human embryo or embryos are destroyed, discarded or knowingly subjected to risk of injury or death." The ruling caught the biomedical research community, which had thought the policy was settled by President Obama's executive order, by surprise. Although an appeals court suspended implementation of the injunction two weeks later, allowing federally funded embryonic stem cell research to continue, as of this writing the matter remains in dispute and may well end up in the Supreme Court. In the following article, Christopher Thomas Scott looks at the ethical issues underlying the stem cell debate, quoting sources from all sides of this complex issue.

Scott is a senior research scholar in the Center for Biomedical Ethics at the Stanford University School of Medicine. He is director of the Program on Stem Cells in Society and has served as a member of the Stem Cell Research Advisory Panel at the medical school. He holds degrees in biological sciences as well as policy and has a wide range of publications, including Stem Cell Now: From the Experiment That Shook the World to the New Politics of Life, *from which this article was taken.*

Nobody, I imagine, will credit me with a desire to limit the
empire of physical science, but I really feel bound to
confess that a great many very familiar and, at the
same time, extremely important phenomena lie
quite beyond its legitimate limits.
THOMAS HUXLEY[1]

The newly fertilized egg, a corpuscle one two-hundredth of an inch in diameter, is not a human being. It is a set of instructions set adrift into the cavity of the womb, wrote E. O. Wilson, a Pulitzer prize–winning zoologist.[2] But where E. O. Wilson seems unperturbed, Charles Krauthammer, M.D., a syndicated columnist and member of the President's Council on Bioethics (PCBE), a 17-member group charged [in the administration of George W. Bush] with advising the president on the ethics of biological innovation, is deeply concerned. "We will, slowly and by increments, have gone from stem cells to embryo farms to factories with fetuses hanging (metaphorically) on meat hooks waiting to be cut open and used by the already born."[3]

The two quotes reflect opposite poles of an emotionally charged debate about the use of human embryonic stem cells (hESCs) for research and medicine. The rhetoric often reveals from which side of the debate the person speaks. Supporters of hESC research sometimes describe the human embryo as nothing more than a ball of cells; opponents mention the embryo as if it were a newborn baby. Others portray the blastocyst as something in between: neither a clump of cells nor a person. All who consider the question of using embryos for research share one thing: passion. Embryonic stem cells touch us deeply, not just because they might cure disease. It is because forms of human life are at stake — living embryos and living persons.

Many ethical questions touch hESC research. What are our moral obligations to the sick among us who could benefit from embryonic stem cell research? What roles do family, religion, and society play, and how do they inform our opinions and decisions? How do we properly explain the benefits and risks of using embryos and cells to the individuals and parents who donate them? Who should benefit from the first therapies, and how will we pay for them? Tackling these questions could fill an entire book. But the ethical question on most people's minds (including people in the federal government) is whether a four- to six-day-old human embryo — the blastocyst — should be used to make lines of hESCs. Adult stem cells taken from a consenting person's body don't raise the same ethical concerns. Adult stem cells made from embryonic stem cells do.

A much more incendiary issue is whether somatic cell nuclear transfer (SCNT) should be used to make cloned humans for medical or other purposes. Here, the ethical positions are unanimous: both sides of the debate overwhelmingly condemn human reproductive cloning. Making a cloned human would require surmounting all the difficulties inherent in nuclear transfer, many of which may never be fully understood. Attempting to overcome these problems in order to achieve a normal birth or to use embryos to make fetuses or human beings for spare parts would amount to the worst forms of illegal and unethical human experimentation. Our moral codes are designed to protect people in our pursuit of knowledge, and humans or fetuses cloned for research purposes fall squarely and unambiguously into this category. Despite the universal agreement on prohibiting human cloning, some, like Charles Krauthammer, worry that if we use embryos for research, unscrupulous persons will use them to create more developed forms of life, including humans. Because of this, they argue, it is best to err on the side of safety and not use embryos at all.

PHILOSOPHY MEETS THE NEW BIOLOGY

Philosophers, theologians, and entire societies are wrestling with these questions, so much so that a new field, bioethics, has emerged to study the advances of medicine and technology and their impact on humankind. Bioethics is a child of the field of medical ethics, the qualities embodied by practitioners of medicine, who are enjoined to heal and not to harm; to (if asked) refuse to extinguish life; and to strictly keep the confidence of their patients. But, 40 years ago, the "new biology" entered the arena and, with it, an avalanche of discovery. Scientists could insert foreign genes into living things and transplant human organs. No longer do we think only about the pros and cons of traditional medical care; we now face the ability of science to change our human future — and change it radically.

Bioethics is still a young field, and the rapid pace of stem cell biology is just one area challenging ethics to stay in step. In academia, dozens of programs in bioethics, most within medical schools, grapple with a wide range of rapidly evolving issues. One of the early thinkers in the field, Albert Jonsen, a specialist in medical ethics and former presidential advisor, writes, "Only half of bioethics counts as an ordinary academic discipline: the half that has original and borrowed theory, principles, and methods. But only part of bioethics lies within the academy, where scholars worry about whether they have a discipline to teach and promote. The other half of bioethics is the public discourse: people of all sorts and professions talking and arguing about bioethical questions."[4]

Jonsen is right about public discourse. Our moral universe is changing and challenging us, impinged upon and steered by ethics debates. Over time classic ethics endeavored to describe our world and the best prescriptions for living in it. The results often translate into laws and public policy — the voice of governments and institutions. When it comes to stem cells, the positions taken by scholars and philosophers are strewn across the map. It is worth exploring the views of a handful of prominent bioethicists — including members of President George W. Bush's ethics council — to see how the discourse on stem cells is shaping up.

THE MORAL STATUS OF THE EMBRYO

Of all the moral dimensions of stem cell research, the human embryo looms largest. Recall that viable embryos may be created two ways: naturally, through the process of conception, or artificially, through either nuclear transfer or *in vitro* fertilization (IVF). In the latter case, removing the inner cell mass (ICM) in order to produce stem cells destroys the embryo. The cells may survive indefinitely, but the embryo is gone. Fertilized eggs kept in a freezer or blastocysts grown in a lab will never develop into a fetus or human because the outer layer of cells, the trophoblast, is missing. Normal development and a live birth require a viable embryo's successful implantation into the uterus, where it will grow to term.

What should we do with leftover embryos from IVF procedures? Are we justified in using them for the purposes of research? Should we create embryos using nuclear transfer so that we may use them for therapies? Do we treat embryos the same as a newborn or a child or even as an adult? The moral status of an embryo — whether we consider it a mere object, a human being, or somewhere in between — is the subject of thousands of pages of opinion, essays, and research. A rough sorting divides the issue into two camps. One group believes that embryos deserve protection and should not be used for research. The other group believes that embryos can be used and embryonic stem cell research should proceed. The divining rod prompting each stance is the moral weight given to the embryo.

[An early stage embryo (known as a blastocyst) is between 0.1 and 0.2 mm in diameter.] If we place a culture dish under a microscope and peer at the embryo at this stage, should we protect it from harm? If not, should it be used to save others from disability, disease, and death? The debate pivots around these two questions.

PROTECT THE EMBRYO

The answers depend, in part, on whether we believe the embryo has a soul or is a person; in essence, whether it is a human being. If so, then we should protect it. [Former] presidential council members Robert P. George and Alfonso Gómez-Lobo — the first a political scientist and the second a philosopher — are clear about where they stand. They write, "A human embryo is a whole living member of the species *Homo sapiens* in the earliest stage of his or her natural development.... The human embryo, then, is a whole (though immature) and distinct human organism — a human being."[5] Their position is based on the fact that human development proceeds along a continuum. Each of us was once a one-celled zygote, embryo, fetus, and an adult. To George and Gómez-Lobo, each stage represents a different version of the same person. If the zygote has the "natural capacity" to become a person, they argue, then it's an either/or matter: "a 'thing' either is or is not a whole human being."

Conservative Christian thinkers agree. Gilbert Meilaender, a Lutheran theologian and member of the president's council, considers the embryo "the weakest and least advantaged of our fellow human beings."[6] Meilaender believes that the embryo's mere presence is enough to make it a person, though we may be barely aware of it during the early stages of a pregnancy or when it is stored for use at a reproductive clinic. He warns that some of his fellow philosophers define the concept of "person" too narrowly, "trying to find some capacity — perhaps self-awareness, reasoning power, or sense of oneself as having a history — that marks the point at which human beings become persons (or cease to be persons)."[7] The Valparaiso theologian might disagree with the English philosopher John Locke (1632–1704), who described a person as "a thinking, intelligent being, that has reason and reflection, that can consider itself as itself, the same thinking thing, in different times and places."[8] The traits Locke describes can be broadly interpreted: humans who have lost or never acquired these abilities may not be persons; animals with these traits could be construed as persons.

"I think it is accurate to state that a person is simply a 'someone who' — a someone who has a history," Meilaender says. "That history begins before we have some of the highest human capacities and, for many of us, it may continue after we have lost those capacities. But we remain the same person throughout the trajectory of our life." Meilaender's concept of personal history — and *personhood* — thus begins before we are conscious of it and continues after we have lost consciousness. Acknowledging this history gives the embryo the same amount of respect that we would give a fully conscious adult human being.

Some philosophers use a different rationale to argue for the protection of embryos. They say that our uncertainties about embryos are enough to give us pause. Although council advisors George and Gómez-Lobo characterize human development as a seamless series of the "same person," those who aren't sure about that claim say that it is impossible to pinpoint when the metaphysical characteristics of soul and personhood begin. Perhaps the blastocyst has a scintilla of personhood at four days — how can we really know? If an embryo is *possibly* a person, they contend, then it follows that destroying an embryo could possibly mean killing a person. Given this doubt, we should leave it alone. The Christian ethicist Robert Song believes that using embryos for research and medicine requires a "burden of proof " that they are *not* persons. "The merely possible personhood of the embryo may *seem* abstract or theoretical in comparison with the concrete hopes for clinical treatments." But it is proof enough, he says. "[F]or all one knows, they are persons, and should be treated as persons."[9]

A similar argument rests on the fact that a one-celled embryo *will* become a person, circumstances permitting. It uses a concept rich with meaning in stem cell biology: potential. A fertilized egg has the potential to become a fully realized person and, when an embryo is destroyed, its potential to become human is destroyed, too. When something dies naturally, as in the case of a fertilized egg that never implants in the uterus, or intentionally, when a less-than-perfect zygote is discarded after an IVF procedure, the occurrence causes us to reflect and wonder what that embryo could have been. President George W. Bush's former chief advisor on bioethics, Leon Kass, puts it this way. "[I] must acknowledge that the human blastocyst is (1) human in origin and (2) *potentially* a mature human being, if all goes well."[10]

The official positions of conservative religions consider the embryo as a human being. The Southern Baptist Convention, noted for their long-standing position on abortion, strenuously opposes human embryo research and calls upon research centers to "cease and desist from research which destroys human embryos, the most vulnerable members of the human community."[11] Both the Orthodox Christian and Methodist churches assert that embryo research is a fundamental violation of human life. The Anglican view, prepared as a brief for the House of Lords in 2002, elevates the moral status of the embryo as sacred, containing "the very beginning of each human being."[12]

The Catholic Church declares that God bestows personhood and a soul at the moment of conception. The official position of the Vatican, however, has shifted over the years. Saint Thomas Aquinas (1225–1274) believed that a human soul was not present at conception, but appeared between 40 and 90 days later.[13] In 1974, the Vatican wrote in its *Declaration on Procured Abortion*, "Respect for human life is called for from the time that the process of generation begins. From the time that the ovum is fertilized, a life is begun which is neither that of the father nor of the mother, it is rather the life of a new human being with his own growth."[14] The church went on to define an embryo as a person in 1987. The instruction, called the *Donum Vitae* (The Gift of Life), explains, "From the time that the ovum is fertilized ... [it] demands the unconditional respect that is morally due to the human being in his bodily and spiritual totality ... [and] his rights as a person must be recognized, among which in the first place is the inviolable right of every innocent human being to life."[15]

For the Vatican, the unique combination of genes resulting from meiosis and fertilization is enough to trigger personhood. Using the *Donum Vitae* as its guide, the church condemns the use of embryos for research. In 2000, it wrote that removing the inner cell mass from an embryo "is a gravely immoral act, and consequently is gravely illicit."[16]

USE THE EMBRYO

On the other side of the moral divide are those who believe that embryos are not people and maintain that we can — indeed must — use them to help humankind. Not surprisingly, many scientists, patients, and doctors hold this view. Moderate and left-leaning philosophers and theologians tend to be in this camp and disagree — at times vehemently — with their conservative colleagues on the moral status of the embryo.

If polls are any indication of American religious sentiment, they show a disagreement between those who profess faith and those who institutionalize it. The fracture is particularly notable among mainstream American Protestants and Catholics. In a Harris Poll conducted in August 2004, 73 percent of Catholics voted in favor of embryonic stem cell research; only 11 percent were against it. The margin of Protestants in favor of research was even larger — 8 to 1. Even among the "evangelical" or "born-again" Christians so important to the conservative political right, only one in five voted against using embryos.[17]

Other exceptions to the "bright line" religious views include the American Presbyterian Church. Its resolution places the respect of sick persons above the respect due the embryo, affirming the use of stem cells "for research that may result in the restoring the health of those suffering from serious illness."[18] A growing number of centrist Catholic theologians don't consider the embryo before two weeks of age an individual human entity. Other moderate Catholics use an ethical middle ground called "proportionate reason," which tolerates a "lesser evil" to bring about a "greater good." Michael Mendiola, a Catholic and professor of Christian ethics in the Graduate Theological Union at Berkeley, California, suggests one version of this compromise: a requirement that researchers consistently seek to move beyond the use of human embryos while allowing their use in the near term.[19]

Lutheran Theologians Ted Peters and Gaymon Bennett use a bioethical principle of beneficence — a moral obligation to act for the benefit of others — to make a case for supporting embryonic stem cell research.[20] They recall the parable of the Good Samaritan, who pursues one goal: to heal a suffering stranger. The duo contrasts positive acts to help others against an instinct to protect the embryo, a position they summarize as "better safe than sorry." Bennett, an affable young religious scholar who studies at the Center for Theology and the Natural Sciences in Berkeley, California, doesn't fit the image of a gray-haired philosopher with a furrowed brow.* He says he wants a just world — where people suffer less.

---

* Bennett is now (2011) the Communications Coordinator for the Science and Religion Course Program at the Center for Theology and the Natural Sciences, at Berkeley.— *ed.*

"I think about how science can help me bring about that kind of world. But I also consider how science can get in the way of achieving that aim."[21] He notes that for most people, the stem cell debate comes down to three questions: What are our responsibilities for (1) people who are sick and injured, (2) the embryo's protection, and (3) the unseen consequences of the research? On question (3), Bennett says, "We shouldn't believe 'anything goes.' Ethics argues against doing science purely for science's sake. We need a philosophy that guides science and we must realize we won't always have a perfect match of scientific and ethical truth."

Even with these cautions in mind, Peters and Bennett say the potential benefits of medicine should come first. Opponents of hESC research maintain that we should uphold human dignity and, as a result, protect the embryo. The two theologians point out that we aren't certain about when an embryo or fetus becomes human. In the meantime, we are certain there is plenty of human suffering, and these people could benefit from discoveries made with embryonic stem cells. Because of this certainty, they argue, we should pursue hESC research.[22]

The Jewish faith's assessment of the early embryo's moral position stands in stark contrast to conservative Christian dogma. Laurie Zoloth is a Jewish philosopher and professor of medical ethics at Northwestern University. Jewish religious law — called *halachah* — uses a defense of justice in all of its deliberations about medicine and health-care. Zoloth describes the mandate *pikauch nefesh*, the duty to save a life and to heal. If healing is mandatory then embryonic stem cells *must* be used. She explains that with the exceptions of the ill-begotten use of murder, adultery, or idolatry, "If one can save a life, one must save a life; if one can heal, one must heal."[23]

Is breaking apart an embryo in the lab murder? *Halachah* says no, it is not considered murder, nor is it considered killing. Zoloth uses an example of Judaic case law to illustrate. "Suppose two men are fighting and as a consequence a pregnant woman is injured as an innocent bystander. If she has a miscarriage, we consider the harm has come to the woman — not to the potential child." The rabbinical text treats pregnancy as a continuous process, with the moral status of the embryo, fetus, and newborn gradually increasing along the way. Pregnancy — along with a significant moral imprint — isn't officially recognized until after 40 days. "The old texts describe the developmental period before 40 days like water," Zoloth says. "It makes practical sense if you think about it. If a pregnancy ended before 40 days, you wouldn't be able to detect a recognizable human form with the naked eye." The same reasoning applies to embryos in a laboratory dish. They don't have true moral status unless they are implanted in a woman and survive until 40 days. Zoloth points out, however, that we should not be careless with embryos and that they should be treated with special consideration and respect.

Jewish religious leaders emphasize the importance of the duty to heal. In a written statement prepared for a government commission on bioethics in 2000, Rabbi Elliot Dorff of the University of Judaism contends, "[I]n light of our divine mandate to seek to maintain life and health, one might even argue that from a Jewish perspective, we have a duty to proceed with that research."[24] In the same session, Yeshiva University's Rabbi Moshe Dovid Tendler extends a warning, "[A] fence that prevents the cure of fatal diseases must not be erected, for then the loss is greater than the benefit. In the Judeo-biblical legislative tradition, a fence that causes pain and suffering is dismantled. Even biblical law is superseded by the duty to save lives."[25]

Interpretations of Islamic law also find support for the use of embryos for research. As in many cultures, Islam's debate about the status of extracorporeal tissue arises from its discussion about cells taken from aborted fetuses for therapies. Opinion and law about embryos and stem cells are sparse, but in a review of both Shi'ite and Sunni interpretations of the Koran, the Islamic scholar Abdulaziz Sachedina mentions that most opinions state that the soul is formed sometime after the early stages of embryogenesis. As a rule, Islam usually accepts abortion before the eightieth day. Like Judaism, Islam permits interventions in nature that will further a greater good for humanity. But Sachedina also notes that there is disagreement among Muslim jurists about whether embryos in IVF clinics have a predefined sanctity, ensuring their protection, or no sanctity, allowing their destruction.[26]

PHILOSOPHICAL ARGUMENTS

Philosophers and ethicists describe the concept of *sentience*, the capacity to feel psychic or physical pleasure or pain. In order to be sentient, an animal or person must be conscious of its existence. Permanently unconscious persons — including those classified neurologically as being in a "persistent vegetative state" — lack sentience. Though we think of them as human, we also acknowledge that they lack an essential quality of "being in the world," that is, relating, speaking, and thinking like other members of society. Such experiences make certain creatures not just a thing, but also a being. In other words, consciousness, whether it is explained behaviorally or neurochemically, is the experience of *being a being*.[27] Sentient beings deserve our respect and demand that we're attentive to the possibility of causing them pain, fear, or discomfort.

Biology isn't adept at defining when a soul becomes present or when a person emerges during development. However, biology can be helpful when we think about sentience. The threshold of sentience can be estimated in developmental and biochemical terms, when the nervous system has matured. When are the sensations of pleasure and pain and an inkling of consciousness possible? At this juncture, it's best to ask a neuroscientist.

Michael Gazzaniga has spent a career at the edge of brain biology and is another member of the PCBE. The formation of the brain is a *tour de force*, a long process that begins early in development. The neuroscientist disagrees with some of his fellow council members about the status of an embryo, and bases his position on what he understands about brain biology. He points out that the human brain isn't viable until gestation has reached six months — about the same time a fetus could survive a premature birth in a hospital's neonatal unit.[28] Working backward through time, the brain's first electrical activity is detected around week six and the major divisions of the brain don't form until week four. The primitive streak — an indentation on the embryo that signals the scant beginnings of a nervous system — appears at 15 days.

In contrast to those who consider an embryo the same moral person at different stages, Gazzaniga believes that moral rights of the developing human begin at six months, coincident with its survival outside the womb. Just as Zoloth describes the early stages of embryogenesis "like water," Gazzaniga uses a perceptual (and emotional) cue to imagine brain function at eight weeks, when the head of the fetus begins to look human. He writes, "I am reacting to a sentiment that wells up in me, a perceptual moment that is stark, defining, and real. The brain at [eight weeks] is hardly a brain that could sustain any serious mental life."[29]

There are other, nuanced arguments made by philosophers and commentators who support hESC research. James Wilson, an emeritus professor of public policy at the University of California, Los Angeles, resigned from the PCBE in May 2005. He wrote in the council's 2002 report, "My view is that people endow a thing with humanity when it appears, or even begins to appear, human — that is, when it resembles a human creature. The more an embryo resembles a person, the more claims it exerts on our moral feelings."[30] Others note that had a modern version of "technological ethics" been present a century earlier, we could well be without air travel, space flight, or the benefits derived from other risky areas of science.[31] A number of scholars respond to religious "sanctity of life" views by pointing out that up to half of fertilized eggs never implant in the uterus or, if implanted, fail to develop. If the Vatican contends that life begins at conception, then, the argument goes, how could God create a system for making babies that destroys half of them?[32] Zoloth says, "Of all the things I don't understand about God's plan, I do understand this: part of the way the world is structured is that every time you become pregnant, you do not produce a living being. I know that one can be a woman of faith and experience a miscarriage and understand that you have not failed."

The assertion that an embryo should not be destroyed because it has the potential to become a person or possibly is a person is countered by a world full of real people, each with a fully realized potential. Professor of ethics and theology James Petersen writes, "How can we let patients who are unmistakably people die to protect embryos that, even if implanted, may or may not turn out to someday become persons? We should not kill people to benefit others, but we should also not let people die to protect human tissue such as sperm or ova, even though such gametes have great potential."[33]

THE PURSUIT OF PERFECTION

Conservative Christian thinkers and commentators, including a number of the president's advisors, brook no argument when it comes to morality and human forms of life. The message from members of this group is clear: "Leave the embryo alone." They believe that carelessly using an embryo for scientific research is the same as carelessly using a person for scientific research. Destroying an embryo is equal to killing a person.

It is not simply a case of Christian morality at work among those who object to hESC research. The connection to personhood recalls longstanding moral instructions from philosophers like Immanuel Kant (1724–1804), who said that persons should never be used as a means for someone else's ends. The Kantian ethic of how we should treat each other is an essential ingredient of our professional codes of medicine — doctors must treat patients with dignity and respect and, above all, "do no harm." If an embryo is a person, then the Kantian imperatives apply.

Whichever side of the debate one chooses, dead philosophers help us only up to a point. It is no exaggeration to say that looking at early embryonic life in the glare of modern technology provokes a visceral response in some, and the feeling translates into a values-laden moral opinion. For example, Michael Gazzaniga uses his "gut feeling" and what he knows about science to determine that the embryo is not a person. The neuroscientist's political colleague was Leon Kass, former chairman of the PCBE. To Kass, the "gut feeling" is a sinking one. His reaction doesn't have much to do with whether the embryo has a moral status — Kass maintains he is "agnostic" on that point. A University of Chicago philosopher with degrees in medicine and biochemistry, Kass says our *hubris* is the danger — Americans have developed a scientific swagger that threatens our humanity. Because of our overconfident attitude, we find ourselves teetering on the precipice of a "slippery slope." Kass writes, "In leading laboratories, academic and industrial, new creators are confidently amassing their powers and quietly honing their skills, while on the street their evangelists are zealously prophesying a posthuman future."[34]

What lies at the bottom of Kass's stance that we have embarked on a perilous decent? An existence akin to Aldous Huxley's *Brave New World*, a futuristic place with an amoral society living in perfect health. *New World*'s inhabitants have technology to blame for the lack of their humanity; children are born in embryo factories and tranquilizing drugs distributed by technocrats control adult behavior. Kass finds a deep resonance with Huxley's dystopic vision and compares it to our devotion to biomedical technologies, including those that deal with the human embryo. He begins with *in vitro* fertilization. The reproductive clinician, Kass believes, subverts family values by becoming a third partner along with the parents of the newly implanted embryo.[35] He is fearful that if left unchallenged, scientists will genetically engineer babies, grow "newborns" in laboratory vats, and use them as helpless factories to produce medical products and human parts.[36] The embryos in his posthuman future are treated as "mere meat" and "human caviar."[37]

Kass admits his images are meant to provoke — Laurie Zoloth describes his views as a "philosophy that demands engagement." Though Kass avers that the embryo probably deserves less respect than a human being, he thinks we should treat it with dignity. After all, each of us begins life as an embryo and if *we* are worthy of dignity, then we are worthy of such respect at every stage of our existence. To experiment with an embryo is to meddle with nature, or worse, to play God. In this worldview, nature and God are intertwined and inseparable. Genetic engineering, genetic testing, *in vitro* fertilization, mood-enhancing drugs, and embryonic stem cells — indeed, any technology that pushes beyond "natural limits" — are listed as dangerous outcomes of our headlong pursuit of perfection.[38] In this very important respect, Kass is in agreement with conservative Christians about the embryo and hESC research. The trouble with biotechnology, writes fellow council member Michael Sandel, is that it represents "the one-sided triumph of willfulness over giftedness, of dominion over reverence, of molding over beholding." It leads, according to Sandel, a Harvard University professor of government, to a confusion "of our role with God's."[39] There is a distinction between using science for therapeutic reasons (antibiotics to overcome an infection) and using science for human enhancement (increasing our lifespans or our capacity for memory) concludes Meilaender. "Here is where the limitlessness of our desire enters in," he warns. "Enhancement deliberately tries to move beyond the normal condition of our species — and there is no end to the ways in which we might like to be 'better.' Either we get a grip on that desire or it will increase its already strong hold on us."[*]

A cadre of commentators who worry about scientific "progress" echoes the *Brave New World* philosophy. If we aren't careful, they say, Huxley's fictional world may come to pass. Among the group is Daniel Callahan, a co-founder of the Hastings Center for Bioethics, a think tank nestled in a tree-lined acreage [about 50 miles north] of New York City. In his 2003 book, *What Price Better Health: Hazards of the Research Imperative*, Callahan writes that biomedical research has become a "moral imperative" with its promise to win the battle against the "diseases of aging." The spoils of war are longer, healthier lives. Our attempts to find ways of living longer shouldn't be a mandate. Callahan contends, "We ought to act in a beneficent way toward our fellow citizens, but there are many ways of doing that, and medical research can claim no more of us than many other worthy ways of spending our time and resources."[40] It's a fair argument: scarce resources can be better spent on preventing illness and disability and teaching people how to take care of their own health. Regenerative medicine seems to fall squarely within Callahan's crosshairs. He writes, "Unless someone can come up with a plausible case that the nation needs everyone to live much longer, and longer than the present steady gain of normalization will bring, there is no reason whatever for government-supported research aimed at maximizing or optimizing lifespans."

Joining Callahan and Kass is Francis Fukuyama. The professor of international political economy at Johns Hopkins University writes in the introduction to his book, *Our Posthuman Future: Consequences of the Biotechnology Revolution*, "The aim of this book is to argue that Huxley was right, that the most significant threat posed by contemporary biotechnology is the possibility that it will alter human nature and thereby move us into a 'posthuman' stage of history."[41]

---

[*]For more on enhancement see Chapter 19.

Another member of the president's council, Fukuyama warns, "New procedures and technologies emerging from research laboratories and hospitals ... can as easily be used to 'enhance' the species as to ease or ameliorate illness."[42] What are Fukuyama's remedies? In terms of the embryo, he sides with Kass: "I believe that human embryos ... are not the moral equivalents of infants, nor are they simply clumps of cells like any other tissue that can be discarded at will."[43] He argues for more regulation, but deems the American government unfit to oversee stem cell research. He cites how our present patchwork of regulations lag behind biomedical science's breakneck pace.[44]

TRUTH-TELLING

Among those who believe that hESC research should wait includes an ethicist who charges the real truth about stem cells has gone missing. The hype about cures — used by the media, stem cell supporters, and scientists alike — obscures the very real possibility that any cures of substance will be a long time coming, if they come at all. This is the sentiment of council member Rebecca Dresser. A professor at Washington University School of Law, Dresser maintains "truth-telling" is an overlooked dimension of stem cell ethics. "Scientists must be clear with patients, egg donors, and the public about the stage of this research. We don't know if it will produce treatments and cures," she says. "Research often surprises, and just as doctors should be honest about a poor prognosis or an uncertain outcome, researchers should be honest about all the things that remain to be looked at and tested."[45]

Dresser cites other, ballyhooed, scientific "revolutions" that have yet come to pass. "My skepticism comes from living through so many examples of excitement, including gene therapy and fetal tissue transplants. A lot of this stuff never works, and it takes a lot longer than people think. If it does produce an incremental benefit, it might only extend their lives for a few years." Dresser's statement might run afoul of critically ill patients, their families, and doctors who regard mere months of extra living as precious commodities. Yet looking deeper into the maw of healthcare reform and the best way to distribute scarce resources, her logic — along with Daniel Callahan's — demands a second thought. Why should we spend all this money at the leading edge of science? Wouldn't it be a much better use of resources to devise, for example, a fair and just means of distributing treatments we currently have to patients who need it? Dresser claims she isn't against hESC research per se. "Look, private funds can be used for stem cell research. And other countries permit it," Dresser states. "There are other exciting areas of research that could benefit from federal funding. It seems to me there ought to be a way to use the funding to benefit patients without violating the strongly held moral views of a large group of people in this country."

Along with nine other members of the president's council, Dresser voted in 2002 for a recommendation to place a four-year moratorium on embryonic stem cell research. At least in some council members' minds, the moratorium was designed to force scientists and supporters to write guidelines and rules to regulate hESC research. As the first anniversary of the PCBB recommendation nears, would Rebecca Dresser vote the same way again? She hesitates for a moment, and says, "Yes."

THE COSTS OF DELAY

"I don't believe for a second that voting repeatedly for a moratorium is any different than an outright ban."[46] This fiery comment comes from Alta Charo, an outspoken and energetic supporter of embryonic stem cell research. Like scientists who make it their business to know the experimental ins and outs of their competitors, Charo, a professor of law and bioethics at the University of Wisconsin, knows and studies the ethical positions of her peers, including the people she disagrees with. No wonder: as a discipline, bioethics is little bigger than even the youthful guild of stem cell biology.[47]

As some philosophers think "retreat" — that science should withdraw to a simpler, more comfortable time — Charo dares to think ahead. To her, the moral priority is the needs of patients, and she's leery of the government — or presidential advisors — slowing things down. She asks, "How do you balance the patient's demands against the government's role to provide safety?" Charo lists diseases where patient advocacy forced regulators to change (AIDS and cancer come to mind), and predicts the same will happen for stem cell research. "People with degenerative diseases will insist that clinical trials begin. Demand will come from parents with kids suffering from juvenile diabetes — nobody fights harder for a kid than a parent. There will be tremendous pressure on the Food and Drug Administration to quickly approve new treatments." She adds that patients and taxpayers alike will want returns on their political and financial investments in states that have passed legislation favoring stem cell research.

Charo's comments reflect the frustration of scientists who claim that politics, not ethics, stand behind pronouncements from the White House and the [2001] executive order prohibiting government funding of new hESC lines. The criticism is that some government advisory bodies — including one with ethics as its focus — are antiscience. The 18-member PCBE originally had only three scientists: now there are two. Elizabeth Blackburn, a professor of biology and physiology at the University of California, San Francisco, was an outspoken opponent of the Bush administration during her rollercoaster tenure on the council. She was removed from the council in 2005. She firmly expresses her dissatisfaction with their deliberations in a paper entitled *Thoughts of a Former Council Member*.[48]

"[A] moratorium is used to gain more information.... But that information can only be gained by performing the same research that the moratorium proposes to halt," she writes. Noting that adult stem cell research alone can't answer important questions about disease, she continues, "But one cannot find answers to questions about oranges by doing all of one's research on apples. Some research on apples will be useful because it will provide information that applies to fruit in general. Diseases, however, are very specific."

Blackburn, like Charo, regards putting science on ice while calling for more regulations as equivalent to maneuvering for an outright ban. "Such regulations may never emerge, allowing opponents ... to accomplish by administrative delay what they have been unable to accomplish by legislation, that is, a *de facto* ban on SCNT."[49] Along with Michael Gazzaniga, Janet Rowley — a geneticist and cancer specialist at the University of Chicago — is one of the two remaining career scientists on the council. She admitted in 2002 that stem cell treatments were largely based on promise. She asserts the reason that evidence was lacking that hESCs could treat Parkinson's and other problems was due to a decades-long government ban on funding embryo research.[50] Without embryos as a source of embryonic stem cell, knowledge is scarce.

Blackburn, Rowley, Charo, Zoloth, and other ethicists, theologians, and patient rights activists remind us that while the government dithers, people suffer. The reality of suffering is very much on Zoloth's mind. "I worked for 20 years as an intensive care unit nurse, and I know what it is to stand beside the body of a broken, sick child and be desperate for ways to heal the baby," she recounts. "Parents who inject their children over and over with insulin, constantly worried they will get it wrong, kids with sickle cell disease; people suffering from suicidal clinical depression — these are *not* trivial matters!" For Zoloth and other ethics scholars who call themselves "justice theorists," what matters is the priority given to certain kinds of medical research, and how best to distribute the discoveries among those who need it. Zoloth insists that medicine that cuts across class boundaries is the best medicine of all. The philosopher lists spinal cord injuries as one problem that plagues developed and undeveloped countries alike, and she applauds the use of stem cell lines to discover drugs for infectious diseases like malaria and tuberculosis, where pathogens make mincemeat of healthy cells.

Can an argument for longer lives with less suffering be reconciled with the contention that science has become a selfish means to a perfect end? Charo says, "Why would you say, 'all enhancements are bad?' " She uses a compelling object lesson. "If you could use genetic engineering to make your offspring resistant to a deadly virus, wouldn't you? Why wouldn't you?" The heated exchange between those who see biotechnology as out of control and those who don't has, according to Charo, stopped the discussion cold. "We need a nuanced, levelheaded approach about which alterations we are willing to accept," she says. The word "nuanced" however, doesn't occur to Arthur Caplan, chair of the Department of Medical Ethics at University of Pennsylvania, when he writes, "Beating up on the pursuit of perfection is silly."[51] We are already creatures of technology, says Caplan, and have been ever since we've been able to probe nature and question our relations to it. There is nothing in our history, he maintains, "that shows why we should not try to improve upon the biological design with which we are endowed. Augmenting breasts or prolonging erections may be vain and even a waste of scarce resources, but seeking to use our knowledge to enhance our vision, memory, learning skills, immunity, or metabolism is not obviously either."

Both Charo and Zoloth see the human responsibility to repair what nature has left unfinished, or as Charo puts it, "The point isn't that we play God, it's that we play human." To them, the goal is not to seek perfection. The task is — and always has been — an incremental, painful, and slow approach toward a better life. Zoloth says, "Thank God, we no longer die of smallpox, plague, and horrible infectious diseases. We should stop worrying about a tiny proportion of our society that might use new technology incorrectly. People are sick! Will some abuse science and medicine? Yes. They do already. I would rather let a few of those slip by than have hundreds or thousands of sick people not be treated."

GUIDANCE AND OVERSIGHT

Charo bristles at criticisms that hESC research needs to wait for better guidance — she's one of the principal authors of the National Academy of Science's (NAS) 132-page report, *Guidelines for Human Embryonic Stem Cell Research.* "There is no way a moratorium can be lifted if the conditions for lifting it are that hESC research must have 'adequate regulations,'" she says. "All someone has to do is say, 'hESC research is inadequately regulated by government' to stop it. There is nothing easier for the government than *not* to act." The fact is, a government agency instructed *not* to fund new embryonic stem cell research — the National Institutes of Health — wasn't about to act anyway. So the NAS, a congressionally mandated group of expert scientists and engineers advising the government since 1863, did. The authors say the report is "designed specifically to provide comprehensive coverage of hESC research ... a system with both local and national components that meets the important goals identified by the other advisory bodies, including the President's Council on Bioethics in its report on somatic cell nuclear transfer."[52]

Among other things, the report recommends that each research center form an ESCRO (embryonic stem cell review oversight) committee, similar to committees that oversee and approve human clinical trial research. To garner a wide range of opinion, the NAS suggests an ESCRO should include a mixture of scientists, ethics, legal professionals, and members of the public. The committee's job is to ensure the research has scientific merit and that certain ethical guidelines are followed. If a scientist wants to make an embryonic stem cell line by using an embryo made by *in vitro* fertilization or by nuclear transfer, the ESCRO must be satisfied that the donors have given consent to use their cells or embryos for research and that no payments exchange hands between the donors and research centers. The group also is instructed to ask whether existing lines of hESCs can be used, recognizing that embryos shouldn't be destroyed unnecessarily.

Along with these questions, there are guidelines to protect the donors of cells and embryos. Donors should be assured that their confidentiality will be protected and told clearly that embryos will be destroyed during the process. A statement of risk is required, especially for women who donate eggs for research — a chemical procedure that stimulates the ovaries to produce extra eggs. Egg donation is an overlooked facet of stem cell ethics. Charo and her colleagues also suggest that both male and female donors be given the option of how they want their cells to be used. For example, some donors may feel fine about their embryo being used to make a cell line for research but uncomfortable if the cells are used to make organs or tissues for transplants.[53] If embryos or gametes come by way of infertility treatments, then the decisions to donate must be free of influence by any researcher interested in using them.

Committees that approve experiments on humans or animals, including hazardous procedures using radiation or infectious agents, have been part of research centers and teaching hospitals for decades. The knock on such groups from critics is that researchers are essentially policing themselves — a fox guarding a henhouse is little protection for the chickens inside. This is a conundrum for any "expert review" process, because often the best people to determine whether a project is scientifically, medically, and ethically sound are the experts themselves. Both Francis Fukuyama and Rebecca Dresser favor broadening oversight of hESC research to include greater participation by the public, although Fukuyama recognizes that members of society at large may not be knowledgeable enough about the science to participate meaningfully.[54] For her part, Dresser proposes something more unconventional. Rather than focus on protecting donors and determining the best medical need, she believes the first task should treat embryos as "moral scarce resources." "If we are serious about giving the embryo some respect, then we should have oversight committees that have an interest in treating them as precious," she states. "We call ourselves a deliberative democracy. Let's engage citizens who feel strongly about protecting an embryo. A real review should have teeth, where people who see the world differently can fight it out and argue about what's best." Both sides of the debate agree that citizen participation is necessary; the question remains what kind of public input will be most effective for ESCRO deliberations.

The NAS report contains other recommendations, including ways to create center-by-center stem cell registries and suggests that lines imported from other laboratories, especially those in other countries, are obtained in ways consistent with the ethical guidelines set down by the NAS. Some of the report follows Britain's lead, where embryo politics aren't so fractious. In the United Kingdom, a centralized agency, the Human Fertilisation and Embryology Authority (HFEA) regulates the research by licensing hESC lines to investigators. The NAS suggests a national authority like the HFEA be organized in the United States. Like the HFEA, the NAS guidelines prohibit researchers from keeping embryos alive past fourteen days, when the neural crest appears.

CAN MICE DO CALCULUS?

Time will tell whether the NAS report will take hold. For now, it represents the only attempt at a national set of hESC guidelines. What surprised many was the report contained a section on a controversial dimension of stem cell research: animal-human chimeras. This [type of] chimera results from human stem cells transplanted into a lab animal. Animals and humans already share cells and tissues. Heart valves from pigs replace human valves damaged by heart disease. We can do experiments on specially engineered strains of mice with a human immune system that would not be permitted on humans. The ethical equations change, however, when transplanting human embryonic or neural stem cells into animals. If a mouse with a functioning brain made entirely of human neurons can be produced, it could be used as an experimental model for Parkinson's, Alzheimer's, or other dementias. New drugs or other treatments could be first tested for their effects on mice before moving on to human clinical trials. How human neurons are damaged by pathogens could be studied in this mouse without risking harm to a human subject.

Trouble is, a mouse with a functioning brain made from human neural stem cells may no longer be a mouse. It could be partly human.

Such a creature would be vastly more mouse than human, experts contend. A mouse's brain is 1/1,000th the size of a human brain and, as a consequence, organized much differently. Neuroscientists claim the differences in "architecture" among animals as the principal reason that mice are not men — or women.[55] Without proof otherwise, experimental animals made with human stem cells could have an altered form of consciousness. This area of neuroscience is still in its infancy, so experiments to make a neural-mouse model will no doubt be closely monitored by ethicists and neuroscientists who wonder what degree of brain complexity is needed to trigger consciousness or even sentience, the ability to feel pleasure and pain.

The NAS guidelines don't prohibit putting human stem cells into an animal brain; but they do stipulate the degree of caution rises as scientists move up the evolutionary ladder. For example, work with primate embryos raises red flags. Putting a human embryonic stem cell into a monkey blastocyst is forbidden because it will integrate and contribute to the development of the primate — resulting in a human-primate chimera. Such an animal may have heightened consciousness, appear human, or have human characteristics embedded in the genes of eggs and sperm, outcomes unnerving to imagine and of deep concern for most people. Certain human-to-human neural stem cell transplants could be quite controversial; fussing with the human brain could positively or negatively affect the way we process sensory information. "We don't know whether we are on thick or thin ice with neural stem cell transplants," Charo warns.

POLICY OR JUST POLITICS?

Ethics isn't limited to street corners, coffee shops, and university corridors. In its most mature form, ethics becomes policy — rules made by society to guide our best attempts to living a good life. More than ever before, positions pounded out by ethicists are being used for political ends, especially in government administrations. The debate has reached every developed country with the capability of biomedical research. What are the consequences of limiting or outlawing embryonic stem cell research? How does the U.S. compare to other governments facing the same challenges?

The moral divide between philosophers has widened to a chasm between politicians. Our state and federal governments have changed — indeed are now changing — our ability to use embryonic stem cells.

ENDNOTES

1. Thomas Huxley, *Evolution and Ethics; Science and Morals* (New York: Prometheus Books 2004), p. 122.

2. Edmund O. Wilson, *On Human Nature* (Boston: Harvard University Press, 1978), p. 53.

3. Charles Krauthammer, Personal statement. *Human Cloning* and *Human Dignity: The Report of the President's Council on Bioethics* (New York: Public Affairs, Leon Kass, ed., 2002), p. 328.

4. Albert R. Jonsen, *The Birth of Bioethics* (New York: Oxford University Press, 1998), p. 348.

5. Robert P. George and Alfonso Gómez-Lobo, "The moral status of the human embryo." *Perspectives in Biology and Medicine*, 48 (2005): pp. 201–210.

6. Gilbert Meilaender, "Some Protestant Reflections." In *The Human Embryonic Stem Cell Debate* (Cambridge: MIT Press, Suzanne Holland, Karen Lebacqz, and Laurie Zoloth, eds., 2001), p. 151.

7. Gilbert Meilaender, This statement and following statements from an interview with author. June 2005.

8. John Locke, *An Essay Concerning Human Understanding*. (Cleveland, Ohio: World, A. D. Woosley, ed., 1964), p. 220.

9. Robert Song, "To be willing to kill a person." In *God and the Embryo: Religious Voices on Stem Cells and Cloning*. (Washington: Georgetown University Press, Brent Waters and Ronald Cole Turner, eds., 2004), p. 102.

10. Leon L. Kass, Life, Liberty and the Pursuit of Dignity: The Challenge for Bioethics. (San Francisco: Encounter Books, 2002), p. 88.

11. Southern Baptist Convention, "Resolution on human embryonic and stem cell research." In *God and the Embryo*, pp. 179–180.

12. Select Committee on Stem Cell Research, "A theologian's brief on the place of the human embryo within the Christian tradition, and the theological principles for evaluating its moral status." In *God and the Embryo*, pp. 190–200.

13. John Haldane and Patrick Lee, "Aquinas on human ensoulment: abortion and the value of life." *Philosophy*, 78 (2003): pp. 255–278.

14. The Holy See declaration can be found at http://www.vatican.va/roman_curia/congregations/cfaith/documents/rc_con_cfaith_doc_19741118_declaration-abortion_en.html.

15. Prosaically described as the "Instruction on Respect for Human Life in Its Origin and the Dignity of Procreation: Replies to Certain Questions of the Day" and found on the Vatican's website: http://www.vatican.va/cfaith/documents/rc_con_cfaith-doc19870222_respect-for-human-life_en.html.

16. The Vatican's "Declaration on the Production and the Scientific and Therapeutic Use of Human Embryonic Stem Cells" can be found at http://www.vatican.va/ roman_curia/pontifical_academies/acdlife/docurnents/rc_pa_acdlife_-doc_20000824_cellule-staminali_en.html.

17. Complete data of Harris Poll #58, August 18, 2004, is available at http:// www.harrisinteractive.com/harris_poll/index.asp?PID=488.

18. Presbyterian Church (USA) Resolution, "Overture 01-50. On adopting a resolution enunciating ethical guidelines for fetal tissue and stem cell research — from the Presbytery of Baltimore." In *God and the Embryo*, pp. 185–189.

19. Michael Mendiola, "Possible approaches from a Catholic perspective." *The Human Embryonic Stem Cell Debate* (Cambridge, MA: MIT Press, 2001), p. 124.

20. Ted Peters and Gaymon Bennett, "A plea for beneficence." *God and the Embryo*, pp. 114–130.

21. Gaymon Bennett. Interview with author. August 2004.

22. Ted Peters and Gaymon Bennett, "Stem Cell Research and the claim of the other in the human subject." *Dialog: A Journal of Theology*, 43 (3) (2004): pp. 184–204.

23. Laurie Zoloth. This statement and following statements from an interview with author. June 2005.

24. Rabbi Elliot M. Dorff, *Ethical Issues in Human Stem Cell Research*, Vol. II (Rockville, MD: Religious Perspectives, 2000), C1. http://www.bioethics.gov/reports/past_-commissions/index.html.

25. Rabbi Moshe Dovid Tendler. Ibid., C2.

26. Abdulaziz Sachedina. Ibid., G1-3.

27. Mary Anne Warren can be consulted for her descriptive examples of sentience of animals in *Moral Status* (Oxford, Clarendon Press, 1997), pp. 52–69.

28. Michael Gazzaniga, *The Ethical Brain* (Washington, D.C: Dana Press, 2005), p. 7.

29. Ibid., 8.

30. James Q. Wilson, Personal statement. In *Human Cloning and Human Dignity*, pp. 347–351.

31. See note 23.

32. See notes 21 and 22.

33. James C. Petersen, "Is the human embryo a human being?" *God and the Embryo*, p. 85.

34. Leon L. Kass. Life, Liberty and the Pursuit of Dignity, 4.

35. Ibid., 101.

36. Ibid., 103.

37. Ibid., 91.

38. The President's Council on Bioethics published a volume dedicated to the *Brave New World* philosophy in 2003. A copy can be obtained from http://bioethics.gov/ reports/beyondtherapy/index.html.

39. Michael J. Sandel. "The case against perfection." *Atlantic Monthly*, April 2004. http://www.theatlantic.com/doc/200404/sandel.

40. Daniel Callahan, *What Price Better Health? Hazards of the Research Imperative* (University of California Press, October 2003), excerpts from Chapter 3 found at http://www.bioethics.gov/background/callahan_paper.html.

41. Francis Fukuyama, *Our Posthuman Society: Consequences of the Biotechnology Revolution* (New York: Farrar, Straus and Giroux, 2002), vii.

42. Francis Fukuyama, "Transhumanism." *Foreign Affairs: The World's Most Dangerous Ideas* (September/October 2004). http://www.foreignpolicy.com/story/cms.php?story_id=2696.

43. Francis Fukuyama, "Human biomedicine and the problem of governance." *Perspectives in Biology and Medicine*, 48 (2005): pp. 195–200.

44. Ibid.

45. Rebecca Dresser. This statement and the following statements from an interview with author. May 2005.

46. Alta Charo. This statement and the following statements from an interview with author. June 2005.

47. About 800 people attended the biggest convention of bioethics professionals in 2005. Over 2,000 people attended the 2005 meeting of the International Society of Stem Cell Research. The ISSCR's first meeting, held in 2002, attracted several hundred participants. Personal communication, Laurie Zoloth and ISSCR representatives.

48. Elizabeth Blackburn, "Thoughts of a former council member." *Perspectives in Biology and Medicine*, 48 (2005): 173.

49. Ibid., 176.

50. Janet Rowley, Personal statement. In *Human Cloning and Human Dignity*, pp. 340–342.

51. Arthur Caplan, "Is it ethical to use enhancement technologies to make us better than well?" *Public Library of Science Biology*, 1 (2004). http://medicine.plosjournals.org.

52. National Research Council. Guidelines for Human Embryonic Stem Cell Research (Washington, D.C.: National Academies Press, 2005), p. 43.

53. See note 52.

54. See note 43.

55. Henry Greely, et al., "Hi, I'm Mickey." Unpublished manuscript furnished by Henry Greely and the Stanford University Center for Biomedical Ethics.

17

Applications, Benefits, and Risks of Synthetic Biology

PRESIDENTIAL COMMISSION FOR THE STUDY OF BIOETHICAL ISSUES

Use of recombinant DNA (rDNA) has become commonplace in many spheres since the techniques of gene-splicing were first developed in the 1970s. Work that at first was done in meticulously isolated laboratories to protect society from unknown risks is now routinely done in high school (and even middle school) biology labs. Entire industries involving such products as genetically engineered foods and medical tests for genetically-linked diseases have grown up around rDNA techniques. What they have in common is that they all start with DNA from existing organisms, take the strands apart, and reassemble them in novel ways. Synthetic biology goes one step further: it involves creating living organisms by assembling DNA from non-living chemical components. This has long been the stuff of science fiction, but it moved closer to reality when, in May 2010, scientists at the J. Craig Venter Institute announced in a paper published in the journal Science *that they had created a self-replicating synthetic genome inside a bacterial cell from non-living chemicals.*

The announcement drew enormous media coverage and stimulated intense discussion of the potential risks and benefits of what many regarded as a step toward the ability to "create life." Reaction from the White House was swift. President Obama called on his recently created Presidential Commission for Study of Bioethical Issues to study, as its first task, the implications of the controversial development and report back within six months. The selection that follows is adapted from Chapter 3 of the Commission's report. It is in written a straightforward — some would say dull — style. But it serves to lay out the basics of synthetic biology and, without going into

From Presidential Commission for the Study of Bioethical Issues, "Applications, Benefits and Risks of Synthetic Biology," chapter 3 from *New Directions: The Ethics of Synthetic Biology and Emerging Technologies*, December 2010.

great technical detail, describes what its applications might be in several different areas. As such, it is a useful introduction to the subject.

The Presidential Commission for Study of Bioethical Issues is the Obama Administration's version of a White House body that has existed through several administrations to advise on the complex ethical, social, and policy issues raised by developments in modern biology. It consists of 13 members including physicians, lawyers, bioethicists, researchers and patient advocates. It is chaired by Amy Gutmann, President of the University of Pennsylvania, and Christopher H. Browne, Distinguished Professor of Political Science at the University, and supported by a sizable professional staff.

Synthetic biology offers opportunities to apply biological and engineering principles to benefit humankind in unprecedented ways. Clean energy sources, targeted medicines and more efficient vaccine production, new chemicals, environmental cleansers, and hardy crops are some of the potential applications of this burgeoning field of science. While most of the fruits of synthetic biology remain in early stages of development, some applications are expected to come to market within a few years.[1] Success in these research efforts will yield new jobs as novel products and product streams develop. The pace of acceleration of synthetic biology is likely to increase dramatically in the years ahead.

Despite its promise, synthetic biology raises concerns about risks to human health, the environment, and biosecurity. Some of these potential harms include unanticipated adverse human health effects, negative environmental effects (anticipated or unanticipated) from field release and dual-use concerns when research undertaken for "legitimate scientific purpose ... may be misused to pose a biologic threat to public health and/or national security."[2]

This chapter provides an overview of the potential applications, benefits, and risks of synthetic biology. Because renewable energy is expected to yield the first large-scale commercial products of synthetic biology, the Commission discusses this area first. Next, the Commission reviews potential health application and benefits. Many products remain in research and development, but a few are nearing commercialization. Finally, the Commission provides a summary of potential agricultural, environmental, and biosecurity applications of synthetic biology, all of which are in more preliminary stages of development. Within these discussions the potential health, security, and other risks are examined, as well as anticipated technical challenges.

RENEWABLE ENERGY APPLICATIONS
OF SYNTHETIC BIOLOGY

In general, biofuels are renewable energy sources derived from biomass, which includes material derived from plants, animals, and organic waste. Several methods can be used to harvest energy from biomass, including burning, chemical treatment, or biodegradation using the metabolic power of microorganisms. Processing biomass into biofuels or electricity through more complex chemical and biochemical reactions, as opposed to simple combustion, limits environmental impact by minimizing the production of waste and decreasing net greenhouse emissions. Current practices for farming biomass for energy use employ a range of biological sources including grains, grasses, oil seed crops, trees, sugar, and corn.

Ethanol is the most common biofuel worldwide. It is produced mainly from corn or sugar cane. Biodiesel, another currently used biofuel, is made from vegetable oils, animal fats, or recycled restaurant grease. There are challenges to widespread commercial development of either of these fuels. For ethanol production, challenges include inefficiencies and energy costs for production, as well as concerns about the volume of plant sources needed and possible collateral impact on food prices. Biodiesel also involves significant energy costs for production.

Promise and Potential Benefits

Biofuels and related products produced through synthetic biology offer the potential to reduce global dependence on fossil fuel, cut harmful emissions, and minimize economic and political volatility surrounding fossil fuel reserves. Some biofuels produced with synthetic biology processes are expected to be available commercially within the next few years. Other research may not yield commercial products for a decade or more. The various synthetic biology alternatives to current biofuel production methods include producing cellulosic ethanol (derived from cell walls rather than corn) and manufacturing other bioalcohols with synthetically manipulated biomass. Biofuel can also be produced from modified algae that use the natural process of photosynthesis to manufacture bio-oils, such as biodiesel, more easily than current chemical processes.[3]

The biochemical conversion of biomass into energy involves chemical reactions performed by biological systems. Enzymes in microorganisms such as bacteria break down biological materials into their component parts, from which energy can be extracted more easily. Perhaps the simplest example of biochemical conversion is a backyard composting bin, in which microorganisms gradually degrade vegetation in the presence of oxygen. As is apparent from the surge of warm air that emerges upon opening the lid of the bin, this form of bioconversion is an energy-yielding process.

Synthetic biologists aim to improve the speed and efficiency of converting biomass into advanced, second- or third-generation biofuels with cleaner and more favorable energy-usage profiles.[4] This challenge may be met by creating "super-fermenting" yeast and bacteria through synthetic biology. These organisms have the potential to boost the power and potential of current industrially used microorganisms by means of new or altered genes. Synthetic biology also offers new biomass sources, or feedstocks, that are more efficient, reliable, low-cost, and scalable than current sources. These include forest and agriculture residues, some grasses, algae, oilseeds, and potentially sewage.[5]

Aside from biofuels, synthetic biology may also play an important environmental role by harnessing energy in novel, cleaner ways than traditional nonrenewable energy production processes. Large global reserves of hydrocarbons, such as oil, gas, shale, and oil sands, might be leveraged with synthetic biology tools. Coal bed methane, for example, is a globally available source of natural gas. Its reserves are vast and largely untapped. Synthetic biology research is underway to harvest this methane through microbial digestion and other processes.[6]

BIOALCOHOLS

Unlike ethanol derived from corn or sugar cane, cellulosic ethanol is made from cellulose fibers, a major component in the cell walls of all plants. Processing plant biomass not used for food, for example, waste corn stalks, straws, grass clippings, prairie grasses, and wood chips, could reduce economic and other pressures imposed by relying on corn for ethanol. However, cellulosic ethanol is a relatively low-yield bioalcohol and, like ethanol fuel derived from more conventional chemistries, still tends to corrode storage and transport equipment.

A potentially more promising bioalcohol made by synthetic biology and used for energy production is butanol. Like ethanol, butanol is produced by the fermentation of sugars and starches or through the breakdown of cellulose. The crude product is then refined to make usable fuel. A particular advantage of butanol (and a similar biofuel called isobutanol) is that it can be used directly in a traditional gasoline-powered engine. It also has a relatively high energy density, resulting in better gas mileage than ethanol.[7] Some bacteria have the built-in enzymes to manufacture butanol, but the natural process is not very fast or high-yield. Synthetic biologists have engineered the easy-to-manipulate bacterium *E. coli* to improve this bacterial biochemical reaction to make butanol more industrially useful.[8]

PHOTOSYNTHETIC ALGAE

Another tool for creating biofuels via synthetic biology is through the use of photosynthetic algae. Algae are low-input, high-yield feedstocks that, under experimental conditions, produce substantially more energy per acre than land crops such as corn or soybeans.[9] To create biofuel from algae, the cells are grown, harvested, and treated chemically or thermally to recover the oil content inside algal cells, the so-called "bio-oil." While experimental yields have not yet been duplicated on a commercial scale, an alternative strategy currently under development with synthetic biology is engineering algal cells to secrete oil continuously through their cell walls and thereby increase yield. This time-saving step may support large-scale industrial operations in the near future.[10]

Proponents of farming algae note that it is biodegradable and therefore relatively harmless to the environment if spilled. Algae can also be grown on land and in water that is otherwise unsuitable for crops and food production. Making bio-oils using algae is expected to be less polluting and more efficient than converting vegetable oils or animal fats into biofuel.[11]

Through its capacity to consume carbon dioxide, algae offer the added benefit of mitigating greenhouse gas emissions. Unlike ethanol, algae-derived bio-oils, such as gasoline, diesel, and jet fuels, have been found to have very similar physical and chemical properties in comparison to currently used petroleum-based products, suggesting that these fuels are likely to be compatible with current transportation technologies and infrastructure.

HYDROGEN FUEL

Hydrogen fuel is an additional area of focus for commercial applications of synthetic biology. Hydrogen is a highly desirable fuel source because it is clean-burning, producing water as a by-product. Hydrogen also has the second highest energy density per unit of weight of any known fuel.[12] Several possible routes to generate biohydrogen are under investigation. One method uses engineered *E. coli* as a host organism to produce hydrogen in 62 addition to other biofuels.[13] Engineered algae are also being examined as sources of biohydrogen.[14] Finally, and perhaps most promisingly, researchers are investigating ways to produce high yields of hydrogen using starch and water via a synthetic enzymatic pathway.[15] The latter system is particularly attractive, as it may enable sugar to be converted into hydrogen fuel inside a vehicle itself. This would mitigate the problem of storage that exists today, as hydrogen takes up inordinate amounts of space at regular atmospheric pressure and compression of the gas requires energy and makes storage both difficult and dangerous.[16]

The synthetic processes being explored, if successful, will differ markedly from the current method of producing hydrogen fuel, which involves converting natural gas using steam. Natural gas techniques are costly, inefficient, and heavily reliant on fossil fuels. The synthetic biology-driven process is expected to cost significantly less while providing substantially higher yields, though research remains early in the developmental pipeline.

Risks and Potential Harms

Synthetic biology offers many potential methods to improve energy production and reduce costs, which deservedly generate attention and enthusiasm. A full assessment of these promising activities requires comparable attention to the current limitations, challenges, and anticipated risks or harms. This assessment is particularly important at this time because renewable energy applications may be the first synthetic biology products to come to market. Contamination by accidental or intentional release of organisms developed with synthetic biology is among the principal anticipated risks. Unlike synthetically produced chemicals, which generally have well-defined and predictable qualities, biological organisms may be more difficult to control. Unmanaged release could, in theory, lead to undesired cross-breeding with other organisms, uncontrolled proliferation, crowding out of existing species, and threats to biodiversity.[17]

Consider biofuel production systems that employ synthetic biology and pond grown algae. One hypothetical, worst-case scenario is a newly engineered type of high-yielding blue-green algae cultivated for biofuel production unintentionally leaking from outdoor ponds and out-competing native algal growth.[18] A durable synthetic biology-derived organism might then spread to natural waterways, where it may thrive, displace other species, and rob the ecosystem of vital nutrients, with negative consequences for the environment.

This scenario is theoretical. Considering it and developing appropriate precautions is nevertheless appropriate because of the rapid development of synthetic biology-generated photosynthetic algae for fuel production and the uncertain nature of the harm that may arise from accidental release. One of the advantages of synthetic biology is that many of the tools being developed include strategies to remediate such risks. Some of the approaches proposed include the engineering of so-called "terminator" genes or "suicide" switches that can be inserted into organisms, precluding them from reproducing or surviving outside of a laboratory or other controlled setting in the absence of unique chemical conditions.[19] Some are clearly sufficient to neutralize the risk of release, and others require further study as synthetic biology progresses.

Another risk in the energy sector is harm to ecosystems from the required dedication of land and other natural resources to production of biomass as feedstock for biofuels. If large areas of land were to be dedicated to biofuel development, this could put new and intense pressures on land, potentially affecting food production, communities, and current ecosystems. Because these applications of synthetic biology are still young, the impact of biofuel production on land use remains unknown. Some argue that efforts to develop and grow additional cellulosic biofuel will dramatically change and adversely impact the way land is used in the United States and abroad.[20] Others suggest that biofuel production can proceed safely with only minor adjustments in current land use practices.[21] Existing biodiverse prairie and meadow grasses may actually enhance the growth of feedstock for second-generation biofuels.[22]

On balance, many anticipate the potential efficiencies and attendant reduction in reliance on fossil fuels offered by energy production using synthetic biology would offset anticipated risks to the environmental ecosystem as it exists today. But considerable uncertainty remains.

HEALTH APPLICATIONS OF SYNTHETIC BIOLOGY

Synthetic biology has the opportunity to advance human health in a variety of ways. Improved production of drugs and vaccines, advanced mechanisms for personalized medicine, and novel, programmable drugs and devices for prevention and healing are among a few of the expected achievements.

Promise and Potential Benefits

There is a long tradition of employing plants and other biological organisms to detect and cure human disease. Genetic engineering technology has been used for more than three decades in medicine to engineer bacteria with the ability to produce commercially relevant molecules like insulin and vaccines for hepatitis B virus and human papillomavirus.[23] Synthetic biology applications related to health build on this history, but most remain early in the research and development pipeline. The quick pace of biomedical research in general, and synthetic biology research in particular, suggests that this could change soon. This research is being conducted at universities and biotechnology or synthetic biology companies in the United States and overseas.[24]

MEDICINES

Synthetic biologists have refined a chemical technique called metabolic engineering to enhance the production of medicines. Through this process, scientists alter an organism's metabolic pathways — the series of chemical reactions that enable the organism to function at the cellular or organism level — in order to better understand and manage how those pathways work. They can redesign these pathways to produce novel products or augment the production of current products, like drugs. Synthetic biology can also be used to engineer molecules and cells that express proteins or pathways responsible for human disease. At some point these products may be used in efficient, large-scale screening methods to identify novel drugs for disease treatment or prevention.

One well-known example of synthetic biology in medicine is the re-engineering of a microorganism to make the antimalarial drug artemisinin more cheaply and efficiently. Malaria affects approximately two to three hundred million people each year and results in between 700,000–1,000,000 deaths, largely among young children in sub-Saharan Africa.[25] Artemisinin is a naturally occurring chemical derived from the plant artemesia, or sweet wormwood. It is an effective malaria treatment, but is difficult to obtain due to limitations on plant yield and high production costs. To address this problem, synthetic biologists at the University of California genetically engineered *E. coli* bacteria to produce a high volume precursor that can be chemically converted to artemisinin.[26] This semi-synthetic artemisinin is being developed today by the pharmaceutical company Sanofi-Aventis in collaboration with the California researchers and the Institute for OneWorld Health. If successful, these efforts should substantially reduce the drug's production cost and increase and stabilize world supply. Full-scale production is expected to begin shortly, with marketing expected in 2012.[27]

VACCINES

Synthetic biology techniques are also being studied and used to accelerate the development of vaccines. Influenza vaccine production is among the key areas of focus. To develop a vaccine, one first needs to identify the virus strain, with its unique genetic code, against which the vaccine will be used. Synthetic biology tools, including rapid, inexpensive DNA sequencing combined with computer modeling, may streamline production time by accelerating this first step.

One industry group is developing a "bank" of synthetically created seed viruses for influenza vaccines that it hopes will enable more rapid vaccine production by reducing virus identification time.[28] DNA-based vaccines created "on-the-spot" to match actual, circulating viral genetic material may be a more efficient process for producing vaccine seed stock in the future.[29] However, these strategies are preliminary and may prove no more efficient or effective than conventional reverse engineering techniques. More research and experience are needed.

ADVANCING BASIC BIOLOGY AND PERSONALIZED MEDICINE

Twenty years ago, cloning, or replicating, a single gene was enormously time consuming. Today, such a task can be done in minutes by a machine, a development that has fueled rapid advances in synthetic biology. The ability to easily manufacture and manipulate DNA in the laboratory has enhanced scientists' productivity and opened new directions for scientific exploration. Researchers see great potential for synthetic biology to advance knowledge of fundamental biological principles. Expanding the DNA "alphabet" beyond its traditional four nucleotides — A, C, G, and T — to include non-naturally occurring nucleotides also gives synthetic biologists more flexibility in studying, detecting, and treating disease. For example, scientists recently used polymerase chain reaction (PCR) with novel nucleotides, a process that increases DNA's information potential and thus enables the manufacture of proteins with new properties.[30] To this end, researchers have already developed diagnostic tests using these DNA nucleotides to screen for human immunodeficiency virus, cystic fibrosis, and other diseases.[31]

In general, personalized medicine aims to apply the science of genomics to develop individually tailored, and thereby more effective, approaches to disease prevention and health care.[32] Synthetic biology offers useful strategies for advancing this goal. Many current cancer treatments focus on non-selective cell killing or on delivery to specific tissues. A growing body of knowledge supporting a molecular classification of tumors may facilitate the development of specifically designed detection devices matched to individual tumors. A synthetic biology approach currently under study is a cancer treatment that focuses on up to six cellular identifiers rather than one, effectively enabling the treatment to be targeted more carefully and precisely toward the cells intended to be killed, while sparing healthy ones.[33]

Custom protein and biological circuit design may eventually enable the delivery of "smart proteins" or programmed cells that self-assemble at disease sites. Similarly, synthetic organisms could be developed to create a trigger to deliver or withhold treatment depending upon a local disease environment (such as low levels of oxygen) and provide targeted killing of cancer cells.[34] These and other novel approaches to tailored disease treatment may substantially improve outcomes and reduce the costs and burden of disease across the population. While the benefits of synthetic biology to health care may prove monumental, significant hurdles remain. With the exception of semi-synthetic artemisinin and potential, near-term improvements in vaccine design, most of the anticipated health benefits of synthetic biology remain in the preliminary research stage. We are unlikely to see commercial applications from much of the biomedically oriented synthetic biology research for many years, although the pace of discovery is unpredictable.

Risks and Potential Harms

In addition to practical challenges, biomedical applications of synthetic biology raise potential risks for humans and the environment that are, in part, similar to those identified in the biofuels discussion and those commonly understood within the biomedical or greater engineering research communities today. Human health risks may arise from adverse effects of intentional or inadvertent release of the organisms engineered using synthetic biology. Infectious diseases may be transmitted to laboratory workers after needle sticks or to family members following airborne transmission of disease agents manipulated using synthetic biology techniques. Risks may also accrue to the wider human community or the environment if organisms proliferate without adequate means to limit reproduction.

Similarly, novel organisms developed with synthetic biology to treat illness may trigger unanticipated adverse effects in patients. The use of cell therapies of bacterial, or potentially, mixed microbial origin may cause infections or unexpected immune responses. New organisms developed with the emerging technology of synthetic biology may pose unusual, if not unprecedented, risks resulting from their potential as biological organisms to reproduce or evolve.

Many of these risks are qualitatively similar to the risks that arise in horticultural biomedical and biotechnology research. There are well-established mechanisms in place to identify and manage future risks. Additionally, as with energy applications, internal mechanisms to reliably contain function and reduce or eliminate these risks are being developed. "Biological isolation," which is also termed "biosafety engineering," aims to build in molecular "brakes" or "seatbelts" that restrain growth or replication of partially or fully synthetic organisms.[35] Synthetic organisms can be engineered to be contained physically or temporally. Additional data are needed to assess how well biologically engineered safeguards, such as "kill switches" that activate after a defined number of generations, will work.

AGRICULTURAL, FOOD, AND ENVIRONMENTAL APPLICATIONS OF SYNTHETIC BIOLOGY

Synthetic biology may also help to shift, if not substantially mitigate, some of the existing threats to our global food supply and environmental health. These potential benefits are in some ways more preliminary than the expectations for energy and health, but research and development in these fields are well underway.

Promise and Potential Benefits

In agriculture, efforts to manipulate crops and breed animals for specific purposes are not new. Many traditional farming practices, from plant breeding to animal husbandry, aim to direct evolution to achieve desired outcomes. Use of recombinant DNA technology, cloning, and other biotechnology tools have enhanced these practices. Taking these activities one step further, synthetic biologists are experimenting with high-yield and disease-resistant plant feedstocks that can be supplemented with efficient and environmentally friendly microorganisms to minimize water use and replace chemical fertilizers.[36] Researchers are altering the properties of plants through methods that combine metabolic components from various organisms in order to gain nutritional benefits, such as higher levels of food-grade protein.[37]

Efforts to remove waste using biological means date to at least 1972, when a researcher at General Electric applied for a patent on a form of *Pseudomonas* bacteria genetically engineered to digest oil slicks.[38] Environmental applications of synthetic biology are generally targeted to pollution control and ecological protection. The impact of naturally occurring oil-devouring microorganisms at the site of the 2010 oil spill off the U.S. Gulf Coast, for example, demonstrated how these organisms could reduce some types of pollution.[39] Synthetic biologists are eager to understand and direct these biological capabilities, or even enhance them, to respond to existing and future waste generated by human activities.

Other environmentally relevant examples of synthetic biology applications include laboratory-constructed microbial consortia, known as synthetic biofilms, which are being developed for use as environmental biosensors. These sensors could be used, for example, to monitor soil for nutrient quality or signs of environmental degradation. The design of biological "wetting agents," or biosurfactants, could increase the efficiency of bioremediation efforts and minimize the extent of damage from pollutants.[40] Biosurfactants are naturally produced by bacteria, yeasts, or fungi and are environmentally friendly in freshwater, marine, and terrestrial ecosystems. Synthetic biology may offer the ability to enhance the features of microbially produced biosurfactants to tailor them to specific spills or otherwise polluted areas.

Risks and Potential Harms

Synthetic biology applications in the context of agriculture, food, and the environment raise concerns broadly similar to those raised about genetic engineering in the past and those discussed above with respect to safety, resource management, and biodiversity. In brief, these risks include harms to humans, plants, or animals from, for example:[41]

- uncontrolled environmental escape or release and attendant disruption to ecosystems,
- new or sturdier pests — animal or plant — that may be difficult to control, and
- increased pesticide resistance and growth of invasive species.

As in the discussion of energy and health applications, the risks may be assessed and managed through existing protections long in use for biomedical and greater engineering research. Synthetic biology applications in the context of agriculture, food, and the environment may require more targeted efforts, however, including use of inbred checks, such as "suicide genes" or "kill switches" to ensure that they cannot propagate unintentionally.

Many potential applications of synthetic biology go well beyond the genetic engineering practiced throughout the biotechnology industry today. In the future, the field may be capable of creating entirely new organisms and systems previously unseen in the world today. Synthetic biology's critics and proponents alike worry that creating new organisms that have uncertain or unpredictable functions, interactions, and properties could affect ecosystems and other species in unknown and adverse ways. The associated risks of escape and contamination may be extremely difficult to assess in advance, as such novel entities may have neither an evolutionary nor an ecological history.[42]

Countering these concerns, at least somewhat, is experience showing that synthetic cells and systems in research settings have tended to be short-lived by comparison to those that have evolved in nature. Scientists have observed that synthetic organisms allowed to develop in the laboratory have consistently evolved toward nonfunctionality.[43] These are encouraging preliminary findings, but they do not eliminate the need for precautions in the event that a future synthetic organism behaves differently than expected outside of the contained laboratory setting.

Another concern related to synthetic biology's impact on natural systems — crops grown for either biofuel or food consumption — is the broader effect on how society views and protects biodiversity. Does a chemically synthesized organism increase or decrease biodiversity, as measured by traditional taxonomy-based classification schemes? This concept becomes important in policy discussions pertaining to the use and potential abuse of land and other natural resources.

BIOSECURITY

Generally, the term "biosecurity" refers to the efforts needed to prevent misuse or mishandling of biological agents and organisms with the intent to do harm. The National Science Advisory Board for Biosecurity (NSABB), an independent federal advisory committee charged with advising the U.S. government on biosecurity issues and "dual use" research — that which may be used for either good or ill — defines the term as follows: "[b]iosecurity refers to the protection, control of, and accountability for high-consequence biological agents and toxins, and critical relevant biological materials and information, to prevent unauthorized possession, loss, theft, misuse, diversion, or intentional release."[44]

Unlike applications and potential applications of synthetic biology in the energy, health, agricultural, and environmental sectors, possible benefits in the biosecurity arena have not garnered significant public attention. Nor have they received comparable investment from academia, industry, or the government. It is nonetheless easy to anticipate some potential benefits.

Synthetic biology may enhance biosecurity by enabling researchers to identify biological agents of concern that may be developed synthetically or semisynthetically. In the same way that the J. Craig Venter Institute "branded" the bacterium it synthesized this year with traceable information in the organism's genetic code, researchers may uniquely tag the genetic code of new organisms that they develop. When combined with other measures to ensure biosecurity, this tagging process may provide an additional and effective deterrent to malicious use.

Similarly, biosecurity may be improved using the techniques discussed above for applications in energy, human health, agriculture, and the environment. As noted, "suicide" genes or terminator technologies built into the genome of a new organism to inhibit growth or survival outside of a contained environment may offer particularly effective means to counter biosecurity threats. Related tools could be crafted to ensure organism death in the face of particular chemicals or contexts. Uncertainties remain, however, with regard to the effectiveness of such strategies.

Concerns about dual use or intentional misuse of synthetic biology to do harm are among the most prominent critiques of this emerging technology. One of the most widely voiced risks attributed to synthetic biology is that it may be used, in the wrong hands, to intentionally create harmful organisms for bioterrorism. Recent examples of virus reconstruction using traditional recombinant DNA techniques fuel these concerns. These examples include the laboratory creation of infectious polio virus, the mycoplasma genome, and the 1918 strain of influenza virus.[45]

Frequently lost in these discussions about synthetic biology risks is recognition that DNA alone is not sufficient to create an independently functioning biological entity, such as a disease-causing virus that could spread. Despite the relative ease of access to known DNA sequences through public databases like GenBank[46] (an annotated collection of all publicly available genetic sequences), and equivalent databases across the globe, most experts in the scientific community agree that mere knowledge of a viral genome is far from sufficient to be able to re-constitute it or create a disease-forming pathogen. Rather, one must have an appropriate host and conditions for a virus to grow. Few individuals or groups today have the financial means or the technical skills to accomplish such ends, even when scientifically feasible. As the many technical challenges in synthetic biology affirm, it is not yet possible to craft functioning biological organisms from synthesized genomic material alone.

Risks and Potential Harms

With regard to biosecurity risks arising from synthetic biology, NSABB has twice issued reports and made recommendations to the federal government — first in 2006 and again in 2010.[47] In 2006, the group focused on synthesis of select agents and toxins, which are defined in law as certain infectious components of identified "select agent viruses," meaning those that the U.S. government has found to pose a severe threat to human health.[48] Following a review of the science at that time, the group made specific recommendations to reduce biosecurity risks, many of which the United States has since implemented, such as the establishment of a screening infrastructure for genetic sequence providers and others.[49]

NSABB's report "Addressing Biosafety Concerns Related to Synthetic Biology," issued in April 2010, offered four specific recommendations to ensure biosecurity in the current field of synthetic biology:

- Synthetic biology should be subject to institutional review and oversight since some aspects of this field pose biosecurity risks.

- Oversight of dual use research should extend beyond the boundaries of life sciences and academia.

- Outreach and education strategies should be developed that address dual use research issues and engage the research communities that are most likely to undertake work under the umbrella of synthetic biology.

- The U.S. government should include advances in synthetic biology and understanding of virulence/pathogenicity in efforts to monitor new scientific findings and technologies.

These recommendations reflect an attempt to balance the considerable potential benefits of synthetic biology with the risks resulting from intentional or unintentional misuse of this technology and its products. Noticeably absent were recommendations to restrict access to genetic sequences separate from those components of Select Agents and toxins already limited by the U.S. Select Agent regulations. In large part, this determination appears to reflect the fact, as noted, that sequences alone will not yield, nor often be sufficient to predict, functions.

NSABB's work is not unique. Many experts and interested groups in the United States and abroad have recently devoted considerable time and energy to evaluating the biosecurity risks of advancing synthetic biology practices.[50] This still-young field benefits from a clear consensus among scientists and policy-makers that biosecurity risks, while perhaps overstated by some, nevertheless are serious and warrant ongoing and proactive re-examination as technical capacity evolves. The tools used to mitigate these risks may also be the tools to mitigate environmental, health, and other potential risks. The tools to address risk depend on an expanding scientific knowledge base as much as potential benefits do.

ENDNOTES

1. Sheridan, C. (2009). Making green. *Nature Biotechnology* 27:1074–1076.

2. Department of Health and Human Services. (2004). National Science Advisory Board for Biosecurity Charter, March 4, 2004; National Science Advisory Board for Biosecurity Charter — Revised, March 10, 2006. Available at: http://oba.od.nih.gov/biosecurity/PDF/NSABB%202010%20Charter_Renewal%20.pdf.

3. Beer, L. L., et al. (2009). Engineering algae for biohydrogen and biofuel production. *Current Opinion in Biotechnology* 20(3):264–271.

4. Savage, D. F., Way J., and P. A. Silver. (2008). Defossiling fuel: How synthetic biology can transform biofuel production. *American Chemical Society Chemical Biology* 3(1):13–16.

5. Rulkens, W. (2008). Sewage sludge as a biomass resource for the production of energy: Overview and assessment of the various options. *Energy Fuels* 22(1):9–15.

6. Synthetic Genomics, Inc. *Hydrocarbon Recovery & Conversion.* Available at: www.syntheticgenomics.com/what/hydrocarbonrecovery.html.

7. Bullis, K. (2007). Forget ethanol. *MIT Technology Review.* Available at: www.technologyreview.com/energy/18443/.

8. Atsumi, S., Hanai, T., and J. C. Liao. (2008). Non-fermentative pathways for synthesis of branched-chain higher alcohols as biofuels. *Nature* 451:86–90.

9. ExxonMobil. *Algae biofuels.* Available at: www.exxonmobil.com/Corporate/ energy_climate_con_vehicle_algae.aspx.

10. Synthetic Genomics, Inc. *Synthetic Genomics and EMRE Fact Sheet.* Available at: www.syntheticgenomics.com/media/emrefact.html.

11. Chisti, Y. (2007). Biodiesel from microalgae. *Biotechnology Advances* 25(3):294–306; Solix. *About Microalgae and Biofuels.* Available at: www.solixbiofuels.com/content/ technology/about_microalgae-biofuels.

12. Demirbas, A. (2009). *Biohydrogen for Future Engine Fuel Demands: Green Energy and Technology Virtual Series.* New York and Dordrecht: Springer. Pages 105–161 at 134.

13. Clomburg, J. M., and R. Gonzales. (2010). Biofuel production in *Escherichia coli*: the role of metabolic engineering and synthetic biology. *Applied Microbiology and Biotechnology* 86:419–434 at 424.

14. Beer, L. L., et al., op cit.

15. Zhang, Y. H., et al. (2007). High-yield hydrogen production from starch and water by a synthetic enzymatic pathway. *PLoS One (Public Library of Science)* 2(5):e456; Science and technology: Gassed up — Synthetic biology. *Economist.* 383(8530): 104. May 24, 2007; Ajudua, C. (2006). Driving: Y. H. Percival Zhang's crazy idea of the year: 'Sugar cars'. *Esquire.* November 30, 2006.

16. Demirbas, A., op cit., at 134.

17. Eggers, J., et al. (2009). Is biofuel policy harming biodiversity in Europe? *Global Change Biology Bioenergy* 1(1):18–34.

18. Snow, A., Professor, Department of Evolution, Ecology & Organismal Biology, Ohio State University. (2010). Benefits and Risks of Synthetic Biology. Presentation to the Presidential Commission for the Study of Bioethical Issues, July 8, 2010. Available at: www.bioethics.gov/transcripts/synthetic-biology/070810/ benefits-and-risks-of-synthetic-biology.html.

19. Callura, J. M., et al. (2010). Tracking, tuning, and terminating microbial physiology using synthetic riboregulators. *Proceedings of the National Academy of Sciences* 107(36):15898–15903.

20. Thomas, J., Programme Manager, ETC Group. (2010). Benefits and Risks of Synthetic Biology. Presentation to the President's Commission for the Study of Bioethical issues, July 8, 2010. Available at: http://www.bioethics.gov/transcripts/ synthetic-biology/070810/benefits-and-risks-of-synthetic-biology.html.

21. Dale, V. H., et al. (2010). Biofuels: Implications for land use and biodiversity. *Ecological Society of America: Biofuels and Sustainability Report.* Available at: www.esa. org/biofuelsreports/files/ESA%20Biofucls%20Report_VH%20Dale%20et%20al.pdf.

22. Tilman, D., Reich., P. B., and J. M. Knops. (2006). Biodiversity and ecosystem stability in a decade-long grassland experiment. *Nature* 441:629–632; Tilman, D., et al.

(2001). Diversity and productivity in a long-term grassland experiment. *Science* 294(5543):843–845.

23. *See* Goeddel, D. V., et al. (1979). Expression in *Escherichia coli* of chemically synthesized genes for human insulin. *Proceedings of the National Academy of Sciences* 76(1):106–110; Mast, E. E., and J. W. Ward (2008). Hepatitis B vaccines. In *Vaccines*, S. Plotkin, W. Orenstein, and P. Offit (cds.). Pages 205–42; Schiller, J. T., Frazer, I. H., and Lowy, D. R. (2008). Human papillomavirus vaccines. In *Vaccines*, S. Plotkin, W. Orenstein, and P. Offit (eds.). Pages 243–258.

24. Rodemeyer, M. (2009). *New Life, Old Bottles: Regulating First-Generation Products of Synthetic Biology*. Washington, D.C.: Woodrow Wilson International Center for Scholars. Available at: www.synbioprojcct.org/process/assets/files/6319/nano_synbio2_electronic_final.pdf.

25. Centers for Disease Control and Prevention. *Malaria*. Available at: www.cdc.gov/MALARIA/.

26. Martin V. J., et al. (2003). Engineering a mevalonate pathway in *Escherichia coli* for production of terpenoids. *Nat Biotechnol*. 21:796–802.

27. Amyris. *Artemisinin — Anti-malarial Therapeutic*. Available at: www.amyrisbiotech.com/markets/artemisinin.

28. Synthetic Genomics. *Press Release: Synthetic Genomics Inc. and J. Craig Venter Institute Form New Company, Synthetic Genomics Vaccines Inc. (SGVI), to Develop Next Generation Vaccines*. October 7, 2010. Available at: www.syntheticgenomics.com/media/press/100710.html.

29. Ibid.

30. Yang, Z., et al. (2010). Expanded genetic alphabets in the polymerase chain reaction. *Angewandte Chemie International Edition* 49(1); 177–180.

31. Benner, S. A. (2004). Understanding nucleic acids using synthetic chemistry. *Accounts of Chemical Research* 37(10):784–797.

32. Feero, E. G., Guttmacher, A. E., and F. S. Collins. (2010). Genomic medicine: An updated primer. *New England Journal of Medicine* 362:2001–2011.

33. Weiss, R., Associate Professor, Department of Biological Engineering and Department of Electrical Engineering and Computer Science, Massachusetts Institute of Technology. (2010). Synthetic Biology: What New Methods and Products are Being Developed? Presentation to the Presidential Commission for the Study of Bioethical Issues, September 13, 2010. Available at: www.bioethics.gov/transcripts/synthetic-biology/091310/synthetic-biology-what-new-methods-and-products-are-being-developed.html.

34. Anderson, J. C., et al. (2006). Environmentally controlled invasion of cancer cells by engineered bacteria. *Journal of Molecular Biology* 355(4):619–627.

35. Church, G. M., Professor of Genetics, Harvard Medical School. (2010). Applications of Synthetic Biology. Presentation to the Presidential Commission for the Study of Bioethical Issues, July 8, 2010. Available at: www.bioethics.gov/transcripts/synthetic-biology/070810/applications-of-synthetic-biology.html.

36. The Joint Bioenergy Institute. *About JBEI*. Available at: www.jbei.org; Synthetic Genomics, Inc. *Agricultural Products*. Available at: www.syntheticgenomics.com/what/agriculture.html.

37. Ibid.

38. *See generally Diamond v. Chakrabarty*, 447 U.S. 303 (1980).

39. Hazen, T. C., et al. (2010). Deep-sea oil plume enriches indigenous oil-degrading bacteria. *Science* 330(6001):204–208.

40. Cameotra, S. S., and R. S. Makkar. (2004). Recent applications of biosurfactants as biological and immunological molecules. *Current Opinion in Microbiology* 7(3):262–266.

41. Snow, A. A., et al. (2005). Genetically engineered organisms and the environment: current status and recommendations. *Ecological Applications* 15:377–404.

42. Norton, B. G., Distinguished Professor of Philosophy, School of Public Policy, Georgia Institute of Technology. (2010). Social Responsibility, Risk Assessment, and Ethics. Presentation to the Presidential Commission for the Study of Bioethical Issues, September 13, 2010. Available at: www.bioethics.gov/transcripts/synthetic-biology/091310/social-responsibility-risk-assessment-and-ethics.html.

43. Collins, J. J., University Professor, William F. Warren Distinguished Professor, Professor of Biomedical Engineering, and Co-Director, Center for BioDynamics, Boston University. (2010). Synthetic Biology: What New Methods and Products are Being Developed? Presentation to the Presidential Commission for the Study of Bioethical Issues, September 13, 2010. Available at: www.bioethics.gov/transcripts/synthetic-biology/091310/synthetic-biology-what-new-methods-and-products-are-being-developed.html

44. NSABB. (2010). *Addressing Biosecurity Concerns Related to Synthetic Biology*. Available at: http://oba.od.nih.gov/biosecurity/pdf/NSABB%20SynBio%20DRAFT%20Report-FINAL%20(2)_6-7-10.pdf.

45. Kodumal, S. J., et al. (2004). Total synthesis of long DNA sequences: Synthesis of a contiguous 32-kb polyketide synthase gene cluster. *Proceedings of the National Academy of Sciences* 101(44):15573–15578; Cello, J., Paul, A. V., and E. Wimmer. (2002). Chemical synthesis of poliovirus cDNA: Generation of infectious virus in the absence of natural template. *Science* 297(5583):1016–1018; Gibson, D. G., et al. (2008). Complete chemical synthesis, assembly, and cloning of a *Mycoplasma genitalium* genome. *Science* 319(5867):1215–1220; Tumpey, T. M., et al. (2005). Characterization of the reconstructed 1918 Spanish influenza pandemic virus. *Science* 310(5745):77–80.

46. National Center for Biotechnology Information. *GenBank overview*. Available at: www.ncbi.nlm.nih.gov/genbank/.

47. NSABB. (2006). *Addressing Biosecurity Concerns Related to the Synthesis of Select Agents*. Available at: http://oba.od.nih.gov/biosecurity/pdf/Final_NSABB_Report_on_Synthetic_Genomics.pdf; NSABB, op cit. (2010).

48. 42 C.F.R. Part 73.

49. Department of Health and Human Services. (2010). *Screening Framework Guidance for Providers of Synthetic Double Stranded DNA*. Available at: www.phe.gov/Preparedness/legal/guidance/syndna/Pages/default.aspx.

50. *See, e.g.*, National Research Council, Board on Life Sciences. (2010). *Sequence-Based Classification of Select Agents: A Brighter Line*. Washington, D.C.: National Academies Press.

18

Five Hard Truths for Synthetic Biology

ROBERTA KWOK

The Presidential Commission report is generally optimistic about the future of synthetic biology. Although the report contains plenty of cautions about the risks and possible harms of the technology, it focuses mainly on the applications and benefits. It also describes developments that are likely to come to fruition in the relatively near future. Roberta Kwok is more skeptical. In the article that follows, which appeared in Nature *a few months before the J. Craig Venter Institute's announcement and nearly a year before the publication of the Presidential Commission's report, she looks at some of the challenges that will need to be overcome if the promise of synthetic biology is to be realized. These challenges "loom at every step in the process," she writes. Concerned with the prospects for scaling up from the laboratory to industrial applications, she quotes a researcher who warns, "There's a lot of biology that gets in the way of the engineering." Nevertheless, Kwok looks for — and finds — ways to overcome these challenges.*

Roberta Kwok *is a freelance science writer based in the San Francisco Bay Area. Her articles have appeared in* Nature, New Scientist, Salon.com, Conservation, Harvard Magazine, *and* ScienceNOW. *She has a bachelor's degree in biology from Stanford University and a graduate certification in science communication from the University of California, Santa Cruz. Kwok is the recipient of the American Geophysical Union's 2010 Walter Sullivan Award for Excellence in Science Journalism.*

To read some accounts of synthetic biology, the ability to manipulate life seems restricted only by the imagination. Researchers might soon program cells to produce vast quantities of biofuel from renewable sources, or to sense the presence of toxins, or to release precise quantities of insulin as a body needs it — all visions inspired by the idea that biologists can extend genetic engineering to be more like the engineering of any hardware. The formula: characterize the genetic sequences that perform needed functions, the 'parts', combine the parts into devices to achieve more complex functions, then insert the devices into cells. As all life is based on roughly the same genetic code, synthetic biology could provide a toolbox of reusable genetic components — biological versions of transistors and switches — to be plugged into circuits at will.

Such analogies don't capture the daunting knowledge gap when it comes to how life works, however. "There are very few molecular operations that you understand in the way that you understand a wrench or a screwdriver or a transistor," says Rob Carlson, a principal at the engineering, consulting and design company Biodesic in Seattle, Washington. And the difficulties multiply as the networks get larger, limiting the ability to design more complex systems. A 2009 review[1] showed that although the number of published synthetic biological circuits has risen over the past few years, the complexity of those circuits — or the number of regulatory parts they use — has begun to flatten out.

Challenges loom at every step in the process, from the characterization of parts to the design and construction of systems. "There's a lot of biology that gets in the way of the engineering," says Christina Agapakis, a graduate student doing synthetic-biology research at Harvard Medical School in Boston, Massachusetts. But difficult biology is not enough to deter the field's practitioners, who are already addressing the five key challenges.

1. Many of the Parts Are Undefined

A biological part can be anything from a DNA sequence that encodes a specific protein to a promoter, a sequence that facilitates the expression of a gene. The problem is that many parts have not been characterized well. They haven't always been tested to show what they do, and even when they have, their performance can change with different cell types or under different laboratory conditions.

The Registry of Standard Biological Parts, which is housed at the Massachusetts Institute of Technology in Cambridge, for example, has more than 5,000 parts available to order, but does not guarantee their quality, says director Randy Rettberg. Most have been sent in by undergraduates participating in the International Genetically Engineered Machine (iGEM) competition, an annual event that started in 2004. In it, students use parts from a 'kit' or develop new ones to design a synthetic biological system. But many competitors do not have the time to characterize the parts thoroughly.

While trying to optimize lactose fermentation in microbes, an iGEM team from the University of Pavia in Italy tested several promoters from the registry by placing them in *Escherichia coli,* a standard laboratory bacterium. Most of the promoters tested by the team worked, but some had little documentation, and one showed no activity. About 1,500 registry parts have been confirmed as working by someone other than the person who deposited them and 50 have reportedly failed, says Rettberg. 'Issues' have been reported for roughly another 200 parts, and it is unclear how many of the remaining parts have been tested.

The registry has been stepping up efforts to improve the quality by curating the collection, encouraging contributors to include documentation on part function and performance, and sequencing the DNA of samples of parts to make sure they match their descriptions, says Rettberg. Meanwhile, synthetic biologists Adam Arkin and Jay Keasling at the University of California, Berkeley, and Drew Endy at Stanford University in Stanford, California are launching a new effort, tentatively called BIOFAB, to professionally develop and characterize new and existing parts. Late last year, the team was awarded US$1.4 million by the National Science Foundation and is hiring staff, says Arkin. Endy, moreover, has proposed methods to reduce some of the variability in measurements from different labs. By measuring promoter activity relative to a reference promoter, rather than looking at absolute activity, Endy's team found that it could eliminate half the variation arising from experimental conditions and instruments.[2]

Measurements are tricky to standardize, however. In mammalian cells, for example, genes introduced into a cell integrate unpredictably into the cell's genome, and neighboring regions often affect expression, says Martin Fussenegger, a synthetic biologist at the Swiss Federal Institute of Technology (ETH) Zurich. "This is the type of complexity that is very difficult to capture by standardized characterization," he says.

2. The Circuitry Is Unpredictable

Even if the function of each part is known, the parts may not work as expected when put together, says Keasling. Synthetic biologists are often caught in a laborious process of trial-and-error, unlike the more predictable design procedures found in other modern engineering disciplines.

"We are still like the Wright Brothers, putting pieces of wood and paper together," says Luis Serrano, a systems biologist at the Centre for Genomic Regulation in Barcelona, Spain. "You fly one thing and it crashes. You try another thing and maybe it flies a bit better."

Bioengineer Jim Collins and his colleagues at Boston University in Massachusetts crashed a lot when implementing a system called a toggle switch in yeast. His lab built one roughly ten years ago in E. coli[3]: the team wanted to make cells express one gene — call it gene A — and then prompt them with a chemical signal to turn off A and express another gene, B. But the cells refused to express B continuously; they always shifted back to expressing A. The problem, says Collins, was that the promoters controlling the two genes were not balanced, so A overpowered B. It took about three years of tweaking the system to make it work, he says.

Computer modelling could help reduce this guesswork. In a 2009 study,[4] Collins and his colleagues created several slightly different versions of two promoters. They used one version of each to create a genetic timer, a system that would cause cells to switch from expressing one gene to another after a certain lag time. They then tested the timer, fed the results back into a computational model and predicted how timers built from other versions would behave. Using such modeling techniques, researchers could optimize computationally rather than test every version of a network, says Collins.

But designs might not have to work perfectly: imperfect ones can be refined using a process called directed evolution, says Frances Arnold, a chemical engineer at the California Institute of Technology in Pasadena. Directed evolution involves mutating DNA sequences, screening their performance, selecting the best candidates and repeating the process until the system is optimized. Arnold's lab, for instance, is using the technique to evolve enzymes involved in biofuel production.

3. The Complexity Is Unwieldy

As circuits get larger, the process of constructing and testing them becomes more daunting. A system developed by Keasling's team,[5] which uses about a dozen genes to produce a precursor of the antimalarial compound artemisinin in microbes, is perhaps the field's most cited success story. Keasling estimates that it has taken roughly 150 person-years of work including uncovering genes involved in the pathway and developing or refining parts to control their expression. For example, the researchers had to test many part variants before they found a configuration that sufficiently increased production of an enzyme needed to consume a toxic intermediate molecule.

"People don't even think about tackling those projects because it takes too much time and money," says Reshma Shetty, co-founder of the start-up firm Ginkgo BioWorks in Boston, Massachusetts. To relieve similar bottlenecks, Ginkgo is developing an automated process to combine genetic parts. The parts have pre-defined flanking sequences, dictated by a set of rules called the BioBrick standard, and can be assembled by robots.

At Berkeley, synthetic biologist J. Christopher Anderson and his colleagues are developing a system that lets bacteria do the work. Engineered *E. coli* cells, called 'assembler' cells, are being equipped with enzymes that can cut and stitch together DNA parts. Other *E. coli* cells, engineered to act as "selection" cells, will sort out the completed products from the leftover parts. The team plans to use virus-like particles called phagemids to ferry the DNA from the assembler to the selection cells. Anderson says that the system could shorten the time needed for one BioBrick assembly stage from two days to three hours.

4. Many Parts Are Incompatible

Once constructed and placed into cells, synthetic genetic circuits can have unintended effects on their host. Chris Voigt, a synthetic biologist at the University of California, San Francisco, ran into this problem while he was a postdoc at Berkeley in 2003. Voigt had assembled genetic parts, mainly from the bacterium *Bacillus subtilis*, into a switch system that was supposed to turn on expression of certain genes in response to a chemical stimulus. He wanted to study the system independently of *B. subtilis'* other genetic networks, so he put the circuit into *E. coli* — but it didn't work.

"You looked under the microscope and the cells were sick," says Voigt. "One day it would do one thing, and another day it would do another thing." He eventually saw in the literature that one of the circuit's parts dramatically disrupted *E. coli*'s natural gene expression. "There was nothing wrong with the design of the circuit," he says. "It was just that one part was not compatible."

Synthetic biologist Lingchong You at Duke University in Durham, North Carolina, and his colleagues found that even a simple circuit, comprising a foreign gene that promoted its own expression, could trigger complex behavior in host cells.[6] When activated in *E. coli*, the circuit slowed down the cells' growth, which in turn slowed dilution of the gene's protein product. This led to a phenomenon called bistability: some cells expressed the gene, whereas others did not.

To lessen unexpected interactions, researchers are developing 'orthogonal' systems that operate independently of the cell's natural machinery. Synthetic biologist Jason Chin of the Medical Research Council Laboratory of Molecular Biology in Cambridge, UK, and his colleagues have created a protein-production system in *E. coli* that is separate from the cell's built-in system.[7] To transcribe DNA into RNA, the team uses a polymerase enzyme that recognizes genes only if they have a specific promoter sequence that is not present in the cell's natural genes. Similarly, the system's orthogonal 'O-ribosomes', which translate RNA into protein, can read only 'O-mRNA' that contains a specific sequence, and O-mRNA is unreadable by natural ribosomes.

A parallel system gives biologists the freedom to tweak components without disrupting the machinery needed for the cell to survive, says Chin. For example, his team has stripped down the DNA sequence encoding part of the O-ribosome to speed up production. This allows the cell to boot up protein manufacture more quickly, he says.

Another solution is to physically isolate the synthetic network from the rest of the cell. Wendell Lim, a synthetic biologist at the University of California, San Francisco, is experimenting with the creation of membrane-bound compartments that would insulate the genetic circuits. Lim's team is working in yeast, but similar principles could be applied to bacterial cells, he says.

5. Variability Crashes the System

Synthetic biologists must also ensure that circuits function reliably. Molecular activities inside cells are prone to random fluctuations, or noise. Variation in growth conditions can also affect behavior. And over the long term, randomly arising genetic mutations can kill a circuit's function altogether.

Michael Elowitz, a synthetic biologist at the California Institute of Technology in Pasadena, observed the cell's capacity for randomness about ten years ago when his team built a genetic oscillator.[8] The system contained three genes whose interactions caused the production of a fluorescent protein to go up and down, making cells blink on and off. However, not all cells responded the same way. Some were brighter, and some were dimmer; some blinked faster, others slower; and some cells skipped a cycle altogether.

Elowitz says that the differences might have arisen for multiple reasons. A cell can express genes in bursts rather than a steady stream. Cells also may contain varying amounts of mRNA and protein-production machinery, such as polymerase enzymes and ribosomes. Furthermore, the number of copies of the genetic circuit in a cell can fluctuate over time.

Jeff Hasty, a synthetic biologist at the University of California, San Diego, and his colleagues described an oscillator with more consistent behavior[9] in 2008. Using a different circuit design and microfluidic devices that allowed fine control of growth conditions, the team made nearly every monitored cell blink at the same rate — though not in sync. And in January 2010, Hasty's team reported the ability to synchronize the blinking by relying on cell-cell communication.[10] But Hasty says that rather than trying to eliminate noise, researchers could use it to their advantage. He notes that in physics, noise can sometimes make a signal easier to detect. "I don't think you can beat it, so I think you ought to try to use it," says Hasty. For example, noise could allow some cells to respond differently to the environment from others, enabling the population to hedge its bets, says Elowitz.

Meanwhile, geneticist George Church at Harvard Medical School in Boston, Massachusetts, is exploring ways to make a bacterial strain more stable. Church says that this might be achieved by introducing more accurate DNA-replication machinery, changing genome sites to make them less prone to mutation and putting extra copies of the genome into cells. Although stability may not be a serious issue for simple systems, it will become important as more components are assembled, he says.

Time to Deliver?

Despite the challenges, synthetic biologists have made progress. Researchers have recently developed devices that allow *E. coli* to count events such as the number of times they have divided and to detect light and dark edges. And some systems have advanced from bacteria to more complex cells. The field is also gaining legitimacy, with a new synthetic-biology centre at Imperial College London and a programme at Harvard University's recently launched Wyss Institute for Biologically Inspired Engineering in Boston. The time has come for synthetic biologists to develop more real-world applications, says Fussenegger. "The field has had its hype phase," he says. "Now it needs to deliver."

Keasling's artemisinin precursor system is approaching commercial reality, with Paris-based pharmaceutical company Sanofi-Aventis aiming to have the product available at an industrial scale by 2012. And several companies are pursuing biofuel production via engineered microbes. But most applications will take time.

As the cost of DNA synthesis continues to drop and more people begin to tinker with biological parts, the field could progress faster, says Carlson. "It's a question of whether the complexity of biology yields to that kind of an effort."

ENDNOTES

1. Purnick, P.E.M. & Weiss, R. *Nature Rev. Mol. Cell Biol.* **10**, 410–422 (2009).

2. Kelly, J.R. et al. *J. Biol. Engineer.* **3**, 4 (2009).

3. Gardner, T.S., Cantor, C.R. & Collins, J.J. *Nature* **403**, 339–342 (2000).

4. Ellis, T., Wang, X. & Collins, J. J. *Nature Biotechnol.* **27**, 465–471 (2009).

5. Ro, D.-K. et al. *Nature* **440**, 940–943 (2006).

6. Tan, C., Marguet, P. & You, L. *Nature Chem. Biol.* **5**, 842–848 (2009).

7. An, W. & Chin, J.W. *Proc. Natl. Acad. Sci. USA* **106**, 8477–8482 (2009).

8. Elowitz, M.B. & Leibler, S. *Nature* **403**, 335–338 (2000).

9. Stricker, J. et al. *Nature* **456**, 516–519 (2008).

10. Danino, T., Mondragón-Palomino, O., Tsimring, L. & Hasty, J. *Nature* **463**, 326–330 (2010).

19

The Case against Perfection

MICHAEL J. SANDEL

Advances in biotechnology have begun to make possible a range of interventions in human development that, until recently, could only be dreamed of. Some of these possibilities, as Michael Sandel says, "present us with a promise and a predicament." The promise is the ability to treat and prevent a range of diseases and alleviate a great deal of human suffering. The predicament is that the same knowledge may enable us to change our very nature — to enhance or choose such specific traits in our children as their height, athletic or musical talents, intelligence, or gender — in other words, to design our offspring. Related technologies may make possible the safe and reliable cloning of individual human beings. Most people would say there is something not quite right about designing a child to certain specifications or, through cloning, creating a child who is genetically identical to a parent or, perhaps, to a sibling who has died.

These prospects are unsettling for many of us. But why? Sandel explores various possible reasons for our discomfort. What is the difference between using medicine to cure and using the same technologies to design or enhance? In exploring these questions, Sandel helps us to articulate the reasons for our unease and, in the process, to explore the ethical dilemmas that face us and the choices that technology may require us to make in the near future.

Michael J. Sandel is the Anne T. and Robert M. Bass Professor of Government at Harvard University; he has taught political philosophy at Harvard since 1980. His highly popular courses include "Justice" and "Ethics, Biotechnology, and the Future of Human Nature." Sandel is the author of several books, including The Case against Perfection: Ethics in the Age of Genetic Engineering, *of which this chapter is the introduction. He served as a member of President George W. Bush's Council on Bioethics. Sandel's*

"The Ethics of Enhancement," reprinted by permission of the publisher from *The Case Against Perfection: Ethics in the Age of Genetic Engineering*, by Michael J. Sandel, pp. 1–24, Cambridge, Mass: The Belknap Press of Harvard University Press, © 2007 by Michael J. Sandel. Adapted and expanded from an original essay published in the Atlantic Monthly, 2004.

undergraduate degree is from Brandeis University; his doctorate is from Oxford University, where he was a Rhodes Scholar. He holds three honorary degrees.

A few years ago, a couple decided they wanted to have a child, preferably a deaf one. Both partners were deaf, and proudly so. Like others in the deaf-pride community, Sharon Duchesneau and Candy McCullough considered deafness a cultural identity, not a disability to be cured. "Being deaf is just a way of life," said Duchesneau. "We feel whole as deaf people and we want to share the wonderful aspects of our deaf community — a sense of belonging and connectedness — with children. We truly feel we live rich lives as deaf people."[1]

In hopes of conceiving a deaf child, they sought out a sperm donor with five generations of deafness in his family. And they succeeded. Their son Gauvin was born deaf.

The new parents were surprised when their story, which was reported in the *Washington Post*, brought widespread condemnation. Most of the outrage focused on the charge that they had deliberately inflicted a disability on their child. Duchesneau and McCullough (who are lesbian partners) denied that deafness is a disability and argued that they had simply wanted a child like themselves. "We do not view what we did as very different from what many straight couples do when they have children," said Duchesneau.[2]

Is it wrong to make a child deaf by design? If so, what makes it wrong — the deafness or the design? Suppose, for the sake of argument, that deafness is not a disability but a distinctive identity. Is there still something wrong with the idea of parents picking and choosing the kind of child they will have? Or do parents do that all the time, in their choice of mate and, these days, in their use of new reproductive technologies?

Not long before the controversy over the deaf child, an ad appeared in the *Harvard Crimson* and other Ivy League student newspapers. An infertile couple was seeking an egg donor, but not just any egg donor. She had to be five feet, ten inches tall, athletic, without major family medical problems, and to have a combined SAT score of 1400 or above. In exchange for an egg from a donor meeting this description, the ad offered payment of $50,000.[3]

Perhaps the parents who offered the hefty sum for a premium egg simply wanted a child who resembled them. Or perhaps they were hoping to trade up, trying for a child who would be taller or smarter than they. Whatever the case, their extraordinary offer did not prompt the public outcry that met the parents who wanted a deaf child. No one objected that height, intelligence, and athletic prowess are disabilities that children should be spared. And yet something about the ad leaves a lingering moral qualm. Even if no harm is involved, isn't there something troubling about parents ordering up a child with certain genetic traits?

Some defend the attempt to conceive a deaf child, or one who will have high SAT scores, as similar to natural procreation in one crucial respect: whatever these parents did to increase the odds, they were not guaranteed the outcome they sought. Both attempts were still subject to the vagaries of the genetic lottery. This defense raises an intriguing question. Why does some element of unpredictability seem to make a moral difference? Suppose biotechnology could remove the uncertainty and allow us to design the genetic traits of our children?

While pondering this question, put aside children for a moment and consider pets. About a year after the furor over the deliberately deaf child, a Texas woman named Julie (she declined to give her last name) was mourning the death of her beloved cat Nick. "He was very beautiful," Julie said. "He was exceptionally intelligent. He knew eleven commands." She had read of a company in California that offered a cat cloning service — Genetic Savings & Clone. In 2001 the company had succeeded in creating the first cloned cat (named CC, for Carbon Copy). Julie sent the company a genetic sample of Nicky, along with the required fee of $50,000. A few months later, to her great delight, she received Little Nicky, a genetically identical cat. "He is identical," Julie proclaimed. "I have not been able to see one difference."[4]

The company's Web site has since announced a price reduction for cat cloning, which now costs a mere $32,000. If the price still seems steep, it comes with a money-back guarantee: "If you feel that your kitten doesn't sufficiently resemble the genetic donor, we'll refund your money in full with no questions asked." Meanwhile, the company's scientists are working to develop a new product line — cloned dogs. Since dogs are harder to clone than cats, the company plans to charge $100,000 or more.[5]

Many people find something odd about the commercial cloning of cats and dogs. Some complain that, with thousands of strays in need of good homes, it is unconscionable to spend a small fortune to create a custom-made pet. Others worry about the number of animals lost during pregnancy in the attempt to create a successful clone. But suppose these problems could be overcome. Would the cloning of cats and dogs still give us pause? What about the cloning of human beings?

ARTICULATING OUR UNEASE

Breakthroughs in genetics present us with a promise and a predicament. The promise is that we may soon be able to treat and prevent a host of debilitating diseases. The predicament is that our newfound genetic knowledge may also enable us to manipulate our own nature — to enhance our muscles, memories, and moods; to choose the sex, height, and other genetic traits of our children; to improve our physical and cognitive capacities; to make ourselves "better than well."[6] Most people find at least some forms of genetic engineering disquieting. But it is not easy to articulate the source of our unease. The familiar terms of moral and political discourse make it difficult to say what is wrong with reengineering our nature.

Consider again the question of cloning. The birth of Dolly the cloned sheep in 1997 brought a torrent of worry about the prospect of cloned human beings. There are good medical reasons to worry. Most scientists agree that cloning is unsafe and likely to produce offspring with serious abnormalities and birth defects. (Dolly died a premature death.) But suppose cloning technology

improves to the point where the risks are no greater than with natural pregnancy. Would human cloning still be objectionable? What exactly is wrong
with creating a child who is a genetic twin of his or her parent, or of an older
sibling who has tragically died, or, for that matter, of an admired scientist, sports
star, or celebrity?

Some say cloning is wrong because it violates the child's right to autonomy.
By choosing in advance the genetic makeup of the child, the parents consign her
to a life in the shadow of someone who has gone before, and so deprive the
child of her right to an open future. The autonomy objection can be raised not
only against cloning but also against any form of bioengineering that allows parents to choose their child's genetic characteristics. According to this objection,
the problem with genetic engineering is that "designer children" are not fully
free; even favorable genetic enhancements (for musical talent, say, or athletic
prowess) would point children toward particular life choices, impairing their
autonomy and violating their right to choose their life plan for themselves.

At first glance, the autonomy argument seems to capture what is troubling
about human cloning and other forms of genetic engineering. But it is not persuasive, for two reasons. First, it wrongly implies that, absent a designing parent,
children are free to choose their physical characteristics for themselves. But none
of us chooses our own genetic inheritance. The alternative to a cloned or genetically enhanced child is not one whose future is unbiased and unbound by particular talents, but a child at the mercy of the genetic lottery.

Second, even if a concern for autonomy explains some of our worries about
made-to-order children, it cannot explain our moral hesitation about people
who seek genetic enhancements for themselves. Not all genetic interventions
are passed down the generations. Gene therapy on nonreproductive (or somatic)
cells, such as muscle cells or brain cells, works by repairing or replacing defective
genes. The moral quandary arises when people use such therapy not to cure a
disease but to reach beyond health, to enhance their physical or cognitive capacities, to lift themselves above the norm.

This moral quandary has nothing to do with impairing autonomy. Only
germline genetic interventions, which target eggs, sperm, or embryos, affect subsequent generations. An athlete who genetically enhances his muscles does not
confer on his progeny his added speed and strength; he cannot be charged with
foisting talents on his children that may push them toward an athletic career.
And yet there is still something unsettling about the prospect of genetically
altered athletes.

Like cosmetic surgery, genetic enhancement employs medical means for nonmedical ends — ends unrelated to curing or preventing disease, repairing injury,
or restoring health. But unlike cosmetic surgery, genetic enhancement is not
merely cosmetic. It is more than skin deep. Even somatic enhancements, which
would not reach our children and grandchildren, raise hard moral questions. If
we are ambivalent about plastic surgery and Botox injections for sagging chins
and furrowed brows, we are all the more troubled by genetic engineering for
stronger bodies, sharper memories, greater intelligence, and happier moods. The
question is whether we are right to be troubled — and if so, on what grounds?

When science moves faster than moral understanding, as it does today, men and women struggle to articulate their unease. In liberal societies, they reach first for the language of autonomy, fairness, and individual rights. But this part of our moral vocabulary does not equip us to address the hardest questions posed by cloning, designer children, and genetic engineering. That is why the genomic revolution has induced a kind of moral vertigo. To grapple with the ethics of enhancement, we need to confront questions largely lost from view in the modern world — questions about the moral status of nature, and about the proper stance of human beings toward the given world. Since these questions verge on theology, modern philosophers and political theorists tend to shrink from them. But our new powers of biotechnology make them unavoidable.

GENETIC ENGINEERING

To see how this is so, consider four examples of bioengineering already on the horizon: muscle enhancement, memory enhancement, height enhancement, and sex selection. In each case, what began as an attempt to treat a disease or prevent a genetic disorder now beckons as an instrument of improvement and consumer choice.

Muscles

Everyone would welcome a gene therapy to alleviate muscular dystrophy and to reverse the debilitating muscle loss that comes with old age. But what if the same therapy were used to produce genetically altered athletes? Researchers have developed a synthetic gene that, when injected into the muscle cells of mice, makes muscles grow and prevents them from deteriorating with age. The success bodes well for human applications. Dr. H. Lee Sweeney, who leads the research, hopes his discovery will cure the immobility that afflicts the elderly. But Dr. Sweeney's bulked-up mice have already attracted the attention of athletes seeking a competitive edge.[7] The gene not only repairs injured muscles but also strengthens healthy ones. Although the therapy is not yet approved for human use, the prospect of genetically enhanced weight lifters, home-run sluggers, linebackers, and sprinters is easy to imagine. The widespread use of steroids and other performance-enhancing drugs in professional sports suggests that many athletes will be eager to avail themselves of genetic enhancement. The International Olympic Committee has already begun to worry about the fact that, unlike drugs, altered genes cannot be detected in urine or blood tests.[8]

The prospect of genetically altered athletes offers a good illustration of the ethical quandaries surrounding enhancement. Should the IOC and professional sports leagues ban genetically enhanced athletes, and if so, on what grounds?

The two most obvious reasons for banning drugs in sports are safety and fairness: Steroids have harmful side effects, and to allow some to boost their performance by incurring serious health risks would put their competitors at an unfair disadvantage. But suppose, for the sake of argument, that muscle-enhancing gene therapy turned out to be safe, or at least no riskier than a rigorous weight-training regime. Would there still be a reason to ban its use in sports? There is something unsettling about the specter of genetically altered athletes lifting SUVs or hitting 650-foot home runs or running a three-minute mile. But what exactly is troubling about these scenarios? Is it simply that we find such superhuman spectacles too bizarre to contemplate, or does our unease point to something of ethical significance?

The distinction between curing and improving seems to make a moral difference, but it is not obvious what the difference consists in. Consider: If it is all right for an injured athlete to repair a muscle tear with the help of genetic therapy, why is it wrong for him to extend the therapy to improve the muscle, and then to return to the lineup better than before? It might be argued that a genetically enhanced athlete would have an unfair advantage over his unenhanced competitors. But the fairness argument against enhancement has a fatal flaw. It has always been the case that some athletes are better endowed, genetically, than others. And yet we do not consider the natural inequality of genetic endowments to undermine the fairness of competitive sports. From the standpoint of fairness, enhanced genetic differences are no worse than natural ones. Moreover, assuming they are safe, genetic enhancements could be made available to all. If genetic enhancement in sports is morally objectionable, it must be for reasons other than fairness.

Memory

Genetic enhancement is possible for brains as well as brawn. In the mid-1990s scientists managed to manipulate a memory-linked gene in fruit flies, creating flies with photographic memories. More recently researchers produced smart mice by inserting extra copies of a memory-related gene into mouse embryos. The altered mice learn more quickly and remember things longer than normal mice. For example, they are better able to recognize objects they have seen before, and to remember that a certain sound leads to an electric shock. The gene the scientists tweaked in mouse embryos is present in human beings as well, and becomes less active as people age. The extra copies installed in the mice were programmed to remain active even in old age, and the improvement was passed on to their offspring.[9]

Of course human memory is more complicated than recalling simple associations. But biotech companies with names like Memory Pharmaceuticals are in hot pursuit of memory-enhancing drugs, or "cognition enhancers," for human beings. One obvious market for such drugs consists of those who suffer from serious memory disorders, such as Alzheimer's and dementia. But the companies also have their sights on a bigger market: the 76 million baby boomers over fifty who are beginning to encounter the natural memory loss that comes with age.[10]

A drug that reversed age-related memory loss would be a bonanza for the pharmaceuticals industry, a "Viagra for the brain."

Such use would straddle the distinction between remedy and enhancement. Unlike a treatment for Alzheimer's it would cure no disease. But insofar as it restored capacities a person once possessed, it would have a remedial aspect. It could also have purely nonmedical uses: for example, by a lawyer cramming to memorize facts for an upcoming trial, or by a business executive eager to learn Mandarin on the eve of his departure for Shanghai.

It might be argued, against the project of memory enhancement, that there are some things we would rather forget. For the drug companies, however, the desire to forget represents not an objection to the memory business but another market segment. Those who want to blunt the impact of traumatic or painful memories may soon be able to take a drug that prevents horrific events from being etched too vividly in memory. Victims of a sexual assault, soldiers exposed to the carnage of war, or rescue workers forced to face the aftermath of a terrorist attack would be able to take a memory-suppressing drug to dull the trauma that might otherwise plague them for a lifetime. If the use of such drugs became widely accepted, they might one day be administered routinely in emergency rooms and military field hospitals.[11]

Some who worry about the ethics of cognitive enhancement point to the danger of creating two classes of human beings — those with access to enhancement technologies, and those who must make do with an unaltered memory that fades with age. And if the enhancements can be passed down the generations, the two classes may eventually become subspecies of human beings — the enhanced and the merely natural. But the worry about access begs the question of the moral status of enhancement itself. Is the scenario troubling because the unenhanced poor are denied the benefits of bioengineering, or because the enhanced affluent are somehow dehumanized? As with muscles, so with memory: The fundamental question is not how to assure equal access to enhancement but whether we should aspire to it. Should we devote our biotechnological ingenuity to curing disease and restoring the injured to health, or should we also seek to improve our lot by reengineering our bodies and minds?

Height

Pediatricians already struggle with the ethics of enhancement when confronted by parents who want to make their children taller. Since the 1980s, human growth hormone has been approved for children with a hormone deficiency that makes them much shorter than average.[12] But the treatment also increases the height of healthy children. Some parents of healthy children who are unhappy with their stature (typically boys) ask for the hormone treatments on the grounds that it should not matter whether a child is short because of a hormone deficiency or because his parents happen to be short. Whatever the cause, the social consequences of shortness are the same in both cases.

In the face of this argument, some doctors began prescribing hormone treatments for children whose short stature was unrelated to any medical problem. By

1996 such "off-label" use accounted for 40 percent of human growth hormone prescriptions.[13] Although it is not illegal to prescribe drugs for purposes the Food and Drug Administration (FDA) has not approved, the pharmaceutical companies cannot promote such use. Seeking to expand its market, one company, Eli Lilly, recently persuaded the FDA to approve its human growth hormone for healthy children whose projected adult height is in the bottom first percentile — under five feet, three inches for boys; four feet, eleven inches for girls.[14] This small concession raises a large question about the ethics of enhancement: If hormone treatments need not be limited to those with hormone deficiencies, why should they be available only to very short children? Why shouldn't all shorter-than-average children be able to seek treatment? And what about a child of average height who wants to be taller so he can make the basketball team?

Critics call the elective use of human growth hormone "cosmetic endocrinology." Health insurance is unlikely to cover it, and the treatments are expensive. Injections are administered up to six times a week, for two to five years, at an annual cost of about $20,000 — all for a potential height gain of two or three inches.[15] Some oppose height enhancement on the grounds that it is collectively self-defeating; as some become taller, others will become shorter relative to the norm. Except in Lake Wobegon, every child cannot be above average in height. As the unenhanced begin to feel shorter, they too might seek treatment, leading to a hormonal arms race that will leave everyone worse off, especially those who cannot afford to buy their way up from shortness.

But the arms-race objection is not decisive on its own. Like the fairness objection to bioengineered muscles and memory, it leaves unexamined the attitudes and dispositions that prompt the drive for enhancement. If we were bothered only by the injustice of adding shortness to the problems of the poor, we could remedy that unfairness by providing publicly subsidized height enhancement. As for the collective-action problem, the innocent bystanders who suffer relative height deprivation could be financially compensated by a tax imposed on those who buy their way to greater height. The real question is whether we want to live in a society where parents feel compelled to spend a fortune to make perfectly healthy kids a few inches taller.

Sex Selection

Perhaps the most alluring nonmedical use of bioengineering is sex selection. For centuries parents have been trying to choose the sex of their children. Aristotle advised men who wanted a boy to tie off their left testicle before intercourse. The Talmud teaches that men who restrain themselves and allow their wives to achieve sexual climax first will be blessed with a son. Other recommended methods have involved timing conception in relation to ovulation, or to the phases of the moon. Today, biotech succeeds where folk remedies failed.[16]

One technique for sex selection arose with prenatal tests using amniocentesis and ultrasound. These medical technologies were developed to detect genetic abnormalities, such as spina bifida and Down syndrome. But they can also reveal the sex of a fetus, allowing for the abortion of a fetus of the undesired sex. Even among those who favor abortion rights, few advocate abortion simply because the mother (or father) does not want a girl. But in societies with powerful cultural preferences for boys, ultrasound sex determination followed by the abortion of female fetuses has become a familiar practice. In India, the number of girls per 1,000 boys has dropped from 962 to 927 in the past two decades. India has banned the use of prenatal diagnosis for sex selection, but the law is rarely enforced. Itinerant radiologists with portable ultrasound machines travel from village to village, plying their trade. One Bombay clinic reported that, of 8,000 abortions it performed, all but one were for purposes of sex selection.[17]

But sex selection need not involve abortion. For couples undergoing in vitro fertilization (IVF), it is possible to choose the sex of the child before the fertilized egg is implanted in the womb. The procedure, known as preimplantation genetic diagnosis (PGD), works like this: Several eggs are fertilized in a petri dish and allowed to grow to the eight-cell stage (for about three days). At that point, the early embryos are tested to determine their sex. Those of the desired sex are implanted; the others are typically discarded. Although few couples are likely to undergo the difficulty and expense of IVF simply to choose the sex of their child, embryo screening is a highly reliable means of sex selection. And as our genetic knowledge increases, it may be possible to use PGD to cull embryos carrying other undesired genetic traits, such as those associated with obesity, height, and skin color. The 1997 science fiction movie *Gattaca* depicts a future in which parents routinely screen embryos for sex, height, immunity to disease, and even IQ. There is something troubling about the *Gattaca* scenario, but it is not easy to identify what exactly is wrong with screening embryos to choose the sex of our children.

One line of objection draws on arguments familiar from the abortion debate. Those who believe that an embryo is a person reject embryo screening on the same grounds that they reject abortion. If an eight-cell embryo growing in a petri dish is morally equivalent to a fully developed human being, then discarding it is no better than aborting a fetus, and both practices are equivalent to infanticide. Whatever its merits, however, this "pro-life" objection is not an argument against sex selection as such. It is an argument against all forms of embryo screening, including PGD carried out to screen for genetic diseases. Because the pro-life objection finds an overriding moral wrong in the means (namely, the discarding of unwanted embryos), it leaves open the question of whether there is anything wrong with sex selection itself.

The latest sex selection technology poses this question on its own unclouded by the matter of an embryo's moral status. The Genetics & IVF Institute, a for-profit infertility clinic in Fairfax, Virginia, now offers a sperm sorting technique that makes it possible for clients to choose the sex of their child before it is conceived. The X-bearing sperm (which produce girls) carry more DNA than Y-bearing sperm (which produce boys); a device called a flow cytometer can separate them. The trademarked process, called MicroSort, has a high rate of success — 91 percent for producing girls, 76 percent for boys. The Genetics & IVF Institute licensed the technology from the U.S. Department of Agriculture, which had developed the process for breeding cattle.[18]

If sex selection by sperm sorting is objectionable it must be for reasons that go beyond the debate about the moral status of the embryo. One such reason is that sex selection is an instrument of sex discrimination, typically against girls, as illustrated by the chilling sex ratios in India and China. And some speculate that societies with substantially more men than women will be less stable, more violent, more prone to crime or war than societies with normal distributions.[19] These are legitimate worries, but the sperm-sorting company has a clever way of addressing them. It offers MicroSort only to couples who want to choose the sex of their child for purposes of family balancing. Those with more sons than daughters can choose a girl, and vice versa. But customers may not use the technology to stock up on children of the same sex, or even to choose the sex of their first-born child. So far, the majority of MicroSort clients have chosen girls.[20]

The case of MicroSort helps us isolate the moral question posed by technologies of enhancement. Put aside familiar debates about safety, embryo loss, and sex discrimination. Imagine that sperm-sorting technologies were employed in a society that did not favor boys over girls, and that wound up with a balanced sex ratio. Would sex selection under those conditions be unobjectionable? What if it became possible to select not only for sex but also for height, eye color, and skin color? What about sexual orientation, IQ, musical ability, and athletic prowess? Or suppose that muscle-enhancement, memory-enhancement, and height-enhancement technologies were perfected to the point where they were safe and available to all. Would they cease to be objectionable?

Not necessarily. In each of these cases, something morally troubling persists. The trouble resides not only in the means but also in the ends being aimed at. It is commonly said that enhancement, cloning, and genetic engineering pose a threat to human dignity. This is true enough. But the challenge is to say *how* these practices diminish our humanity. What aspects of human freedom or human flourishing do they threaten?

ENDNOTES

1. Margarette Driscoll, "Why We Chose Deafness for Our Children," *Sunday Times* (London). April 14, 2002. See also Liza Mundy, "A World of Their Own," *Washington Post*, March 31, 2002, p. W22.

2. Driscoll, "Why We Chose Deafness."

3. See Gina Kolata, "$50,000 Offered to Tall, Smart Egg Donor," *New York Times*, March, 3, 1999, p. A10.

4. Alan Zarembo, "California Company Clones a Woman's Cat for $50,000," *Los Angeles Times*, December 23, 2004.

5. See Web site for Genetic Savings & Clone, at http://www.savingsandclone.com; Zarembo, "California Company Clones a Woman's Cat."

6. The phrase "better than well" is from Carl Elliott, *Better Than Well: American Medicine Meets the American Dream* (New York: W.W. Norton, 2003), who in turn cites Peter D. Kramer, *Listening to Prozac*, rev. ed. (New York: Penguin, 1997).

7. E. M. Swift and Don Yaeger, "Unnatural Selection," *Sports Illustrated*, May 14, 2001, p. 86; H. Lee Sweeney, "Gene Doping," *Scientific American*, July 2004, pp. 62–69.

8. Richard Sandomir, "Olympics: Athletes May Next Seek Genetic Enhancement," *New York Times*, March 21, 2002, p. 6.

9. Rick Weiss, "Mighty Smart Mice," *Washington Post*, September 2, 1999, p. A1; Richard Saltus, "Altered Genes Produce Smart Mice, Tough Questions," *Boston Globe*, September 2, 1999, p. A1; Stephen S. Hall, "Our Memories, Our Selves," *New York Times Magazine*, February 15, 1998, p. 26.

10. Hall, "Our Memories, Our Selves," p. 26; Robert Langreth, "Viagra for the Brain," *Forbes*, February 4, 2002; David Tuller, "Race Is On for a Pill to Save the Memory," *New York Times*, July 29, 2003; Tim Tully et al., "Targeting the CREB Pathway for Memory Enhancers," *Nature 2* (April 2003): 267–277; www.memorypharma.com.

11. Ellen Barry, "Pill to Ease Memory of Trauma Envisioned," *Boston Globe*, November 18, 2002, p. A1; Robin Maranz Henig, "The Quest to Forget," *New York Times Magazine*, April 4, 2004, pp. 32–37; Gaia Vince, "Rewriting Your Past," *New Scientist*, December 3, 2005, p. 32.

12. Marc Kaufman, "FDA Approves Wider Use of Growth Hormone," *Washington Post*, July 26, 2003, p. A12.

13. Patricia Callahan and Leila Abboud, "A New Boost for Short Kids," *Wall Street Journal*, June 11, 2003.

14. Kaufman, "FDA Approves Wider Use of Growth Hormone"; Melissa Healy, "Does Shortness Need a Cure?" *Los Angeles Times*, August 11, 2003.

15. Callahan and Abboud, "A New Boost for Short Kids."

16. Talmud, *Niddah* 31b, cited in Miryam Z. Wahrman, *Brave New Judaism: When Science and Scripture Collide* (Hanover, NH: Brandeis University Press, 2002), p. 126; Meredith Wadman, "So You Want a Girl?" *Fortune*, February 19, 2001, p. 174; Karen Springen, "The Ancient Art of Making Babies," *Newsweek*, January 26, 2004, p. 51.

17. Susan Sachs, "Clinics' Pitch to Indian Emigrés: It's a Boy," *New York Times*, August 15, 2001, p. A1; Seema Sirohi, "The Vanishing Girls of India," *Christian Science Monitor*, July 30, 2001, p. 9; Mary Carmichael, "No Girls, Please," *Newsweek*, January 26, 2004; Scott Baldauf, "India's 'Girl Deficit' Deepest among Educated," *Christian Science Monitor*, January 13, 2006, p. 1; Nicholas Eberstadt, "Choosing the Sex of Children: Demographics," presentation to President's Council on Bioethics, October 17, 2002, at www.bioethics.gov/transcripts/oct02/session2.html; B. M. Dickens, "Can Sex Selection Be Ethically Tolerated?" *Journal of Medical Ethics* 28 (December 2002): 335–336; "Quiet Genocide: Declining Child Sex Ratios," *Statesman* (India), December 17, 2001.

18. See the Genetics & IVF Institute Web site, at www.microsoft.net; see also Meredith Wadman "So You Want a Girl?"; Lisa Belkin, "Getting the Girl," *New York Times Magazine*, July 25, 1999; Claudia Kalb, "Brave New Babies," *Newsweek*, January 26, 2004, pp. 45–52.

19. Felicia R. Lee, "Engineering More Sons than Daughters: Will It Tip the Scales toward War?" *New York Times*, July 3, 2004, p. B7; David Glenn, "A Dangerous Surplus of Sons?" *Chronicle of Higher Education*, April 30, 2004, p. A14; Valerie M. Hudson and Andrea M. den Boer, *Bare Branches: Security Implications of Asia's Surplus Male Population* (Cambridge, MA: MIT Press, 2004).

20. See www.microsoft.net.

20

Some Possible Legal and Social Implications of Advances in Neuroscience

HENRY T. GREELY[1]

A technology that would allow one to know what other people are really thinking — not what they are saying but what is actually going on in their minds — would be an incredibly powerful tool with enormous social and legal consequences. While such a tool does not yet exist, the field of neuroscience is moving rapidly in a direction that suggests that someday it might be a possibility. Henry Greely considers some of the potential implications, principally from the standpoint of the legal system. Knowing whether an individual is telling the truth, whether that person's memory of an event is real and accurate, whether he or she is biased against certain groups — all of these notions are central to many legal disputes. Neuroscience, one of the fastest-growing fields in the life sciences, offers the prospect of being able to determine some of these things. But how certain must the science be for judges and juries to base life-and-death decisions on its findings? The situations in which neuroscience might be used in legal proceedings and the issues that such uses might raise are discussed in this chapter.

Henry T. ("Hank") Greely is Deane F. and Kate Edelman Johnson Professor of Law at Stanford University Law School. Prior to joining the Stanford Law School faculty in 1985, he was a partner at the law firm of Tuttle &

From "Prediction, Litigation, Privacy, and Property: Some Possible Legal and Social Implications of Advances," from *Neuroscience and the Law: Brain, Mind, and the Scales of Justice*," pp. 114–142, by Henry T. Greely. © 2004 Dana Press and the AAAS. Reprinted with permission.

Taylor and served as staff assistant to the Secretary of Energy. Greely specializes in the legal implications of new biomedical technologies, especially those related to genetics, neuroscience, and stem cells. He chairs the steering committee of the Stanford Center for Biomedical Ethics and serves as director of Stanford's Interdisciplinary Group on Neuroscience and Society, and director of its Program in Neuroethics. His articles on legal aspects of genetics, neuroscience, stem cells, and other areas of bioscience have appeared in a wide range of legal journals, as well as such major newspapers as the Philadelphia Inquirer *and the* San Jose Mercury News.

"There's no art/To find the mind's construction in the face:/He was a gentleman on whom I built/An absolute trust."[2]

The lament of Duncan, King of Scotland, for the treason of the Thane of Cawdor, his trusted nobleman, echoes through time as we continue to feel the sting of not *knowing* the minds of those people with whom we deal. From "We have a deal" to "Will you still love me tomorrow?" we continue to live in fundamental uncertainty about the minds of others. Duncan himself emphasized this by immediately giving his trust to Cawdor's conqueror, one Macbeth, with fatal consequences. But at least some of this uncertainty may be about to lift, for better or for worse.

Neuroscience is rapidly increasing our knowledge of the functioning, and malfunctioning, of that intricate three-pound organ, the human brain. In expanding our understanding of something so central to human existence, science is necessarily provoking changes in both our society and its laws. This paper seeks to forecast and explore the social and legal changes that neuroscience might bring in four areas: prediction, litigation, confidentiality and privacy, and patents....

Two notes of caution are in order. First, this paper may appear to paint a gloomy picture of future threats and abuses. In fact, the technologies discussed seem likely to have benefits far outweighing their harms. It is the job of people looking for ethical, legal, and social consequences of new technologies to look disproportionately for troublesome consequences — or, at least, that's the convention. Second, as Niels Bohr (probably) said, "It is always hard to predict things, especially the future."[3] This paper builds on experience gained in studying the ethical, legal, and social implications of human genetics over the last decade. That experience, for me and for the whole field, has included both successes and failures. In neuroscience, as in genetics, accurately envisioning the future is particularly difficult, as one must foresee successfully both what changes will occur in the science and how they will affect society. I am confident about only two things concerning this paper: first, it discusses at length some things that will never happen; and second, it ignores what will prove to be some of the most important social and legal implications of neuroscience. Nonetheless, I hope the paper will be useful as a guide to beginning to think about these issues.

PREDICTION

Advances in neuroscience may well improve our ability to make predictions about an individual's future. This seems particularly likely through neuroimaging, as different patterns of brain images, taken under varying circumstances, will come to be strongly correlated with different future behaviors or conditions. The images may reveal the *structure* of the living brain, through technologies such as computed axial tomography (CAT) scans or magnetic resonance imaging (MRI), or they may show how different parts of the brain *function*, through positron-emission tomography (PET) scans, single-photon-emission computed tomography (SPECT) scans, or functional magnetic resonance imaging (fMRI).

Neuroscience might make many different kinds of predictions about people. It might predict, or reveal, mental illness, behavioral traits, and cognitive abilities, among other things. For the purposes of this paper, I have organized these predictive areas not by the nature of the prediction but by who might use the predictions: the health care system, the criminal justice system, schools, businesses, and parents.

That new neuroscience methods are used to make predictions is not necessarily good or bad. Our society makes predictions about people all the time: when a doctor determines a patient's prognosis, when a judge (or a legislature) sentences a criminal, when colleges use the Scholastic Aptitude Test, and when automobile liability insurers set rates. But although prediction is common, it is not always uncontroversial.

The Analogy to Genetic Predictions

The issues raised by predictions based on neuroscience are often similar to those raised by genetic predictions. Indeed, in some cases the two areas are the same — genetic analysis can powerfully predict several diseases of the brain, including Huntington's disease and some cases of early-onset Alzheimer's disease. Experience of genetic predictions teaches at least three important lessons.

First, a claimed ability to predict may not, in fact, exist. Many associations between genetic variations and various diseases have been claimed, only to fail the test of replication. Interestingly, many of these failures have involved two mental illnesses, schizophrenia and bipolar disorder.

Second, and more important, the strength of the predictions can vary enormously. For some genetic diseases, prediction is overwhelmingly powerful. As far as we know, the only way a person with the genetic variation that causes Huntington's disease can avoid dying of that disease is to die first from something else. On the other hand, the widely heralded "breast cancer genes," BRCA 1 and BRCA 2, though they substantially increase the likelihood that a woman will be diagnosed with breast or ovarian cancer, are not close to determinative. Somewhere between 50 and 85 percent of women born with a pathogenic mutation in either of those genes will get breast cancer; 20 to 30 percent (well under half) will get ovarian cancer. Men with a mutation in BRCA 2 have a hundredfold greater risk of breast cancer than average men — but their chances are still under

5 percent. A prediction based on an association between a genetic variation and a disease, even when true, can be very strong, very weak, or somewhere in between. The popular perception of genes as extremely powerful is probably a result of ascertainment bias: the diseases first found to be caused by genetic variations were examples of very powerful associations *because* powerful associations were the easiest to find. If, as seems likely, the same holds true for predictions from neuroscience, such predictions will need to be used very carefully.

Finally, the use of genetic predictions has proven controversial, both in medical practice and in social settings. Much of the debate about the uses of human genetics has concerned its use in predicting the health or traits of patients, insureds, employees, fetuses, and embryos. Neuroscience seems likely to raise many similar issues.

Health Care

Much of health care is about prediction — predicting the outcome of a disease, predicting the results of a treatment for a disease, predicting the risk of getting a disease. When medicine, through neuroscience, genetics, or other methods, makes an accurate prediction that leads to a useful intervention, the prediction is clearly valuable. But predictions also can cause problems when they are inaccurate (or are perceived inaccurately by patients). Even if the predictions are accurate, they still have uncertain value if no useful interventions are possible. These problems may justify regulation of predictive neuroscientific medical testing.

Some predictive tests are inaccurate, either because the scientific understanding behind them is wrong or because the test is poorly performed. In other cases the test may be accurate in the sense that it gives an accurate assessment of the probability of a certain result, but any individual patient may not have the most likely outcome. In addition, patients or others may misinterpret the test results. In genetic testing, for example, a woman who tests positive for a BRCA 1 mutation may believe that a fatal breast cancer is inevitable, when, in fact, her lifetime risk of breast cancer is between 50 and 85 percent, and her chance of dying from a breast cancer is roughly one-third of the risk of diagnosis. Alternatively, a woman who tests negative for the mutation may falsely believe that she has *no* risk for breast cancer and might stop breast self-examinations or mammograms to her harm. Even very accurate tests may not be very useful. Genetic testing to predict Huntington's disease is quite accurate, yet, with no useful medical interventions, a person may find fore-knowledge of Huntington's disease not only unhelpful but psychologically or socially harmful. These concerns have led to widespread calls for regulation of genetic testing.[4]

The same issues can easily arise in neuroscience. Neuroimaging, for example, might easily lead to predictions, with greater or lesser accuracy, that an individual will be diagnosed with one of a variety of neurodegenerative diseases. Such imaging tests may be inaccurate, may present information patients find difficult to evaluate, and may provide information of dubious value and some harm. One might want to regulate some such tests along the lines proposed for genetic tests:

proof that the test was effective at predicting the condition in question, assessment of the competency of those performing the test, required informed consent so that patients appreciate the test's possible consequences, and mandatory posttest counseling to ensure that patients understand the results.

The Food and Drug Administration (FDA) has statutory jurisdiction over the use of drugs, biologicals, and medical devices. It requires proof that covered products are both safe and effective. The FDA has asserted that it has jurisdiction over genetic tests as medical devices, but it has chosen to impose significant regulation only on genetic tests sold by manufacturers as kits to clinical laboratories, physicians, or consumers. Tests done as "home brews" by clinical laboratories have been subject only to very limited regulation, which does not include proof of safety or efficacy. Neuroscience tests might well be subject to even less FDA regulation. If the test used an existing, approved medical device, such as an MRI machine, no FDA approval of this additional use would be necessary. The test would be part of the "practice of medicine," expressly not regulated by the FDA.

The FDA also implements the Clinical Laboratory Improvement Amendments Act (CLIA), along with the Centers for Disease Control and Prevention and the Centers for Medicare and Medicaid Services. CLIA sets standards for the training and working conditions of clinical laboratory personnel and requires periodic testing of laboratories' proficiency at different tests. Unless the tests were done in a clinical laboratory — through, for example, pathological examination of brain tissue samples or analysis of chemicals from the brain — neuroscience testing would also seem to avoid regulation under CLIA.

At present, neuroscience-based testing, particularly through neuroimaging using existing (approved) devices, seems to be entirely unregulated except, to a very limited extent, by malpractice law. One important policy question should be whether to regulate such tests, through government action or by professional self-regulation.

Criminal Justice

The criminal justice system makes predictions about individuals' future behavior in sentencing, parole, and other decisions, such as civil commitment for sex offenders.[5] The trend in recent years has been to limit the discretion of judges and parole boards in using predictions by setting stronger sentencing guidelines and mandatory sentences. Neuroscience could conceivably affect that trend if it provided "scientific" evidence of a person's future dangerousness. Such evidence might be used to increase sentencing discretion — or it might provide yet another way to limit such discretion.[6]

One can imagine neuroscience tests that could predict a convicted defendant was particularly likely to commit dangerous future crimes by showing that he has, for example, poor control over his anger, his aggressiveness, or his sexual urges. This kind of evidence has been used in the past; neuroscience may come up with ways that either are more accurate or that *appear* more accurate (or more impressive). For example, two papers[7] have already linked criminality to variations in the gene for monoamine oxidase A, a protein that plays an important role in the brain. Genetic tests may seem more scientific and more impressive to a judge, jury, or parole board than a psychologist's report. The use of neuroscience to make these predictions raises at least two issues: Are neuroscience tests for future dangerousness or lack of self-control valid at all? If so, how accurate do they need to be before they should be used?

The law has had experience with claims that inherent violent tendencies can be tested for. The XYY syndrome was widely discussed and accepted, in the literature though not by the courts,[8] in the late 1960s and early 1970s. Men born with an additional copy of the Y chromosome were said to be much more likely to become violent criminals. Further research revealed, about a decade later, that XYY men were somewhat more likely to have low intelligence and to have long arrest records, typically for petty or property offenses. They did not have a higher than average predisposition to violence.

If, unlike XYY syndrome, a tested condition were shown to predict reliably future dangerousness or lack of control, the question would then become how accurate the test must be in order for it to be used. A test of dangerousness or lack of control that was only slightly better than flipping coins should not be given much weight; a perfect test could be. At what accuracy level should the line be set?

The Supreme Court has recently spoken twice on the civil commitment of sexual offenders, both times reviewing a Kansas statute.[9] The Kansas act authorizes civil commitment of a "sexually violent predator," defined as "any person who has been convicted of or charged with a sexually violent offense and who suffers from a mental abnormality or personality disorder which makes the person likely to engage in repeat acts of sexual violence."[10] In *Kansas v. Hendricks*, the Court held the state law constitutional against a substantive due process claim because it required, in addition to proof of dangerousness, proof of the defendant's lack of control. "This admitted lack of volitional control, coupled with a prediction of future dangerousness, adequately distinguishes Hendricks from other dangerous persons who are perhaps more properly dealt with exclusively through criminal proceedings."[11] It held that Hendricks's commitment survived attack on ex post facto and double jeopardy grounds because the commitment procedure was neither criminal nor punitive.[12]

Five years later, the Court revisited this statute in *Kansas v. Crane*.[13] It held that the Kansas statue could be applied constitutionally only if there were a determination of the defendant's lack of control and not just proof of the existence of a relevant "mental abnormality or personality disorder":

> It is enough to say that there must be proof of serious difficulty in
> controlling behavior. And this, when viewed in light of such features of
> the case as the nature of the psychiatric diagnosis, and the severity of the
> mental abnormality itself, must be sufficient to distinguish the dangerous
> sexual offender whose serious mental illness, abnormality, or disorder
> subjects him to civil commitment from the dangerous but typical
> recidivist convicted in an ordinary criminal case.[14]

We know then that, at least in civil commitment cases related to prior sexually violent criminal offenses, proof that the particular defendant had limited power to control his actions is constitutionally necessary. There is no requirement that this evidence, or proof adduced in sentencing or parole hearings, convince the trier of fact beyond a reasonable doubt. The Court gives no indication of how strong that evidence must be or how its scientific basis would be established. Would any evidence that passed *Daubert* or *Frye* hearings be sufficient for civil commitment (or for enhancing sentencing or denying parole), or would some higher standard be required?[*]

It is also interesting to speculate on how evidence of the accuracy of such tests would be collected. It is unlikely that a state or federal criminal justice system would allow a randomized double-blind trial, performing the neuroscientific dangerousness or volition tests on all convicted defendants at the time of their conviction and then releasing them to see which ones would commit future crimes. That judges, parole boards, or legislatures would insist on rigorous scientific proof of connections between neuroscience evidence and future mental states seems doubtful.

Schools

Schools commonly use predictions of individual cognitive abilities. Undergraduate and graduate admissions are powerfully influenced by applicants' scores on an alphabet's worth of tests: ACT, SAT, LSAT, MCAT, and GRE, among others. Even those tests, such as the MCAT, that claim to test knowledge rather than aptitude, use the applicant's tested knowledge as a predictor of her ability to function well in school, either because she has that background knowledge or because her acquisition of the knowledge demonstrates her abilities. American primary and secondary education uses aptitude tests less frequently, although some tracking does go on. And almost all of those schools use grading (after a certain level), which the school or others — such as other schools, employers, and parents — can use to make predictions.

It is conceivable that neuroscience could provide other methods of testing ability or aptitude. Of course, the standard questions of the accuracy of those tests would apply. Tests that are highly inaccurate usually should not be used. But even assuming the tests are accurate, they would raise concerns. While they might be used only positively — as Dr. Alfred Binet intended his early intelligence test to be used, to identify children who need special help — to

---

[*] *Daubert v. Merrell Dow Pharmaceuticals* is a 1993 decision of the U.S. Supreme Court that set a new standard for the admissibility of scientific evidence in a trial. The court ruled that the trial judge must act as a "gatekeeper" and determine whether the evidence is relevant to the case at hand and whether it is scientifically valid, for example whether it was arrived at using the scientific method and whether it was subject to peer review. Under the previous standard, *Frye v. United States* (a decision of the D.C. Circuit Court dating from 1923), scientific evidence was admissible if "the thing from which the deduction is made" was "sufficiently established to have gained general acceptance in the particular field in which it belongs." The *Daubert* decision applies only to U.S. federal courts. State courts do not have a uniform standard; some use *Daubert*, others use *Frye*. – Ed.

the extent that they were used to deny students, especially young children, opportunities, they would seem more troubling.

It is not clear why a society that uses aptitude tests so commonly for admission into elite schools should worry about the tests' neuroscience equivalents. The SAT and similar aptitude tests claim that student preparation or effort will not substantially affect the tests' results, just as, presumably, preparation (at least in the short term) seems unlikely to alter neuroscience tests of aptitude. The existing aptitude tests, though widely used, remain controversial. Neuroscience tests, particularly if given and acted upon at an early age, are likely to exacerbate the discomfort we already feel with predictive uses of aptitude tests in education.

Businesses

Perhaps the most discussed social issue in human genetics has been the possible use — or abuse — of genetic data by businesses, particularly insurers and employers. Most, but not all, commentators have favored restrictions on the use of genetic information by health insurers and employers.[15] And legislators have largely agreed. Over 45 states and, to some extent, the federal government restrict the use of genetic information in health insurance. Eleven states impose limits on the use of genetic information by life insurers, but those constraints are typically weak. About 30 states limit employer-ordered genetic testing or the use of genetic information in employment decisions, as does, to some very unclear extent, the federal government, through the Americans with Disabilities Act.[16] And 2004 might be the year when broad federal legislation against "genetic discrimination" is finally passed.[17] [In fact, the Genetic Information Nondiscrimination Act — GINA — did not pass both houses of Congress until 2008. It was signed into law by President George W. Bush on May 21, 2008. — Ed.] Should similar legislation be passed to protect people against "neuroscience" discrimination?

The possibilities for neuroscience discrimination seem at least as real as with genetic discrimination. A predictive test showing that a person has a high likelihood of developing schizophrenia, bipolar disorder, early-onset Alzheimer's disease, early-onset Parkinson's disease, or Huntington's disease could certainly provide insurers or employers with an incentive to avoid that person. To the extent one believes that health coverage should be universal or that employment should be denied or terminated only for good cause, banning "neuroscientific discrimination" might be justified as an incremental step toward this good end. Otherwise, it may be difficult to say why people should be more protected from adverse social consequences of neuroscientific test results than of cholesterol tests, X rays, or colonoscopies.

Special protection for genetic tests has been urged on the ground that genes are more fundamental, more deterministic, and less the result of personal actions or chance than other influences on health. Others have argued against such "genetic exceptionalism," denying special power to genes and contending that special legislation about genetics only confirms in the public a false view of genetic determinism. Still others, including me, have argued that the public's particularly strong fear of genetic test results, even though exaggerated, justifies regulation in order to gain concrete benefits from reducing that fear. The same arguments could be played out with respect to predictive neuroscience tests. Although this is an open empirical question, it does seem likely that the public's perception of the fundamental or deterministic nature of genes does not exist with respect to neuroscience.

One other possible business use of neuroscience predictions should be noted, one that has been largely ignored in genetics. Neuroscience might be used in marketing. Firms might use neuroscience techniques on test subjects to enhance the appeal of their products or the effectiveness of their advertising. Individuals or focus groups could, in the future, be examined under fMRI. At least one firm, Brighthouse Institute for Thought Sciences, has embraced this technology and, in a press release from 2002, announced "its intentions of revolutionizing the marketing industry."[18]

More alarmingly, if neuromonitoring devices were perfected that could study a person's mental function without his or her knowledge, information intended to predict a consumer's preferences might be collected for marketing purposes. Privacy regulation seems appropriate for the undisclosed monitoring in the latter example. Regulating the former seems less likely, although it might prove attractive if such neuroscience-enhanced market research proved too effective an aid to selling.

Parents

The prenatal use of genetic tests to predict the future characteristics of fetuses, embryos, or as-yet-unconceived offspring is one of the most controversial and interesting issues in human genetics. Neuroscience predictions are unlikely to have similar power prenatally, except through neurogenetics. It is possible that neuroimaging or other nongenetic neuroscience tests might be performed on a fetus during pregnancy. Structural MRI has been used as early as about 24 weeks to look for major brain malformations, following up on earlier suspicious sonograms. At this point, no one appears to have done fMRI on the brain of a fetus; the classic method of stimulating the subject and watching which brain regions react would be challenging in utero, though not necessarily impossible. In any event, fetal neuroimaging seems likely to give meaningful results only for serious brain problems and even then at a fairly late stage of fetal development so that the most plausible intervention, abortion, would be rarely used and only in the most extreme cases.[19]

Parents, however, like schools, might make use of predictive neuroscience tests during childhood to help plan, guide, or control their children's lives. Of course, parents already try to guide their children's lives, based on everything from good data to wishful thinking about a child's abilities. Would neuroscience change anything? It might be argued that parents would take neuroscience testing more seriously than other evidence of a child's abilities because of its scientific nature, and thus perhaps exaggerate its accuracy. More fundamentally, it could be argued that, even if the test predictions were powerfully accurate, too extreme parental control over a child's life is a bad thing. From this perspective, any procedures that are likely to add strength to parents' desire or ability to exercise that control should be discouraged. On the other hand, society vests parents with enormous control over their children's upbringing, intervening only in strong cases of abuse. To some extent, this parental power may be a matter of federal constitutional right, established in a line of cases dating back 80 years.[20]

This issue is perhaps too difficult to be tackled. It is worth noting, though, that government regulation is not the only way to approach it. Professional self-regulation, insurance coverage policies, and parental education might all be methods to discourage any perceived overuse of children's neuroscience tests by their parents.

LITIGATION USES

Predictions may themselves be relevant in some litigation, particularly the criminal cases discussed above, but other, nonpredictive uses of neuroscience might also become central to litigated cases. Neuroscience *might* be able to provide relevant, and possibly determinative, evidence of a witness's mental state at the time of testimony, ways of eliciting or evaluating a witness's memories, or other evidence relevant to a litigant's claims. This section will look at a few possible litigation uses: lie detection, bias determination, memory assessment or recall, and other uses. Whether any of these uses is scientifically possible remains to be seen. It is also worth noting that the extent of the use of any of these methods will also depend on their cost and intrusiveness. A method of, for example, truth determination that required an intravenous infusion or examination inside a full-scale MRI machine would be used much less than a simple and portable headset.

The implications of any of these technologies for litigation seem to depend largely on four evidentiary issues. First, will the technologies pass the *Daubert*[21] or *Frye*[22] tests for the admissibility of scientific evidence? Second, if they are held sufficiently scientifically reliable to pass *Daubert* or *Frye*, are there other reasons to forbid or to compel the admissibility of the results of such technologies when used voluntarily by a witness? Third, would the refusal — or the agreement — of a witness to use one of these technologies itself be admissible in evidence? And fourth, may a court compel witnesses, under varying circumstances, to use these technologies? The answers to these questions will vary with the setting (especially criminal or civil), with the technology, and with other circumstances of the case, but they provide a useful framework for analysis.

Detecting Lies or Compelling Truth

The concept behind current polygraph machines dates back to the early twentieth century.[23] They seek to measure various physiological reactions associated with anxiety, such as sweating, breathing rate, and blood pressure, in the expectation that those signs of nervousness correlate with the speaker's knowledge that what he is saying is false. American courts have generally, but not universally, rejected them, although they are commonly used by the federal government for various security clearances and investigations.[24] It has been estimated that their accuracy is about 85 to 90 percent.[25]

Now imagine that neuroscience leads to new ways to determine whether or not a witness is telling a lie or even to compel a witness to tell the truth. A brain-imaging device might, for example, be able to detect patterns or locations of brain activity known from experiments to be highly correlated with the subject's consciousness of falsehood. (I will refer to this as "lie detection.") Alternatively, drugs or other stimuli might be administered that made it impossible for a witness to do anything but tell the truth — an effective truth serum. (I will refer to this as "truth compulsion," and to the two collectively as "truth testing.") Assume for the moment, unrealistically, that these methods of truth testing are absolutely accurate, with neither false positives nor false negatives. How would, and should, courts treat the results of such truth testing? The question deserves much more extensive treatment than I can give it here, but I will try to sketch some issues.

Consider first the nonscientific issues of admissibility. One argument against admissibility was made by four justices of the Supreme Court in *United States v. Scheffer*,[26] a case involving a blanket ban on the admissibility of polygraph evidence. Scheffer, an enlisted man in the Air Force working with military police as an informant in drug investigations, wanted to introduce the results of a polygraph examination at his court-martial for illegal drug use.[27] The polygraph examination, performed by the military as a routine part of his work as an informant, showed that Scheffer denied illegal drug use during the same period that a urine test detected the presence of methamphetamine.[28] Military Rule of Evidence 707, promulgated by President George H. W. Bush in 1991, provides that "notwithstanding any other provision of law, the results of a polygraph examination, the opinion of a polygraph examiner, or any reference to an offer to take, failure to take, or taking of a polygraph examination, shall not be admitted into evidence."

The court-martial refused to admit Scheffer's evidence on the basis of Rule 707. His conviction was overturned by the Court of Appeals for the Armed Forces, which held that this per se exclusion of all polygraph evidence violated the Sixth Amendment.[29] The Supreme Court reversed in turn, upholding Rule 707, but in a fractured opinion. Justice Thomas wrote the opinion announcing the decision of the Court, which found the rule constitutional on three grounds: continued question about the reliability of polygraph evidence, the need to "preserve the jury's core function of making credibility determinations in criminal trials," and the avoidance of collateral litigation.[30] Justices Rehnquist, Scalia, and Souter joined the Thomas opinion in full. Justice Kennedy, joined by Justices O'Connor, Ginsburg, and Breyer, concurred in the section of the Thomas opinion based on reliability of polygraph evidence. Those four justices did not agree with the other two grounds.[31] Justice Stevens dissented, finding that the reliability of polygraph testing was already sufficiently well established to invalidate any per se exclusion.[32]

Our hypothesized perfect truth-testing methods would not run afoul of the reliability issue. Nor, assuming the rules for admitted "truth-tested" evidence were sufficiently clear, would collateral litigation appear to be a major concern. Such testing would seem, however, even more than the polygraph, to evoke the concerns of the four justices about invading the sphere of the jury even when the witness had agreed to the use. Although at this point Justice Thomas's concern lacks the fifth vote it needs to become a binding precedent, the preservation of the jury's role might be seen by some courts as rising to a constitutional level under a federal or state constitutional right to a jury trial in criminal or civil cases. This issue could certainly be used as a policy argument against allowing such evidence, and, as an underlying concern of the judiciary, it might influence judicial findings under *Daubert* or *Frye* about the reliability of the methods.[33] Assuming robust proof of reliability, it is hard to see any other strong argument against the admission of this kind of evidence. (Whether Justice Thomas's rationale, either as a constitutional or a policy matter, would apply to nonjury trials seems more doubtful.)

On the other hand, some defendants might have strong arguments *for* the admission of such evidence, at least in criminal cases. Courts have found in the Sixth Amendment, perhaps in combination with the Fifth Amendment, a constitutional right for criminal defendants to present evidence in their own defense. Scheffer made this very claim, that Rule 707, in the context of his case, violated his constitutional right to present a defense. The Supreme Court has two lines of cases dealing with this right. In *Chambers v. Mississippi*, the Court resolved the defendant's claim by balancing the importance of the evidence to the defendant's case with the reliability of the evidence.[34] In *Rock v. Arkansas*, a criminal defendant alleged that she could remember the events only after having her memory "hypnotically refreshed."[35] The Court struck down Arkansas's per se rule against hypnotically refreshed testimony on the ground that the rule, as a per se rule, was arbitrary and therefore violated the Sixth Amendment rights of a defendant to present a defense and to testify in her own defense. The *Rock* opinion also stressed that the Arkansas rule prevented the defendant from telling her own story in any meaningful way. That might argue in favor of the admissibility of a criminal defendant's own testimony, under truth compulsion, as opposed to an examiner giving his or her expert opinion about the truthfulness of the witness's statements based on the truth detector results. These constitutional arguments for the admission of such evidence would not seem to arise with the prosecution's case or with either the plaintiff's or the defendant's case in a civil matter (unless some state constitutional provisions were relevant).[36]

Assuming "truth-tested" testimony were admissible, should either a party's, or a witness's, offer or refusal to undergo truth testing be admissible in evidence as relevant to his or her honesty? Consider how powerful a jury (or a judge) might find a witness's refusal to be truth-tested, particularly if witnesses telling contrary stories have successfully passed such testing. Such a refusal could well prove fatal to the witness's credibility.

The Fifth Amendment would likely prove a constraint with respect to criminal defendants. The fact that a defendant has invoked the Fifth Amendment's privilege against self-incrimination cannot normally be admitted into evidence or considered by the trier of fact. Otherwise, the courts have held, the defendant would be penalized for having invoked the privilege. A defendant who takes the stand might well be held to have waived that right and so might be impeached by his refusal to undergo truth testing. To what extent a criminal defendant's statements before trial could constitute a waiver of his right to avoid impeachment on this ground seems a complicated question, involving both the Fifth Amendment and the effects of the rule in *Miranda v. Arizona*.[37] These complex issues would require a paper of their own; I will not discuss them further here.

Apart from a defendant in a criminal trial, it would seem that any other witnesses should be impeachable for their refusal to be truth-tested; they might invoke the privilege against self-incrimination, but the trier of fact, in weighing their credibility in this trial, would not be using that information against them. And this should be true for prosecution witnesses as well as defense witnesses. Both parties and nonparty witnesses at civil trials would seem generally to be impeachable for their refusal to be truth-tested, except in some jurisdictions that hold that a civil party's invocation of the Fifth Amendment may not be commented upon even in a civil trial.

It seems unlikely that a witness's *willingness* to undergo truth testing would add anything to the results of a test in most cases. It might, however, be relevant, and presumably admissible, if for some reason the test did not work on that witness or, unbeknownst to the witness at the time she made the offer, the test results turned out to be inadmissible.

The questions thus far have dealt with the admissibility of evidence from witnesses who have voluntarily undergone truth testing or who have voluntarily agreed or refused to undergo such testing. Could, or should, either side have the power to compel a witness to undergo either method of truth testing? At its simplest, this might be a right to retest a witness tested by the other side, a claim that could be quite compelling if the results of these methods, like the results of polygraphy, were believed to be significantly affected by the means by which the test was administered — not just the scientific process but the substance and style of the questioning. More broadly, could either side compel a witness, in a criminal or a civil case, to undergo such truth testing either as part of a courtroom examination or in pretrial discovery?

Witnesses certainly can be compelled to testify, at trial or in deposition. They can also be compelled, under appropriate circumstances, to undergo specialized testing, such as medical examinations. (The latter procedures typically require express authorization from the court rather than being available as of right to the other side.) Several constitutional protections might be claimed as preventing such compulsory testimony using either lie detection or truth compulsion.

A witness might argue that the method of truth testing involved was so great an intrusion into the person's bodily (or mental) integrity as to "shock the conscience" and violate the Fifth or Fourteenth Amendment, as did the stomach pumping in *Rochin v. California*.[38] A test method involving something like the wearing of headphones might seem quite different from one involving an intravenous infusion of a drug or envelopment in the coffinlike confines of a fullsized MRI machine. The strength of such a claim might vary according to whether the process was lie detection and merely verified (or undercut) the witness's voluntarily chosen words, or whether it was truth compulsion and interfered with the witness's ability to choose her own words.

The Fifth Amendment's privilege against self-incrimination would usually protect those who choose to invoke it (and who have not been granted immunity). As noted above, that would not necessarily protect either a party in a civil case or a nondefendant witness in a criminal case from impeachment for invoking the privilege.

Would a witness have a possible Fourth Amendment claim that such testing, compelled by court order, was an unreasonable search and seizure by the government? I know of no precedent for considering questioning itself as a search or seizure, but this form of questioning could be seen as close to searching the confines of the witness's mind. In that case, would a search warrant or other court order suffice to authorize the test against a Fourth Amendment claim? And, if it were seen in that light, could a search warrant be issued for the interrogation of a person under truth testing outside the context of any pending criminal or civil litigation — and possibly even outside the context of an arrest and Miranda rights that follow it? If this seems implausible, consider what an attractive addition statutory authorization of such "mental searches" might seem to the Bush administration or to Congress in the next version of the USA PATRIOT Act.[39]

In some circumstances, First Amendment claims might be plausible. Truth compulsion might be held to violate in some respects the right not to speak, although the precedents on this point are quite distant, involving a right not to be forced to say, or to publish, specific statements. It also seems conceivable that some religious groups could object to these practices and might be able to make a free exercise clause argument against such compelled speech.

These constitutional questions are many and knotty. Equally difficult is the question whether some or all of them might be held to be waived by witnesses who either had undergone truth testing themselves or had claimed their own truthfulness, thus "putting it in question." And, of course, even if parties or witnesses have no constitutional rights against being ordered to undergo truth testing, that does not resolve the policy issue of whether such rights should exist as a matter of statute, rule, or judicial decision.

Parties and witnesses are not the only relevant actors in trials. Truth testing might also be used in voir dire. Prospective jurors are routinely asked about their knowledge of the parties or of the case or about their relevant biases. Could a defendant claim that his right to an unbiased juror was infringed if such methods were not used and hence compel prospective jurors to undergo truth testing? Could one side or the other challenge for cause a prospective juror who was unwilling to undergo such testing? In capital cases, jurors are asked whether they could vote to convict in light of a possible death penalty; truth testing might be demanded by the prosecution to make sure the prospective jurors are being honest.

It is also worth considering how the existence of such methods might change the pretrial maneuvers of the parties. Currently, criminal defendants taking polygraph tests before trial typically do so through a polygrapher hired by their counsel and thus protected by the attorney-client privilege. That may change. Whatever rules are adopted concerning the admissibility of evidence from truth testing will undoubtedly affect the incentives of the parties, in civil and criminal cases, to undergo truth testing. This may, in turn, have substantial, and perhaps unexpected, repercussions for the practices of criminal plea bargaining and civil settlement. As the vast majority of criminal and civil cases are resolved before trial, the effects of truth testing could be substantial.

Even more broadly, consider the possible effects of truth testing on judicial business generally. Certainly not every case depends on the honesty of witness testimony. Some hinge on conclusions about reasonableness or negligence; others are determined by questions of law. Even factual questions might be the focus of subjectively honest, but nevertheless contradictory, testimony from different witnesses. Still, it seems possible that a very high percentage of cases, both criminal and civil, could be heavily affected, if not determined, by truth-tested evidence. If truth testing reduced the number of criminal trials tenfold, that would surely raise Justice Thomas's concern about the proper role of the jury, whether or not that concern has constitutional implications. It would also have major effects on the workload of the judiciary and, perhaps, on the structure of the courts.

The questions raised by a perfect method of truth testing are numerous and complicated. They are also probably unrealistic, given that no test will be perfect. Most of these questions would require reconsideration if truth testing turned out to be only 99.9 percent accurate, or 99 percent accurate, or 90 percent accurate. That reconsideration would have to examine not just overall "accuracy" but the rates of both false positives (the identification of a false statement as true) and false negatives (the identification of a true statement as false), as those may have different implications. Similarly, decisions on admissibility might differ if accuracy rates varied with a witness's age, sex, training in "beating" the machine, or other traits. And, of course, proving the accuracy of such methods as they are first introduced or as they are altered will be a major issue in court systems under the *Daubert* or *Frye* tests.

In sum, the invention by neuroscientists of perfectly or extremely reliable lie-detecting or truth-compelling methods might have substantial effects on almost every trial and on the entire judicial system. How those effects would play out in light of our current criminal justice system, including the constitutional protections of the Bill of Rights, is not obvious.

Determining Bias

Evidence produced by neuroscience may play other significant roles in the courtroom. Consider the possibility of testing, through neuroimaging, whether a witness or a juror reacts negatively to particular groups. Already, neuroimaging work is going on that looks for — and finds — differences in the reaction of a subject's brain to people of different races. If that research is able to associate certain patterns of activity with negative bias, its possible use in litigation could be widespread.

As with truth testing, courts would have to decide whether bias testing met *Daubert* or *Frye*, whether voluntary test results would be admissible, whether a party's or witness's refusal or agreement to take the test could be admitted into evidence, and whether the testing could ever be compelled. The analysis on these points seems similar to that for truth testing, with the possible exception of a lesser role for the privilege against self-incrimination.

If allowed, neuroscience testing for racial bias might be used where bias was a relevant fact in the case, as in claims of employment discrimination based on race. It might be used to test any witness for bias for or against a party of a particular race. It might be used to test jurors to ensure that they were not biased against parties because of race. One could even, barely, imagine it being used to test judges for bias, perhaps as part of a motion to disqualify for bias. And, of course, such bias testing need not be limited to bias based on race, nationality, sex, or other protected groups. One could seek to test, in appropriate cases, for bias against parties or witnesses based on their occupation (the police, for example), their looks (too fat, too thin), their voices (a Southern accent, a Boston accent), or many other characteristics.

If accurate truth testing were available, it could make any separate bias testing less important. Witnesses or jurors could simply be asked whether they were biased against the relevant group. On the other hand, it is possible that people might be able to answer honestly that they were not biased, when they were in fact biased. Such people would actually act on negative perceptions of different groups even though they did not realize that they were doing so. If the neuroimaging technique were able to detect people with that unconscious bias accurately, it might still be useful in addition to truth testing.

Bias testing might even force us to reevaluate some truisms. We say that the parties to litigation are entitled to unbiased judges and juries, but we mean that they are entitled to judges and juries that are not demonstrably biased in a context where demonstrating bias is difficult. What if demonstrating bias becomes easy — and bias is ubiquitous? Imagine a trial in which neuroimaging shows that all the prospective jurors are prejudiced against a defendant who looks like a stereotypical Hell's Angel because they think he looks like a criminal. Or what if the only potential jurors who didn't show bias were themselves members of quasi-criminal motorcycle gangs? What would the defendant's right to a fair trial mean in that context?

Evaluating or Eliciting Memory

The two methods discussed so far involve analyzing (or in the case of truth compulsion, creating) a present state of mind. It is conceivable that neuroscience might also provide courts with at least three relevant tools concerning memory. In each case, courts would again confront questions of the reliability of the tools, their admissibility with the witness's permission, the impeaching of witnesses for failing to use the tools, and the compelling of a witness to use such a memory enhancing tool.

The first tool might be an intervention, pharmacological or otherwise, that improved a witness's ability to remember events. It is certainly conceivable that researchers studying memory-linked diseases might create drugs that help people retrieve old memories or retrieve them in more detail. This kind of intervention would not be new in litigation. The courts have seen great controversy over the past few years over "repressed" or "recovered" memories, typically traumatic early childhood experiences brought back to adult witnesses by therapy or hypnosis. Similarly, some of the child sex abuse trials over the past decade have featured testimony from young children about their experiences. In both cases, the validity of these memories has been questioned. We do know from research that people will often come to remember, in good faith, things that did not happen, particularly when those memories have been suggested to them.[40] Similar problems might arise with "enhanced" memories.[41]

A second tool might be the power to assess the validity of a witness's memory. What if neuroscience could give us tools to distinguish between "true" and "false" memory? One could imagine different parts of a witness's brain being used while recounting a "true" memory, a "false" memory, or a creative fiction. Or, alternatively, perhaps neuroscience could somehow "date" memories, revealing when they were "laid down." These methods seem more speculative than either truth testing or bias testing, but if either one (or some other method of testing memory) turned out to be feasible, courts would, after the *Daubert* or *Frye* hearings, again face questions of admitting testimony concerning their voluntary use, allowing comment on a witness's refusal to take a test, and possibly compelling their use.

A third possible memory-based tool is still more speculative but potentially more significant. There have long been reports that electrical stimulation can, sometimes, trigger a subject to have what appears to be an extremely detailed and vivid memory of a past scene, almost like reliving the experience. At this point, we do not know whether such an experience is truly a memory or is more akin to a hallucination; if it is a memory, how to reliably call it up; how many memories might potentially be recalled in this manner; or, perhaps most important, how to recall any specific memory. Whatever filing system the brain uses for memories seems to be, at this point, a mystery. Assume that it proves possible to cause a witness to recall a specific memory in its entirety, perhaps by localizing the site of the memory first through neuroimaging the witness while she calls up her existing memories of the event. A witness could then, perhaps, *relive* an event important to trial, either before trial or on the witness stand. One can even, just barely, imagine a technology that might be able to "read out" the witness's memories, intercepted as neuronal firings, and translate them directly into voice, text, or the equivalent of a movie for review by the finder of fact. Less speculatively, one can certainly imagine a drug that would improve a person's ability to retrieve specific long-term memories.

While a person's authentic memories, no matter how vividly they are recalled, may not be an accurate portrayal of what actually took place, they would be more compelling testimony than that provided by typically foggy recollections of past events. Once again, if the validity of these methods were established, the key questions would seem to be whether to allow the admission of evidence from such a recall experience, voluntarily undertaken; whether to admit the fact of a party's or witness's refusal or agreement to use such a method; and whether, under any circumstances, to compel the use of such a technique.[42]

Other Litigation-Related Uses

Neuroscience covers a wide range of brain-related activities. The three areas sketched above are issues where neuroscience could conceivably have an impact on almost any litigation, but neuroscience might also affect any specific kind of litigation where brain function was relevant. Consider four examples.

The most expensive medical malpractice cases are generally so-called bad baby cases. In these cases, children are born with profound brain damage. Damages can be enormous, sometimes amounting to the cost of round-the-clock nursing care for 70 years. Evidence of causation, however, is often very unclear. The plaintiff parents allege that the defendants managed the delivery negligently, which led to a lack of oxygen that in turn caused the brain damage. Defendants, in addition to denying negligence, usually claim that the damage had some other, often unknown, cause. Jurors are left with a family facing a catastrophic situation and no strong evidence about what caused it. Trial verdicts, and settlements, can be extremely high, accounting in part for the high price of malpractice insurance for obstetricians. If neuroscience could reliably distinguish between brain damage caused by oxygen deprivation near birth and that caused earlier, these cases would have more accurate results, in terms of compensating families only when the damage was caused around the time of delivery. Similarly, if fetal neuroimaging could reveal serious brain damage before labor, those images could be evidence about the cause of the damage. (One can even imagine obstetricians insisting on prenatal brain scans before delivery in order to establish a baseline.) A more certain determination of causation should also lead to more settlements and less wasteful litigation. (Of course, in cases where neuroscience showed that the damage was consistent with lack of oxygen around delivery, the defendants' negligence would still be in question.)

In many personal injury cases, the existence of intractable pain may be an issue. In some of those cases there may be a question whether the plaintiff is exaggerating the extent of the pain. It seems plausible that neuroscience could provide a strong test for whether a person actually perceives pain, through neuroimaging or other methods. It might be able to show whether signals were being sent by the sensory nerves to the brain from the painful location on the plaintiff's body. Alternatively, it might locate a region of the brain that is always activated when a person feels pain or a pattern of brain activation that is always found during physically painful experiences. Again, by reducing uncertainty about a very subjective (and hence falsifiable) aspect of a case, neuroscience could improve the litigation system.

A person's competency is relevant in several legal settings, including disputed guardianships and competency to stand trial. Neuroscience might be able to establish some more objective measures that could be considered relevant to competency. (It might also reveal that what the law seems pleased to regard as a general, undifferentiated competency does not, in fact, exist.) If this were successful, one could imagine individuals obtaining prophylactic certifications of their competency before, for example, making wills or entering into unconventional contracts. The degree of mental ability is also relevant in capital punishment, where the Supreme Court has recently held that executing the mentally retarded violates the Eighth Amendment.[43] Neuroscience might supply better, or even determinative, evidence of mental retardation. Or, again, it may be that neuroscience would force the courts to recognize that "mental retardation" is not a discrete condition.

Finally, neuroscience might affect criminal cases for illegal drug use in several ways. Neuroscience might help determine whether a defendant was "truly" addicted to the drug in question, which could have some consequences for guilt and sentencing. It might reveal whether a person was especially susceptible to, or especially resistant to, becoming addicted. Or it could provide new ways to block addiction, or even pleasurable sensations, with possible consequences for sentencing and treatment. Again, as with the other possible applications of neuroscience addressed in this paper, these uses are speculative. It would be wrong to count on neuroscience to solve, *deus ex machina*, our drug problems. It does not seem irresponsible, however, to consider the possible implications of neuroscience breakthroughs in this area.[44]

ENDNOTES

1. I want to thank particularly my colleagues John Barton, George Fisher, and Tino Cuellar for their helpful advice on intellectual property, evidentiary issues, and neuroscience predictions in the criminal justice system, respectively. I also want to thank the participants at the AAAS/Dana Foundation workshop on law and neuroscience for their useful comments, as well as colleagues and students who made suggestions at talks on these topics I gave at Stanford during the fall of 2003. Last, but not least, I want to thank my research assistant, Melanie Blunschi, for her able help.

2. Shakespeare, *Macbeth*, act 1, scene 4, lines 11–14.

3. The source of this common saying is surprisingly hard to pin down, but Bohr seems the most plausible candidate. See Henry T. Greely, *Trusted Systems and Medical Records: Lowering Expectations, Stan. L. Rev.* 52: 1585, 1591 n. 9 (2000). [The saying has also been attributed to Yogi Berra – Ed.]

4. See, for example, Secretary's Advisory Committee on Genetic Testing, *Enhancing the Oversight of Genetic Tests: Recommendations of the SACGT*, National Institutes of Health (July 2000), report available at http://www4.od.nih.gov/oba/sacgt/reports/oversight_report.htm; N. A. Holtzman and M. S. Watson, eds., *Promoting Safe and Effective Genetic Testing in the United States: Final Report of the Task Force on Genetic Testing* (Baltimore: Johns Hopkins University Press, 1997); and Barbara A. Koenig, Henry T. Greely, Laura McConnell, Heather Silverberg, and Thomas A. Raffin, "PGES Recommendations on Genetic Testing for Breast Cancer Susceptibility." *Journal of Women's Health* (June 1998) 7: 531–545.

5. Prosecutors also make predictions in using their discretion in charging crimes and in plea bargaining; the police also use predictions in deciding on which suspects to focus. My colleague Tino Cuellar pointed out to me that neuroscience data, from a current prosecution or investigation of an individual or from earlier investigations of

that person, might play a role in deciding the criminal charge or whether to plea bargain.

6. The implications of neuroscientific assessments of a person's state of mind at the time of the crime for criminal liability are discussed in Professor [Stephen J.] Morse's paper [Chapter 9 in the book in which this article was originally published.]. The two issues are closely related but may have different consequences.

7. See H. G. Brunner, M. Nelen, X. O. Breakefield, H. H. Ropers, and B. A. van Oost, "Abnormal Behavior Associated with a Point Mutation in the Structural Gene for Monoamine Oxidase A." *Science* 262: 5133–5136 (October 22, 1993), discussed in V. Morrell "Evidence Found for a Possible 'Aggression' Gene." *Science* 260: 1722–1724 (June 18, 1993); and Avshalon Caspi, Joseph McClay, Terrie E. Moffitt, Jonathan Mill, Judy Martin, Ian W. Craig, Alan Taylor, and Richie Poulton, "Role of Genotype in the Cycle of Violence in Maltreated Children." *Science* 297: 851–854 (August 2, 2002), discussed in Erik Stokstad, "Violent Effects of Abuse Tied to Gene." *Science* 297: 752 (August 2, 2002).

8. See the discussion of the four unsuccessful efforts to use XYY status as a defense in criminal cases in Deborah W. Denno, "Human Biology and Criminal Responsibility: Free Will or Free Ride?" 137 U. PA. L. REV. 613, 620–622 (1988).

9. See two excellent recent discussions of these cases: Stephen J. Morse, *Uncontrollable Urges and Irrational People*, VA. L. REV. 88 (2002): 1025; and Peter C. Pfaffenroth, *The Need for Coherence: States' Civil Commitment of Sex Offenders in the Wake of Kansas v. Crane*, STAN. L. REV. 55 (2003): 2229.

10. Kan. Stat. Ann. §59–29a02(a) (2003).

11. 521 U.S. 346, 360 (1997).

12. Ibid.

13. 534 U.S. 407 (2002).

14. Ibid., p. 413.

15. For a representative sample of views, see Kathy L. Hudson, Karen H. Rothenberg, Lori B. Andrews, Mary Jo Ellis Kahn, and Francis S. Collins, "Genetic Discrimination and Health Insurance: An Urgent Need for Reform," *Science* 270 (1995): 391 (broadly favoring a ban on discrimination); Richard A. Epstein, *The Legal Regulation of Genetic Discrimination: Old Responses to New Technology*, B.U.L. REV. 74 (1994): 1 (opposing a ban on the use of genetic information in employment discrimination); Henry T. Greely, *Genotype Discrimination: The Complex Case for Some Legislative Protection*, U. PA. L. REV. 149 (2001): 1483 (favoring a carefully drawn ban, largely to combat exaggerated fears of discrimination); and Colin S. Diver and Jane M. Cohen, *Genophobia: What Is Wrong with Genetic Discrimination?* U. PA. L. REV. 149 (2001): 1439 (opposing a ban on its use in health insurance).

16. For the most up-to-date information on state law in this area, see Ellen W. Clayton, "Ethical, Legal, and Social Implications of Genomic Medicine." *New Eng. J. Med.* 349 (2003): 342.

17. After considering, but not adopting, similar legislation since 1997, the Senate in October 2003 passed the Genetic Information NonDiscrimination Act, S. 1053. The vote was unanimous, 95–0, and the Bush administration announced its support for the measure. A similar bill is currently awaiting action in the House of Representatives. See Aaron Zitner, "Senate Blocks Genetic Discrimination," *Los Angeles Times*, October 15, 2003, sec. 1, p. 16.

18. "Brighthouse Institute for Thought Sciences Launches First 'Neuromarketing' Research Company," press release (June 22, 2002) found at http://www.prweb. com/releases/2002/6/prweb40936.php.

19. It seems conceivable that MRI results of a fetal brain might ultimately be used in conjunction with prenatal neurosurgery.

20. See, for example, *Pierce v. Society of Sisters*, 268 U.S. 510 (1925); *Meyer v. Nebraska*, 262 U.S. 390 (1923).

21. *Daubert v. Merrell Dow Pharmaceuticals*, 516 U.S. 869; 116 S. Ct. 189; 133 L. Ed. 2d 126 (1993).

22. *Frye v. United States*, 54 App. D.C. 46, 293 F. 1013 (1923, D.C. Cir.).

23. A National Academy of Sciences panel examining polygraph evidence dated the birth of the polygraph machine to William Marston, between 1915 and 1921. Committee to Review the Scientific Evidence on the Polygraph, National Research Council, *The Polygraph and Lie Detection* (2003) pp. 291–297. Marston was the polygraph examiner whose testimony was excluded in *Frye v. United States*.

24. See the discussion in *United States v. Scheffer*, 523 U.S. 303, 310–11 (1998). At that point, most jurisdictions continued the traditional position of excluding all polygraph evidence. Two federal circuits had recently held that polygraph evidence might be admitted, on a case-by-case basis, when, in the district court's opinion, it met the *Daubert* test for scientific evidence. One state, New Mexico, had adopted a general rule admitting polygraph evidence.

25. Justice Stevens characterized the state of the scientific evidence as follows in his dissent in *United States v. Scheffer*:

    There are a host of studies that place the reliability of polygraph tests at 85 percent to 90 percent. While critics of the polygraph argue that accuracy is much lower, even the studies cited by the critics place polygraph accuracy at 70 percent. Moreover, to the extent that the polygraph errs, studies have repeatedly shown that the polygraph is more likely to find innocent people guilty than vice versa. Thus, exculpatory polygraphs — like the one in this case — are likely to be more reliable than inculpatory ones.

    United States v. Scheffer, 523 U.S. 303, 333 (1998) (Stevens, J., dissenting) (footnotes omitted).

    A committee of the National Academy of Sciences has recently characterized the evidence as follows:

    Notwithstanding the limitations of the quality of the empirical research and the limited ability to generalize to real-world settings, we conclude that in populations of examinees such as those represented in the polygraph research literature, untrained in countermeasures, specific-incident polygraph tests can discriminate lying from truth telling at rates well above chance, though well below perfection.

    Committee to Review the Scientific Evidence on the Polygraph, p. 4.

26. 523 U.S. 303 (1998).

27. Ibid., p. 305.

28. Ibid., p. 306.

29. 44 M.J. 442 (1996).

30. 532 U.S. at 312–313.

31. Ibid., p. 318.

32. Ibid., p. 320.

33. I owe this useful insight to Professor Fisher.

34. 410 U.S. 284 (1973).

35. 483 U.S. 44 (1987).

36. A constitutional right to admit such evidence might also argue for a constitutional right for indigent defendants to have the government pay the cost of such truth testing, which might be small or great.

37. 396 U.S. 868 (1969).

38. 342 U.S. 165 (1952).

39. Uniting and Strengthening America by Providing Appropriate Tools Required to Intercept and Obstruct Terrorism Act ("USA PATRIOT Act") of 2001, PL 107–156 (2001).

40. As with bias detection, truth testing could limit the need for such memory assessment when the witness was conscious of the falsity of the memory. Memory assessment, however, could be useful in cases where the witness had actually come to believe in the accuracy of a questioned "false" memory.

41. It is quite plausible that researchers might create drugs that help people make, retain, and retrieve new memories, important in conditions such as Alzheimer's disease. One can imagine giving such a drug in advance to someone whom you expected to witness an important event — although providing such a person with a video recorder might be an easier option.

42. Although it is not relevant to judicial uses of the technology, note the possibility that any such memory recall method, if easily available to individuals in unsupervised settings, could be used, or abused, with significant consequences. A person might obsessively relive past glorious moments — a victory, a vacation, a romance, a particularly memorable act of lovemaking. A depressed person might dwell compulsively on bad memories. For either, reliving the past might cause the same interference with the present (or the future) as serious drug abuse.

43. *Atkins v. Virginia*, 536 U.S. 304 (2003).

44. At the same time, neuroscience could give rise to new drugs or drug equivalents. A neuroscience-devised trigger of pleasurable sensations — say, that would cause powerful orgasms — could function effectively as a powerful drug of abuse.

PART VI

Contemporary Technological Dilemmas: Information and Communications Technology

Whereas many of the social impacts of the new biology and other biomedical advances are speculative and in the future, the impacts of computers and information technology are being felt right now. One can hardly think or talk about technology without considering computers. In fact, in many contexts (for example, the "Technology Services" department of many organizations), "technology" is assumed to *mean* computers.

Computers, especially personal computers, are an integral part of most people's lives in the United States in the early twenty-first century. Increasingly, moreover, having a PC or a Mac means being connected to the Internet. Computers began decades ago to have substantial effects on human work, on power and control in society, and on social and economic equity. But the Internet, which during the 1990s exploded into an entirely new medium of communication, has intensified these effects, added new ones, and accelerated the pace at which they are being felt. Little of this was foreseen or planned. For starters, the engineers and scientists responsible for developing computers, and even the heads of the companies that produced the early versions, completely failed to see the extent to which computers would permeate society. In the first chapter in Part VI, historian Paul Ceruzzi of the Smithsonian Institution conducts a kind of retrospective technology assessment, looking at early expectations of the usefulness and impact of computers and finding these views remarkably myopic.

Following Ceruzzi, Wendell Berry, farmer, author, and poet, tells us why he rejects the computer and does his writing instead by daylight on a manual typewriter. Berry, who first published this essay in 1987, describes himself as a conservationist. If so, he is a rather extreme one. His essay expresses a profound distrust of government, large corporations, and other centralized institutions.

On the other hand, Deborah Johnson, a philosopher and ethicist, takes the existence of computers and their wide use in society as a given. She asks about the ethical issues they raise. Are they the same kinds of issues raised by other technologies and other areas of society? Or is there something unique about "computer ethics?" Nicholas Carr's chapter, which follows Johnson's, asks a rather different, but no less provocative question: "Is Google Making Us Stupid?" In a way, the question is an updated version of Marshall McLuhan's famous phrase, "The medium is the message." McLuhan was writing about television and other media of the mid- twentieth century and suggesting that our interactions with these media shape the way in which we see the world, indeed the nature of our consciousness. Carr makes a similar point about the Internet.

Part VI wraps up with two chapters on a somewhat more technical issue, but one that has major implications for the way in which computer networks are likely to develop in the future. This is the issue of "net neutrality," the matter of whether Internet service providers are allowed to discriminate among the different kinds of content and applications that they carry. Consumer advocates and others favoring an open Internet argue that network owners (ISPs) must not do so, that they must treat all content similarly. Others argue that discriminating among uses is the only way that rapidly increasing network traffic can be managed intelligently. Chapters 25 and 26 present these two opposing points of view.

21

An Unforeseen Revolution: Computers and Expectations, 1935–1985

PAUL CERUZZI

Paul Ceruzzi's fine essay, "An Unforeseen Revolution: Computers and Expectations, 1935–1985," is an excellent way to put the subject of information and communications technology in perspective. Ceruzzi looks back at the early forecasts of the societal impact of computers. He finds that the computer pioneers of the 1940s assumed that perhaps half a dozen of the giant new machines would serve the world's needs for the foreseeable future. As Joseph Corn notes in the introduction to his book, Imagining Tomorrow, *in which this reading was first published, this "dazzling failure of prophecy" is explained by the fact that most of the computer pioneers were physicists who viewed the new devices as equipment for their experiments and found it hard to imagine that their inventions might be applied to entirely different fields, such as payroll processing, trading recorded music, publishing books, and making animated films. More recently, since Corn's words were written some years ago, he fails to mention (because they did not exist) the convergence of computing with mobile communications and the remarkable growth of texting, mobile e-mail and web access, and all of the other ways in which iPhones, iPads, Blackberrys, Androids, etc. have changed our lives — not to mention Facebook, Twitter, and other social networking applications. The impact of computers on society has been staggering, and it is sobering*

Paul Ceruzzi, "An Unforeseen Revolution: Computers and Expectations, 1935–1985," From *Imagining Tomorrow: History, Technology and the American Future*, edited by Joseph J. Corn. Reprinted by permission of the author.

to realize how little of this impact was anticipated by those most responsible for developing and introducing this new technology.

Paul Ceruzzi is curator of aerospace electronics and computing in the Space History Division at the Smithsonian's National Air and Space Museum in Washington, D.C. He holds a Ph.D. from the University of Kansas and B.A. from Yale, both in American Studies. He is the author of A History of Modern Computing *(2nd ed., 2003) and several other books.*

The "computer revolution" is here. Computers seem to be everywhere: at work, at play, and in all sorts of places in between. There are perhaps half a million large computers in use in America [in 1986], seven or eight million personal computers, five million programmable calculators, and millions of dedicated microprocessors built into other machines of every description. [*Editor's Note*: Since this article was written, the number of personal computers in use has increased vastly. The *Computer Industry Almanac* reported that the number of PCs in use worldwide exceeded 1.2 billion in 2008. The United States, which accounts for about 22 percent of these, is forecast to have more PCs than people by 2013.]

The changes these machines are bringing to society are profound, if not revolutionary. And, like many previous revolutions, the computer revolution is happening very quickly. The computer as defined today did not exist in 1950. Before World War II, the word *computer* meant a human being who worked at a desk with a calculating machine, or something built by a physics professor to solve a particular problem, used once or twice, and then retired to a basement storeroom. Modern computers — machines that do a wide variety of things, many having little to do with mathematics or physics — emerged after World War II from the work of a dozen or so individuals in England, Germany, and the United States. The "revolution," however one may define it, began only when their work became better known and appreciated.

The computer age dawned in the United States in the summer of 1944, when a Harvard physics instructor named Howard Aiken publicly unveiled a giant electromechanical machine called the Mark I. At the same time, in Philadelphia, J. Presper Eckert, Jr., a young electrical engineer, and John Mauchly, a physicist, were building the ENIAC, which, when completed in 1945, was the world's first machine to do numerical computing with electronic rather than mechanical switches.

Computing also got under way in Europe during the war. In 1943, the British built an electronic machine that allowed them to decode intercepted German radio messages. They built several copies of this so-called Colossus, and by the late 1940s general-purpose computers were being built at a number of British institutions. In Germany, Konrad Zuse, an engineer, was building computers out of used telephone equipment. One of them, the Z4, survived the war and had a long and productive life at the Federal Technical Institute in Zurich.

These machines were the ancestors of today's computers. They were among the first machines to have the ability to carry out any sequence of arithmetic operations, keep track of what they had just done, and adjust their actions accordingly. But machines that only solve esoteric physics problems or replace a few human workers, as those computers did, do not a revolution make. The computer pioneers did not foresee their creations as doing much more than that. They had no glimmering of how thoroughly the computer would permeate modern life. The computer's inventors saw a market restricted to a few scientific, military, or large-scale business applications. For them, a computer was akin to a wind tunnel: a vital and necessary piece of apparatus, but one whose expense and size limited it to a few installations.

For example, when Howard Aiken heard of the plans of Eckert and Mauchly to produce and market a more elegant version of the ENIAC, he was skeptical. He felt they would never sell more than a few of them, and he stated that four or five electronic digital computers would satisfy all the country's computing needs.[1] In Britain in 1951, the physicist Douglas Hartree remarked, "We have a computer here in Cambridge; there is one in Manchester and one at the [National Physical Laboratory]. I suppose there ought to be one in Scotland, but that's about all."[2] Similar statements appear again and again in the folklore of computing.[3] This perception clearly dominated early discussions about the future of the new technology.[4] At least two other American computer pioneers, Edmund Berkeley and John V. Atanasoff, also recall hearing estimates that fewer than ten computers would satisfy all of America's computing needs.[5]

By 1951, about half a dozen electronic computers were running, and in May of that year companies in the United States and England began producing them for commercial customers. Eckert and Mauchly's dream became the UNIVAC — a commercial electronic machine that for a while was a synonym for *computer*, as *Scotch Tape* is for cellophane tape or *Thermos* is for vacuum bottles. It was the star of CBS's television coverage of the 1952 presidential election when it predicted, with only a few percent of the vote gathered, Eisenhower's landslide victory over Adlai Stevenson. With this election, Americans in large numbers suddenly became aware of this new and marvelous device. Projects got under way at universities and government agencies across the United States and Europe to build computers. Clearly, there was a demand for more than just a few of the large scale machines.

But not many more. The UNIVAC was large and expensive, and its market was limited to places like the U.S. Census Bureau, military installations, and a few large industries. (Only the fledgling aerospace industry seemed to have an insatiable appetite for those costly machines in the early years.) Nonetheless, UNIVAC and its peers set the stage for computing's next giant leap, from one of-a-kind special projects built at universities to mass-produced products designed for the world of commercial and business data processing, banking, sales, routine accounting, and inventory control.

Yet, despite the publicity accorded the UNIVAC, skepticism prevailed. The manufacturers were by no means sure of how many computers they could sell. Like the inventors before them, the manufacturers felt that only a few commercial computers would saturate the market. For example, an internal IBM study regarding the potential market for a computer called the Tape Processing Machine (a prototype of which had been completed by 1951) estimated that there was a market for no more than 25 machines of its size.[6] Two years later,

IBM developed a smaller computer for business use, the Model 650, which was designed to rent for $3,000 a month — far less than the going price for large computers like the UNIVAC, but nonetheless a lot more than IBM charged for its other office equipment. When it was announced in 1953, those who were backing the project optimistically foresaw a market for 250 machines. They had to convince others in the IBM organization that this figure was not inflated.[7]

As it turned out, businesses snapped up the 650 by the thousands. It became the Model T of computers, and its success helped establish IBM as the dominant computer manufacturer it is today [— or it was for many years, anyway — Ed.]. The idea finally caught on that a private company could manufacture and sell computers — of modest power, and at lower prices than the first monsters — in large quantities. The 650 established the notion of the computer as a machine for business as well as for science, and its success showed that the low estimates of how many computers the world needed were wrong.

Why the inventors and the first commercial manufacturers underestimated the computer's potential market by a wide margin is an interesting question for followers of the computer industry and for historians of modern technology. There is no single cause that accounts for the misperception. Rather, three factors contributed to the erroneous picture of the computer's future: a mistaken feeling that computers were fragile and unreliable; the institutional biases of those who shaped policies toward computer use in the early days; and an almost universal failure, even among the computer pioneers themselves, to understand the very nature of computing (how one got a computer to do work, and just how much work it could do).

It was widely believed that computers were unreliable because their vacuum-tube circuits were so prone to failure. Large numbers of computers would not be built and sold, it was believed, because their unreliability made them totally unsuitable for routine use in a small business or factory. (Tubes failed so frequently they were plugged into sockets to make it easy to replace them. Other electronic components were more reliable and so were soldered in place.) Eckert and Mauchly's ENIAC had 18,000 vacuum tubes. Other electronic computers got by with fewer, but they all had many more than most other electronic equipment of the day. The ENIAC was a room-sized Leviathan whose tubes generated a lot of heat and used great quantities of Philadelphia's electric power. Tube failures were indeed a serious problem, for if even one tube blew out during a computation it might render the whole machine inoperative. Since tubes are most likely to blow out within a few minutes after being switched on, the ENIAC's power was left on all the time, whether it was performing a computation or not.

Howard Aiken was especially wary of computers that used thousands of vacuum tubes as their switching elements. His Mark I, an electromechanical machine using parts taken from standard IBM accounting equipment of the day, was much slower but more rugged than computers that used vacuum tubes. Aiken felt that the higher speeds vacuum tubes offered did not offset their tendency to burn out. He reluctantly designed computers that used vacuum tubes, but he always kept the numbers of tubes to a minimum and used electromechanical relays wherever he could.[8] Not everyone shared Aiken's wariness, but his arguments against using vacuum-tube circuits were taken seriously by many other computer designers, especially those whose own computer projects were shaped by the policies of Aiken's Harvard laboratory.

That leads to the next reason for the low estimates: Scientists controlled the early development of the computer, and they steered postwar computing projects away from machines and applications that might have a mass market. Howard Aiken, John von Neumann, and Douglas Hartree were physicists or mathematicians, members of a scientific elite. For the most part, they were little concerned with the mundane payroll and accounting problems that business faced every day.

Such problems involved little in the way of higher mathematics, and their solutions contributed little to the advancement of scientific knowledge. Scientists perceived their own place in society as an important one but did not imagine that the world would need many more men like themselves. Because their own needs were satisfied by a few powerful computers, they could not imagine a need for many more such machines. Even at IBM, where commercial applications took precedence, scientists shaped the perceptions of the new invention. In the early 1950s, the mathematician John von Neumann was a part-time consultant to the company, where he played no little role in shaping expectations for the new technology.

The perception of a modest and limited future for electronic computing came, most of all, from misunderstandings of its very nature. The pioneers did not really understand how humans would interact with machines that worked at the speed of light, and they were far too modest in their assessments of what their inventions could really do. They felt they had made a breakthrough in numerical calculating, but they missed seeing that the breakthrough was in fact a much bigger one. Computing turned out to encompass far more than just doing complicated sequences of arithmetic. But just how much more was not apparent until much later, when other people gained familiarity with computers. A few examples of objections raised to computer projects in the early days will make this clear.

When Howard Aiken first proposed building an automatic computer, in 1937, his colleagues at Harvard objected. Such a machine, they said, would lie idle most of the time, because it would soon do all the work required of it. They were clearly thinking of his proposed machine in terms of a piece of experimental apparatus constructed by a physicist; after the experiment is performed and the results gathered, such an apparatus has no further use and is then either stored or dismantled so that the parts can be reused for new experiments. Aiken's proposed "automatic calculating machine," as he called it in 1937, was perceived that way. After he had used it to perform the calculations he wanted it to perform, would the machine be good for anything else? Probably not. No one had built computers before. One could not propose building one just to see what it would look like; a researcher had to demonstrate the need for a machine with which he could solve a specific problem that was otherwise insoluble. Even if he could show that only with the aid of a computer could he solve the problem, that did not necessarily justify its cost.[9]

Later on, when the much faster electronic computers appeared, this argument surfaced again. Mechanical computers had proved their worth, but some felt that electronic computers worked so fast that they would spew out results much faster than human beings could assimilate them. Once again, the expensive computer would lie idle, while its human operators pondered over the results of a few minutes of its activity. Even if enough work was found to keep an electronic computer busy, some felt that the work could not be fed into the machine rapidly enough to keep its internal circuits busy.[10]

Finally, it was noted that humans had to program a computer before it could do any work. Those programs took the form of long lists of arcane symbols punched into strips of paper tape. For the first electronic computers, it was mostly mathematicians who prepared those tapes. If someone wanted to use the computer to solve a problem, he was allotted some time during which he had complete control over the machine; he wrote the program, fed it into the computer, ran it, and took out the results. By the early 1950s, computing installations saw the need for a staff of mathematicians and programmers to assist the person who wanted a problem solved, since few users would be expected to know the details of programming each specific machine. That meant that every computer installation would require the services of skilled mathematicians, and there would never be enough of them to keep more than a few machines busy. R. F. Clippinger discussed this problem at a meeting of the American Mathematical Society in 1950, stating, "In order to operate the modern computing machine for maximum output, a staff of perhaps twenty mathematicians of varying degrees of training are required. There is currently such a shortage of persons trained for this work that machines are not working full time."[11] Clippinger forecast a need for 2,000 such persons by 1960, implying that there would be a mere 100 computers in operation by then.

These perceptions, which lay behind the widely held belief that computers would never find more than a limited (though important) market in the industrialized world, came mainly from looking at the new invention strictly in the context of what it was replacing: calculating machines and their human operators. That context was what limited the pioneers' vision.

Whenever a new technology is born, few see its ultimate place in society. The inventors of radio did not foresee its use for broadcasting entertainment, sports, and news; they saw it as a telegraph without wires. The early builders of automobiles did not see an age of "automobility"; they saw a "horseless carriage." Likewise, the computer's inventors perceived its role in future society in terms of the functions it was specifically replacing in contemporary society. The predictions that they made about potential applications for the new invention had to come from the context of "computing" that they knew. Though they recognized the electronic computer's novelty, they did not see how it would permit operations fundamentally different from those performed by human computers.

Before there were digital computers, a mathematician solved a complex computational problem by first recasting it into a set of simpler problems, usually involving only the four ordinary operations of arithmetic — addition, subtraction, multiplication, and division. Then he would take this set of more elementary problems to human computers who would do the arithmetic with the aid of mechanical desktop calculators. He would supply these persons with the initial input data, books of logarithmic and trigonometric tables, paper on which to record intermediate results, and instructions on how to proceed. Depending on the computer's mathematical skill, the instructions would be more or less detailed. An unskilled computer had to be told, for example, that the product of two negative numbers is a positive number; someone with more mathematical training might need only a general outline of the computation.[12]

The inventors of the first digital computers saw their machines as direct replacements for this system of humans, calculators, tables, pencils and paper, and instructions. We know this because many early experts on automatic computing used the human computing process as the standard against which the new electronic computers were compared. Writers of early textbooks on "automatic computing" started with the time a calculator took to multiply two ten-digit numbers. To that time they added the times for the other operations: writing and copying intermediate results, consulting tables, and keying in input values. Although a skilled operator could multiply two numbers in ten or twelve seconds, in an eight-hour day he or she could be expected to perform only 400 such operations, each of which required about seventy-two seconds.[13] The first electronic computers could multiply two ten-digit decimal numbers in about 0.003 second; they could copy and read internally stored numbers even faster. Not only that, they never had to take a coffee break, stop for a meal, or sleep; they could compute as long as their circuits were working.

Right away, these speeds radically altered the context of the arguments that electronic components were too unreliable to be used in more than a few computers. It was true that tubes were unreliable and that the failure of even one during a calculation might vitiate the results. But the measure of reliability was the number of operations between failures, not the absolute number of hours the machine was in service. In terms of the number of elementary operations it could do before a tube failed, a machine such as ENIAC turned out to be quite reliable after all. If it could be kept running for even one hour without a tube failure, during that hour it could do more arithmetic than the supposedly more reliable mechanical calculators could do in weeks. Eventually the ENIAC's operators were able to keep it running for more than twenty hours a day, seven days week. Computers were reliable enough long before the introduction of the transistor provided a smaller and more rugged alternative to the vacuum tube.

So an electronic computer like the ENIAC could do the equivalent of about thirty million elementary operations in a day — the equivalent of the work of 75,000 humans. By that standard, five or six computers of the ENIAC's speed and size could do the work of 400,000 humans. However, measuring electronic computing power by comparing it with that of humans makes no sense. It is like measuring the output of a steam engine in "horsepower." For a one- or two-horsepower engine, the comparison is appropriate, but it would be impossible to replace a locomotive with an equivalent number of horses. So it is with computing power. But the human measure was the only one the pioneers knew. Recall that between 1945 and 1950 the ENIAC was the only working electronic computer in the United States. At its public dedication in February 1946, Arthur Burks demonstrated the machine's powers to the press by having it add a number to itself over and over again — an operation that reporters could easily visualize in terms of human abilities. Cables were plugged in, switches set, and a few numbers keyed in. Burks then said to the audience, "I am now going to add 5,000 numbers together," and pushed a button on the machine. The ENIAC took about a second to add the numbers.[14]

Almost from the day the first digital computers began working, they seldom lay idle. As long as they were in working order, they were busy, even long after they had done the computations for which they were built.

As electronic computers were fundamentally different from the human computers they replaced, they were also different from special-purpose pieces of experimental apparatus. The reason was that the computer, unlike other experimental apparatus, was programmable. That is, the computer itself was not just "a machine," but at any moment it was one of an almost infinite number of machines, depending on what its program told it to do. The ENIAC's users programmed it by plugging in cables from one part of the machine to another (an idea borrowed from telephone switchboards). This rewiring essentially changed it into a new machine for each new problem it solved. Other early computers got their instructions from punched strips of paper tape; the holes in the tape set switches in the machine, which amounted to the same kind of rewiring effected by the ENIAC's plugboards. Feeding the computer a new strip of paper tape transformed it into a completely different device that could do something entirely different from what its designers had intended it to do. Howard Aiken designed his Automatic Sequence Controlled Calculator to compute tables of mathematical functions, and that it did reliably for many years. But in between that work it also solved problems in hydrodynamics, nuclear physics, and even economics.[15]

The computer, by virtue of its programmability, is not a machine like a printing press or a player piano — devices that are configured to perform a specific function.[16] By the classical definition, a machine is a set of devices configured to perform a specific function: One employs motors, levers, gears, and wire to print newspapers; another uses motors, levers, gears, and wire to play a prerecorded song. A computer is also made by configuring a set of devices, but its function is not implied by that configuration. It acquires its function only when someone programs it. Before that time it is an abstract machine, one that can do "anything." (It can even be made to print a newspaper or play a tune.) To many people accustomed to the machines of the Industrial Revolution, a machine having such general capabilities seemed absurd, like a toaster that could sew buttons on a shirt. But the computer was just such a device; it could do many things its designers never anticipated.

The computer pioneers understood the concept of the computer as a general-purpose machine, but only in the narrow sense of its ability to solve a wide range of mathematical problems. Largely because of their institutional backgrounds, they did not anticipate that many of the applications computers would find would require the sorting and retrieval of nonnumeric data. Yet, outside the scientific and university milieu, especially after 1950, it was just such work in industry and business that underlay the early expansion of the computer industry. Owing to the fact that the first computers did not do business work, the misunderstanding persisted that anything done by a computer was somehow more "mathematical" or precise than that same work, done by other means. Howard Aiken probably never fully understood that a computer could not only be programmed to do different mathematical problems but could also do problems having little to do with mathematics. In 1956, he made the following statement, "… if it should ever turn out that the basic logics of a machine designed for the numerical solution of differential equations coincide with the logics of a machine intended to make bills for a department store, I would regard this as the most amazing coincidence that I have ever encountered."[17] But the logical design of modern computers for scientific work in fact coincides with the logical design of computers for business purposes. It is a "coincidence," all right, but one fully intended by today's computer designers.

The question remained whether electronic computers worked too fast for humans to feed work into them. Engineers and computer designers met the problem of imbalance of speeds head-on, by technical advances at both the input and output stages of computing. To feed in programs and data, they developed magnetic tapes and disks instead of tedious plugboard wiring or slow paper tape. For displaying the results of a computation, high-speed line printers, plotters, and video terminals replaced the slow and cumbersome electric typewriters and card punches used by the first machines.

Still, the sheer bulk of the computer's output threatened to inundate the humans who ultimately wanted to use it. But that was not a fatal fault, owing (again) to the computer's programmability. Even if in the course of a computation a machine handles millions of numbers, it need not present them all as its output. The humans who use the computer need only a few numbers, which the computer's program itself can select and deliver. The program may not only direct the machine to solve a problem, it also may tell the machine to select only the "important" part of the answer and suppress the rest.

Ultimately, the spread of the computer beyond physics labs and large government agencies depended on whether people could write programs that would solve different types of problems and that would make efficient use of the high internal speed of electronic circuits. That challenge was not met by simply training and hiring armies of programmers (although sometimes it must have seemed that way). It was met by taking advantage of the computer's ability to store its programs internally. By transforming the programming into an activity that did not require mathematical training, computer designers exploited a property of the machine itself to sidestep the shortage of mathematically trained programmers.

Although the computer pioneers recognized the need for internal program storage, they did not at first see that such a feature would have such a significant effect on the nature of programming. The idea of storing both the program and data in the same internal memory grew from the realization that the high speed at which a computer could do arithmetic made sense only if it got its instructions at an equally high speed. The plugboard method used with the ENIAC got instructions to the machine quickly but made programming awkward and slow for humans. In 1944, Eckert proposed a successor to the ENIAC (eventually called the EDVAC), whose program would be supplied not by plugboards but by instructions stored on a high-speed magnetic disk or drum.

In the summer of 1944, John von Neumann first learned (by chance) of the ENIAC project, and within a few months he had grasped that giant machine's fundamentals — and its deficiencies, which Eckert and Mauchly hoped to remedy with their next computer. Von Neumann then began to develop a general theory of computing that would influence computer design to the present day.[18] In a 1945 report on the progress of the EDVAC, he stated clearly the concept of the stored program and how a computer might be organized around it.[19] Von Neumann was not the only one to do that, but it was mainly from his report and others following it that many modern notions of how best to design a computer originated.

For von Neumann, programming a digital computer never seemed to be much of an intellectual challenge; once a problem was stated in mathematical terms, the "programming" was done. The actual writing of the binary codes that got a computer to carry out that program was an activity he called coding, and from his writings it is clear that he regarded the relationship of coding to programming as similar to that of typing to writing. That "coding" would be as difficult as it turned out to be, and that there could emerge a profession devoted to that task, seems not to have occurred to him. That was due in part to von Neumann's tremendous mental abilities and in part to the fact that the problems that interested him (such as long-range weather forecasting and complicated aspects of fluid dynamics)[20] required programs that were short relative to the time the computer took to digest the numbers. Von Neumann and Herman Goldstine developed a method (still used today) of representing programs by flow charts. However, such charts could not be fed directly into a machine. Humans still had to do that, and for those who lacked von Neumann's mental abilities, the job remained as difficult as ever.

The intermediate step of casting a problem in the form of a flow chart, whatever its benefits, did not meet the challenge of making it easy for nonspecialists to program a computer. A more enduring method came from reconsidering, once again, the fact that the computer stored its program internally.

In his reports on the EDVAC, von Neumann had noted the fact that the computer could perform arithmetic on (and thus modify) its instructions as if they were data, since both were stored in the same physical device.[21] Therefore, the computer could give itself new orders. Von Neumann saw this as a way of getting a computer with a modest memory capacity to generate the longer sequences of instructions needed to solve complex problems. For von Neumann, that was a way of condensing the code and saving space.

However, von Neumann did not see that the output of a computer program could be, rather than numerical information, another program. That idea seemed preposterous at first, but once implemented it meant that users could write computer programs without having to be skilled mathematicians. Programs could take on forms resembling English and other natural languages. Computers then would translate these programs into long complex sequences of ones and zeroes, which would set their internal switches. One even could program a computer by simply selecting from a "menu" of commands (as at an automated bank teller) or by paddles and buttons (as on a computerized video game). A person need not even be literate to program.

That innovation, the development of computer programs that translated commands simple for humans to learn into commands the computer needs to know, broke through the last barrier to the spread of the new invention.[22] Of course, the widespread use of computers today owes a lot to the technical revolution that has made the circuits so much smaller and cheaper. But today's computers-on-a-chip, like the "giant brains" before them, would never have found a large market had a way not been found to program them. When the low-cost, mass-produced integrated circuits are combined with programming languages and applications packages (such as those for word processing) that are fairly easy for the novice to grasp, all limits to the spread of computing seem to drop away. Predictions of the numbers of computers that will be in operation in the future become meaningless.

What of the computer pioneers' early predictions? They could not foresee the programming developments that would spread computer technology beyond anything imaginable in the 1940s. Today, students with pocket calculators solve the mathematical problems that prompted the pioneers of that era to build the first computers. Furthermore, general-purpose machines are now doing things, such as word processing and game playing, that no one then would have thought appropriate for a computer. The pioneers did recognize that they were creating a new type of machine, a device that could do more than one thing depending on its programming. It was this understanding that prompted their notion that a computer could do "anything." Paradoxically, the claim was more prophetic than they could ever have known. Its implications have given us the unforeseen computer revolution amid which we are living.

ENDNOTES

1. Harold Bergstein, "An Interview with Eckert and Mauchly," *Datamation* 8, no. 4 (1962), pp. 25–30.
2. Simon Lavington, *Early British Computers* (Bedford, MA: Digital Press, 1980), p. 104.
3. See, for example, John Wells, "The Origins of the Computer Industry: A Case Study in Radial Technological Change," Ph.D. Diss., Yale University, 1978, pp. 93, 96, 119; Robert N. Noyce, "Microelectronics," *Scientific American* 237 (September 1977), p. 674; Edmund C. Berkeley, "Sense and Nonsense about Computers and Their Applications," in *Proceedings of World Computer Pioneer Conference*, Llandudno, Wales, 1970, also in Phillip J. Davis and Reuben Hersh (eds.), *The Mathematical Experience* (New York: Houghton Mifflin, 1981).
4. See, for example, the proceedings of two early conferences: Symposium on Large-Scale Digital Calculation Machinery, Annals of Harvard University Computation Laboratory, vol. 16, 1949; The Moore School Lecturers: Theory and Techniques for Design of Electronic Digital Computers, lectures given at Moore School of Electrical Engineering, University of Pennsylvania, 1946 (Cambridge, MA: MIT Press, 1986).
5. Georgia G. Mollenhoff, "John V. Atanasoff, DP Pioneer," *Computerworld* 8, no. 11 (1974), pp. 1, 13.

6. Byron E. Phelps, *The Beginnings of Electronic Computation*, IBM Corporation Technical Report TR–00.2259, Poughkeepsie, NY, 1971, p. 19.

7. Cuthbert C. Hurd, "Early IBM Computers: Edited Testimony," *Annals of the History of Computing* 3 (1981), pp. 162–82.

8. Anthony Oettinger, "Howard Aiken," *Communications* ACM 5 (1962), pp. 298–9, 352.

9. Henry Tropp, "The Effervescent Years: A Retrospective," *IEEE Spectrum* 11 (February 1974), pp. 70–81.

10. For an example of this argument, and a refutation of it, see John von Neumann, *Collected Works*, vol. 5 (Oxford: Pergamon, 1961), pp. 182, 365.

11. R. F. Clippinger, "Mathematical Requirements of the Personnel of a Computing Laboratory," *American Mathematical Monthly* 57 (1950), p. 439; Edmund Berkeley, *Giant Brains, or Machines That Think* (New York: Wiley, 1949), pp. 108–9.

12. Ralph J. Slutz, "Memories of the Bureau of Standards SEAC," in N. Metropolis, J. Howlett, and G. Rota (eds.), *A History of Computing in the Twentieth Century* (New York: Academic, 1980), pp. 471–7.

13. In a typical computing installation of the 1930s, humans worked, with mechanical calculators that could perform the four elementary operations of arithmetic, on decimal numbers having up to ten digits, taking a few seconds per operation. Although the machines were powered by electric motors, the arithmetic itself was always done by mechanical parts — gears, wheels, racks, and levers. The machines were sophisticated and complex, and they were not cheap; good ones cost hundreds of dollars. For a survey of early mechanical calculators and early computers, see Francis J. Murray, *Mathematical Machines*, vol. 1: *Digital Computers* (New York: Columbia University Press, 1961); see also Engineering Research Associates, *High-Speed Computing Devices* (New York: McGraw-Hill, 1950; Cambridge, MA: MIT Press, 1984).

14. Quoted in Nancy Stern, *From ENIAC to UNIVAC* (Bedford, MA: Digital Press, 1981), p. 87.

15. Oettinger, "Howard Aiken."

16. Abbott Payson Usher, *A History of Mechanical Inventions*, second edition (Cambridge, MA: Harvard University Press, 1966), p. 117.

17. Howard Aiken, "The Future of Automatic Computing Machinery," in *Elektronische Rechenmaschinen und Informationsverarbeitung*, proceedings of a symposium, published in *Nachrichtentechnische Fachberichte*, no. 4 (Braunschweig: Vieweg, 1956), pp. 32–34.

18. Herman H. Goldstine, *The Computer from Pascal to von Neumann* (Princeton, NJ: Princeton University Press, 1972), p. 182.

19. Von Neumann's "First Draft of a Report on the EDVAC" was circulated in typescript for many years. It was not meant to be published, but it nonetheless had an influence on nearly every subsequent computer design. The complete text has been published for the first time as an appendix to Nancy Stern's *From ENIAC to UNIVAC*.

20. Von Neumann, *Collected Works*, vol. 5, pp. 182, 236.

21. Martin Campbell-Kelley, "Programming the EDVAC," *Annals of the History of Computing* 2 (1980), p. 15.

22. For a discussion of the concept of high-level programming languages and how they evolved, see H. Wexelblatt (ed.), *History of Programming Languages* (New York: Academic, 1981), especially the papers on FORTRAN, BASIC, and ALGOL.

22

Why I Am Not Going to Buy a Computer

WENDELL BERRY

Wendell Berry is not impressed by the hundreds of millions of computers being used by other people around the world. His short essay — concise and spare — explains why he prefers a thirty-year-old manual typewriter to a PC or even an electric typewriter. The essay, originally published in the New England Review *and* Bread Loaf Quarterly *in 1987, was reprinted in* Harper's *and is followed by several letters to the editor that* Harper's *received, together with Berry's response. It is a simple, elegant indictment of centralization, bigness, and consumption-driven technological society that some will resonate with and others will find utterly absurd.*

A writer and farmer, Wendell Berry lives in Lane's Landing, a 125-acre homestead near Port Royal, Kentucky, and is a former member of the English faculty at the University of Kentucky. "Why I Am Not Going to Buy a Computer" is included in a book of his essays entitled, What Are People For? *Berry's other writings include several novels and collections of short stories, poems, and essays. In March 2011 he received the 2010 National Medal of Humanities from President Obama.*

Like almost everybody else, I am hooked to the energy corporations, which I do not admire. I hope to become less hooked to them. In my work, I try to be as little hooked to them as possible. As a farmer, I do almost all of my work with horses. As a writer, I work with a pencil or a pen and a piece of paper.

My wife types my work on a Royal standard typewriter bought new in 1956 and as good now as it was then. As she types, she sees things that are wrong and marks them with small checks in the margins. She is my best critic because she is the one most familiar with my habitual errors and weaknesses. She also understands, sometimes better than I do, what ought to be said. We have, I think, a literary cottage industry that works well and pleasantly. I do not see anything wrong with it.

A number of people, by now, have told me that I could greatly improve things by buying a computer. My answer is that I am not going to do it. I have several reasons, and they are good ones.

The first is the one I mentioned at the beginning. I would hate to think that my work as a writer could not be done without a direct dependence on strip-mined coal. How could I write conscientiously against the rape of nature if I were, in the act of writing, implicated in the rape? For the same reason, it matters to me that my writing is done in the daytime, without electric light.

I do not admire the computer manufacturers a great deal more than I admire the energy industries. I have seen their advertisements, attempting to seduce struggling or failing farmers into the belief that they can solve their problems by buying yet another piece of expensive equipment. I am familiar with their propaganda campaigns that have put computers into public schools in need of books. That computers are expected to become as common as TV sets in "the future" does not impress me or matter to me. I do not own a TV set. I do not see that computers are bringing us one step nearer to anything that does matter to me: peace, economic justice, ecological health, political honesty, family and community stability, good work.

What would a computer cost me? More money, for one thing, than I can afford, and more than I wish to pay to people whom I do not admire. But the cost would not be just monetary. It is well understood that technological innovation always requires the discarding of the "old model" — the "old model" in this case being not just our old Royal standard, but my wife, my critic, my closest reader, my fellow worker. Thus (and I think this is typical of present-day technological innovation), what would be superseded would be not only something, but somebody. In order to be technologically up to date as a writer, I would have to sacrifice an association that I am dependent upon and that I treasure.

My final and perhaps my best reason for not owning a computer is that I do not wish to fool myself. I disbelieve, and therefore strongly resent, the assertion that I or anybody else could write better or more easily with a computer than with a pencil. I do not see why I should not be as scientific about this as the next fellow: When somebody has used a computer to write work that is demonstrably better than Dante's, and when this better is demonstrably attributable to the use of a computer, then I will speak of computers with a more respectful tone of voice, though I still will not buy one.

To make myself as plain as I can, I should give my standards for technological innovation in my own work. They are as follows:

1. The new tool should be cheaper than the one it replaces.
2. It should be at least as small in scale as the one it replaces.
3. It should do work that is clearly and demonstrably better than the one it replaces.

4. It should use less energy than the one it replaces.

5. If possible, it should use some form of solar energy, such as that of the body.

6. It should be repairable by a person of ordinary intelligence, provided that he or she has the necessary tools.

7. It should be purchasable and repairable as near to home as possible.

8. It should come from a small, privately owned shop or store that will take it back for maintenance and repair.

9. It should not replace or disrupt anything good that already exists, and this includes family and community relationships.

1987

After the foregoing essay, first published in the *New England Review and Bread Loaf Quarterly*, was reprinted in *Harper's*, the *Harper's* editors published the following letters in response and permitted me a reply.

W. B.

LETTERS

Wendell Berry provides writers enslaved by the computer with a handy alternative: Wife — a low-tech, energy-saving device. Drop a pile of handwritten notes on Wife and you get back a finished manuscript, edited while it was typed. What computer can do that? Wife meets all of Berry's uncompromising standards for technological innovation: She's cheap, repairable near home, and good for the family structure. Best of all, Wife is politically correct because she breaks a writer's "direct dependence on strip-mined coal."

History teaches us that Wife can also be used to beat rugs and wash clothes by hand, thus eliminating the need for the vacuum cleaner and washing machine, two more nasty machines that threaten the act of writing.

Gordon Inkeles
Miranda, Calif.

I have no quarrel with Berry because he prefers to write with pencil and paper; that is his choice. But he implies that I and others are somehow impure because we choose to write on a computer. I do not admire the energy corporations, either. Their shortcoming is not that they produce electricity but how they go about it. They are poorly managed because they are blind to long-term consequences. To solve this problem, wouldn't it make more sense to correct the precise error they are making rather than simply ignore their product? I would be happy to join Berry in a protest against strip mining, but I intend to keep plugging this computer into the wall with a clear conscience.

James Rhoads
Battle Creek, Mich.

I enjoyed reading Berry's declaration of intent never to buy a personal computer in the same way that I enjoy reading about the belief systems of unfamiliar tribal cultures. I tried to imagine a tool that would meet Berry's criteria for superiority to his old manual typewriter. The clear winner is the quill pen. It is cheaper, smaller, more energy efficient, human powered, easily repaired, and nondisruptive of existing relationships.

Berry also requires that this tool must be "clearly and demonstrably better" than the one it replaces. But surely we all recognize by now that "better" is in the mind of the beholder. To the quill-pen aficionado, the benefits obtained from elegant calligraphy might well outweigh all others.

I have no particular desire to see Berry use a word processor; if he doesn't like computers, that's fine with me. However, I do object to his portrayal of this reluctance as a moral virtue. Many of us have found that computers can be an invaluable tool in the fight to protect our environment. In addition to helping me write, my personal computer gives me access to up-to-the-minute reports on the workings of the EPA and the nuclear industry. I participate in electronic bulletin boards on which environmental activists discuss strategy and warn each other about urgent legislative issues. Perhaps Berry feels that the Sierra Club should eschew modern printing technology, which is highly wasteful of energy, in favor of having its members hand-copy the club's magazines and other mailings each month?

Nathaniel S. Borenstein
Pittsburgh, Pa.

The value of a computer to a writer is that it is a tool not for generating ideas but for typing and editing words. It is cheaper than a secretary (or a wife!) and arguably more fuel efficient. And it enables spouses who are not inclined to provide free labor more time to concentrate on their own work.

We should support alternatives both to coal-generated electricity and to IBM-style technocracy. But I am reluctant to entertain alternatives that presuppose the traditional subservience of one class to another. Let the PCs come and the wives and servants go seek more meaningful work.

Toby Koosman
Knoxville, Tenn.

Berry asks how he could write conscientiously against the rape of nature if in the act of writing on a computer he was implicated in the rape. I find it ironic that a writer who sees the underlying connectedness of things would allow his diatribe against computers to be published in a magazine that carries ads for the National Rural Electric Cooperative Association, Marlboro, Phillips Petroleum, McDonnell Douglas, and yes, even Smith Corona. If Berry rests comfortably at night, he must be using sleeping pills.

Bradley C. Johnson
Grand Forks, N.D.

WENDELL BERRY REPLIES

The foregoing letters surprised me with the intensity of the feelings they expressed. According to the writers' testimony, there is nothing wrong with their computers; they are utterly satisfied with them and all that they stand for. My correspondents are certain that I am wrong and that I am, moreover, on the losing side, a side already relegated to the dustbin of history. And yet they grow huffy and condescending over my tiny dissent. What are they so anxious about?

I can only conclude that I have scratched the skin of a technological fundamentalism that, like other fundamentalisms, wishes to monopolize a whole society and, therefore, cannot tolerate the smallest difference of opinion. At the slightest hint of a threat to their complacency, they repeat, like a chorus of toads, the notes sounded by their leaders in industry. The past was gloomy, drudgery-ridden, servile, meaningless, and slow. The present, thanks only to purchasable products, is meaningful, bright, lively, centralized, and fast. The future, thanks only to more purchasable products, is going to be even better. Thus, consumers become salesmen, and the world is made safer for corporations.

I am also surprised by the meanness with which two of these writers refer to my wife. In order to imply that I am a tyrant, they suggest by both direct statement and innuendo that she is subservient, characterless, and stupid — a mere "device" easily forced to provide meaningless "free labor." I understand that it is impossible to make an adequate public defense of one's private life, and so I will only point out that there are a number of kinder possibilities that my critics have disdained to imagine: that my wife may do this work because she wants to and likes to, that she may find some use and some meaning in it, that she may not work for nothing. These gentlemen obviously think themselves feminists of the most correct and principled sort, and yet they do not hesitate to stereotype and insult, on the basis of one fact, a woman they do not know. They are audacious and irresponsible gossips.

In his letter, Bradley C. Johnson rushes past the possibility of sense in what I said in my essay by implying that I am or ought to be a fanatic. That I am a person of this century and implicated in many practices that I regret is fully acknowledged at the beginning of my essay. I did not say that I proposed to end forthwith all my involvement in harmful technology, for I do not know how to do that. I said merely that I want to limit such involvement and to a certain extent I do know how to do that. If some technology does damage to the world — as two of [these] letters seem to agree that it does — then why is it not reasonable, and indeed moral, to try to limit one's use of that technology? Of course, I think that I am right to do this.

I would not think so, obviously, if I agreed with Nathaniel S. Borenstein that "'better' is in the mind of the beholder." But if he truly believes this, I do not see why he bothers with his personal computer's "up-to-the-minute reports on the workings of the EPA and the nuclear industry" or why he wishes to be warned about "urgent legislative issues." According to his system, the "better" in a bureaucratic, industrial, or legislative mind is as good as the "better" in his. His mind apparently is being subverted by an objective standard of some sort, and he had better look out.

Borenstein does not say what he does after his computer has drummed him awake. I assume from his letter that he must send donations to conservation organizations and letters to officials. Like James Rhoads, at any rate, he has a clear conscience. But this is what is wrong with the conservation movement. It has a clear conscience. The guilty are always other people, and the wrong is always somewhere else; that is why Borenstein finds his "electronic bulletin board" so handy. To the conservation movement, it is only production that causes environmental degradation; the consumption that supports the production is rarely acknowledged to be at fault. The ideal of the run-of-the-mill conservationist is to impose restraints upon production without limiting consumption or burdening the consciences of consumers.

But virtually all of our consumption now is extravagant, and virtually all of it consumes the world. It is not beside the point that most electrical power comes from strip-mined coal. The history of the exploitation of the Appalachian coal fields is long, and it is available to readers. I do not see how anyone can read it and plug in any appliance with a clear conscience. If Rhoads can do so, that does not mean that his conscience is clear; it means that his conscience is not working.

To the extent that we consume, in our present circumstances, we are guilty. To the extent that we guilty consumers are conservationists, we are absurd. But what can we do? Must we go on writing letters to politicians and donating to conservation organizations until the majority of our fellow citizens agree with us? Or can we do something directly to solve our share of the problem?

I am a conservationist. I believe wholeheartedly in putting pressure on the politicians and in maintaining the conservation organizations. But I wrote my little essay partly in distrust of centralization. I don't think that the government and the conservation organizations alone will ever make us a conserving society. Why do I need a centralized computer system to alert me to environmental crises? That I live every hour of every day in an environmental crisis I know from all my senses. Why then is not my first duty to reduce, so far as I can, my own consumption?

Finally, it seems to me that none of my correspondents recognizes the innovativeness of my essay. If the use of a computer is a new idea, then a newer idea is not to use one.

23

Computer Ethics

DEBORAH G. JOHNSON

The many roles that computers play in society raise a host of ethical and legal issues: privacy, cybercrime, ownership of intellectual property, liability for damages, accountability, and more. But to what extent are these issues unique to computers, and to what extent are they simply new areas of application for well-established ethical and legal principles? Many of these issues have developed as computers and their uses have grown and permeated society. The advent of the Internet has intensified issues of computer ethics and created new and more complex ones. And, as computer technology continues to evolve, new and more difficult ethical issues are likely to arise. Deborah Johnson, one of the most respected voices in this area, probes the field of computer ethics in a systematic manner that provides an effective introduction and a set of guideposts to structure our thinking about its many dimensions.

Deborah Johnson is chair of the Department of Science, Technology, and Society and Anne Shirley Carter Olsson Professor of Applied Ethics in the School of Engineering and Applied Science at the University of Virginia. Johnson holds a Ph.D. in philosophy from the University of Kansas and has taught at Rensselaer Polytechnic Institute and Georgia Institute of Technology. She is the author or editor of several books, including Computer Ethics, *the third edition of which was published in 2001, and many articles. This essay appeared first as a chapter in* The Blackwell Guide to the Philosophy of Computing and Information *(2003), edited by Luciano Floridi.*

Deborah G. Johnson, "Computer Ethics" from *The Blackwell Guide to the Philosophy of Computing and Information*, ed. Luciano Floridi. © 2004 by Blackwell Publishing Ltd.

INTRODUCTION

From the moment of their invention, computers have generated complex social, ethical, and value concerns. These concerns have been expressed in a variety of ways, from the science fiction stories of Isaac Asimov (1970) to a dense three-volume treatise on social theory by Manuel Castells (1996, 1997, 1998), and with much in between. Generally, the literature describes the social consequences of computing, speculates on the meaning of computation and information technology in human history, and creatively predicts the future path of development of computer technology and social institutions around it. A small, though steadily increasing, number of philosophers has focused specifically on the *ethical issues*.

As computer technology evolves and gets deployed in new ways, certain issues persist — issues of privacy, property rights, accountability, and social values. At the same time, seemingly new and unique issues emerge. The ethical issues can be organized in at least three different ways: according to the type of technology; according to the sector in which the technology is used; and according to ethical concepts or themes. In this chapter I will take the third approach. However, before doing so it will be useful to briefly describe the other two approaches.

The first is to organize the ethical issues by type of technology and its use. When computers were first invented, they were understood to be essentially sophisticated calculating machines, but they seemed to have the capacity to do that which was thought to be uniquely human — to reason and exhibit a high degree of rationality; hence, there was concern that computers threatened ideas about what it means to be human. In the shadow of the Second World War, concerns quickly turned to the use of computers by governments to centralize and concentrate power. These concerns accompanied the expanding use of computers for record-keeping and the exponential growth in the scale of databases, allowing the creation, maintenance, and manipulation of huge quantities of personal information. This was followed by the inception of software control systems and video games, raising issues of accountability — liability and property rights. This evolution of computer technology can be followed through to more recent developments including the Internet, simulation and imaging technologies, and virtual reality systems. Each one of these developments was accompanied by conceptual and moral uncertainty. What will this or that development mean for the lives and values of human beings? What will it do to the relationship between government and citizen? Between employer and employee? Between businesses and consumers?

A second enlightening approach is to organize the issues according to the sector in which they occur. Ethical issues arise in real-world contexts, and computer-ethical issues arise in the contexts in which computers are used. Each context or sector has distinctive issues, and if we ignore this context we can miss important aspects of computer-ethical issues. For example, in dealing with privacy protection in general, we might miss the special importance of privacy protection for *medical records* where confidentiality is so essential to the doctor–patient relationship. Similarly, one might not fully understand the appropriate role for computers in education were one not sensitive to distinctive goals of education.

Both of these approaches — examining issues by types and uses of particular technologies, and sector by sector — are important and illuminating; however, they take us too far afield of the philosophical issues. The third approach — the approach to be taken in this chapter — is to emphasize ethical concepts and themes that persist across types of technology and sectors. Here the issues are sorted by their philosophical and ethical content. In this chapter I divide the issues into two broad categories: (1) metatheoretical and methodological issues, and (2) traditional and emerging issues.

METATHEORETICAL AND METHODOLOGICAL ISSUES

Perhaps the deepest philosophical thinking on computer-ethical issues has been reflection on the field itself — its appropriate subject matter, its relationship to other fields, and its methodology. In a seminal piece entitled "What is Computer Ethics?" Moor (1985) recognized that when computers are first introduced into an environment, they make it possible for human beings (individuals and institutions) to do things they couldn't do before, and this creates *policy vacuums*. We do not have rules, policies, and conventions on how to behave with regard to the new possibilities. Should employers monitor employees to the extent possible with computer software? Should doctors perform surgery remotely? Should I make copies of proprietary software? Is there any harm in me taking on a pseudo-identity in an online chatroom? Should companies doing business online be allowed to sell the transaction-generated information they collect? These are examples of policy vacuums created by computer technology.

Moor's account of computer ethics has shaped the field of computer ethics with many computer ethicists understanding their task to be that of helping to fill policy vacuums. Indeed, one of the topics of interest in computer ethics is to understand this activity of filling policy vacuums. This will be addressed later on.

The Connection Between Technology and Ethics

While Moor's account of computer ethics remains influential, it leaves several questions unanswered. Hence, discussion and debate continue around the question of why there is or should be a field of computer ethics and what the focus of the field should be.

In one of the deeper analyses, Floridi (1999) argues for a metaphysical foundation for computer ethics. He provides an account of computer ethics in which information has status such that destroying information can itself be morally wrong. In my own work I have tried to establish the foundation of computer ethics in the nonobvious connection between technology and ethics (Johnson 2001).

Why is technology of relevance to ethics? What difference can technology make to human action? To human affairs? To moral concepts or theories?

Two steps are involved in answering these questions. The first step involves fully recognizing something that Moor's account acknowledges, namely that technology often makes it possible for human beings to do what they could not do without it. Think of spaceships that take human beings to the moon; think of imaging technology that allows us to view internal organs; or think of computer viruses that wreak havoc on the Internet.

Of course, it is not just that human beings can do what they couldn't do before. It is also that we can do the same sorts of things we did before, only in new ways. As a result of technology, we can travel, work, keep records, be entertained, communicate, and engage in warfare *in new ways*. When we engage in these activities using computer technology, our actions have different properties, properties that may change the character of the activity or action-type. Consider the act of writing with various technologies. When I write with paper and pencil, the pencil moves over paper; when I write using a typewriter, levers and gears move; when I write using a computer, electronic impulses change configurations in microchips. So, the physical events that take place when I write are very different when I use computer technology.

Using action theory, the change can be characterized as a change in the possible act tokens of an act type. An act type is a kind of action (e.g. reading a book, walking) and an act token is a particular instance of an act type. An act token is an instance of the act type performed by a particular person, at a particular time, and in a particular place. For example, "Jan is, at this moment, playing chess with Jim in Room 200 of Thornton Hall on the campus of the University of Virginia" is an act token of the act type "playing chess." When technology is involved in the performance of an act type, a new set of act tokens may become possible. It is now possible, for example, to "play chess" while sitting in front of a computer and not involving another human being. Instead of manually moving three-dimensional pieces, one presses keys on a keyboard or clicks on a mouse. Thus, when human beings perform actions with computers, new sets of tokens (of act types) become possible. Most important, the new act tokens have properties that are distinct from other tokens of the same act type.

Computer technology instruments human action in ways that turn very simple movements into very powerful actions. Consider hardly-visible finger movements on a keyboard. When the keyboard is connected to a computer and the computer is connected to the Internet, and when the simple finger movements create and launch a computer virus, those simple finger movements can wreak havoc in the lives of thousands (even millions) of people. The technology has instrumented an action not possible without it. To be sure, individuals could wreak havoc on the lives of others before computer technology, but not in this way and perhaps not quite so easily. Computer technology is not unique among technologies in this respect; other technologies have turned simple movements of the body into powerful actions, e.g., dynamite, automobiles.

Recognizing the intimate connection between technology and human action is important for stopping the deflection of human responsibility in technology-instrumented activities, especially when something goes wrong. Hence, the hacker cannot avoid responsibility for launching a virus on grounds that he simply moved his fingers while sitting in his home. Technology does nothing independent of human initiative; though, of course, sometimes human beings cannot foresee what it is they are doing with technology.

Thus, the first step in understanding the connection between computer technology and ethics is to acknowledge how intimate the connection between (computer) technology and human action can be. The second step is to connect human action to ethics. This step may seem too obvious to be worthy of mention since ethics is often understood to be exclusively the domain of human action. Even so, computer technology changes the domain of human action; hence, it is worth asking whether these changes have moral significance. Does the involvement of computer technology — in a human situation — have moral significance? Does the *instrumentation* of human action affect the character of ethical issues, the nature of ethical theory, or ethical decision-making?

The involvement of computer technology has moral significance for several reasons. As mentioned earlier, technology creates new possibilities for human action and this means that human beings face ethical questions they never faced before. Should we develop biological weapons and risk a biological war? Should I give my organs for transplantation? In the case of computer technology, is it wrong to monitor keystrokes of employees who are using computers? To place cookies on computers when the computers are used to visit a website? To combine separate pieces of personal data into a single comprehensive portfolio of a person?

When technology changes the properties of tokens of an act type, the moral character of the act type can change. In workplace monitoring, for example, while it is generally morally acceptable for employers to keep track of the work of employees, the creation of software that allows the employer to record and analyze every keystroke an employee makes raises the question in a new way. The rights of employers and employees have to be reconsidered in light of this new possibility. Or to use a different sort of example, when it comes to property rights in software, the notion of property and the stakes in owning and copying are significantly different when it comes to computer software because computer software has properties unlike that of anything else. Most notably, software can be replicated with no loss to the owner in terms of possession or usefulness (though, of course, there is a loss in the value of the software in the marketplace).

So, computers and ethics are connected insofar as computers make it possible for humans to do things they couldn't do before and to do things they could do before but in new ways. These changes often have moral significance.

APPLIED AND SYNTHETIC ETHICS

To say that computer technology creates new tokens of an act type may lead some to categorize computer ethics as a branch of applied or practical ethics. Once a computer ethical issue is understood to involve familiar act types, it might be presumed, all that is necessary to resolve the issue is to use moral principles and theories that generally apply to the act type. For example, if the situation involves honesty in communicating information, simply follow the principle, "tell the truth," with all its special conditions and caveats. Or, if the situation involves producing some positive and negative effects, simply do the utilitarian calculation. This account of computer ethics is, however, as controversial as is the notion of "applied ethics" more generally.

For one thing, computer technology and the human situations arising around it are not always so easy to understand. As Moor has pointed out, often there are conceptual muddles (1985). What is software? What is a computer virus? How are we to conceptualize a search engine? A cookie? A virtual harm? In other words, computer ethicists do more than "apply" principles and theories; they do conceptual analysis. Moreover, the analysis of a computer-ethical issue often involves synthesis, synthesis that creates an understanding of both the technology and the ethical situation. A fascinating illustration of this is the case of a virtual rape (Dibbell 1993). Here a character in a multi-user virtual reality game rapes another character. Those participating in the game are outraged and consider the behavior of the real person controlling the virtual characters offensive and bad. The computer ethical issue involves figuring out what, if anything, wrong the real person controlling the virtual character has done. This involves understanding how the technology works, what the real person did, figuring out how to characterize the actions, and then recommending how the behavior should be viewed and responded to. Again, analysis of this kind involves more than simply "applying" principles and theories. It involves conceptual analysis and interpretation. Indeed, the synthetic analysis may have implications that reflect back on the meaning of, or our understanding of, familiar moral principles and theories.

To be sure, philosophical work in computer ethics often does involve drawing on and extending the work of well-known philosophers and making use of familiar moral concepts, principles, and theories. For example, computer ethical issues have frequently been framed in utilitarian, deontological, and social contract theory. Many scholars writing about the Internet have drawn on the work of existentialist philosophers such as Søren Kierkegaard (Dreyfus 1999; Prosser and Ward 2000) and Gabriel Marcel (Anderson 2000). The work of Jürgen Habermas has been an important influence on scholars working on computer-mediated communication (Ess 1996). Recently van den Hoven (1999) has used Michael Walzer's "spheres of justice" to analyze the information society; Cohen (2000) and Introna (2001) have used Emmanuel Levinas to understand Internet communication; Adams and Ofori-Amanfo (2000) have been connecting feminist ethics to computer ethics; and Grodzinsky (1999) has developed virtue theory to illuminate computer ethics.

Nevertheless, while computer ethicists often draw on, extend, and "apply" moral concepts and theories, computer ethics involves much more than this. Brey (2000) has recently argued for an approach that he labels "disclosive computer ethics." The applied ethics model, he notes, emphasizes controversial issues for which the ethical component is transparent. Brey argues that there are many nontransparent issues, issues that are not so readily recognized. Analysis must be done to "disclose" and make visible the values at stake in the design and use of computer technology. A salient example here is work by Introna and Nissenbaum (2000) on search engines. They show how the design of search engines is laden with value choices. In order to address those value choices explicitly, the values embedded in search engine design must be uncovered and disclosed. This may sound simple, but in fact uncovering the values embedded in technology involves understanding how the technology works and how it affects human behavior and human values.

Setting aside what is the best account of computer ethics, it should be clear that a major concern of the field is to understand its domain, its methodology, its reason for being, and its relationship to other areas of ethical inquiry. As computer technology evolves and gets deployed in new ways, more and more ethical issues are likely to arise.

TRADITIONAL AND EMERGING ISSUES

"Information society" is the term often used (especially by economists and sociologists) to characterize societies in which human activity and social institutions have been significantly transformed by computer and information technology. Using this term, computer ethics can be thought of as the field that examines ethical issues distinctive to "an information society." Here I will focus on a subset of these issues, those having to do with professional ethics, privacy, cyber crime, virtual reality, and general characteristics of the Internet.

Ethics for Computer Professionals

In an information society, a large number of individuals are educated for and employed in jobs that involve development, maintenance, buying and selling, and use of computer and information technology. Indeed, an information society is dependent on such individuals — dependent on their special knowledge and expertise and on their fulfilling correlative social responsibilities. Expertise in computing can be deployed recklessly or cautiously, used for good or ill, and the organization of information technology experts into occupations/professions is an important social means of managing that expertise in ways that serve human well-being.

An important philosophical issue here has to do with understanding and justifying the social responsibilities of computer experts. Recognizing that justification of the social responsibilities of computer experts is connected to more general notions of duty and responsibility, computer ethicists have drawn on a variety of traditional philosophical concepts and theories, but especially social contract theory.

Notice that the connection between being a computer expert and having a duty to deploy that expertise for the good of humanity cannot be explained simply as a causal relationship. For one thing, one can ask "why?" Why does the role of computer expert carry with it social responsibilities? For another, individuals acting in occupational roles are typically not acting simply as individual autonomous moral agents; they act as employees of companies or agencies, and may not be involved in the decisions that most critically determine project outcomes. Hence, there is a theoretical problem in explaining why and to what extent individuals acting in occupational roles are responsible for the effects of their work.

Social contract theory provides an account of the connection between occupational roles and social responsibilities. A social contract exists between members of an occupational group and the communities or societies of which they are a part. Society (states, provinces, communities) allows occupational groups to form professional organizations, to make use of educational institutions to train their members, to control admission, and so on, but all of this is granted in exchange for a commitment to organize and control the occupational group in ways that benefit society. In other words, a profession and its members acquire certain privileges in exchange for accepting certain social responsibilities.

The substantive content of those responsibilities has also been a topic of focus for computer ethicists. Computer professional groups have developed and promulgated codes of professional and ethical conduct that delineate in broad terms what is and is not required of computer experts. See, for example, the ACM [Association for Computing Machinery — the premier membership organization for computer professionals] Code of Ethics and Professional Conduct or the Code of Conduct of the British Computer Society. Since these codes are very general, there has been a good deal of discussion as to their appropriate role and function. Should they be considered comparable to law? Should there be enforcement mechanisms and sanctions for those who violate the code? Or should codes of conduct aim at inspiration? If so, then they should merely consist of a statement of ideals and need not be followed "to the letter" but only in spirit.

At least one computer ethicist has gone so far as to argue that the central task of the field of computer ethics is to work out issues of professional ethics for computer professionals. Gotterbarn (1995: 21) writes that the "only way to make sense of 'Computer Ethics' is to narrow its focus to those actions that are within the control of the individual *moral* computer professional."

While Gotterbarn's position is provocative, it is not at all clear that it is right. For one thing, many of the core issues in computer ethics are social value and policy issues, such as privacy and property rights. These are issues for all citizens, not just computer professionals. Moreover, many of the core issues faced by computer professionals are not unique to computing; they are similar to issues facing other occupational groups: What do we owe our clients? Our employers? When are we justified in blowing the whistle? How can we best protect the public from risk? Furthermore, since many computer professionals work in private industry, many of the issues they face are general issues of business ethics. They have to do with buying and selling, advertising, proprietary data, competitive practices, and so on. Thus, it would be a mistake to think that all of the ethical issues surrounding computer and information technology are simply ethical issues for computer professionals. Computer experts face many complex and distinctive issues, but these are only a subset of the ethical issues surrounding computer and information technology.

Privacy

In an "information society" privacy is a major concern in that much (though by no means all) of the information gathered and processed is information about individuals. Computer technology makes possible a previously unimaginable magnitude of data collection, storage, retention, and exchange. Indeed, computer technology has made information collection a built-in feature of many activities, for example, using a credit card, making a phone call, browsing the web. Such information is often referred to as transaction-generated information or TGI.

Computer ethicists often draw on prior philosophical and legal analysis of privacy and focus on two fundamental questions: What is privacy? Why is it of value? These questions have been contentious and privacy often appears to be an elusive concept. Some argue that privacy can be reduced to other concepts such as property or liberty; some argue that privacy is something in its own right and that it is intrinsically valuable; yet others argue that while not intrinsically valuable, privacy is instrumental to other things that we value deeply — friendship, intimacy, and democracy.

Computer ethicists have taken up privacy issues in parallel with more popular public concerns about the social effects of so much personal information being gathered and exchanged. The fear is that an "information society" can easily become a "surveillance society." Here computer ethicists have drawn on the work of Bentham and Foucault suggesting that all the data being gathered about individuals may create a world in which we effectively live our daily lives in a panopticon (Reiman 1995). "Panopticon" is the shape of a structure that Jeremy Bentham designed for prisons. In a panopticon, prison cells are arranged in a circle with the inside wall of each cell made of glass so that a guard, sitting in a guard tower situated in the center of the circle, can see everything that happens in each and every cell. The effect is not two-way; that is, the prisoners cannot see the guard in the tower. In fact, a prison guard need not be in the guard tower for the panopticon to have its effect; it is enough that prisoners believe they are being watched. When individuals believe they are being watched, they adjust their behavior accordingly; they take into account how the watcher will perceive their behavior. This influences individual behavior and how individuals see themselves.

While computerized information-gathering does not physically create the structure of a panopticon, it does something similar insofar as it makes a good deal of individual behavior available for observation. Thus, data collection activities of an information society could have the panopticon effect. Individuals would know that most of what they do can be observed and this could influence how they behave. When human behavior is monitored, recorded, and tracked, individuals could become intent on conforming to norms for fear of negative consequences. If this were to happen to a significant extent, it might incapacitate individuals in acting freely and thinking critically — capacities necessary to realize democracy. In this respect, the privacy issues around computer technology go to the heart of freedom and democracy.

It might be argued that the panoptic effect will not occur in information societies because data collection is invisible so that individuals are unaware they are being watched. This is a possibility, but it is also possible that as individuals become more and more accustomed to information societies, they will become more aware of the extent to which they are being watched. They may come to see how information gathered in various places is put together and used to make decisions that affect their interactions with government agencies, credit bureaus, insurance companies, educational institutions, employers, etc.

Concerns about privacy have been taken up in the policy arena, with a variety of legislation controlling and limiting the collection and use of personal data. An important focus here has been comparative analyses of policies in different countries — for they vary a good deal. The American approach has been piecemeal, with separate legislation for different kinds of records (i.e., medical records, employment histories, credit records), whereas several European countries have comprehensive policies that specify what kind of information can be collected under what conditions in *all* domains. Currently the policy debates are pressured by the intensification of global business. Information-gathering organizations promise data subjects that they will only use information in certain ways; yet, in a global economy, data collected in one country — with a certain kind of data protection — can flow to another country where there is no or different protection. An information-gathering organization might promise to treat information in a certain way, and then send the information abroad where it is treated in a completely different way, thus breaking the promise made to the data subject. To assure that this does not happen, a good deal of attention is currently being focused on working out international arrangements and agreements for the flow of data across national boundaries.

Cybercrime and Abuse

While the threats to privacy described above arise from *uses* of computer and information technology, other threats arise from *abuses*. As individuals and companies do more and more electronically, their privacy and property rights become ever more important, and these rights are sometimes threatened by individuals who defy the law or test its limits. Such individuals may seek personal gain or may just enjoy the challenge of figuring out how to *crack* security mechanisms. They are often called *hackers* or *crackers*. The term *hacker* used to refer to individuals who simply loved the challenge of working on programs and figuring out how to do complex things with computers, but did not necessarily break the law. *Crackers* were those who broke the law. However, the terms are now used somewhat interchangeably to refer to those who engage in criminal activity.

The culture of hackers and crackers has been of interest not only because of the threat posed by their activities, but also because the culture of hackers and crackers represents an alternative vision of how computer technology might be developed and used, one that has intrigued philosophers. Hackers and crackers often defend their behavior by arguing for a much more open system of computing with a freer flow of information, creating an environment in which individuals can readily share tools and ideas. In particular, the culture suggests that a policy of no ownership of software might lead to better computing. This issue goes to the heart of philosophical theories of property, raising traditional debates about the foundations of property, especially intellectual property.

Some draw on Locke's labor theory of property and argue that software developers have a natural right to control the use of their software. Others, such as me, argue that while there are good utilitarian reasons for granting ownership in software, natural rights arguments do not justify private ownership of software (Johnson 2001). There is nothing inherently unfair about living in a world in which one does not own and cannot control the use of software one has created.

Nevertheless, currently, in many industrialized countries there are laws against copying and distributing proprietary software, and computer ethicists have addressed issues around violations of these laws. Conceptually, some have wondered whether there is a difference between familiar crimes such as theft or harassment and parallel crimes done using computers. Is there any morally significant difference between stealing (copying and selling copies of) a software program and stealing a car? Is harassment via the Internet morally any different than face-to-face harassment? The question arises because actions and interactions on the Internet have some distinguishing features. On the Internet, individuals can act under the shroud of a certain kind of anonymity. They can disguise themselves through the mediation of computers. This together with the reproducibility of information in computer systems makes for a distinctive environment for criminal behavior. One obvious difference in cybertheft is that the thief does not deprive the owner of the use of the property. The owner still has access to the software, though of course the market value of the software is diminished when there is rampant copying.

Computer ethicists have taken up the task of trying to understand and conceptualize cybercrimes as well as determining how to think about their severity and appropriate punishment. Criminal behavior is nothing new, but in an information society new types of crimes are made possible, and the actions necessary to catch criminals and prevent crimes are different.

Internet Issues

Arguably the Internet is the most powerful technological development of the late twentieth century. The Internet brings together many industries, but especially the computer, telecommunications, and media enterprises. It brings together and provides a forum for millions of individuals and businesses around the world. It is not surprising, then, that the Internet is currently a major focus of attention for computer ethicists. The development of the Internet has involved moving many basic social institutions from a paper and ink medium to the electronic medium. The question for ethicists is this: is there anything ethically distinctive about the Internet? (A parallel question was asked in the last section with regard to cybercrime.)

The Internet seems to have three features that make it unusual or special. First, it has an unusual scope in that it provides many-to-many communication on a global scale. Of course, television and radio as well as the telephone are global in scale, but television and radio are one-to-many forms of communication, and the telephone, which is many-to-many, is expensive and more difficult to use. With the Internet, individuals and companies can have much more frequent communication with one another, in real time, at relatively low cost, with ease and with visual as well as sound components. Second, the Internet facilitates a certain kind of anonymity. One can communicate extensively with individuals across the globe (with ease and minimal cost), using pseudonyms or real identities, and yet one never has to encounter the others face-to-face. This type of anonymity affects the content and nature of the communication that takes place on the Internet. The third special feature of the Internet is its reproducibility. When put on the Internet, text, software, music, and video can be duplicated *ad infinitum*. They can also be altered with ease. Moreover, the reproducibility of the medium means that all activity on the Internet is recorded and can be traced.

These three features of the Internet — global many-to-many scope, anonymity, and reproducibility — have enormous positive as well as negative potential. The global, many-to-many scope can bring people from around the globe closer together, relegating geographic distance to insignificance. This feature is especially freeing to those for whom travel is physically challenging or inordinately expensive. At the same time, these potential benefits come with drawbacks; one of the drawbacks is that this power also goes to those who would use it for heinous purposes. Individuals can — while sitting anywhere in the world, with very little effort — launch viruses and disrupt communication between others. They can misrepresent themselves and dupe others on a much larger scale than before the Internet.

Similarly, anonymity has both benefits and dangers. The kind of anonymity available on the Internet frees some individuals by removing barriers based on physical appearance. For example, in contexts in which race and gender may get in the way of fair treatment, the anonymity provided by the Internet can eliminate bias; for example, in on-line education, race, gender, and physical appearance are removed as factors affecting student-to-student interactions as well as the teacher evaluations of students. Anonymity may also facilitate participation in beneficial activities such as discussions among rape victims or battered wives or ex-cons where individuals might be reluctant to participate unless they had anonymity.

Nevertheless, anonymity leads to serious problems of accountability and for the integrity of information. It is difficult to catch criminals who act under the shroud of anonymity. And anonymity contributes to the lack of integrity of electronic information. Perhaps the best illustration of this is information one acquires in chatrooms on the Internet. It is difficult (though not impossible) to be certain of the identities of the persons with whom one is chatting. The same person may be contributing information under multiple identities; multiple individuals may be using the same identity; participants may have vested interests in the information being discussed (e.g., a participant may be an employee of the company/product being discussed). When one can't determine the real source of information or develop a history of experiences with a source, it is impossible to gauge the trustworthiness of the information.

Like global scope and anonymity, reproducibility also has benefits and dangers. Reproducibility facilitates access to information and communication; it allows words and documents to be forwarded (and downloaded) to an almost infinite number of sites. It also helps in tracing cybercriminals. At the same time, however, reproducibility threatens privacy and property rights. It adds to the problems of accountability and integrity of information arising from anonymity. For example, when I am teaching a class, students can now send their assignments to me electronically. This saves time, is convenient, saves paper, etc. At the same time, however, the reproducibility of the medium raises questions about the integrity of the assignments. How can I be sure the student wrote the paper and didn't download it from the web?

When human activities move to the Internet, features of these activities change and the changes may have ethical implications. The Internet has led to a wide array of such changes. The task of computer ethics is to ferret out these changes and address the policy vacuums they create.

Virtual Reality

One of the most philosophically intriguing capacities of computer technology is "virtual reality systems." These are systems that graphically and aurally represent environments, environments into which individuals can project themselves and interact. Virtual environments can be designed to represent real-life situations and then used to train individuals for those environments, e.g., pilot training programs. They can also be designed to do just the opposite, that is, to create environments with features radically different from the real world, e.g., fantasy games. Ethicists have just begun to take up the issues posed by virtual reality, and the issues are deep (Brey 1999). The meaning of actions in virtual reality is what is at stake as well as the moral accountability of individual behavior in virtual systems. When one acts in virtual systems one "does" something, though it is not the action represented. For example, killing a figure in a violent fantasy game is not the equivalent of killing a real person. Nevertheless, actions in virtual systems can have real-world consequences; for example, violence in a fantasy game may have an impact on the real player or, as another example, the pilot flying in the flight simulator may be judged unprepared for real flight. As human beings spend more and more time in virtual systems, ethicists will have to analyze what virtual actions mean and what, if any, accountability individuals bear for their virtual actions.

CONCLUSION

This chapter has covered only a selection of the topics addressed by philosophers working in the field of computer ethics. Since computers and information technology are likely to continue to evolve and become further integrated into the human and natural world, new ethical issues are likely to arise. On the other hand, as we become more and more accustomed to acting with and through computer technology, the difference between "ethics" and "computer ethics" may well disappear.

REFERENCES

Adams, A. and Ofori-Amanfo, J. 2000. "Does gender matter in computer ethics?" *Ethics and Information Technology* 2(1): pp. 37–47.

Anderson, T. C. 2000. "The body and communities in cyberspace: a Marcellian analysis." *Ethics and Information Technology* 2(3): pp. 153–8.

Asimov, I. 1970. *I, Robot*. Greenwich, CT: Fawcett Publications.

Brey, P. 1999. "The ethics of representation and action in virtual reality." *Ethics and Information Technology* 1(1): pp. 5–14.

Brey, P. 2000. "Disclosive computer ethics." *Computers & Society*, Dec.: pp. 10–16.

Castells, M. 1996. *The Rise of the Network Society*. Malden, MA: Blackwell Publishers.

———— 1997. *The Power of Identity*. Malden, MA: Blackwell Publishers.

———— 1998. *The End of Millennium*. Malden, MA: Blackwell Publishers.

Cohen, R. A. 2000. "Ethics and cybernetics: Levinasian reflections." *Ethics and Information Technology* 2(1): pp. 27–35.

Dibbell, J. 1993. "A rape in cyberspace: how an evil clown, a Haitian trickster spirit, two wizards, and a cast of dozens turned a database into a society." *The Village Voice*, Dec. 23: pp. 36–42.

Dreyfus, H. L. 1999. "Anonymity versus commitment: the dangers of education on the Internet." *Ethics and Information Technology* 1(1): pp. 15–21.

Ess, C., ed. 1996. *Philosophical Perspectives on Computer-Mediated Communication*. Albany: State University of New York Press.

Floridi, L. 1999. "Information ethics: on the philosophical foundation of computer ethics." *Ethics and Information Technology* 1(1): pp. 37–56.

Gotterbarn, D. 1995. "Computer ethics: responsibility regained." In D. G. Johnson and H. Nissenbaum, eds., *Computers, Ethics and Social Values*. Englewood Cliffs, NJ: Prentice Hall, pp. 18–24.

Grodzinsky, F. S. 1999. "The practitioner from within: revisiting the virtues." *Computers & Society* 29(1): pp. 9–15.

Introna, L. D. 2001. "Virtuality and morality." *Philosophy in the Contemporary World* 8(1): pp. 31–39.

———— and Nissenbaum, H. 2000. "Shaping the web: why the politics of search engines matters." *The Information Society* 16(3): pp. 169–85.

Johnson, D. G. 2001. *Computer Ethics*, 3rd ed. Upper Saddle River, NJ: Prentice Hall.

Moor, J. 1985. "What is computer ethics?" *Metaphilosophy* 16(4): pp. 266–75.

Prosser, B. T. and Ward, A. 2000. "Kierkegaard and the Internet: existential reflections on education and community." *Ethics and Information Technology* 2(3): pp. 167–80.

Reiman, J. H. 1995. "Driving to the panopticon: a philosophical exploration of the risks to privacy posed by the highway technology of the future." *Computer and High Technology Law Journal* 11: pp. 27–44.

van den Hoven, J. 1999. "Privacy and the varieties of informational wrongdoing." *Australian Journal of Professional and Applied Ethics* 1(1): pp. 30–43.

24

Is Google Making Us Stupid? What the Internet Is Doing to Our Brains

NICHOLAS CARR

Marshall McLuhan's pioneering study, Understanding Media: The Extensions of Man, *was one of the most talked-about books of the 1960s. McLuhan proposed that it was the media themselves, rather than their content, that shaped human consciousness and, by extension, human society. McLuhan was writing about television, radio, film, newspapers, and other media of that era. The Internet was still years away.*

Today the Internet is arguably the dominant medium and its influence on us and our society is even more profound than the media of McLuhan's era. In the following essay, which appeared first in The Atlantic, *Nicholas Carr explores the nature of that influence. The Net, he claims, has changed the way we relate to and absorb information, the way we think. The price we pay for having instant access to the rich store of information available today is a loss in our ability to concentrate and focus. Will we be better off as a result of having the world of information literally at our fingertips? Carr is not sure. This essay does not answer the question that its title asks metaphorically. But it gives us pause and, perhaps, a chance to stop and think about where this uniquely influential technology is leading us.*

Nicholas Carr has written for the New York Times, *the* Wall Street Journal, Wired, *the* Financial Times *and other publications. He writes the popular blog* Rough Type. *Carr has a B.A. from Dartmouth College and an M.A. in English and American Literature and Language from Harvard. He expands on the ideas discussed in this essay in his 2010 book,* The Shallows: What the Internet Is Doing to Our Brains.

Nicholas Carr, "Is Google Making Us Stupid?" *The Atlantic* (July/August 2008). Reprinted by permission of the author.

"Dave, stop. Stop, will you? Stop, Dave. Will you stop, Dave?" So the supercomputer HAL pleads with the implacable astronaut Dave Bowman in a famous and weirdly poignant scene toward the end of Stanley Kubrick's *2001: A Space Odyssey*. Bowman, having nearly been sent to a deep-space death by the malfunctioning machine, is calmly, coldly disconnecting the memory circuits that control its artificial "brain." "Dave, my mind is going," HAL says, forlornly. "I can feel it. I can feel it."

I can feel it, too. Over the past few years I've had an uncomfortable sense that someone, or something, has been tinkering with my brain, remapping the neural circuitry, reprogramming the memory. My mind isn't going — so far as I can tell — but it's changing. I'm not thinking the way I used to think. I can feel it most strongly when I'm reading. Immersing myself in a book or a lengthy article used to be easy. My mind would get caught up in the narrative or the turns of the argument, and I'd spend hours strolling through long stretches of prose. That's rarely the case anymore. Now my concentration often starts to drift after two or three pages. I get fidgety, lose the thread, begin looking for something else to do. I feel as if I'm always dragging my wayward brain back to the text. The deep reading that used to come naturally has become a struggle.

I think I know what's going on. For more than a decade now, I've been spending a lot of time online, searching and surfing and sometimes adding to the great databases of the Internet. The Web has been a godsend to me as a writer. Research that once required days in the stacks or periodical rooms of libraries can now be done in minutes. A few Google searches, some quick clicks on hyperlinks, and I've got the telltale fact or pithy quote I was after. Even when I'm not working, I'm as likely as not to be foraging in the Web's info-thickets, reading and writing e-mails, scanning headlines and blog posts, watching videos and listening to podcasts, or just tripping from link to link to link. (Unlike footnotes, to which they're sometimes likened, hyperlinks don't merely point to related works; they propel you toward them.)

For me, as for others, the Net is becoming a universal medium, the conduit for most of the information that flows through my eyes and ears and into my mind. The advantages of having immediate access to such an incredibly rich store of information are many, and they've been widely described and duly applauded. "The perfect recall of silicon memory," *Wired*'s Clive Thompson has written, "can be an enormous boon to thinking." But that boon comes at a price. As the media theorist Marshall McLuhan pointed out in the 1960s, media are not just passive channels of information. They supply the stuff of thought, but they also shape the process of thought. And what the Net seems to be doing is chipping away my capacity for concentration and contemplation. My mind now expects to take in information the way the Net distributes it: in a swiftly moving stream of particles. Once I was a scuba diver in the sea of words. Now I zip along the surface like a guy on a Jet Ski.

I'm not the only one. When I mention my troubles with reading to friends and acquaintances — literary types, most of them — many say they're having similar experiences. The more they use the Web, the more they have to fight to stay focused on long pieces of writing. Some of the bloggers I follow have also begun mentioning the phenomenon. Scott Karp, who writes a blog about online media, recently confessed that he has stopped reading books altogether. "I was a lit major in college, and used to be [a] voracious book reader," he wrote. "What happened?" He speculates on the answer: "What if I do all my reading on the web not so much because the way I read has changed, i.e., I'm just seeking convenience, but because the way I THINK has changed?"

Bruce Friedman, who blogs regularly about the use of computers in medicine, also has described how the Internet has altered his mental habits. "I now have almost totally lost the ability to read and absorb a longish article on the web or in print," he wrote earlier this year. A pathologist who has long been on the faculty of the University of Michigan Medical School, Friedman elaborated on his comment in a telephone conversation with me. His thinking, he said, has taken on a "staccato" quality, reflecting the way he quickly scans short passages of text from many sources online. "I can't read *War and Peace* anymore," he admitted. "I've lost the ability to do that. Even a blog post of more than three or four paragraphs is too much to absorb. I skim it."

Anecdotes alone don't prove much. And we still await the long-term neurological and psychological experiments that will provide a definitive picture of how Internet use affects cognition. But a recently published study of online research habits , conducted by scholars from University College London, suggests that we may well be in the midst of a sea change in the way we read and think. As part of the five-year research program, the scholars examined computer logs documenting the behavior of visitors to two popular research sites, one operated by the British Library and one by a U.K. educational consortium, that provide access to journal articles, e-books, and other sources of written information. They found that people using the sites exhibited "a form of skimming activity," hopping from one source to another and rarely returning to any source they'd already visited. They typically read no more than one or two pages of an article or book before they would "bounce" out to another site. Sometimes they'd save a long article, but there's no evidence that they ever went back and actually read it. The authors of the study report:

It is clear that users are not reading online in the traditional sense; indeed there are signs that new forms of "reading" are emerging as users "power browse" horizontally through titles, contents pages and abstracts going for quick wins. It almost seems that they go online to avoid reading in the traditional sense.

Thanks to the ubiquity of text on the Internet, not to mention the popularity of text-messaging on cell phones, we may well be reading more today than we did in the 1970s or 1980s, when television was our medium of choice. But it's a different kind of reading, and behind it lies a different kind of thinking — perhaps even a new sense of the self. "We are not only *what* we read," says Maryanne Wolf, a developmental psychologist at Tufts University and the author of *Proust and the Squid: The Story and Science of the Reading Brain.* "We are *how* we read." Wolf worries that the style of reading promoted by the Net, a style that puts "efficiency" and "immediacy" above all else, may be weakening our capacity for the kind of deep reading that emerged when an earlier technology, the printing press, made long and complex works of prose commonplace. When we read online, she says, we tend to become "mere decoders of information." Our ability to interpret text, to make the rich mental connections that form when we read deeply and without distraction, remains largely disengaged.

Reading, explains Wolf, is not an instinctive skill for human beings. It's not etched into our genes the way speech is. We have to teach our minds how to translate the symbolic characters we see into the language we understand. And the media or other technologies we use in learning and practicing the craft of reading play an important part in shaping the neural circuits inside our brains. Experiments demonstrate that readers of ideograms, such as the Chinese, develop a mental circuitry for reading that is very different from the circuitry found in those of us whose written language employs an alphabet. The variations extend across many regions of the brain, including those that govern such essential cognitive functions as memory and the interpretation of visual and auditory stimuli. We can expect as well that the circuits woven by our use of the Net will be different from those woven by our reading of books and other printed works.

Sometime in 1882, Friedrich Nietzsche bought a typewriter — a Malling-Hansen Writing Ball, to be precise. His vision was failing, and keeping his eyes focused on a page had become exhausting and painful, often bringing on crushing headaches. He had been forced to curtail his writing, and he feared that he would soon have to give it up. The typewriter rescued him, at least for a time. Once he had mastered touch-typing, he was able to write with his eyes closed, using only the tips of his fingers. Words could once again flow from his mind to the page.

But the machine had a subtler effect on his work. One of Nietzsche's friends, a composer, noticed a change in the style of his writing. His already terse prose had become even tighter, more telegraphic. "Perhaps you will through this instrument even take to a new idiom," the friend wrote in a letter, noting that, in his own work, his "'thoughts' in music and language often depend on the quality of pen and paper."

"You are right," Nietzsche replied, "our writing equipment takes part in the forming of our thoughts." Under the sway of the machine, writes the German media scholar Friedrich A. Kittler, Nietzsche's prose "changed from arguments to aphorisms, from thoughts to puns, from rhetoric to telegram style."

The human brain is almost infinitely malleable. People used to think that our mental meshwork, the dense connections formed among the 100 billion or so neurons inside our skulls, was largely fixed by the time we reached adulthood. But brain researchers have discovered that that's not the case. James Olds, a professor of neuroscience who directs the Krasnow Institute for Advanced Study at George Mason University, says that even the adult mind "is very plastic." Nerve cells routinely break old connections and form new ones. "The brain," according to Olds, "has the ability to reprogram itself on the fly, altering the way it functions."

As we use what the sociologist Daniel Bell has called our "intellectual technologies" — the tools that extend our mental rather than our physical capacities — we inevitably begin to take on the qualities of those technologies. The mechanical clock, which came into common use in the 14th century, provides a compelling example. In *Technics and Civilization*, the historian and cultural critic Lewis Mumford described how the clock "disassociated time from human events and helped create the belief in an independent world of mathematically measurable sequences." The "abstract framework of divided time" became "the point of reference for both action and thought."

The clock's methodical ticking helped bring into being the scientific mind and the scientific man. But it also took something away. As the late MIT computer scientist Joseph Weizenbaum observed in his 1976 book, *Computer Power and Human Reason: From Judgment to Calculation*, the conception of the world that emerged from the widespread use of timekeeping instruments "remains an impoverished version of the older one, for it rests on a rejection of those direct experiences that formed the basis for, and indeed constituted, the old reality." In deciding when to eat, to work, to sleep, to rise, we stopped listening to our senses and started obeying the clock.

The process of adapting to new intellectual technologies is reflected in the changing metaphors we use to explain ourselves to ourselves. When the mechanical clock arrived, people began thinking of their brains as operating "like clockwork." Today, in the age of software, we have come to think of them as operating "like computers." But the changes, neuroscience tells us, go much deeper than metaphor. Thanks to our brain's plasticity, the adaptation occurs also at a biological level.

The Internet promises to have particularly far-reaching effects on cognition. In a paper published in 1936, the British mathematician Alan Turing proved that a digital computer, which at the time existed only as a theoretical machine, could be programmed to perform the function of any other information-processing device. And that's what we're seeing today. The Internet, an immeasurably powerful computing system, is subsuming most of our other intellectual technologies. It's becoming our map and our clock, our printing press and our typewriter, our calculator and our telephone, and our radio and TV.

When the Net absorbs a medium, that medium is re-created in the Net's image. It injects the medium's content with hyperlinks, blinking ads, and other digital gewgaws, and it surrounds the content with the content of all the other media it has absorbed. A new e-mail message, for instance, may announce its arrival as we're glancing over the latest headlines at a newspaper's site. The result is to scatter our attention and diffuse our concentration.

The Net's influence doesn't end at the edges of a computer screen, either. As people's minds become attuned to the crazy quilt of Internet media, traditional media have to adapt to the audience's new expectations. Television programs add text crawls and pop-up ads, and magazines and newspapers shorten their articles, introduce capsule summaries, and crowd their pages with easy-to-browse info-snippets. When, in March of this year, the *New York Times* decided to devote the second and third pages of every edition to article abstracts, its design director, Tom Bodkin, explained that the "shortcuts" would give harried readers a quick "taste" of the day's news, sparing them the "less efficient" method of actually turning the pages and reading the articles. Old media have little choice but to play by the new-media rules.

Never has a communications system played so many roles in our lives — or exerted such broad influence over our thoughts — as the Internet does today. Yet, for all that's been written about the Net, there's been little consideration of how, exactly, it's reprogramming us. The Net's intellectual ethic remains obscure.

About the same time that Nietzsche started using his typewriter, an earnest young man named Frederick Winslow Taylor carried a stopwatch into the Midvale Steel plant in Philadelphia and began a historic series of experiments aimed at improving the efficiency of the plant's machinists. With the approval of Midvale's owners, he recruited a group of factory hands, set them to work on various metal-working machines, and recorded and timed their every movement as well as the operations of the machines. By breaking down every job into a sequence of small, discrete steps and then testing different ways of performing each one, Taylor created a set of precise instructions — an "algorithm," we might say today — for how each worker should work. Midvale's employees grumbled about the strict new regime, claiming that it turned them into little more than automatons, but the factory's productivity soared.

More than a hundred years after the invention of the steam engine, the Industrial Revolution had at last found its philosophy and its philosopher. Taylor's tight industrial choreography — his "system," as he liked to call it — was embraced by manufacturers throughout the country and, in time, around the world. Seeking maximum speed, maximum efficiency, and maximum output, factory owners used time-and-motion studies to organize their work and configure the jobs of their workers. The goal, as Taylor defined it in his celebrated 1911 treatise, *The Principles of Scientific Management*, was to identify and adopt, for every job, the "one best method" of work and thereby to effect "the gradual substitution of science for rule of thumb throughout the mechanic arts." Once his system was applied to all acts of manual labor, Taylor assured his followers, it would bring about a restructuring not only of industry but of society, creating a utopia of perfect efficiency. "In the past the man has been first," he declared; "in the future the system must be first."

Taylor's system is still very much with us; it remains the ethic of industrial manufacturing. And now, thanks to the growing power that computer engineers and software coders wield over our intellectual lives, Taylor's ethic is beginning to govern the realm of the mind as well. The Internet is a machine designed for the efficient and automated collection, transmission, and manipulation of information, and its legions of programmers are intent on finding the "one best method" — the perfect algorithm — to carry out every mental movement of what we've come to describe as "knowledge work."

Google's headquarters, in Mountain View, California — the Googleplex — is the Internet's high church, and the religion practiced inside its walls is Taylorism. Google, says its chief executive, Eric Schmidt, is "a company that's founded around the science of measurement," and it is striving to "systematize everything" it does. Drawing on the terabytes of behavioral data it collects through its search engine and other sites, it carries out thousands of experiments a day, according to the *Harvard Business Review*, and it uses the results to refine the algorithms that increasingly control how people find information and extract meaning from it. What Taylor did for the work of the hand, Google is doing for the work of the mind.

The company has declared that its mission is "to organize the world's information and make it universally accessible and useful." It seeks to develop "the perfect search engine," which it defines as something that "understands exactly what you mean and gives you back exactly what you want." In Google's view, information is a kind of commodity, a utilitarian resource that can be mined and processed with industrial efficiency. The more pieces of information we can "access" and the faster we can extract their gist, the more productive we become as thinkers.

Where does it end? Sergey Brin and Larry Page, the gifted young men who founded Google while pursuing doctoral degrees in computer science at Stanford, speak frequently of their desire to turn their search engine into an artificial intelligence, a HAL-like machine that might be connected directly to our brains. "The ultimate search engine is something as smart as people — or smarter," Page said in a speech a few years back. "For us, working on search is a way to work on artificial intelligence." In a 2004 interview with *Newsweek*, Brin said, "Certainly if you had all the world's information directly attached to your brain, or an artificial brain that was smarter than your brain, you'd be better off." Last year, Page told a convention of scientists that Google is "really trying to build artificial intelligence and to do it on a large scale."

Such an ambition is a natural one, even an admirable one, for a pair of math whizzes with vast quantities of cash at their disposal and a small army of computer scientists in their employ. A fundamentally scientific enterprise, Google is motivated by a desire to use technology, in Eric Schmidt's words, "to solve problems that have never been solved before," and artificial intelligence is the hardest problem out there. Why wouldn't Brin and Page want to be the ones to crack it?

Still, their easy assumption that we'd all "be better off" if our brains were supplemented, or even replaced, by an artificial intelligence is unsettling. It suggests a belief that intelligence is the output of a mechanical process, a series of discrete steps that can be isolated, measured, and optimized. In Google's world, the world we enter when we go online, there's little place for the fuzziness of contemplation. Ambiguity is not an opening for insight but a bug to be fixed. The human brain is just an outdated computer that needs a faster processor and a bigger hard drive.

The idea that our minds should operate as high-speed data-processing machines is not only built into the workings of the Internet, it is the network's reigning business model as well. The faster we surf across the Web — the more links we click and pages we view — the more opportunities Google and other companies gain to collect information about us and to feed us advertisements. Most of the proprietors of the commercial Internet have a financial stake in collecting the crumbs of data we leave behind as we flit from link to link — the more crumbs, the better. The last thing these companies want is to encourage leisurely reading or slow, concentrated thought. It's in their economic interest to drive us to distraction.

Maybe I'm just a worrywart. Just as there's a tendency to glorify technological progress, there's a countertendency to expect the worst of every new tool or machine. In Plato's *Phaedrus*, Socrates bemoaned the development of writing.

He feared that, as people came to rely on the written word as a substitute for the knowledge they used to carry inside their heads, they would, in the words of one of the dialogue's characters, "cease to exercise their memory and become forgetful." And because they would be able to "receive a quantity of information without proper instruction," they would "be thought very knowledgeable when they are for the most part quite ignorant." They would be "filled with the conceit of wisdom instead of real wisdom." Socrates wasn't wrong — the new technology did often have the effects he feared — but he was shortsighted. He couldn't foresee the many ways that writing and reading would serve to spread information, spur fresh ideas, and expand human knowledge (if not wisdom).

The arrival of Gutenberg's printing press, in the 15th century, set off another round of teeth gnashing. The Italian humanist Hieronimo Squarciafico worried that the easy availability of books would lead to intellectual laziness, making men "less studious" and weakening their minds. Others argued that cheaply printed books and broadsheets would undermine religious authority, demean the work of scholars and scribes, and spread sedition and debauchery. As New York University professor Clay Shirky notes, "Most of the arguments made against the printing press were correct, even prescient." But, again, the doomsayers were unable to imagine the myriad blessings that the printed word would deliver.

So, yes, you should be skeptical of my skepticism. Perhaps those who dismiss critics of the Internet as Luddites or nostalgists will be proved correct, and from our hyperactive, data-stoked minds will spring a golden age of intellectual discovery and universal wisdom. Then again, the Net isn't the alphabet, and although it may replace the printing press, it produces something altogether different. The kind of deep reading that a sequence of printed pages promotes is valuable not just for the knowledge we acquire from the author's words but for the intellectual vibrations those words set off within our own minds. In the quiet spaces opened up by the sustained, undistracted reading of a book, or by any other act of contemplation, for that matter, we make our own associations, draw our own inferences and analogies, foster our own ideas. Deep reading, as Maryanne Wolf argues, is indistinguishable from deep thinking.

If we lose those quiet spaces, or fill them up with "content," we will sacrifice something important not only in our selves but in our culture. In a recent essay, the playwright Richard Foreman eloquently described what's at stake:

I come from a tradition of Western culture, in which the ideal (my ideal) was the complex, dense and "cathedral-like" structure of the highly educated and articulate personality — a man or woman who carried inside themselves a personally constructed and unique version of the entire heritage of the West. [But now] I see within us all (myself included) the replacement of complex inner density with a new kind of self — evolving under the pressure of information overload and the technology of the "instantly available."

As we are drained of our "inner repertory of dense cultural inheritance," Foreman concluded, we risk turning into "'pancake people' — spread wide and thin as we connect with that vast network of information accessed by the mere touch of a button."

I'm haunted by that scene in *2001*. What makes it so poignant, and so weird, is the computer's emotional response to the disassembly of its mind: its despair as one circuit after another goes dark, its childlike pleading with the astronaut — "I can feel it. I can feel it. I'm afraid" — and its final reversion to what can only be called a state of innocence. HAL's outpouring of feeling contrasts with the emotionlessness that characterizes the human figures in the film, who go about their business with an almost robotic efficiency. Their thoughts and actions feel scripted, as if they're following the steps of an algorithm. In the world of *2001*, people have become so machinelike that the most human character turns out to be a machine. That's the essence of Kubrick's dark prophecy: as we come to rely on computers to mediate our understanding of the world, it is our own intelligence that flattens into artificial intelligence.

25

Net Neutrality 101

SAVE THE INTERNET

Savetheinternet.com is an activism and lobbying campaign that describes itself as "a coalition of two million everyday people who have banded together with thousands of nonprofit organizations, businesses and bloggers to protect Internet freedom. http://savetheinternet.com/faq" It is coordinated by a nonprofit group called "Free Press" devoted to reforming the media. Among those listed as members of the coalition are activist Professor Lawrence Lessig, Craig Newmark (founder of craigslist.org), and the American Civil Liberties Union. This short article, taken from Save the Internet's web site, presents the organization's case for net neutrality, the principle that Internet service providers may not discriminate among different forms of content and applications by charging them different rates or by prioritizing their transmission based on their political or economic substance, or the producers' willingness or ability to pay for preferential treatment. More information can be found on the coalition's web site. For a two-minute animated cartoon version of this article see http://www.youtube.com/watch?v=L11kLmWha6o.

When we log onto the Internet, we take lots of things for granted. We assume that we'll be able to access whatever Web site we want, whenever we want to go there. We assume that we can use any feature we like — watching online video, listening to podcasts, searching, e-mailing and instant messaging — anytime we choose. We assume that we can attach devices like wireless routers, game controllers or extra hard drives to make our online experience better.

What makes all these assumptions possible is "Network Neutrality," the guiding principle that preserves the free and open Internet. Net Neutrality means that Internet service providers may not discriminate between different kinds of content and applications online. It guarantees a level playing field for all Web sites and Internet technologies. But all that could change.

Save the Internet, "Net Neutrality 101," http://www.savetheinternet.com/net-neutrality-101. Reprinted by permission.

The biggest cable and telephone companies would like to charge money for smooth access to Web sites, speed to run applications, and permission to plug in devices. These network giants believe they should be able to charge Web site operators, application providers and device manufacturers for the right to use the network. Those who don't make a deal and pay up will experience discrimination: Their sites won't load as quickly, and their applications and devices won't work as well. Without legal protection, consumers could find that a network operator has blocked the Web site of a competitor, or slowed it down so much that it's unusable.

The network owners say they want a "tiered" Internet. If you pay to get in the top tier, your site and your service will run fast. If you don't, you'll be in the slow lane.

What's the Problem Here?

Discrimination: The Internet was designed as an open medium. The fundamental idea since the Internet's inception has been that every Web site, every feature and every service should be treated without discrimination. That's how bloggers can compete with CNN or *USA Today* for readers. That's how up-and-coming musicians can build underground audiences before they get their first top-40 single. That's why when you use a search engine, you see a list of the sites that are the closest match to your request — not those that paid the most to reach you. Discrimination endangers our basic Internet freedoms.

Double-dipping: Traditionally, network owners have built a business model by charging consumers for Internet access. Now they want to charge you for access to the network, and then charge you again for the things you do while you're online. They may not charge you directly via pay-per-view Web sites. But they will charge all the service providers you use. These providers will then pass those costs along to you in the form of price hikes or new charges to view content.

Stifling innovation: Net Neutrality ensures that innovators can start small and dream big about being the next eBay or Google without facing insurmountable hurdles. Unless we preserve Net Neutrality, startups and entrepreneurs will be muscled out of the marketplace by big corporations that pay for a top spot on the Web. On a tiered Internet controlled by the phone and cable companies, only their own content and services — or those offered by corporate partners that pony up enough "protection money" — will enjoy life in the fast lane.

The End of the Internet?

Make no mistake: The free-flowing Internet as we know it could very well become history. What does that mean? It means we could be headed toward a pay-per-view Internet where Web sites have fees. It means we may have to pay a network tax to run voice-over-the-Internet phones, use an advanced search engine, or chat via Instant Messenger. The next generation of inventions will be shut out of the top-tier service level. Meanwhile, the network owners will rake in even greater profits.

26

Managing Broadband Networks

GEORGE OU

A somewhat more dispassionate and technically detailed look at the issue of net neutrality is contained in a report titled "Managing Broadband Networks: A Policymaker's Guide," of which the following article is the executive summary. The report was prepared under the auspices of the Information Technology and Innovation Foundation (ITIF), a non-partisan Washington-based think tank founded in 2006 and devoted to public policy issues related to innovation, productivity, and the digital economy. The report contends that the fears of those who advocate net neutrality result from a "lack of understanding of the history of the Internet, the economics of the ISP industry, and the science of network engineering." Aimed at helping policymakers understand these issues and develop a more balanced approach to network management, the article describes the basic elements of broadband networks and some of the misconceptions about their operations. It concludes with a number of recommendations for policymakers, essentially suggesting that legislating net neutrality is undesirable and likely to be counterproductive.

The author of the report, George Ou, is a senior analyst at ITIF, working out of Silicon Valley. He has served as Technical Director and Editor at Large for TechRepublic and ZDNet. A technical journalist with a background in information technology, Ou is the founder of the web site, ForMortals.com, whose banner reads, "Technology for Mortals: Because technology isn't just for geeks."

The Internet has changed the face of communications, commerce, and indeed the world. And over time the Internet itself has changed too. Until recently, most Americans at home accessed the Internet using telephone dial-up connections

George Ou, *Managing Broadband Networks: A Policymaker's Guide* (Washington, DC: The Information Technology and Innovation Foundation), executive summary, pp. 1–5. Reprinted by permission.

rather than today's faster broadband connections. With slower connections, home users limited themselves to a few basic online activities, such as email and web browsing, which perform passably well even on a slow network. In this environment, the need for Internet service providers (ISPs) to manage their networks to ensure the best possible experience for their customers was limited.

Today most Americans connect to the Internet over broadband connections that are in some cases 400 times faster than the dial-up connections of the late 1990s. But it is precisely because of these new bigger "pipes" that ISPs are finding that they need to more actively manage their networks. Broadband networks have enabled the rise of new applications, including those that need to be managed if they are to work effectively (e.g., voice over Internet Protocol, online gaming, video conferencing, and Internet Protocol–based TV) and those that can cause other applications to fail on an unmanaged network (e.g., many peer-to-peer (P2P) applications).

With this exciting transformation of the Internet into the universal communication platform of the future, network engineers face an array of daunting challenges. Specifically, to provide customers a good Internet service and operate their networks efficiently, ISPs must be able to do two very important things: 1) allocate limited bandwidth fairly among users; and, 2) apply network management tools to shape traffic from multiple applications. ISPs can and should do these things in a fair and nondiscriminatory manner. Thus, they should strive to ensure that customers who pay for the same tier of service get roughly the same bandwidth at a given level of usage, eliminate harmful variations of delay (i.e., jitter), make consumers' broadband service more conducive to using multiple applications simultaneously, while at the same time treating other applications and content fairly.

Unfortunately, network management solutions have come under heavy criticism from many advocates of "net neutrality." The issue of network management came to the fore when Comcast limited the ability of peer-to-peer (P2P) users to operate in upload-only mode whenever P2P traffic exceeded 50 percent of total upstream capacity of the entire neighborhood. More generally, the issue of network management refers to whether and to what extent ISPs can manage their networks to ensure quality of service for the majority of their customers.

Strong advocates of net neutrality argue that ISPs should have little flexibility to manage their networks and that the solution to any kinds of network congestion or other network performance challenges can and should be solved by simply adding more network capacity — primarily in the form of "bigger pipes." Indeed, they fear that using efficient network management techniques may enable network operators to abuse their power, thereby stifling free speech and civic expression and erecting unfair barriers to other companies seeking to distribute digital content or applications. Moreover, some proponents of net neutrality fear that any improvement in the efficiency of the Internet will eliminate the motivation of ISPs to expand network capacity by "building bigger pipes." As we transition to a ubiquitous digital world, bigger pipes are necessary — and public policy should support their deployment — but they are not a substitute for network management. We need to not just expand network capacity, but also build networks that are better and more intelligently managed.

Many if not most of the fears of the proponents of net neutrality stem from a lack of understanding of the history of the Internet, the economics of the ISP industry, and the science of network engineering. This guide is intended to help policymakers better understand how broadband networks and the applications that run on them work, and calls for a balanced approach to the regulation of broadband network management. A balanced approach should be based on reality: both the economic realities of building broadband networks and the scientific realities of network engineering. In addition, it should provide ISPs the flexibility they need to manage complex networks while also ensuring oversight to ensure that network management practices are not being applied in anti-competitive ways.

Effective policy in this area must be based on facts. Unfortunately much of the debate over broadband network management to date has been informed more by rhetoric and emotion than by an actual examination of how advanced networks and the applications that run on them work. By providing policymakers with this guide, ITIF hopes to better inform this debate.

KEY FINDINGS AND CONCLUSIONS

- **Packet–switched networks, like the Internet, have advantages, but also disadvantages.** Packet-switched networks like the Internet were invented for their flexibility and efficiency, characteristics which are optimum for data applications. But they have two key deficiencies in the absence of network management: 1) inability to equitably allocate bandwidth; and 2) high jitter, which are essentially micro-congestion storms that last tens or hundreds of milliseconds, and which can disrupt real-time applications such as VoIP, online gaming, video conferencing, and IPTV.

- **The Internet and its predecessor ARPANET became the first adopter of packet-switching networks because it was more efficient and flexible than the circuit-switching telephone network.** Unlike telephone networks which only connected a small percentage of users at any given time, packet-switched networks allow everyone to be on the network at the same time and dynamically divide up the resources among the active users. If few users are on the network, then those users get a lot of resources allocated to them. If many users are on the network, then each user gets fewer resources but no user is locked out. This dynamic expansion and contraction of bandwidth makes packet switching networks very efficient, but the allocation of bandwidth can become disproportionate whenever applications like P2P resist reallocations of bandwidth. Network management can balance the allocation of bandwidth such that each customer in the same service tier gets an equitable share of the total bandwidth.

- **Network management techniques, such as quality of service (QoS) mechanisms, make a packet-switched network more conducive to simultaneous application usage.** Network management techniques such as QoS essentially carve out virtual circuits within a packet-switched network by providing the necessary resources and performance characteristics that real-time applications need. This gives a packet-switched network the real-time characteristics of a circuit-switched network while maintaining the robustness and flexibility of a packet-switched network.

- **Even since its early days, the Internet has been a managed network.** The Internet has had basic network management mechanisms built into it since its inception, although these mechanisms have undergone and continue to undergo much refinement as usage patterns on the Internet change. Since 1987, for example, computers have used a revised version of the transmission control protocol (TCP) that includes a network congestion control mechanism developed by computer scientist Van Jacobson to slow down endpoints and prevent network meltdown.

- **Peer-to-peer (P2P) applications pose special challenges to broadband networks.** P2P users on unmanaged networks can use a disproportionately high amount of bandwidth and cause network congestion. In Japan, for example, P2P users represent 10 percent of the total broadband population but account for 65 to 90 percent of traffic on the network. By running multiple TCP flows (i.e., connections) per file transfer, P2P applications can effectively circumvent the Jacobson algorithm intended to allocate bandwidth. As a result, P2P applications can maximize the use of available bandwidth, sometimes at the expense of other applications, such as VoIP and video conferencing, which require low latency and jitter.

- **An ISP that dynamically allocates its network capacity can always offer its customers far more unguaranteed bandwidth than its guaranteed minimum level of service.** Because broadband networks are shared, it is more efficient to give consumers access to speeds that can increase when there is less congestion. Since only 1 to 10 percent of network users are active at any point in time, packet switching networks can dynamically allocate 10 to 100 times more bandwidth to each active user. If a network can be built to guarantee 1 megabit per second (Mbps) of performance for each user, for example, it can just as easily offer the customer 1 Mbps of guaranteed performance and up to 20 Mbps of unguaranteed performance. But building a network that provided a guaranteed performance of 20 Mbps, for example, would be much more expensive and require much higher monthly costs for the consumer.

- **One goal of network management is to fairly allocate bandwidth between paying customers.** Fairness dictates that customers who are paying for the same tier of broadband service from a broadband provider should get roughly the same bandwidth at a given level of usage. Fair bandwidth allocation shouldn't just measure instantaneous bandwidth usage, duration should also be factored in to the equitable distribution of bandwidth. If one application or one customer uses the network hundreds or thousands of times more frequently than another application or customer, it isn't unreasonable to let the short duration application or customer get a short boost in bandwidth over the long duration application or customer.

- **To achieve fair bandwidth allocations, protocol-agnostic schemes are the best solution.** ISPs can use protocol-agnostic network management systems (systems that measure the aggregate bandwidth consumption of each customer and not what protocols they are using) to ensure that bandwidth is shared fairly between customers. Early network management systems that used less accurate protocol-specific schemes to allocate bandwidth between customers worked well most of the time but experienced occasional problems. These protocol agnostic solutions are being evaluated by broadband providers. A key downside of protocol-agnostic network management systems is that they are often too expensive for smaller ISPs to deploy.

- **Another goal of network management is to better share network resources between many different applications.** Different types of applications have different network requirements. Real-time applications (e.g., VoIP) are most sensitive to network jitter. Video streaming applications (e.g., YouTube) have moderate fixed bandwidth requirements and moderate jitter tolerance. Interactive applications (e.g., web browsing) have brief bursts in bandwidth that could disrupt real-time or streaming applications. Background applications (e.g., P2P applications) are designed to be unattended with no one waiting for an instant response.

- **Packets should be ordered logically with priority given to real-time applications first, streaming applications second, interactive applications third, and background applications last.** In order for all applications efficiently and fairly share an Internet connection, those with higher duration and higher bandwidth consumption (e.g., P2P) are given lower priority than applications with lower duration and lower bandwidth consumption (e.g., VoIP applications). This does not mean P2P applications are being mistreated because they still receive the highest average bandwidth from the network.

- **To better enable multiple applications to share an Internet connection, protocol-specific schemes are necessary.** Application protocols that require low packet delay must be identified and must be protected against high variations in packet delay (e.g., jitter) and Quality of Service network management techniques are the mechanism that provides that protection.

- **Wireless networks require more management than wired networks.** Wireless networks require more network management than wired networks because they have less bandwidth available and it must be shared more frequently. Furthermore, multiple radio transmitters sharing the same wireless frequency in the same geographic location results in a high probability of radio interference which can bring networks to a halt. These unique challenges of wireless networks require the most elaborate network management system of all in the form of a centralized scheduler which coordinates the transmission slots for network users as tightly and efficiently as possible without collision.

- **Wireless network management enables innovation.** Intelligent wireless networks will ultimately spur more adoption and usage of wireless broadband, which facilitates more mobile e-commerce and enables more innovation and generation of wealth.

RESPONDING TO COMMON MISPERCEPTIONS
ABOUT NETWORK MANAGEMENT

- **Network management techniques, such as QoS, do not put low priority applications on a "dirt road."** QoS gives higher prioritization to applications that have lower bandwidth, lower duration, and higher sensitivity to packet delay. In spite of this, applications that are given the least priority still end up receiving the highest average bandwidth from the network. But with this logical prioritization scheme in place, low priority applications like P2P applications interfere less with other applications sharing the same network. This in turn allows P2P applications to operate freely without any artificial constraints on when to use them or how much bandwidth to allocate to them which are commonly used on unmanaged networks.

- **Building more bandwidth, while desirable, does not eliminate the need for network management.** Advancing the digital economy requires higher speed broadband. However, higher speed networks will not preclude the need for network management. First, as network capacity grows, network demand also grows, as new kinds of applications emerge to take advantage of the capacity. Second, networks with plenty of spare unused capacity on average can still suffer instantaneous shortages at peak times of the day. Third, networks operating at low utilization levels can still suffer packet delay in the form of jitter.

- **Metered pricing and usage caps alone will not solve the problem of network congestion.** Metered pricing and bandwidth usage caps are legitimate tools for ensuring the efficient use of networks, but they cannot control instantaneous bursts in demand nor can they deal with the problem of jitter and the inability of dumb networks to gracefully support multiple applications. Only advanced network management techniques like quality of service can deal with these challenges.

POLICY IMPLICATIONS

- **Legislation and regulations should not limit efforts by ISPs to fairly use network management to overcome technical challenges and maintain a high quality Internet service for their customers.** As described in this report, ISPs face many technical challenges to manage network congestion and support various online applications. Network management is a necessary and important component of broadband networks, and policymakers should support its use. However, this freedom to manage the network is not a license for ISPs to behave in anti-competitive ways such as blocking legitimate websites or unreasonably degrading services that users have paid to access. Neither should ISPs unreasonably discriminate against any content or service on the open Internet.

- **Policymakers should be cognizant of the effects of certain proposed legislation on the use of network management.** Some proposed net neutrality bills ban differentiated pricing for enhanced QoS and would have undesirable and unintended consequences. One intent of these bills is to facilitate more open Internet bandwidth for broadband consumers, but the result may be just the opposite. Not allowing network operators to prioritize their own IPTV content above other Internet content, for example, will simply push those cable TV-like services onto private circuits that share the same physical network. That would result in less Internet bandwidth being available on a permanent basis for broadband consumers even when they are not using their IPTV service.

- **The federal government has a key role to ensure openness and fair play on the Internet.** However, it should do this with sensible rules. Policies should strive to prevent any potential abuse without eliminating the ability of ISPs to manage their networks in ways that produce the best possible user experience for the largest number of users, and without eliminating incentives to build the next generation broadband network. Toward that end the FCC should oversee broadband providers and ensure that their ISP network management practices are open, transparent and not harmful to competition. And the ISP industry should continue its efforts to develop and abide by industry codes of good conduct regarding network management that include, but are not limited to, fuller and more transparent disclosure to consumers of network management practices.

CONCLUSION

The Internet in all its glory has never had a perfect architecture. There have always been conflicts between users and applications competing for scarce network resources. Network management is necessary to fairly allocate bandwidth between customers and seamlessly support multiple applications on shared network connections.

The Internet and broadband technology are continuing to evolve at a fairly rapid rate, and neither shows any signs of maturing. Network engineers continue to find new solutions to improve the Internet experience for all users. This situation makes it very difficult, if not impossible, to predict where the market and technology will evolve. The Internet is so valuable precisely because it is open to anyone, for any use, and for any business model, but participation has always required varying levels of payment for varying levels of service between willing parties. Given this environment, it is best for policymakers not to issue blanket prohibitions on network management technology and existing business models. Instead, policies should focus on creating better transparency for all Internet companies along with FCC oversight to ensure that broadband providers are managing networks in ways that are not unfair or anticompetitive.

PART VII

Governance and Globalization

U ltimately, the future of technology and society will be shaped to a significant extent by the actions of government. Looking back on the technologies discussed in the first six parts of this book, it is clear that the shape of
virtually all of them has been influenced by government funding, government
regulation, or some other type of government activity or policy. Likewise,
these technologies have contributed to the shape of society in the past, are helping to shape it today, and will do so in the future. One of the most significant
ways in which technology is shaping society is through globalization. The next-
to-last chapter in this section of *Technology and the Future* addresses the government dimension of the technology-society relationship, while the final chapter
provides a vivid close-up picture of one aspect of globalization.

Chapter 27 is a short piece that I wrote originally for an encyclopedia of
science, technology, and society. In it, I discuss several aspects of the relationship
between government and technology, including government support for the
development of technology through direct investment in research and development; indirect investment such as subsidies within the tax system; and other
means, such as creating an innovation-friendly economic and political environment, and forcing technological change by setting regulatory standards that cannot be met with existing technologies. Although my frame of reference is mainly
the United States, the chapter also devotes some attention to institutions and
situations in other countries.

The final chapter is an excerpt from Thomas L. Friedman's best-selling book,
The World is Flat. Friedman describes, in his typically readable terms, a visit to a call
center in Bangalore, India, in which hundreds of young Indians, trained to imitate
American accents, staff telephone lines on which they do everything from promoting credit cards to helping callers solve computer problems. The point of this

entertaining vignette is to illustrate the globalization of innovation and its impacts on the world economy. As Friedman points out, even as jobs such as those in the call center have been outsourced to India and other emerging economies, the income generated by those jobs has helped to increase demand for American goods and services in those countries.

27

Government and Technology

ALBERT H. TEICH

Governments worldwide are deeply involved with technology. In this chapter, which I prepared originally for an encyclopedia of science, technology, and society, I discuss briefly the role of governments as promoters, regulators, and users of technology. "Briefly" is a key word here because the encyclopedia, a nearly 700-page opus edited by Sal Restivo of Rensselaer Polytechnic Institute, includes nearly 150 entries covering an enormous range of topics from abortion to robots to the Tuskegee Project (an infamous study in which a U.S. government agency deceived a group of African-American men with syphilis into serving as an untreated control group for many years in order to test the effectiveness of penicillin). The breadth of the book's coverage placed severe limits on the length of individual entries.

Despite its brevity, this chapter, like the rest of Technology and the Future, *treats technology broadly, discussing topics ranging from regulation of pharmaceuticals to use of technical information by legislative bodies, to the role of the military in technology development. Also, like the book as a whole, the chapter raises more questions than it answers and will serve, I hope, to provoke deeper reflection and further study of the topics with which it deals.*

When this chapter appeared in the eleventh edition of Technology and the Future, *it was the first time since the book was originally published in 1972 that I had included a chapter of my own. I am currently (as of mid-2011), Senior Policy Advisor at the American Association for the Advancement of Science in Washington, DC, where I was for the previous 20 years Director of Science and Policy Programs. Additional information about my background can be found in the "About the Editor" page at the beginning of the book and online at* http://www.alteich.com/al.

Governments have been involved with technology throughout human history, at least since the days of the Pharaohs in ancient Egypt. Military technology was essential to the power of medieval governments, and modern governments employ technology to stimulate economic growth, improve their citizens' standards of living, and pursue missions in many other areas, including environment, public health, and defense. The involvement of governments with technology can be described under three broad headings: promotion or development of technology; regulation of technology; and use of technology and technical information in government policy making.

GOVERNMENT'S ROLE IN TECHNOLOGY DEVELOPMENT

Governments support the development of technology both directly and indirectly. Direct funding of research and development (R&D) provides government with a means of shaping technologies according to public policies. In fiscal year 2010 the U.S. federal government spent an estimated $148.5 billion, or about four percent of the overall federal budget, on R&D. [These figures have been updated from the original.— Ed.]

Some government-funded R&D provides the foundation for development of products intended to be manufactured and sold by industry, such as electric cars or improved airport screening devices. Other government investments help build the nation's long-range scientific and technological strength; examples are the National Nanotechnology Initiative in the United States and the Sixth Framework Programme of the European Union. Direct funding of R&D is a major function of government in virtually all industrialized countries and has grown sharply in the past half-century, in concert with the increasingly technological nature of society and the growing role of technology in the world economy.

In the United States, direct federal government support for development of commercial technologies is politically controversial. The history of federal efforts to promote industrial technology goes back at least to the 1920s, but virtually all such initiatives have become enmeshed in disputes between political leaders who advocate an activist role for government in the nation's economy and those who see government's role as more limited and subordinate to the market. During the past decade, one focus of controversy has been the Advanced Technology Program [now the Technology Innovation Program] of the Department of Commerce, a relatively small program that provides subsidies for firms to do R&D on technologies whose chances of succeeding are too small to attract private investors but whose potential payoffs are great. Republican presidents and congressional leaders have sought to kill the program at every opportunity, while Democrats have stood fast in its defense. Programs of this nature are more readily accepted in many other nations, whose governments are less concerned with issues of what is or is not appropriate for government. In France, for example, ANVAR (Agence Nationale de Valorisation de la Recherche, called the French

Agency for Innovation in English), promotes and finances innovation in French industry, particularly in small and medium-sized enterprises and facilitates the emergence of new products and processes.

Many state governments in the United States, eager to attract or retain high-paying jobs in technology-based industries, also subsidize commercial technological development. Michigan is using funds acquired from the settlement of a huge multistate lawsuit against the tobacco industry to leverage investment in biotechnology businesses in order to build a "life sciences corridor" in the southern part of the state. Pennsylvania's Ben Franklin Partnership has invested more than $300 million of state funds in technology development since its founding in 1982.

A large share of government investment in R&D in most countries is primarily intended to serve government's own needs, for example, strengthening military capabilities, building better roads and bridges, or providing a scientific basis for regulating food and drug safety or the environment. This kind of R&D can also help to strengthen technology-based industry. In some cases, the resulting technologies may be adapted for commercial uses or may be "dual-use," directly serving commercial as well as government users. In the United States, the Department of Defense (DOD) is an important source of such funding. Slightly more than half of all federal funding for R&D in the United States typically comes from the defense portion of the federal budget in any given year. Among the civilian technologies that originated or were supported in early stages by DOD R&D funds are the Internet, microelectronics and integrated circuits, optical fibers, and many aeronautical and space technologies. Other U.S. agencies that support technology development for government use are the National Aeronautics and Space Administration (NASA), the Department of Energy, and the Department of Homeland Security.

Governments also provide indirect support for technology development. Some of this support takes the form of subsidies to the private sector through tax codes. Most industrial nations encourage industrial firms to invest in R&D by allowing 100 percent of R&D expenses to be deducted from a firm's income tax. Australia, where industrial investment in R&D has long been regarded as insufficient for the nation's long-term economic growth, allows a 125 percent deduction. Some nations, including the United States, Canada, Japan and France, also allow firms that increase their R&D spending to take a certain percentage of the increase (20 percent in the case of the United States) as a tax credit. With this mechanism, governments can increase industrial investment in R&D while allowing individual firms to choose technologies and R&D projects according to their own needs and judgment.

Other indirect mechanisms that governments use to support technology development include regulation and creation of a suitable environment for technological innovation — for example, by providing protection for intellectual property. To force the development of technology, government may establish a future regulatory standard that it knows cannot be met with existing technology. Such a standard puts pressure on firms in the affected industry to conduct R&D and develop technology that can meet the standard. The best-known American example of technology forcing is the Clean Air Act Amendments of 1970, which required automakers to reduce the exhaust emissions of new vehicles by 90 percent in four to five years. This legislation, and the mandate three years later for eliminating leaded gasoline, led to the implementation of the catalytic converter — although this was not accomplished within the time frame specified in the law.

If they hope to profit from their innovations, firms and organizations that conduct R&D, as well as individual inventors, need to establish property rights in them. Governments provide the means for protecting such rights through patents and copyrights in order to create an environment that will encourage technological innovation. The U.S. Constitution provides the basis for patent protection, and the legal system allows innovators to defend their patents when others threaten to infringe on them. In recent years, developments in information technology as well as in the life sciences have posed new challenges to traditional concepts of intellectual property, raising issues such as whether life forms or DNA sequences can be patented, what kinds of rights apply to computer code, and whether it is possible or desirable to protect the rights of intellectual property owners in a world where those properties (such as music, movies, and books) can be readily duplicated by almost anyone with a computer and shared worldwide on the Internet.

Another important way in which governments are involved with technology development is through the establishment of standards. From keeping exact time to ensuring that one person's or company's inch, centimeter, or kilogram is exactly the same as another's, or that a bolt with a certain thread specification fits into a nut with that thread, or that a nation's television receivers are compatible with its broadcasters, standards are fundamental to technology, commerce, and trade. In the United States, the National Institute of Standards and Technology (NIST) is responsible for these functions. NIST laboratories develop new physical standards and measurement methods. It also provides basic reference standards and works with industry to calibrate measuring instruments to those standards and with international organizations to ensure compatibility with other nations' standards.

REGULATION OF TECHNOLOGY

As they develop and as they affect society, technologies raise issues that create demands for government regulation. These issues may involve human health and safety or the environment; allocation of technological resources, such as the electromagnetic spectrum; protection of consumers from fraudulent or defective products; social goals, such as bringing the benefits of technology to diverse populations or geographic regions; or political goals, such as preventing the acquisition of technologies by foreign enemies, economic rivals, or terrorists. At times, the issues may also involve ethics, as in the case of research involving human embryos and reproductive cloning.

Virtually all countries have government agencies that regulate technology. In the United States, several federal agencies are responsible for regulation to protect human health and safety, including the Food and Drug Administration, the

Occupational Safety and Health Administration, the Environmental Protection Agency, and the Nuclear Regulatory Commission. In Canada, the Health Products and Food Branch of Health Canada performs functions similar to the U.S. Food and Drug Administration. In Germany, the analogous agency is the Federal Institute for Drugs and Medical Devices.

Among the products that the U.S. Food and Drug Administration (FDA) regulates are vaccines and other biologics, such as blood and blood products; cosmetics; medical devices, such as pacemakers and contact lenses; foods, with regard to processing and contamination; and prescription, as well as over-the-counter, drugs. Before a prescription drug can be marketed in the United States, it must go through an elaborate approval process. Based on animal studies and human clinical trials, the FDA must determine (1) whether the drug is safe and effective in its proposed use(s), and whether its benefits outweigh its risks; (2) whether the drug's proposed labeling is appropriate, and what it should contain; and (3) whether the methods used in manufacturing and quality control are satisfactory. The process often takes years and costs millions of dollars. The considerations are similar in most other countries, although the judgments of risks and benefits may differ among them. Because the regulatory process often creates long delays between the discovery or invention of a new drug and its availability to patients, and because of the high costs involved, drug regulation is often the subject of controversy. Controversies also arise in regulation of the environmental effects of technologies or in regard to safety issues. The U.S. Environmental Protection Agency and its counterparts in other nations, such as Environment Canada and the Swedish Environmental Protection Agency (Naturvårdsverket), are charged with the enforcement of laws intended to prevent or remediate environmental pollution. Preventing pollution of rivers, lakes, and other bodies of water imposes costs on firms whose production processes create potential pollutants. The same is true of sources of air pollution, such as that produced by coal-burning power plants, oil refineries, and automobiles. Those who are asked to pay these costs quite naturally resist, generally arguing that the presumed benefits do not justify the costs. The disputes often focus on uncertainties in the data on which the regulations are based.

Probably the most significant controversy of this nature in the United States in the early twenty-first century relates to the problem of global climate change. A strong consensus has developed among scientists that the earth's surface temperature is rising; that it is rising at an accelerating rate; that the rise is being caused by human activities, especially the increase of atmospheric carbon dioxide due to the burning of fossil fuels; and that the increase is likely to cause serious problems in the next 50 to 100 years, including greater climate instability and a significant rise in sea level. Most of the nations in the world have agreed to take action to slow or halt the rise. This action will be very costly, but failure to act could be even more costly. The United States, which has the world's largest economy and is the [second] largest emitter of carbon dioxide and other greenhouse gases [China became number one in 2007 – Ed.], would bear the largest share of the costs. The federal government and much of the U.S. business community have resisted taking action, arguing that there are too many uncertainties — regarding how much the climate is changing, what the potential impacts are, and what may be causing the changes. The dilemma is a central one in the regulation of technology: How certain must one be in order to take a regulatory action, especially when that action is likely to be costly?

The controversy over genetically modified organisms (GMOs), especially in foods, is similar. Guided by the "precautionary principle," which holds that "when an activity threatens harm to human health or the environment, precautionary measures should be taken even if some cause-and-effect relationships are not fully established scientifically," most European nations assert that GMOs should not be allowed in foods. United States regulators, arguing that there is no persuasive scientific evidence that GMOs are harmful, and citing many benefits, have generally rejected the European position.

USE OF TECHNICAL INFORMATION IN GOVERNMENT DECISION MAKING

As the global change and GMO issues illustrate, technology is an increasingly important factor in the programs that governments undertake, in the problems that confront them, and in the policies that they develop in response to, or in anticipation of, these problems. These policies require specialized knowledge that governments must either maintain internally or obtain from outside sources. The government agencies that use technology or fund R&D have engineers and scientists on their staffs. Some, like NASA, have a substantial number; others have relatively few. Virtually all of these agencies, however, have technical advisory committees that supplement their in-house capabilities.

At the top levels, governments of most industrialized countries have bodies that provide science and technology advice to their leaders. Since World War II, the president of the United States has had a science and technology advisor, situated throughout most of the period in the Executive Office of the President. In the administration of President George W. Bush, the advisor became a special assistant to the president, serving as director of the White House Office of Science and Technology Policy and also as co-chair of an external advisory group known as the President's Council of Advisors on Science and Technology. The influence of the advisor and the advisory councils and committees has waxed and waned depending on the nature of the issues facing the president, the power structure within the White House, and the president's personality and degree of interest in scientific and technological matters.

Departments and ministries often have their own science and technology advisory committees as well. In the United States, the Department of Energy, the Environmental Protection Agency, the Department of Defense, and many other agencies have such committees. United States government agencies also obtain technical advice from the National Research Council (NRC), which is the operating arm of the National Academies of Science and Engineering and of the Institute of Medicine. With a staff of over 1,000, the NRC conducts hundreds of studies each year to provide government agencies with authoritative advice on topics ranging from super-computing to smallpox. Agencies also obtain information and advice through studies conducted by universities, nonprofit institutions (such as the RAND Corporation), and private firms under contracts and grants.

Although executive branch agencies and their counterparts have many resources for science and technology information and advice, the situation is different for legislative bodies. Members of parliament in most nations have very limited personal and committee staffs. With relatively few positions available, staff members must be generalists: those with technical expertise are rare, except on specialized committees. Supplementing these staffs are such bodies as the Library of the House of Commons in the United Kingdom. The Library produces research papers, a small fraction of which are devoted to science and technology. The United Kingdom, however, also has a small Parliamentary Office of Science and Technology (POST), which provides more specialized advice on technical topics. Since its establishment in 1989, POST has produced reports for Parliament on subjects ranging from broadband Internet access to stem cell research.

Things are different in the U.S. Congress. It is not uncommon for senators to have personal staffs ranging from 50 to 100. Representatives' staffs are smaller, but they are still considerably larger than their parliamentary counterparts in other nations. Senators and representatives who have committee assignments relating to technology or science, or who have major research facilities in their constituencies, can therefore afford to hire some staff with technical qualifications. In addition, science and engineering associations have since 1973 maintained fellowship programs that make Ph.D.-level scientists and engineers, selected through national competitions, available to members of Congress for one-year assignments. Other nations are beginning to initiate such programs as well. Switzerland has established one on a small scale, and the United Kingdom, Australia, Japan, and South Africa are all considering doing so.

The Office of Technology Assessment (OTA), created by the U.S. Congress in 1972, was the first governmental body devoted exclusively to conducting studies and providing advice to a legislature on the impacts of technology on society. The agency conducted hundreds of studies for Congress on subjects ranging from advanced networking technology to AIDS to the lumber industry. It was unique among agencies serving the U.S. Congress not just in the range of its work, but also in the depth of its technical expertise and in the long-term view it brought to its studies.

In 1995, in what was officially called an economy move, the U.S. Congress eliminated funding for OTA. Other nations (such as the United Kingdom), which had followed the U.S. example in establishing parliamentary offices of technology assessment, did not follow the U.S. lead in abolishing these offices. Today, at least ten European nations plus the European Parliament are served by technology assessment organizations. These bodies conduct policy studies of issues raised by scientific and technological developments, many of which seek to anticipate the future impacts of technologies under development or the impacts of current societal trends. Some conduct "participatory assessments," engaging members of the public in their analyses.

OUTLOOK

The vast amount of resources that governments, industrial firms, universities, and other organizations worldwide are investing in research and development and the growing demand for technological products and technological solutions to the problems of poverty, illness, environmental degradation, and global insecurity virtually ensure that the rate of technological change will only accelerate in the twenty-first century. The changes will continue to pose new challenges for government. Some of these challenges may be foreseen; most will not. When researchers for the U.S. Department of Defense developed a means of linking mainframe computers at a few select laboratories in the late 1960s, no one involved foresaw the immense changes their innovation, forerunner of the Internet, would engender in publishing, commerce, entertainment, and many other fields. And no one imagined that this innovation would provide a means for bored teenagers to wreak havoc on computers halfway around the world or that industry and government would need to spend millions of dollars protecting against such threats. The course that emerging technologies — nanotechnology, biotechnology, robotics, and more — will take in coming years is uncertain. What is certain, however, is that the future of government and the future of technology are inseparably linked.

BIBLIOGRAPHY

Branscomb, Lewis M., and James H. Keller, eds. *Investing in Innovation: Creating a Research and Innovation Policy That Works*. Cambridge, MA: MIT Press, 1998. An attempt to defuse the ideological arguments about government support of commercial technology.

Flamm, Kenneth. *Creating the Computer: Government, Industry, and High Technology*. Washington, DC: The Brookings Institution, 1988. Traces the roots of the various technologies that converged to make modern computers and information technology possible; documents the role of several governments, including the United States, the United Kingdom, Japan, and Germany in the development of these technologies.

Greenberg, Daniel S. *Science, Money, and Politics*. Chicago: University of Chicago Press, 2001. Although nominally about science, its interactions with government, and its ethical transgressions, this book is also relevant to government's technology policies.

Hart, David M. *Forged Consensus: Science, Technology, and Economic Policy in the United States, 1921–1953*. Princeton, NJ: Princeton University Press, 1998. Makes a strong case that the events and policy decisions of the period about which he writes continue to have a strong influence on contemporary science and technology policy.

Heimann, C. F. Larry. *Acceptable Risks: Politics, Policy, and Risky Technologies*. Ann Arbor, MI: University of Michigan Press, 1997. The politics and policy of dealing with high risk technologies and the disasters they sometimes cause, using examples from space flight and pharmaceuticals.

Kleinman, Daniel, ed. *Science, Technology, and Democracy*. Albany, NY: State University of New York Press, 2000. A collection of essays on citizen involvement in government policy making for science and technology.

Mani, Sunil. *Government, Innovation, and Technology Policy: An International Comparative Analysis*. Cheltenham, UK.: Edward Elgar, 2002. Analysis of the role of government in commercial technology development in eight countries.

Morgan, M. Granger, and Jon Peha, eds. *Science and Technology Advice for Congress*. Washington, DC: RFF Press, 2003. Papers from a conference on Congress's need for technical information and whether the Office of Technology Assessment should be resurrected to fill it.

National Research Council. *The Digital Dilemma: Intellectual Property in the Information Age*. Washington, DC: National Academies Press, 2000. An attempt to clarify the issues surrounding digitized intellectual property by a blue-ribbon committee convened by the U.S. National Academy of Sciences; includes policy and research recommendations.

Sarewitz, Daniel. *Frontiers of Illusion: Science, Technology, and the Politics of Progress*. Philadelphia: Temple University Press, 1996. A sharp critique of the myths that guide science and technology policy in the United States, by a former congressional staff member.

Stokes, Donald E. *Pasteur's Quadrant: Basic Science and Technological Innovation*. Washington, DC: Brookings Institution Press, 1997. A seminal work on the interaction of science with technology.

U.S. National Science Foundation, Division of Science Resources Statistics. *Science and Engineering Indicators — 2004*. Arlington, VA: National Science Foundation, 2004. Published every other year, this is the most comprehensive authoritative source of statistics on science and technology in the United States; the full text and tables are available online at http://www.nsf.gov/sbe/srs/seind/start.htm.

Vig, Norman J., and Herbert Paschen. *Parliaments and Technology: The Development of Technology Assessment in Europe*. Albany, NY: State University of New York Press, 1999. A unique attempt to compare technology assessment mechanisms in a number of different countries.

28

The World Is Flat

THOMAS L. FRIEDMAN

The concluding article in Technology and the Future *is largely an account of journalist Thomas Friedman's visit to a call center in Bangalore, India. By weaving together his observations of the scene there and his accounts of conversations with some of the people he meets, and placing them in the context of his acute understanding of global economic, social, and political trends, he paints a vivid picture of a world irreversibly changed by technology. The call center is located in Southern India (Bangalore is sometimes referred to as India's Silicon Valley), but from the standpoint of technology it could be anywhere on earth. What brought it to Bangalore is the confluence of talented young people willing and able to work for wages considerably lower than those in the United States or Europe, the presence of advanced telecommunications technology, and a community of motivated entrepreneurs. With his stories, Friedman illustrates how these factors are "flattening" the world—entangling the world's economies and societies with one another at a breathtaking pace.*

Thomas Friedman is a journalist and columnist with The New York Times, *for which he writes a twice-weekly column. He has written extensively on the Middle East, globalization, technology, terrorism, and climate change, as well as many other issues. In addition to* The World Is Flat: A Brief History of the Twenty-First Century, *the 2005 book from which this article is taken, he is the author of four other books. Friedman is the winner of three Pulitzer Prizes. His undergraduate degree is from Brandeis University. He also holds an M. Phil. from the University of Oxford.*

Do you know what an Indian call center sounds like?
While filming the documentary about outsourcing, the TV crew and I spent an evening at the Indian-owned "24/7 Customer" call center in Bangalore.

The call center is a cross between a co-ed college frat house and a phone bank raising money for the local public TV station. There are several floors with rooms full of twenty-somethings — some twenty-five hundred in all — working the phones. Some are known as "outbound" operators, selling everything from credit cards to phone minutes. Others deal with "inbound" calls — everything from tracing lost luggage for U.S. and European airline passengers to solving computer problems for confused American consumers. The calls are transferred here by satellite and undersea fiber-optic cable. Each vast floor of a call center consists of clusters of cubicles. The young people work in little teams under the banner of the company whose phone support they are providing. So one corner might be the Dell group, another might be flying the flag of Microsoft. Their working conditions look like those at your average insurance company. Although I am sure that there are call centers that are operated like sweatshops, 24/7 is not one of them.

Most of the young people I interviewed give all or part of their salary to their parents. In fact, many of them have starting salaries that are higher than their parents' retiring salaries. For entry-level jobs into the global economy, these are about as good as it gets.

I was wandering around the Microsoft section around six p.m. Bangalore time, when most of these young people start their workday to coincide with the dawn in America, when I asked a young Indian computer expert there a simple question: What was the record on the floor for the longest phone call to help some American who got lost in the maze of his or her own software?

Without missing a beat he answered, "Eleven hours."

"Eleven hours?" I exclaimed.

"Eleven hours," he said.

I have no way of checking whether this is true, but you do hear snippets of some oddly familiar conversations as you walk the floor at 24/7 and just listen over the shoulders of different call center operators doing their things. Here is a small sample of what we heard that night while filming for Discovery Times. It should be read, if you can imagine this, in the voice of someone with an Indian accent trying to imitate an American or a Brit. Also imagine that no matter how rude, unhappy, irritated, or ornery the voices are on the other end of the line, these young Indians are incessantly and unfailingly polite.

Woman call center operator: "Good afternoon, may I speak with ...?" (Someone on the other end just slammed down the phone.)

Male call center operator: "Merchant services, this is Jerry, may I help you?" (The Indian call center operators adopt Western names of their own choosing. The idea, of course, is to make their American or European customers feel more comfortable. Most of the young Indians I talked to about this were not offended but took it as an opportunity to have some fun. While a few just opt for Susan or Bob, some really get creative.)

Woman operator in Bangalore speaking to an American: "My name is Ivy Timberwoods and I am calling you ..."

Woman operator in Bangalore getting an American's identity number: "May I have the last four digits of your Social Security?"

Woman operator in Bangalore giving directions as though she were in Manhattan and looking out her window: "Yes, we have a branch on Seventy-fourth and Second Avenue, a branch at Fifty-fourth and Lexington ..."

Male operator in Bangalore selling a credit card he could never afford himself: "This card comes to you with one of the lowest APR ..."

Woman operator in Bangalore explaining to an American how she screwed up her checking account: "Check number six-six-five for eighty-one dollars and fifty-five cents. You will still be hit by the thirty-dollar charge. Am I clear?"

Woman operator in Bangalore after walking an American through a computer glitch: "Not a problem, Mr. Jassup. Thank you for your time. Take care. Bye-bye."

Woman operator in Bangalore after someone has just slammed down the phone on her: "Hello? Hello?"

Woman operator in Bangalore apologizing for calling someone in America too early: "This is just a courtesy call, I'll call back later in the evening ..."

Male operator in Bangalore trying desperately to sell an airline credit card to someone in America who doesn't seem to want one: "Is that because you have too many credit cards, or you don't like flying, Mrs. Bell?"

Woman operator in Bangalore trying to talk an American out of her computer crash: "Start switching between memory okay and memory test ..."

Male operator in Bangalore doing the same thing: "All right, then, let's just punch in three and press Enter ..."

Woman operator in Bangalore trying to help an American who cannot stand being on the help line another second: "Yes, ma'am, I do understand that you are in a hurry right now. I am just trying to help you out ..."

Woman operator in Bangalore getting another phone slammed down on her: "Yes, well, so what time would be goo ..."

Same woman operator in Bangalore getting another phone slammed down on her: "Why, Mrs. Kent, it's not a ..."

Same woman operator in Bangalore getting another phone slammed down on her: "As a safety back ... Hello?"

Same woman operator in Bangalore looking up from her phone: "I definitely have a bad day!"

Woman operator in Bangalore trying to help an American woman with a computer problem that she has never heard before: "What is the problem with this machine, ma'am? The monitor is burning?"

There are currently about 245,000 Indians answering phones from all over the world or dialing out to solicit people for credit cards or cell phone bargains or overdue bills. These call center jobs are low-wage, low-prestige jobs in America, but when shifted to India they become high-wage, high-prestige jobs. The esprit de corps at 24/7 and other call centers I visited seemed quite high, and the young people were all eager to share some of the bizarre phone conversations they've had with Americans who dialed 1-800-HELP, thinking they would wind up talking to someone around the block, not around the world.

C. M. Meghna, a 24/7 call center female operator, told me, "I've had lots of customers who call in [with questions] not even connected to the product that we're dealing with. They would call in because they had lost their wallet or just to talk to somebody. I'm like, 'Okay, all right, maybe you should look under the bed [for your wallet] or where do you normally keep it,' and she's like, 'Okay, thank you so much for helping.'"

Nitu Somaiah: "One of the customers asked me to marry him."

Sophie Sunder worked for Delta's lost-baggage department: "I remember this lady called from Texas," she said, "and she was, like, weeping on the phone. She had traveled two connecting flights and she lost her bag and in the bag was her daughter's wedding gown and wedding ring and I felt so sad for her and there was nothing I could do. I had no information.

"Most of the customers were irate," said Sunder. "The first thing they say is, 'Where's my bag? I want my bag now!' We were like supposed to say, 'Excuse me, can I have your first name and last name?' 'But where's my bag!' Some would ask which country am I from? We are supposed to tell the truth, [so] we tell them India. Some thought it was Indiana, not India! Some did not know where India is. I said it is the country next to Pakistan."

Although the great majority of the calls are rather routine and dull, competition for these jobs is fierce — not only because they pay well, but because you can work at night and go to school during part of the day, so they are stepping-stones toward a higher standard of living. P. V. Kannan, CEO and cofounder of 24/7, explained to me how it all worked: "Today we have over four thousand associates spread out in Bangalore, Hyderabad, and Chennai. Our associates start out with a take-home pay of roughly $200 a month, which grows to $300 to $400 per month in six months. We also provide transportation, lunch, and dinner at no extra cost. We provide life insurance, medical insurance for the entire family — and other benefits."

Therefore, the total cost of each call center operator is actually around $500 per month when they start out and closer to $600 to $700 per month after six months. Everyone is also entitled to performance bonuses that allow them to earn, in certain cases, the equivalent of 100 percent of their base salary. "Around 10 to 20 percent of our associates pursue a degree in business or computer science during the day hours," said Kannan, adding that more than one-third are taking some kind of extra computer or business training, even if it is not toward a degree. "It is quite common in India for people to pursue education through their twenties — self-improvement is a big theme and actively encouraged by parents and companies. We sponsor an MBA program for consistent performers [with] full-day classes over the weekend. Everyone works eight hours a day, five days a week, with two fifteen-minute breaks and an hour off for lunch or dinner."

Not surprisingly, the 24/7 customer call center gets about seven hundred applications a day, but only 6 percent of applicants are hired. Here is a snippet from a recruiting session for call center operators at a women's college in Bangalore:

Recruiter 1: "Good morning, girls."

Class in unison: "Good morning, ma'am."

Recruiter 1: "We have been retained by some of the multinationals here to do the recruitment for them. The primary clients that we are recruiting [for] today are Honeywell. And also for America Online."

The young women — dozens of them — then all lined up with their application forms and waited to be interviewed by a recruiter at a wooden table. Here is what some of the interviews sounded like:

Recruiter 1: "What kind of job are you looking at?"

Applicant 1: "It should be based on accounts, then, where I can grow, I can grow in my career."

Recruiter 1: "You have to be more confident about yourself when you're speaking. You're very nervous. I want you to work a little on that and then get in touch with us."

Recruiter 2 to another applicant: "Tell me something about yourself."

Applicant 2: "I have passed my SSC with distinction. Second P also with distinction. And I also hold a 70 percent aggregate in previous two years." (This is Indian lingo for their equivalents of GPA and SAT scores.)

Recruiter 2: "Go a little slow. Don't be nervous. Be cool."

The next step for those applicants who are hired at a call center is the training program, which they are paid to attend. It combines learning how to handle the specific processes for the company whose calls they will be taking or making, and attending something called "accent neutralization class." These are daylong sessions with a language teacher who prepares the new Indian hires to disguise their pronounced Indian accents when speaking English and replace them with American, Canadian, or British ones — depending on which part of the world they will be speaking with. It's pretty bizarre to watch. The class I sat in on was being trained to speak in a neutral middle-American accent. The students were asked to read over and over a single phonetic paragraph designed to teach them how to soften their *t*'s and to roll their *r*'s.

Their teacher, a charming eight-months-pregnant young woman dressed in a traditional Indian sari, moved seamlessly among British, American, and Canadian accents as she demonstrated reading a paragraph designed to highlight phonetics. She said to the class, "Remember the first day I told you that the Americans flap the 'tuh' sound? You know, it sounds like an almost 'duh' sound — not crisp and clear like the British. So I would not say" — here she was crisp and sharp — " 'Betty bought a bit of better butter' or 'Insert a quarter in the meter.' But I would say" — her voice very flat — " 'Insert a quarter in the meter' or 'Betty bought a bit of better butter.' So I'm just going to read it out for you once, and then we'll read it together. All right? 'Thirty little turtles in a bottle of bottled water. A bottle of bottled water held thirty little turtles. It didn't matter that each turtle had to rattle a metal ladle in order to get a little bit of noodles.'

"All right, who's going to read first?" the instructor asked. Each member of the class then took a turn trying to say this tongue twister in an American accent. Some of them got it on the first try, and others, well, let's just say that you wouldn't think they were in Kansas City if they answered your call to Delta's lost-luggage number.

After listening to them stumble through this phonetics lesson for half an hour, I asked the teacher if she would like me to give them an authentic version — since I'm originally from Minnesota, smack in the Midwest, and still speak like someone out of the movie *Fargo*. Absolutely, she said. So I read the following paragraph: "A bottle of bottled water held thirty little turtles. It didn't matter that each turtle had to rattle a metal ladle in order to get a little bit of noodles, a total turtle delicacy ... The problem was that there were many turtle battles for less than oodles of noodles. Every time they thought about grappling with the haggler turtles their little turtle minds boggled and they only caught a little bit of noodles."

The class responded enthusiastically. It was the first time I ever got an ovation for speaking Minnesotan. On the surface, there is something unappealing about the idea of inducing other people to flatten their accents in order to compete in a flatter world. But before you disparage it, you have to taste just how hungry these kids are to escape the lower end of the middle class and move up. If a little accent modification is the price they have to pay to jump a rung of the ladder, then so be it — they say.

"This is a high-stress environment," said Nilekani, the CEO of Infosys, which also runs a big call center. "It is twenty-four by seven. You work in the day, and then the night, and then the next morning." But the working environment, he insisted, "is not the tension of alienation. It is the tension of success. They are dealing with the challenges of success, of high-pressure living. It is not the challenge of worrying about whether they would have a challenge."

That was certainly the sense I got from talking to a lot of the call center operators on the floor. Like any explosion of modernity, outsourcing is challenging traditional norms and ways of life. But educated Indians have been held back so many years by both poverty and a socialist bureaucracy that many of them seem more than ready to put up with the hours. And needless to say, it is much easier and more satisfying for them to work hard in Bangalore than to pack up and try to make a new start in America. In the flat world they can stay in India, make a decent salary, and not have to be away from families, friends, food, and culture. At the end of the day, these new jobs actually allow them to be more Indian. Said Anney Unnikrishnan, a personnel manager at 24/7, "I finished my MBA and I remember writing the GMAT and getting into Purdue University. But I couldn't go because I couldn't afford it. I didn't have the money for it. Now I can, [but] I see a whole lot of American industry has come into Bangalore and I don't really need to go there. I can work for a multinational sitting right here. So I still get my rice and sambar [a traditional Indian dish], which I eat. I don't need to, you know, learn to eat coleslaw and cold beef. I still continue with my Indian food and I still work for a multinational. Why should I go to America?"

The relatively high standard of living that she can now enjoy — enough for a small apartment and car in Bangalore — is good for America as well. When you look around at 24/7's call center, you see that all the computers are running Microsoft Windows. The chips are designed by Intel. The phones are from Lucent. The air-conditioning is by Carrier, and even the bottled water is by

Coke. In addition, 90 percent of the shares in 24/7 are owned by U.S. investors. This explains why, although the United States has lost some service jobs to India in recent years, total exports from American-based companies — merchandise and services — to India have grown from $2.5 billion in 1990 to $5 billion in 2003. So even with the outsourcing of some service jobs from the United States to India, India's growing economy is creating a demand for many more American goods and services.

What goes around, comes around.

Nine years ago, when Japan was beating America's brains out in the auto industry, I wrote a column about playing the computer geography game Where in the World is Carmen Sandiego? with my nine-year-old daughter, Orly. I was trying to help her by giving her a clue suggesting that Carmen had gone to Detroit, so I asked her, "Where are cars made?" And without missing a beat she answered, "Japan."

Ouch!

Well, I was reminded of that story while visiting Global Edge, an Indian software design firm in Bangalore. The company's marketing manager, Rajesh Rao, told me that he had just made a cold call to the VP for engineering of a U.S. company, trying to drum up business. As soon as Mr. Rao introduced himself as calling from an Indian software firm, the U.S. executive said to him, *"Namaste,"* a common Hindi greeting. Said Mr. Rao, "A few years ago nobody in America wanted to talk to us. Now they are eager." And a few even know how to say hello in proper Hindu fashion. So now I wonder: If I have a granddaughter one day, and I tell her I'm going to India, will she say, "Grandpa, is that where software comes from?"

No, not yet, honey. Every new product — from software to widgets — goes through a cycle that begins with basic research, then applied research, then incubation, then development, then testing, then manufacturing, then deployment, then support, then continuation engineering in order to add improvements. Each of these phases is specialized and unique, and neither India nor China nor Russia has a critical mass of talent that can handle the whole product cycle for a big American multinational. But these countries are steadily developing their research and development capabilities to handle more and more of these phases. As that continues, we really will see the beginning of what Satyam Cherukuri, of Sarnoff, an American research and development firm, has called "the globalization of innovation" and an end to the old model of a single American or European multinational handling all the elements of the development product cycle from its own resources. More and more American and European companies are outsourcing significant research and development tasks to India, Russia, and China.

According to the information technology office of the state government in Karnataka, where Bangalore is located, Indian units of Cisco Systems, Intel, IBM, Texas Instruments, and GE have already filed 1,000 patent applications with the U.S. Patent Office. Texas Instruments alone has had 225 U.S. patents awarded to its Indian operation. "The Intel team in Bangalore is developing microprocessor chips for high-speed broadband wireless technology, to be launched in 2006," the Karnataka IT office said, in a statement issued at the end of 2004, and "at GE's John F. Welch Technology Centre in Bangalore, engineers are developing new ideas for aircraft engines, transport systems and plastics." Indeed, GE over the years has frequently transferred Indian engineers who worked for it in the United States back to India to integrate its whole global research effort. GE now even sends non-Indians to Bangalore. Vivek Paul is the president of Wipro Technologies, another of the elite Indian technology companies, but he is based in Silicon Valley to be close to Wipro's American customers. Before coming to Wipro, Paul managed GE's CT scanner business out of Milwaukee. At the time he had a French colleague who managed GE's power generator business for the scanners out of France.

"I ran into him on an airplane recently," said Paul, "and he told me he had moved to India to head up GE's high-energy research there."

I told Vivek that I love hearing an Indian who used to head up GE's CT business in Milwaukee but now runs Wipro's consulting business in Silicon Valley tell me about his former French colleague who has moved to Bangalore to work for GE. That is a flat world.

E very time I think I have found the last, most obscure job that could be outsourced to Bangalore, I discover a new one. My friend Vivek Kulkarni used to head the government office in Bangalore responsible for attracting high technology global investment. After stepping down from that post in 2003, he started a company called B2K, with a division called Brickwork, which offers busy global executives their own personal assistant in India. Say you are running a company and you have been asked to give a speech and a PowerPoint presentation in two days. Your "remote executive assistant" in India, provided by Brickwork, will do all the research for you, create the PowerPoint presentation, and e-mail the whole thing to you overnight so that it is on your desk the day you have to deliver it.

"You can give your personal remote executive assistant their assignment when you are leaving work at the end of the day in New York City, and it will be ready for you the next morning," explained Kulkarni. "Because of the time difference with India, they can work on it while you sleep and have it back in your morning." Kulkarni suggested I hire a remote assistant in India to do all the research for this book. "He or she could also help you keep pace with what you want to read. When you wake up, you will find the completed summary in your in-box." (I told him no one could be better than my longtime assistant, Maya Gorman, who sits ten feet away!)

Having your own personal remote executive assistant costs around $1,500 to $2,000 a month, and given the pool of Indian college grads from which Brickwork can recruit, the brainpower you can hire dollar-for-dollar is substantial. As Brickwork's promotional material says, "India's talent pool provides companies access to a broad spectrum of highly qualified people. In addition to fresh graduates, which are around 2.5 million per year, many qualified homemakers are entering the job market." India's business schools, it adds, produce around eighty-nine thousand MBAs per year.

"We've had a wonderful response," said Kulkarni, with clients coming from two main areas. One is American health-care consultants, who often need lots of numbers crunched and PowerPoint presentations drawn up. The other, he said, are American investment banks and financial services companies, which often need to prepare glossy pamphlets with graphs to illustrate the benefits of an IPO or a proposed merger. In the case of a merger, Brickwork will prepare those sections of the report dealing with general market conditions and trends, where most of the research can be gleaned off the Web and summarized in a standard format. "The judgment of how to price the deal will come from the investment bankers themselves," said Kulkarni. "We will do the lower-end work, and they will do the things that require critical judgment and experience, close to the market." The more projects his team of remote executive assistants engages in, the more knowledge they build up. They are full of ambition to do their higher problem solving as well, said Kulkarni. "The idea is to constantly learn. You are always taking an examination. There is no end to learning ... There is no real end to what can be done by whom."

Credits

These pages constitute an extension of the copyright page. We have made every effort to trace the ownership of all copyrighted material and to secure permission from copyright holders. In the event of any question arising as to the use of any material, we will be pleased to make the necessary corrections in future printings. Thanks are due to the following authors, publishers, and agents for permission to use the material indicated.

Chapter 1. 3–12: Leo Marx, "Does Improved Technology Mean Progress?" from *Technology Review* (January, 1987), pp. 33–41. © 1987 *Technology Review*. Reprinted with permission.

Chapter 2. 13–22: From *Beyond Engineering: How Society Shapes Technology* by Robert Pool, © 1997 by Robert Pool. Used by permission of Oxford University Press, Inc.

Chapter 3. 23–33: From *The Shock of the Old: Technology and Global History Since 1900* by David Edgerton. © 2007 David Edgerton. Reprinted by permission of Oxford University Press.

Chapter 4. 34–41: Alvin M. Weinberg, "Can Technology Replace Social Engineering?" Reprinted by permission.

Chapter 5. 42–50: From *Blaming Technology: The Irrational Search for Scapegoats* by Samuel C. Florman. Copyright © 1981 by the author and reprinted with permission of St. Martin's Press, LLC.

Chapter 6. 51–68: "Do Artifacts Have Politics?" from *Daedalus, Journal of the American Academy of Arts and Sciences*, from the issue entitled, "Modern Technology: Problem or Opportunity?" Winter 1980, Vol. 109, No. 1. Reprinted by permission of the author.

Chapter 7. 71–80: From *Technology and Culture* 10:4 (1969), pp. 489–536. © Society for the History of Technology. Reprinted with permission of The Johns Hopkins University Press.

Chapter 23. 287–300: Deborah G. Johnson, "Computer Ethics" from *The Blackwell Guide to the Philosophy of Computing and Information*, ed. Luciano Floridi. © 2004 by Blackwell Publishing Ltd.

Chapter 24. 301–309: Nicholas Carr, "Is Google Making Us Stupid?" *The Atlantic* (July/August 2008). Reprinted by permission of the author.

Chapter 25. 310–311: Save the Internet, "Net Neutrality 101," http://www .savetheinternet.com/net-neutrality-101. Reprinted by permission.

Chapter 26. 312–319: George Ou, *Managing Broadband Networks: A Policymaker's Guide* (Washington, DC: The Information Technology and Innovation Foundation), executive summary, pp. 1–5. Reprinted by permission.

Chapter 27. 323–331: From Albert Teich, "Government and Technology," in *Science, Technology, and Society: An Encyclopedia*, pp. 170–175. © 2005 Oxford University Press, New York.

Chapter 28. 332–340: Excerpt from *THE WORLD IS FLAT: A BRIEF HISTORY OF THE TWENTY-FIRST CENTURY* [Updated and Expanded] [Further Updated and Expanded] by Thomas L. Friedman. Copyright © 2005, 2006, 2007 by Thomas L. Friedman. Reprinted by permission of Farrar, Straus and Giroux, LLC and International Creative Management.